MEGAMAN™ NT WARRIOR

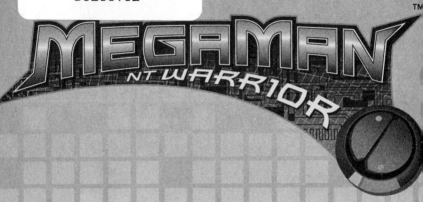

MEGAMAN
NT WARRIOR

Vol. 8
Action Edition

Story and Art by Ryo Takamisaki

English Adaptation/Gary Leach
Translation/Koji Goto
Touch-Up & Lettering/Gia Cam Luc
Cover Design & Graphic Design/Mark Schumann
Special Thanks/Hiromi Kadowaki & Jessica Villat
Editor/Eric Searleman

Managing Editor/Annette Roman
Director of Production/Noboru Watanabe
Editorial Director/Alvin Lu
Sr. Director of Acquisitions/Rika Inouye
Vice President of Sales & Marketing/Liza Coppola
Publisher/Hyoe Narita

© 2001 Ryo TAKAMISAKI/Shogakukan Inc. © CAPCOM Co.,
Ltd. ™ and ® are trademarks of CAPCOM Co., Ltd. First
published by Shogakukan Inc. in Japan as "Rokkuman
Eguze." New and adapted artwork © 2005 VIZ Media, LLC.
All rights reserved. The stories, characters, and incidents
mentioned in this publication are entirely fictional.

No portion of this book may be reproduced or transmitted in
any form or by any means without written permission from
the copyright holders.

Printed in the U.S.A.

Published by VIZ Media, LLC
P.O. Box 77064
San Francisco, CA 94107

Action Edition
10 9 8 7 6 5 4 3 2 1
First printing, August 2005

For advertising rates or media kit,
e-mail advertising@viz.com

CONTENTS

PARENTAL ADVISORY
MEGAMAN NT WARRIOR is rated A and is
recommended for readers of all ages. This
volume contains fantasy violence.

www.viz.com
store.viz.com

Vol. 8

Story and Art by
Ryo Takamisaki

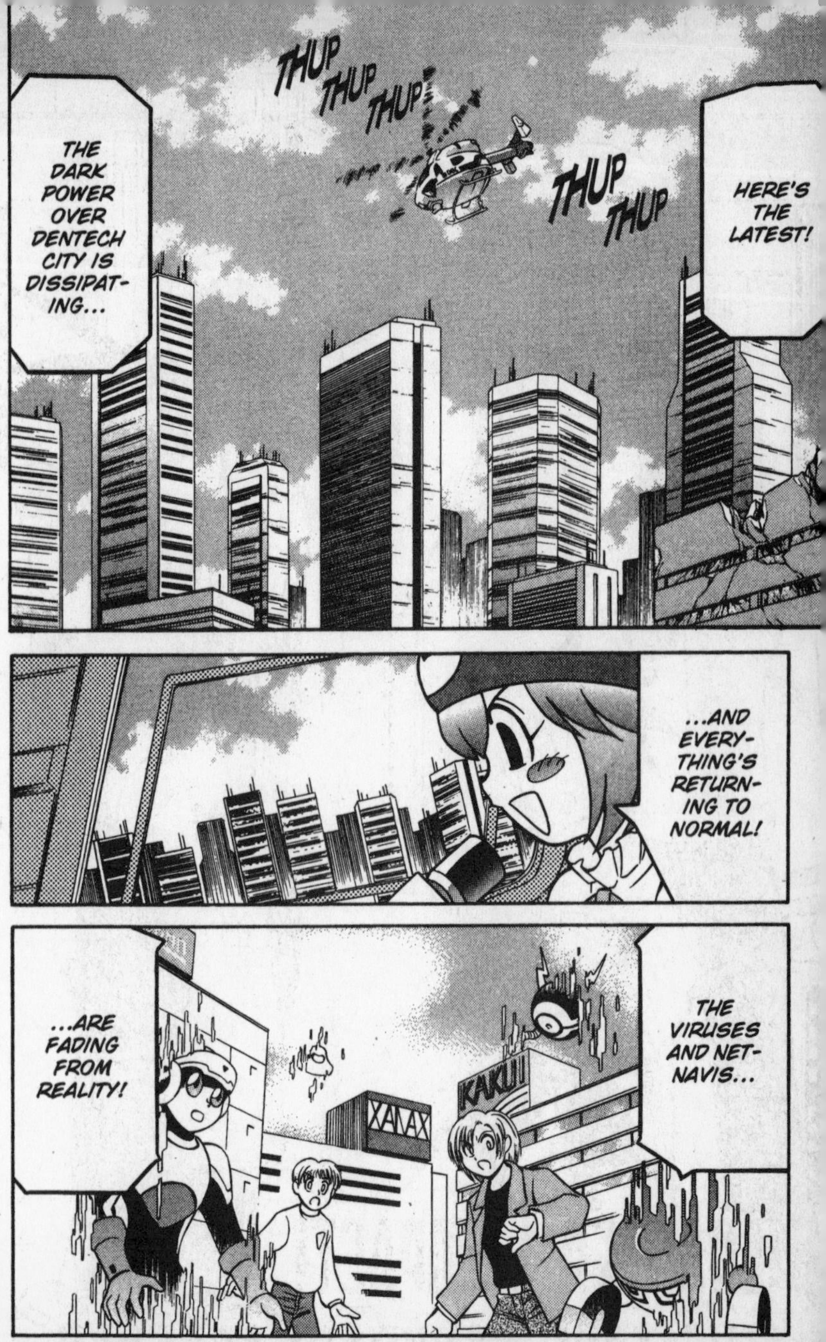
HERE'S THE LATEST!
THUP THUP
THUP THUP THUP
THE DARK POWER OVER DENTECH CITY IS DISSIPAT-ING...
...AND EVERY-THING'S RETURN-ING TO NORMAL!
THE VIRUSES AND NET-NAVIS...
XANAX
...ARE FADING FROM REALITY!

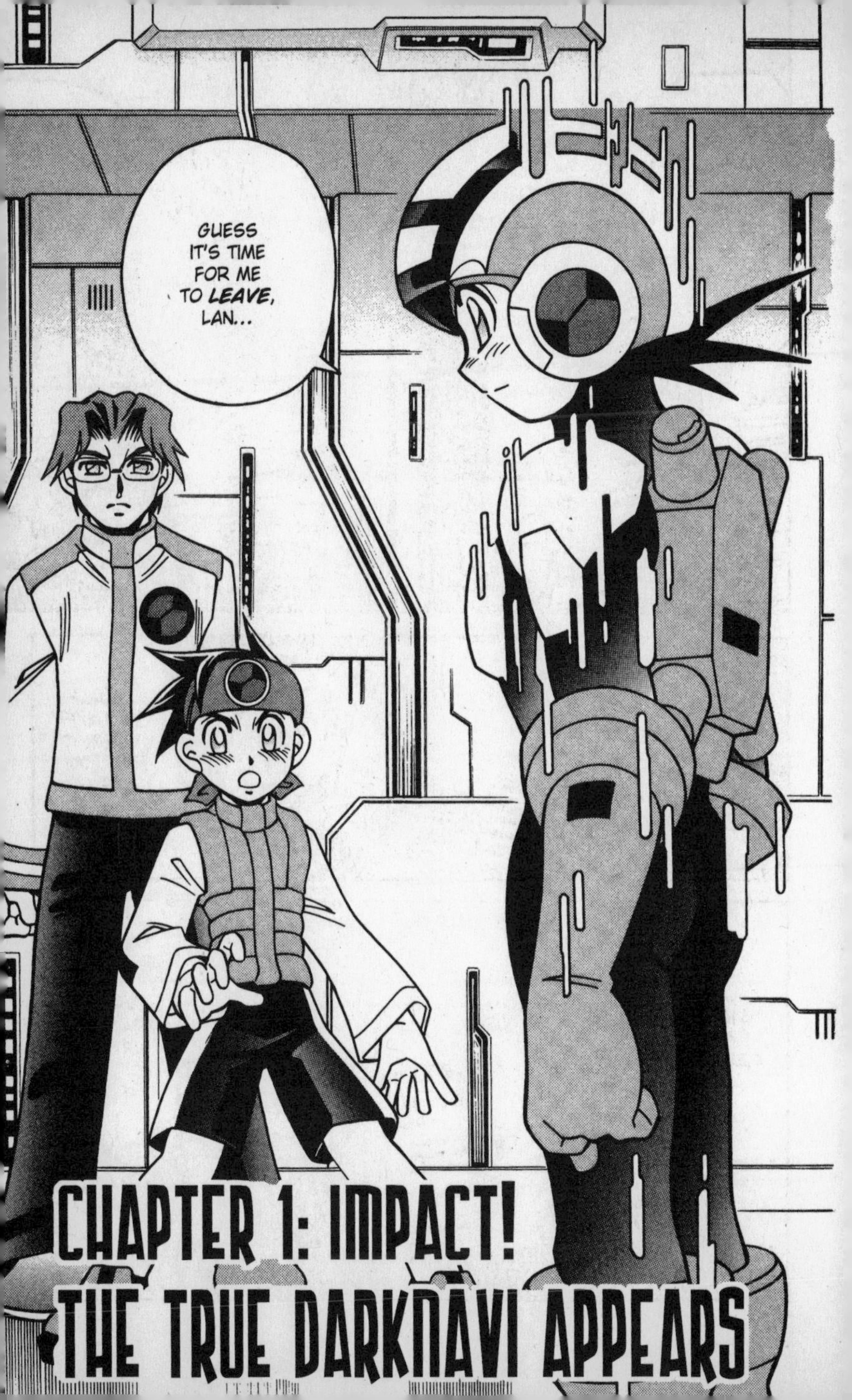
GUESS IT'S TIME FOR ME TO LEAVE, LAN...
CHAPTER 1: IMPACT! THE TRUE DARKNAVI APPEARS

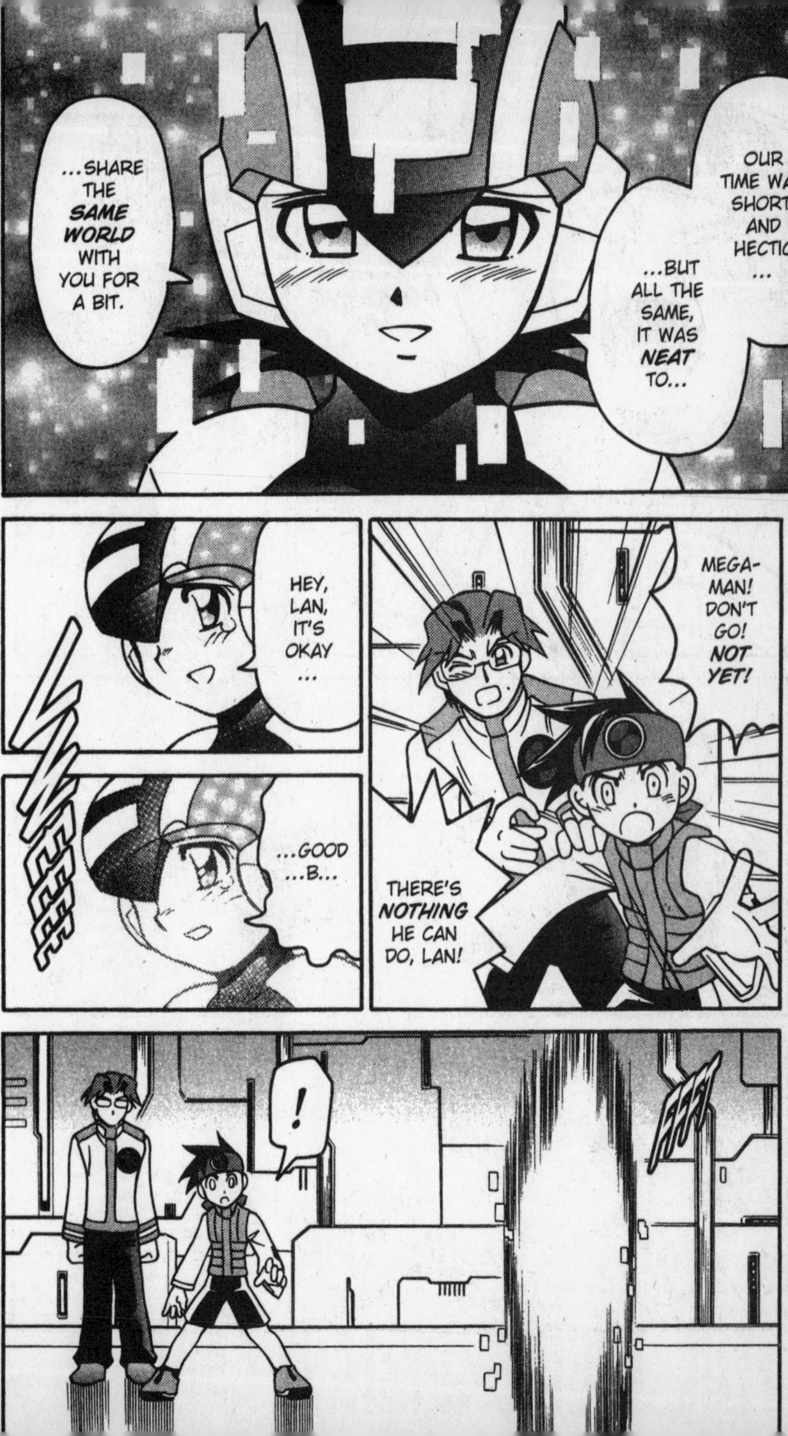

OUR TIME WAS SHORT, AND HECTIC ...
...BUT ALL THE SAME, IT WAS NEAT TO...
...SHARE THE SAME WORLD WITH YOU FOR A BIT.
MEGA-MAN! DON'T GO! NOT YET!
THERE'S NOTHING HE CAN DO, LAN!
HEY, LAN, IT'S OKAY ...
VWEEEE
...GOOD ...B...
!

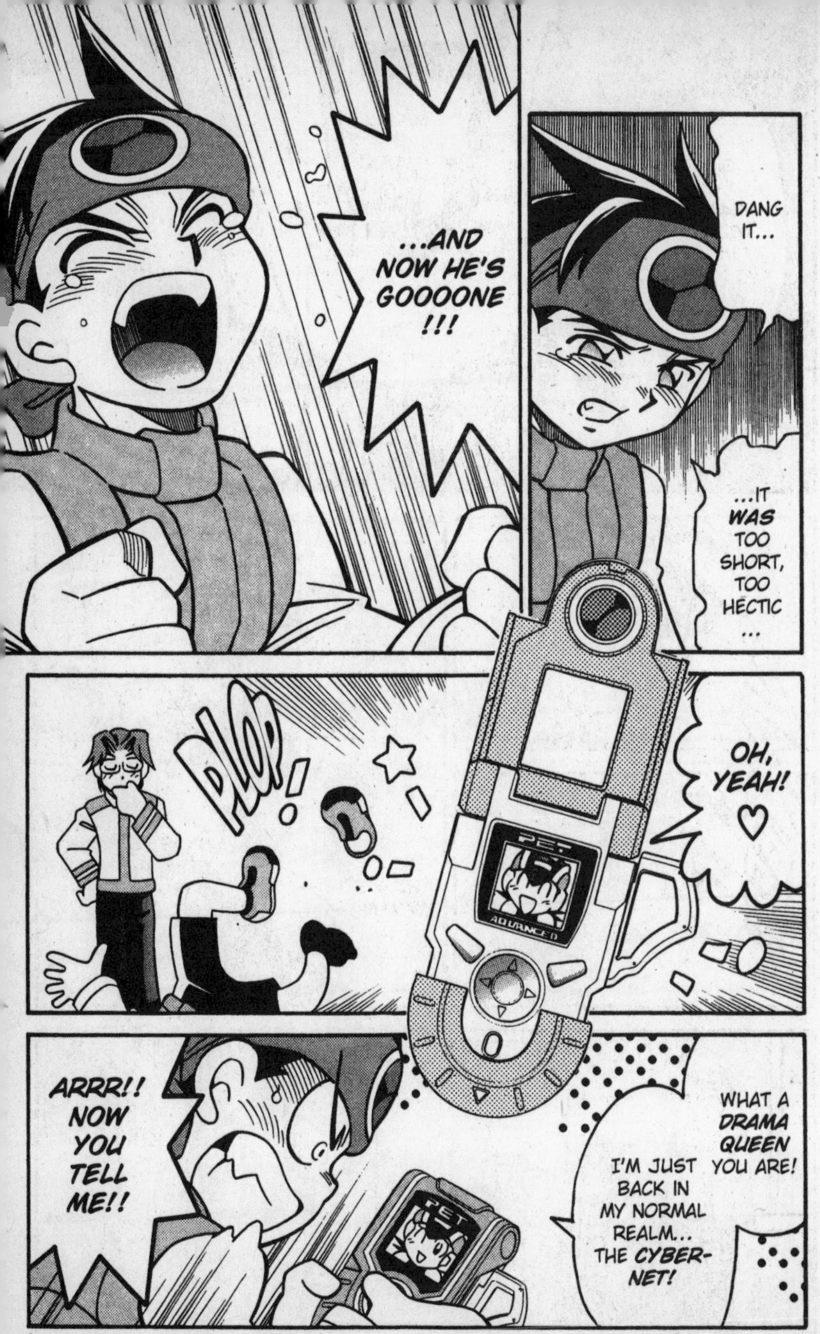
DANG IT...
...IT WAS TOO SHORT, TOO HECTIC...
...AND NOW HE'S GOOOONE!!!
OH, YEAH! ♡
PLOP!
P.E.T.
ADVANCED
WHAT A DRAMA QUEEN YOU ARE!
I'M JUST BACK IN MY NORMAL REALM... THE CYBER-NET!
ARRR!! NOW YOU TELL ME!!

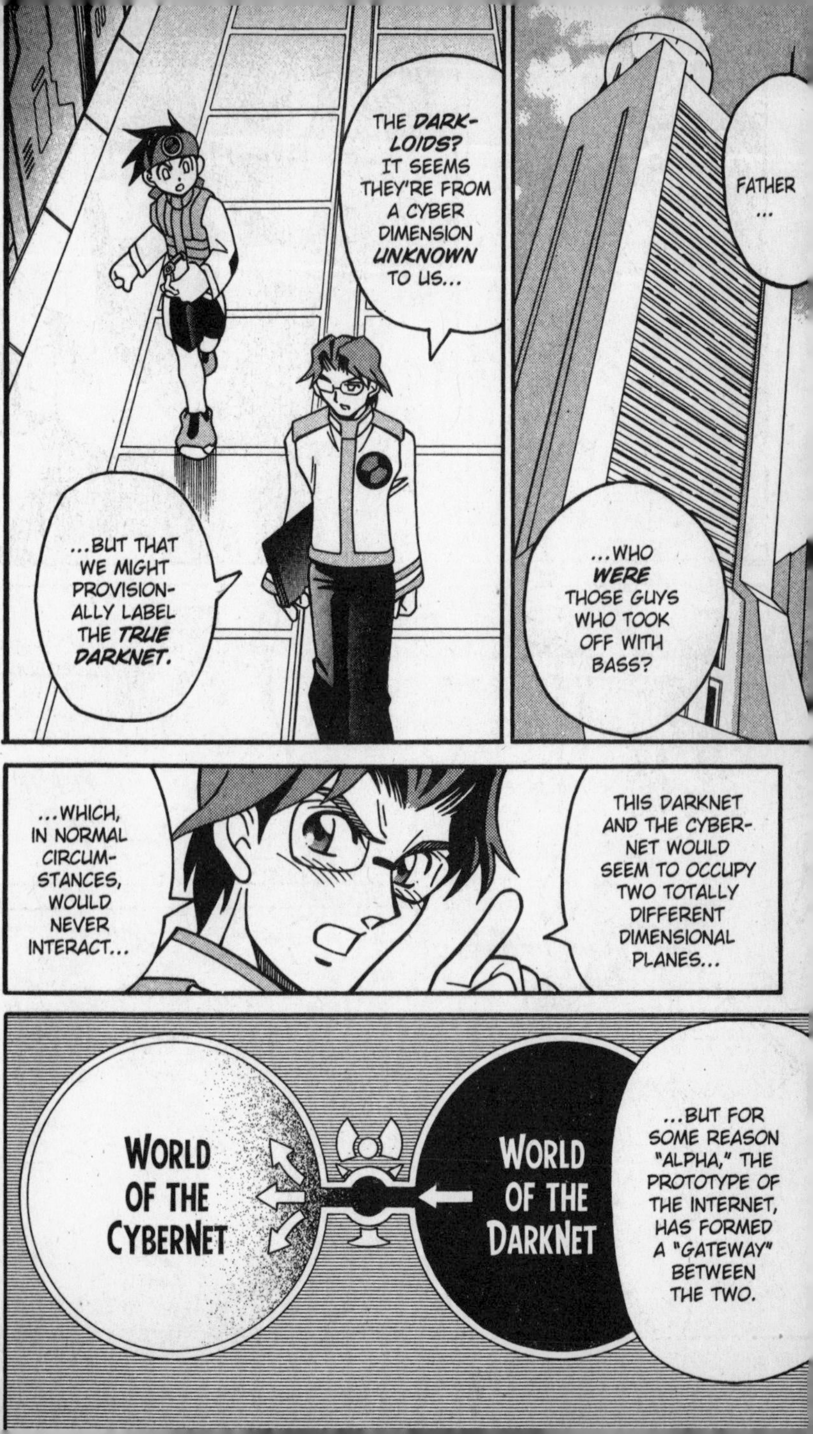
FATHER ...
...WHO WERE THOSE GUYS WHO TOOK OFF WITH BASS?
THE DARK-LOIDS? IT SEEMS THEY'RE FROM A CYBER DIMENSION UNKNOWN TO US...
...BUT THAT WE MIGHT PROVISION-ALLY LABEL THE TRUE DARKNET.
THIS DARKNET AND THE CYBER-NET WOULD SEEM TO OCCUPY TWO TOTALLY DIFFERENT DIMENSIONAL PLANES...
...WHICH, IN NORMAL CIRCUM-STANCES, WOULD NEVER INTERACT...
...BUT FOR SOME REASON "ALPHA," THE PROTOTYPE OF THE INTERNET, HAS FORMED A "GATEWAY" BETWEEN THE TWO.
WORLD OF THE DARKNET
WORLD OF THE CYBERNET

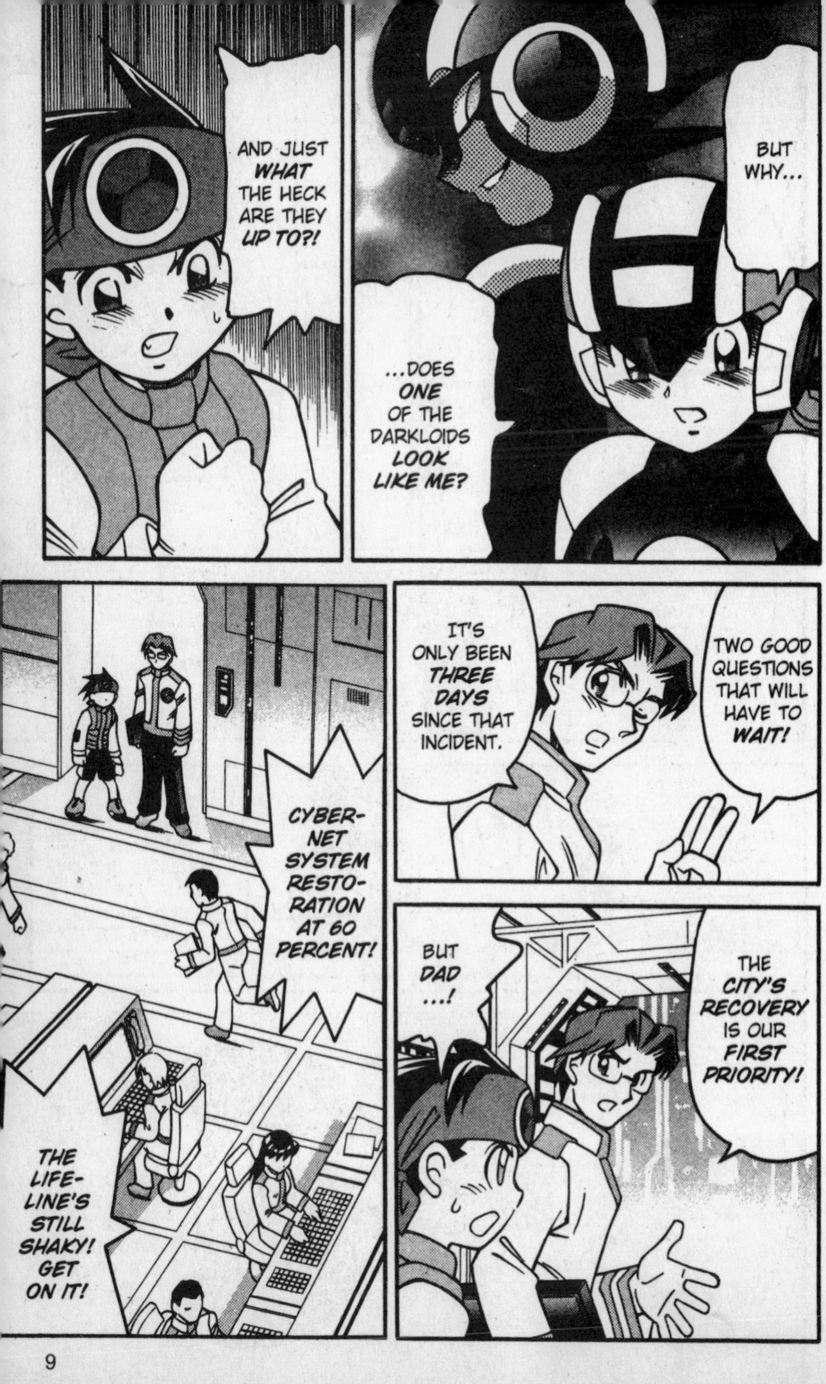
BUT WHY...
...DOES ONE OF THE DARKLOIDS LOOK LIKE ME?
AND JUST WHAT THE HECK ARE THEY UP TO?!
TWO GOOD QUESTIONS THAT WILL HAVE TO WAIT!
IT'S ONLY BEEN THREE DAYS SINCE THAT INCIDENT.
THE CITY'S RECOVERY IS OUR FIRST PRIORITY!
BUT DAD ...!
CYBER-NET SYSTEM RESTO-RATION AT 60 PERCENT!
THE LIFE-LINE'S STILL SHAKY! GET ON IT!

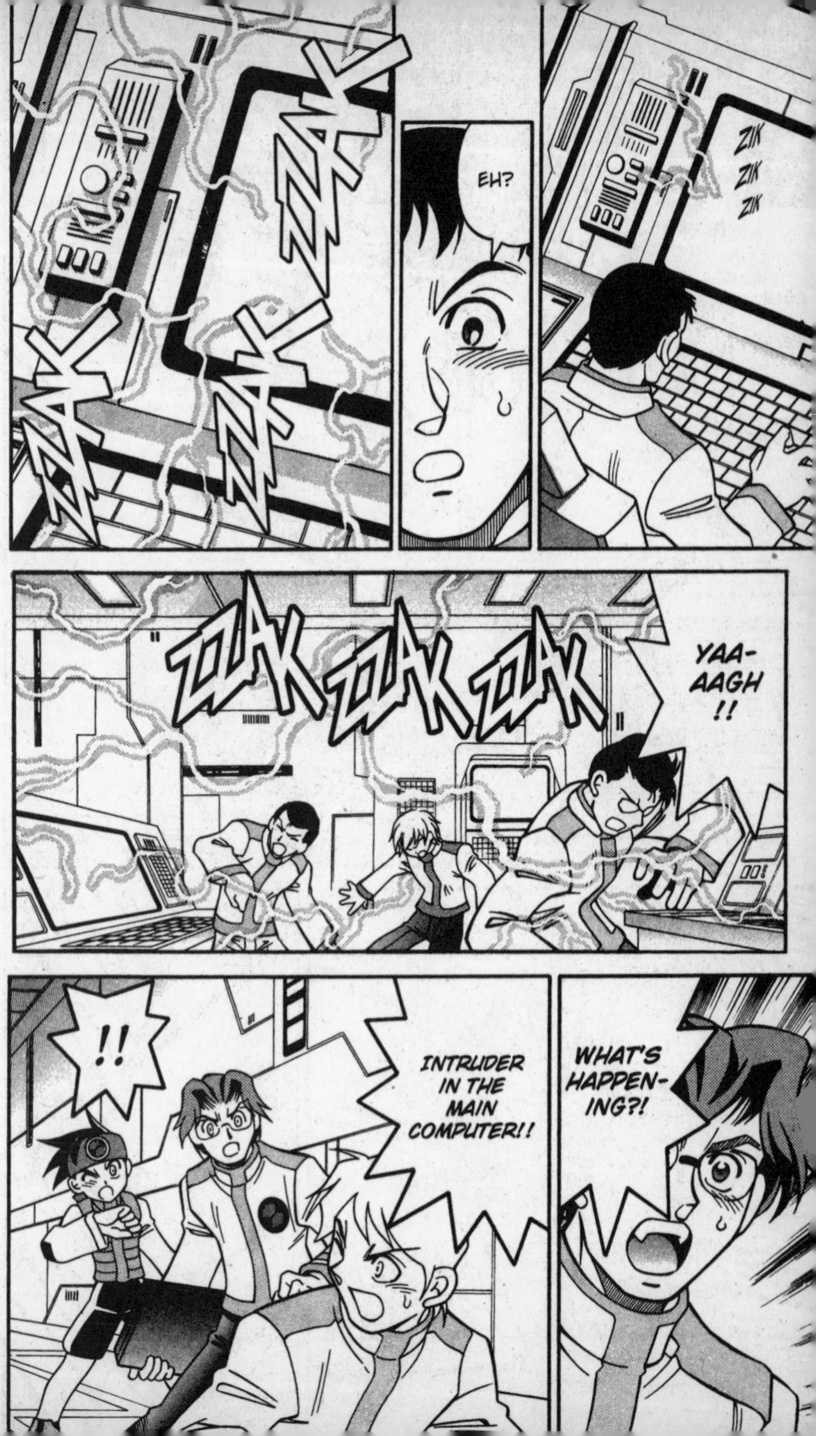
ZIK ZIK ZIK
EH?
ZZAK ZZAK ZZAK
YAAA-AAGH!!
ZZAK ZZAK ZZAK
WHAT'S HAPPEN-ING?!
INTRUDER IN THE MAIN COMPUTER!!
!!

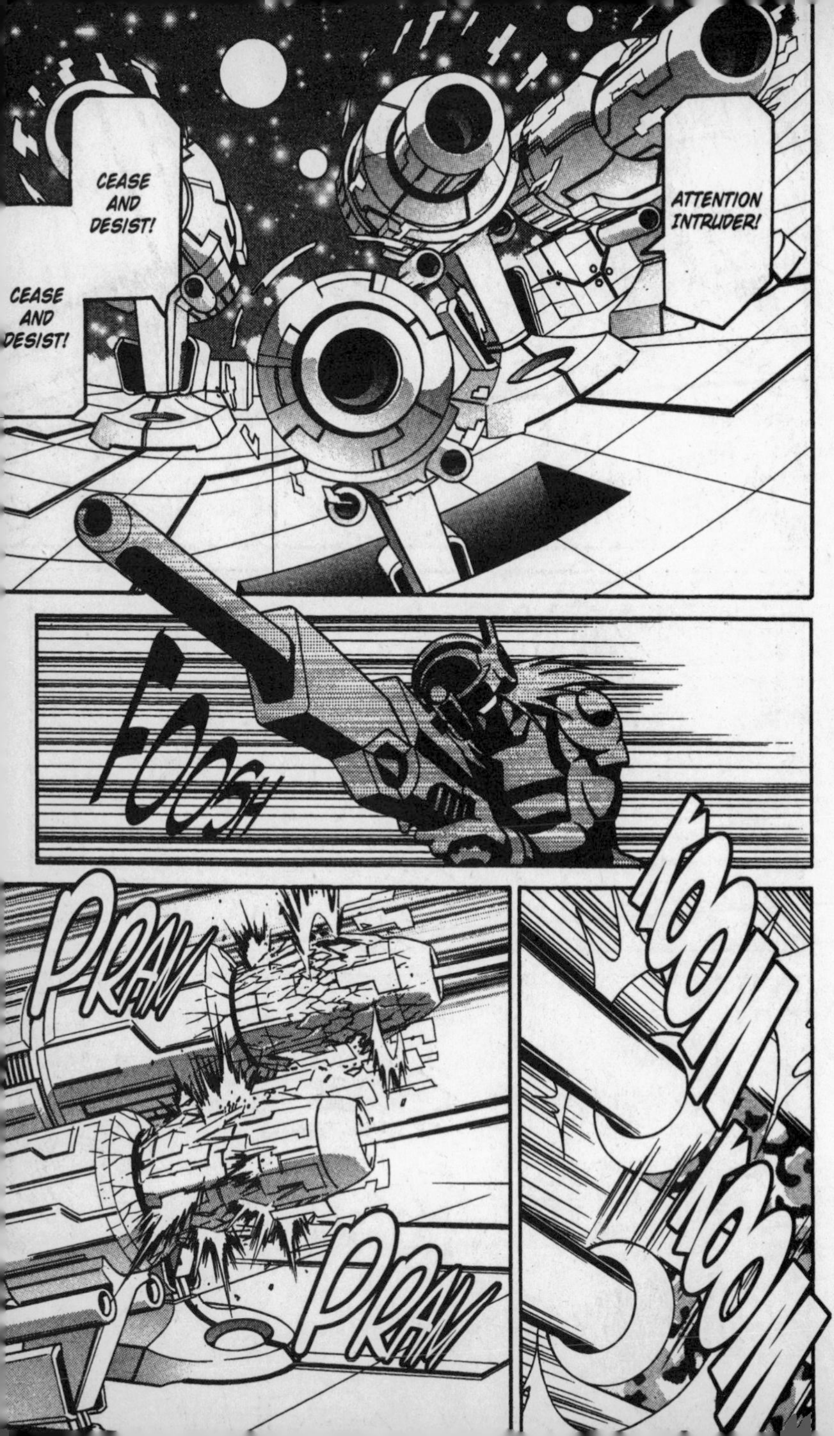
ATTENTION INTRUDER!
CEASE AND DESIST!
CEASE AND DESIST!
FOOSH
KOOM
KOOM
PRAN
PRAN

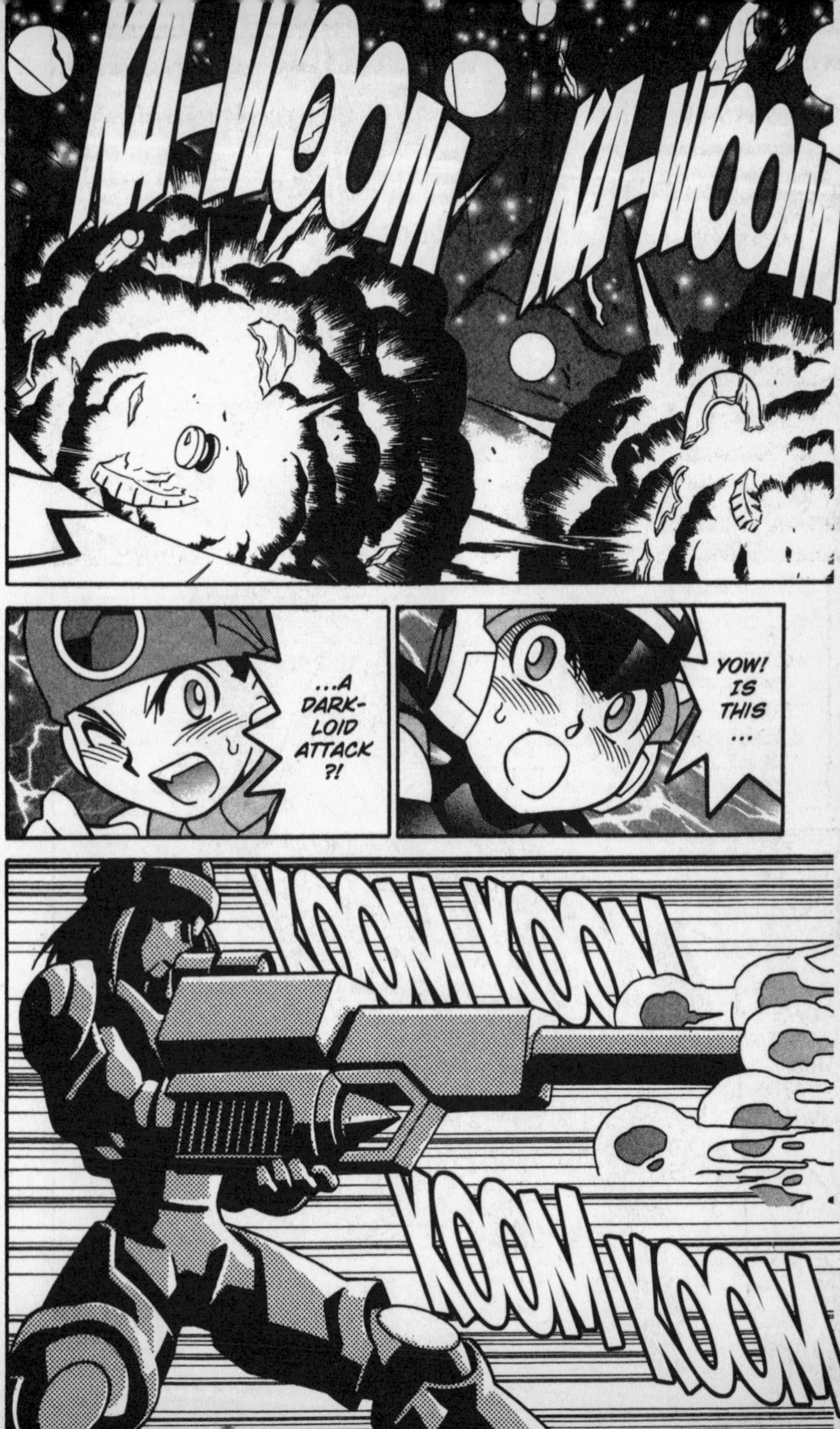
KA-WOOM KA-WOOM
YOW! IS THIS ...
...A DARK-LOID ATTACK ?!
KOOM KOOM
KOOM KOOM

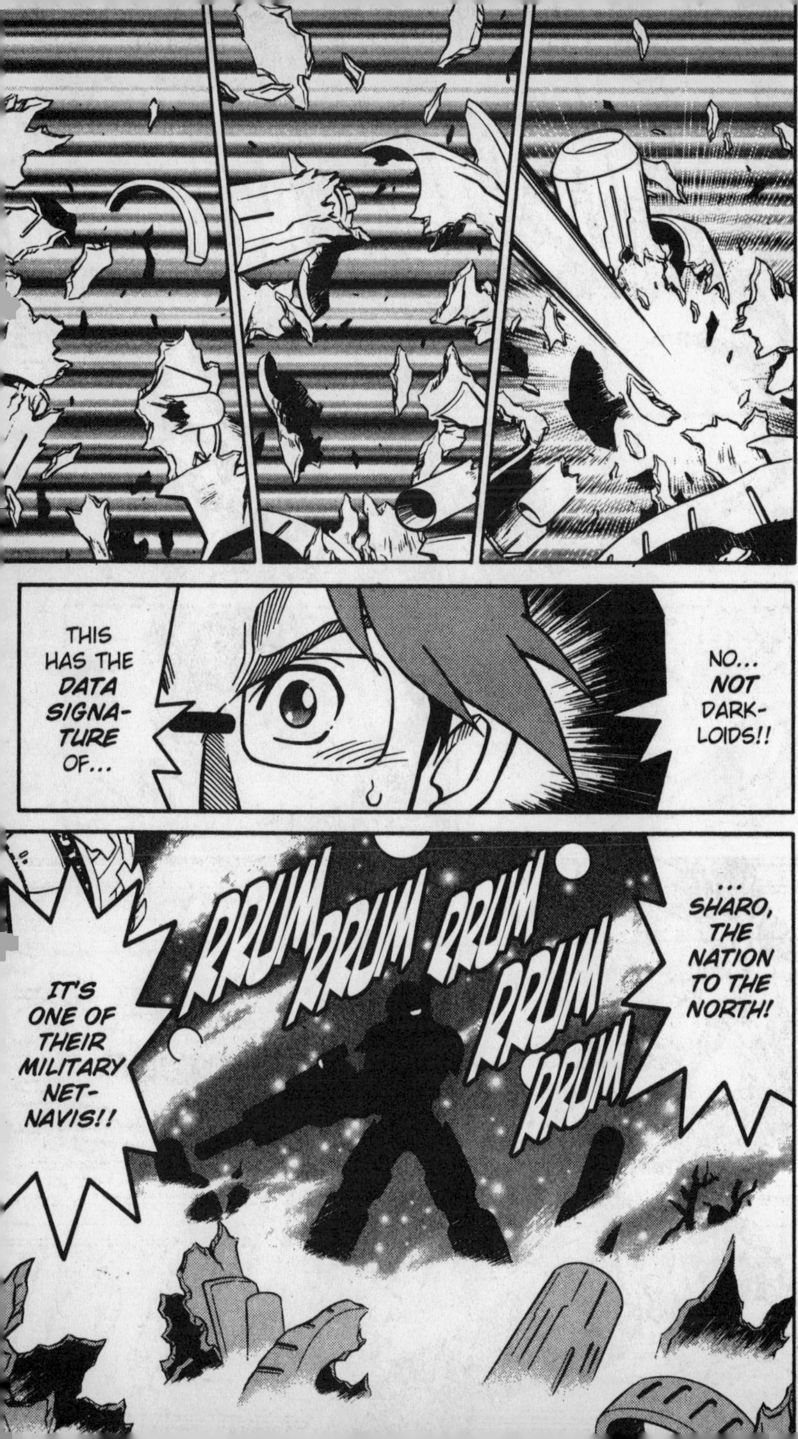
NO... NOT DARK-LOIDS!!
THIS HAS THE DATA SIGNA-TURE OF...
... SHARO, THE NATION TO THE NORTH!
RRUM RRUM RRUM RRUM RRUM
IT'S ONE OF THEIR MILITARY NET-NAVIS!!

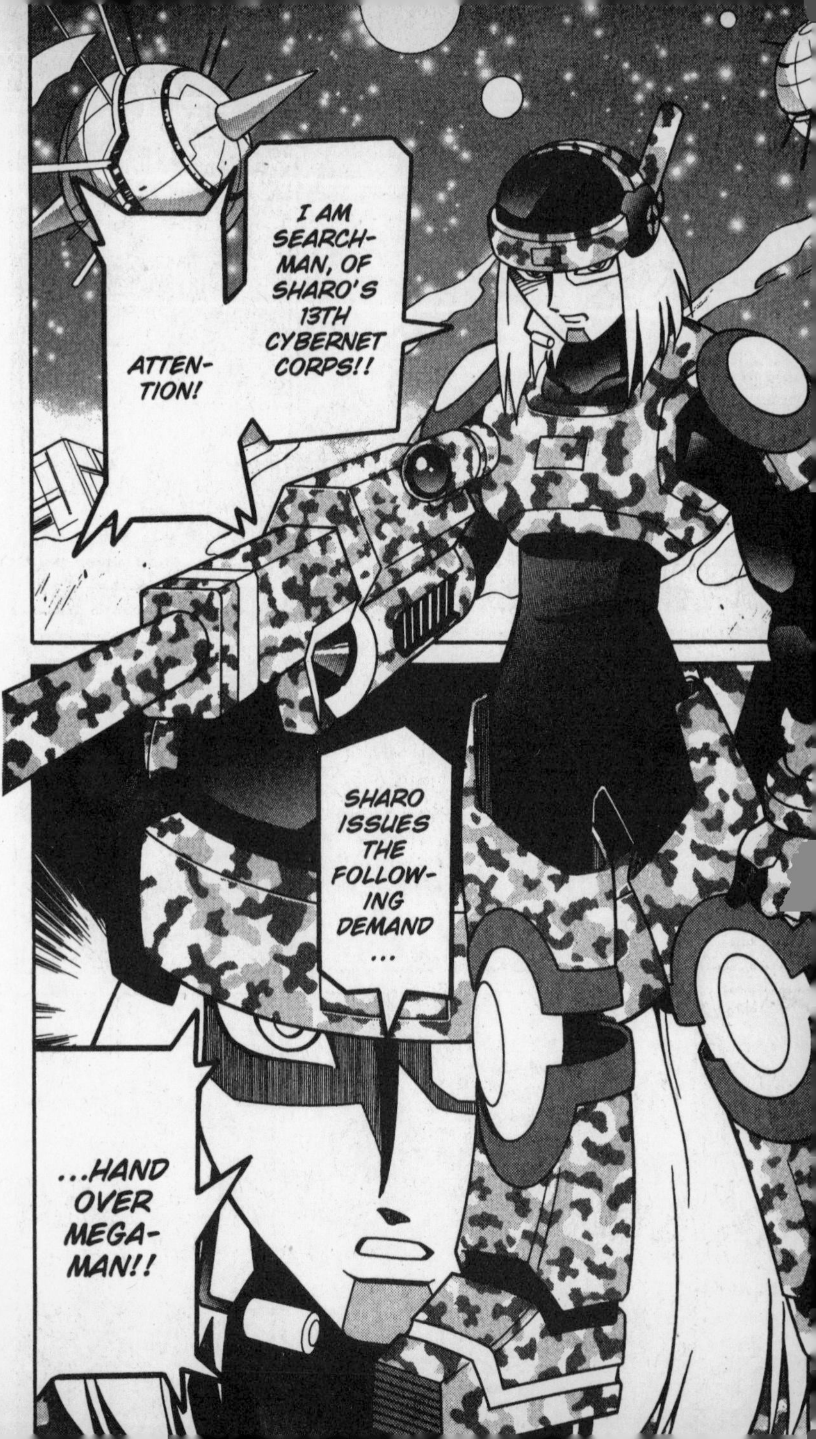
ATTEN-TION!
I AM SEARCH-MAN, OF SHARO'S 13TH CYBERNET CORPS!!
SHARO ISSUES THE FOLLOW-ING DEMAND ...
...HAND OVER MEGA-MAN!!

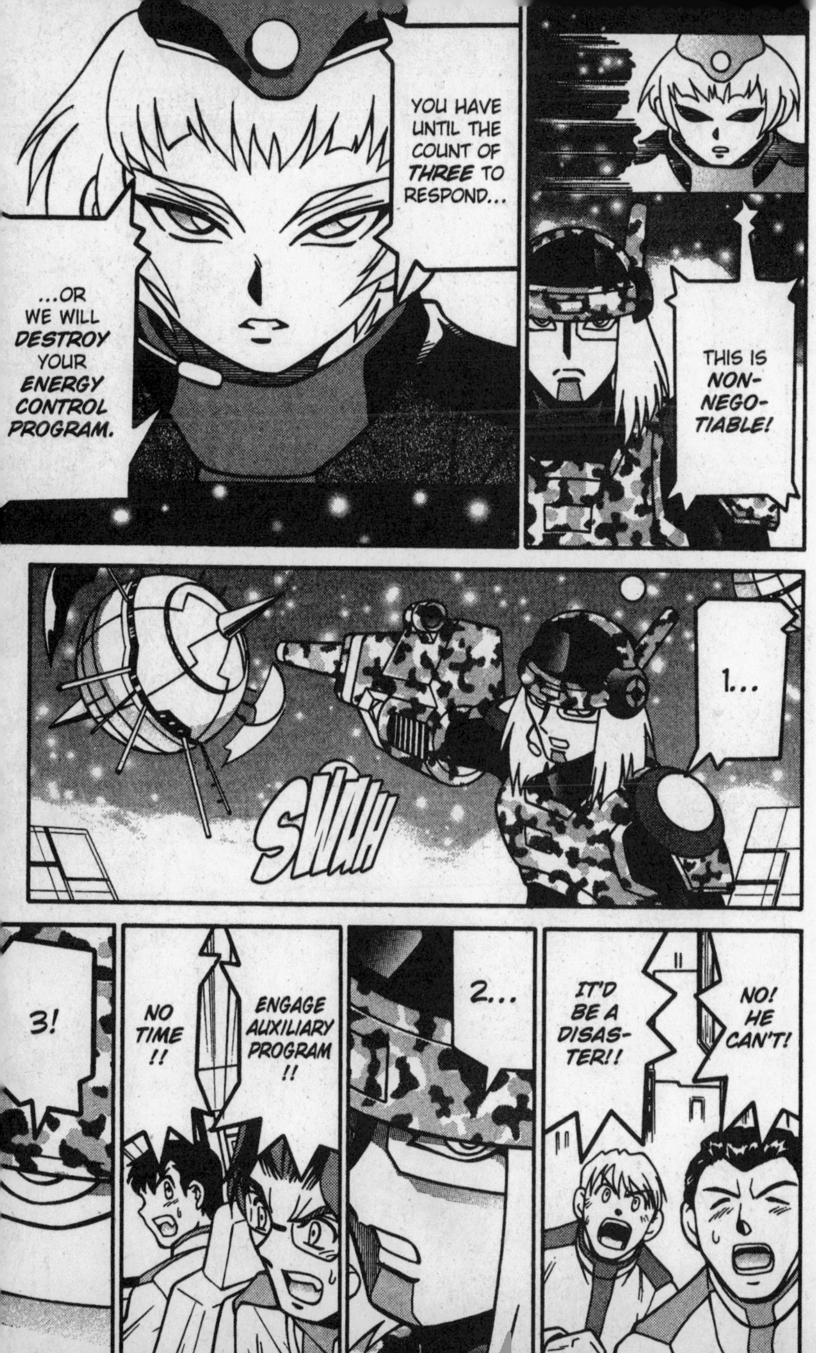
THIS IS NON-NEGOTIABLE!
YOU HAVE UNTIL THE COUNT OF THREE TO RESPOND...
...OR WE WILL DESTROY YOUR ENERGY CONTROL PROGRAM.
1...
SWHH
NO! HE CAN'T!
IT'D BE A DISASTER!!
2...
ENGAGE AUXILIARY PROGRAM!!
NO TIME!!
3!

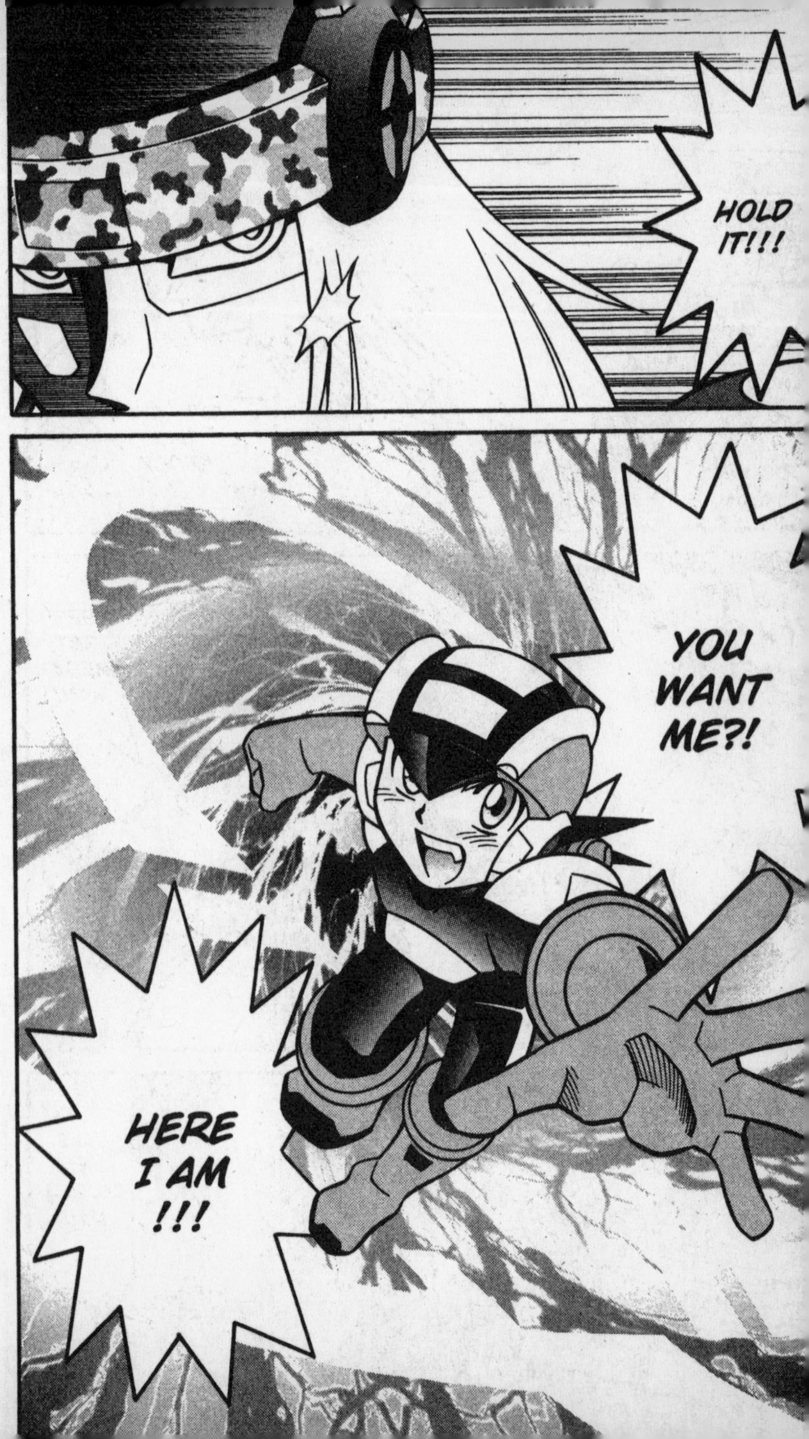
HOLD IT!!!
YOU WANT ME?!
HERE I AM !!!

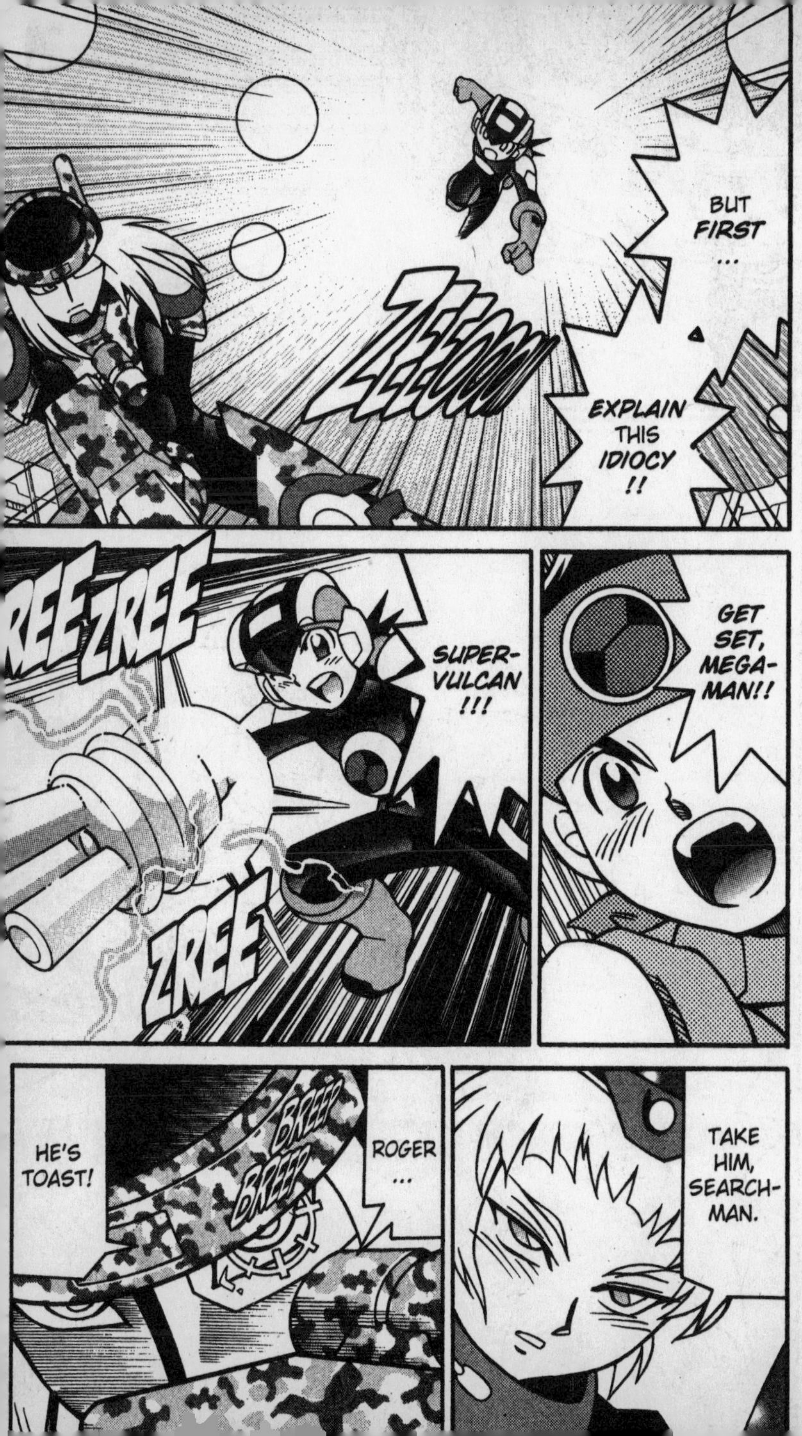
BUT FIRST ...
EXPLAIN THIS IDIOCY !!
GET SET, MEGA-MAN!!
SUPER-VULCAN !!!
ZREE ZREE
ZREE
TAKE HIM, SEARCH-MAN.
ROGER ...
BREEP BREEP
HE'S TOAST!

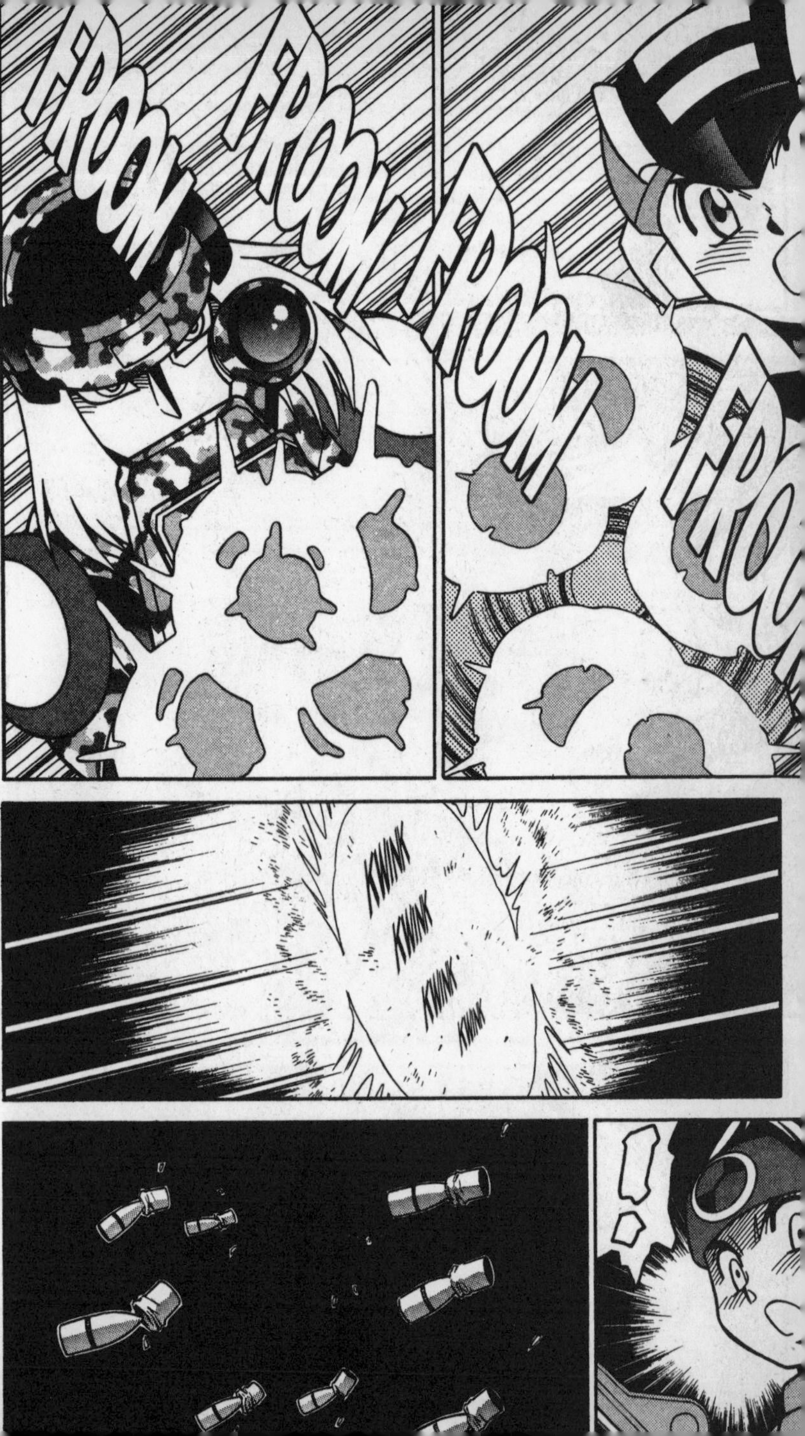
FROO
FROOM
FROOM
FROOM
FROOM
KWINK
KWINK
KWINK
KWINK
!!

H-HOLY YIKES!!

SPLUK

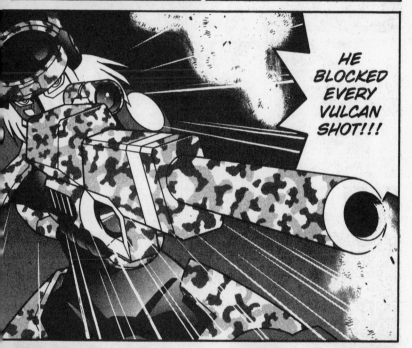

HE BLOCKED EVERY VULCAN SHOT!!!

TAKE COVER, MEGA-MAN!!

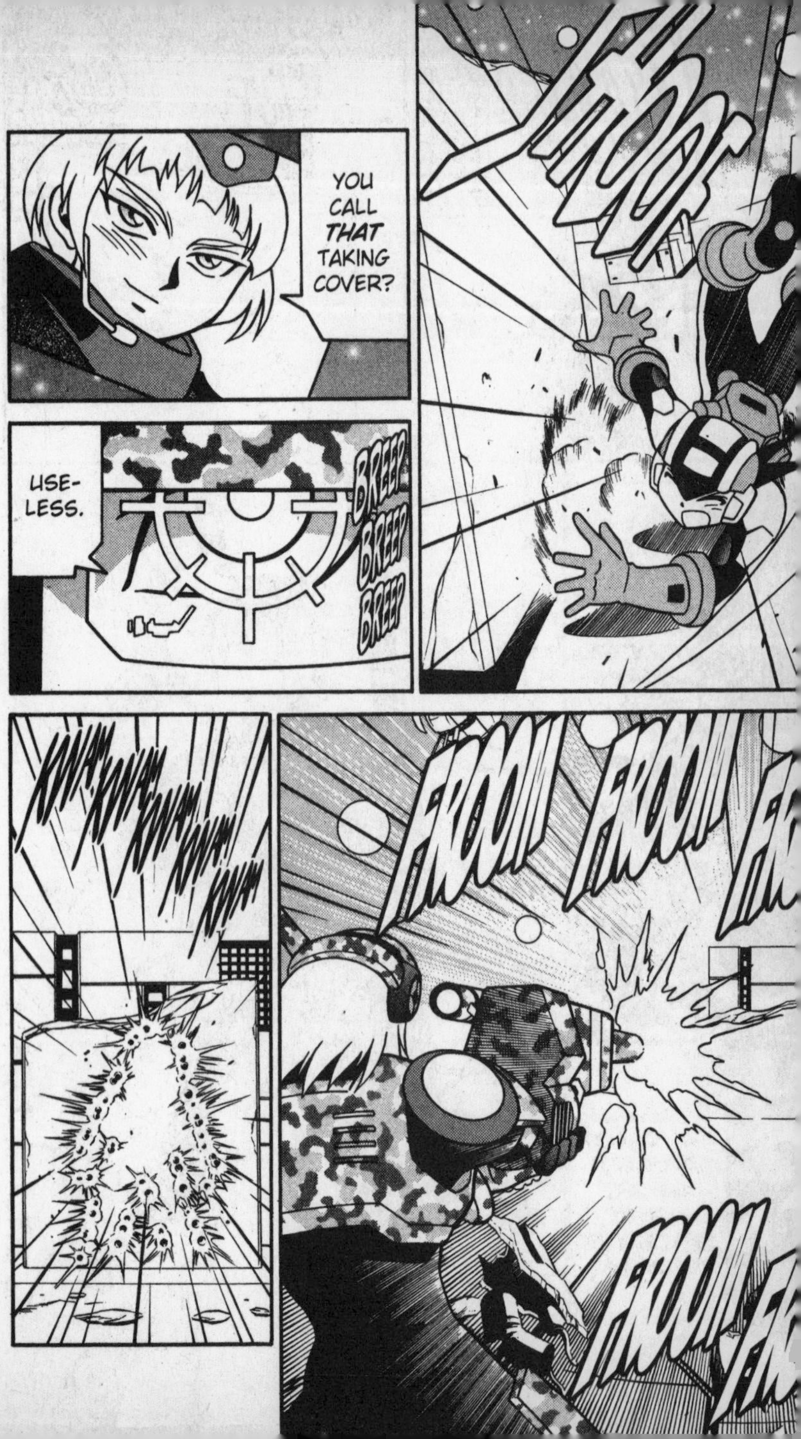
YOU CALL THAT TAKING COVER?
USE-LESS.
BREEP BREEP BREEP BREEP
FROOM FROOM
FROOM

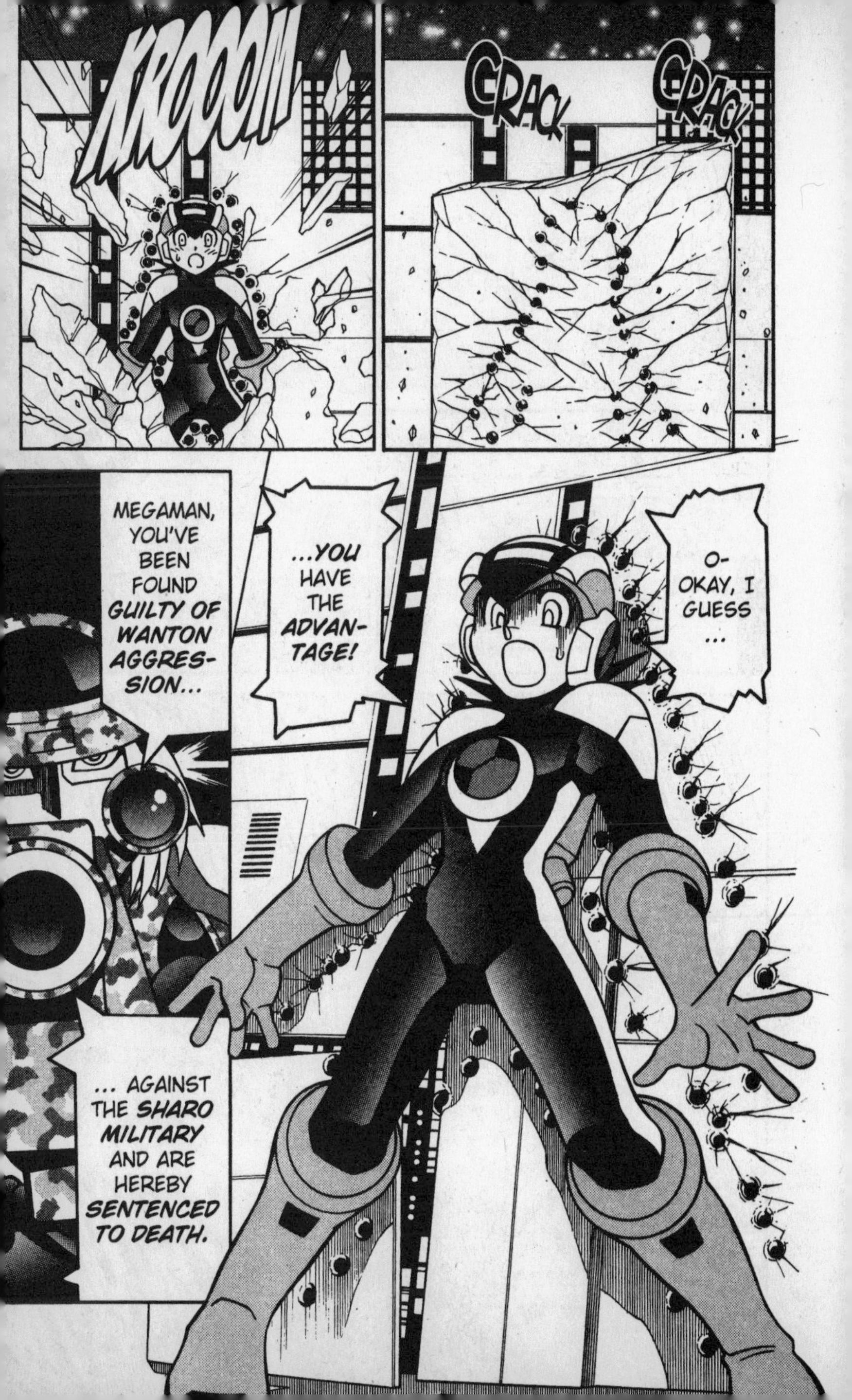
CRACK
CRACK
KROOOM
O-OKAY, I GUESS ...
...YOU HAVE THE ADVANTAGE!
MEGAMAN, YOU'VE BEEN FOUND GUILTY OF WANTON AGGRESSION...
... AGAINST THE SHARO MILITARY AND ARE HEREBY SENTENCED TO DEATH.

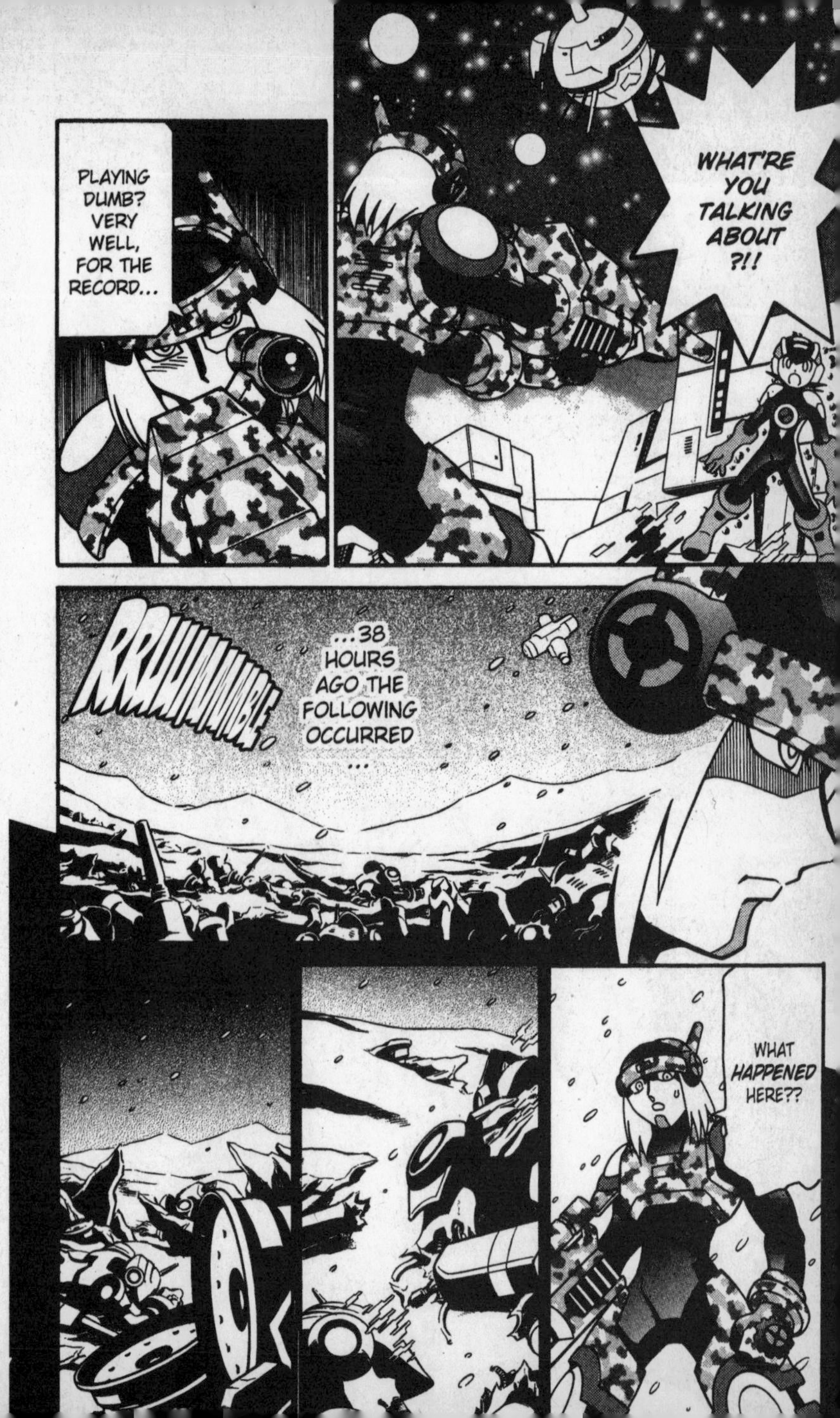
WHAT'RE YOU TALKING ABOUT ?!!
PLAYING DUMB? VERY WELL, FOR THE RECORD...
RRUMMMBLE
...38 HOURS AGO THE FOLLOWING OCCURRED ...
WHAT HAPPENED HERE??

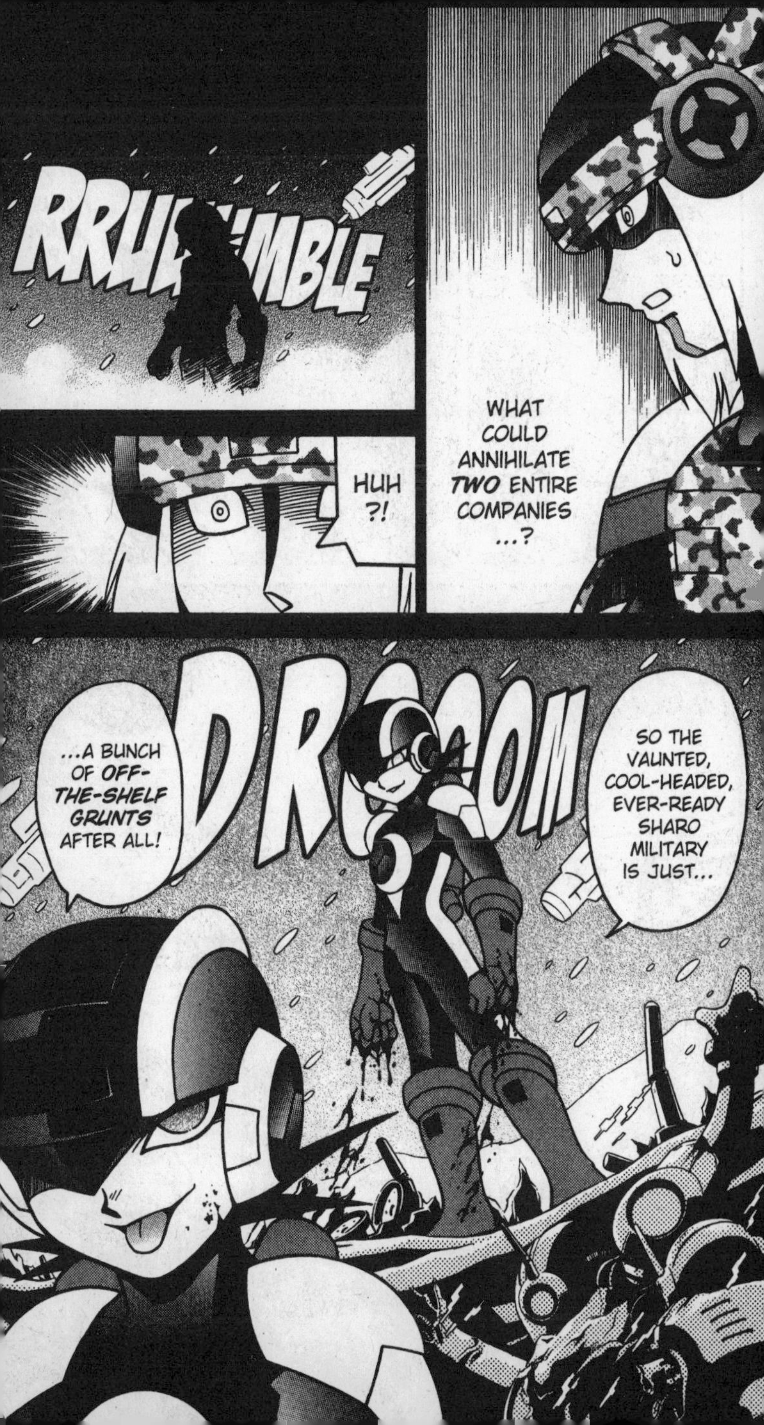
WHAT COULD ANNIHILATE **TWO** ENTIRE COMPANIES ...?
RRU MBLE
HUH ?!
SO THE VAUNTED, COOL-HEADED, EVER-READY SHARO MILITARY IS JUST...
DR OOOM
...A BUNCH OF **OFF-THE-SHELF GRUNTS** AFTER ALL!

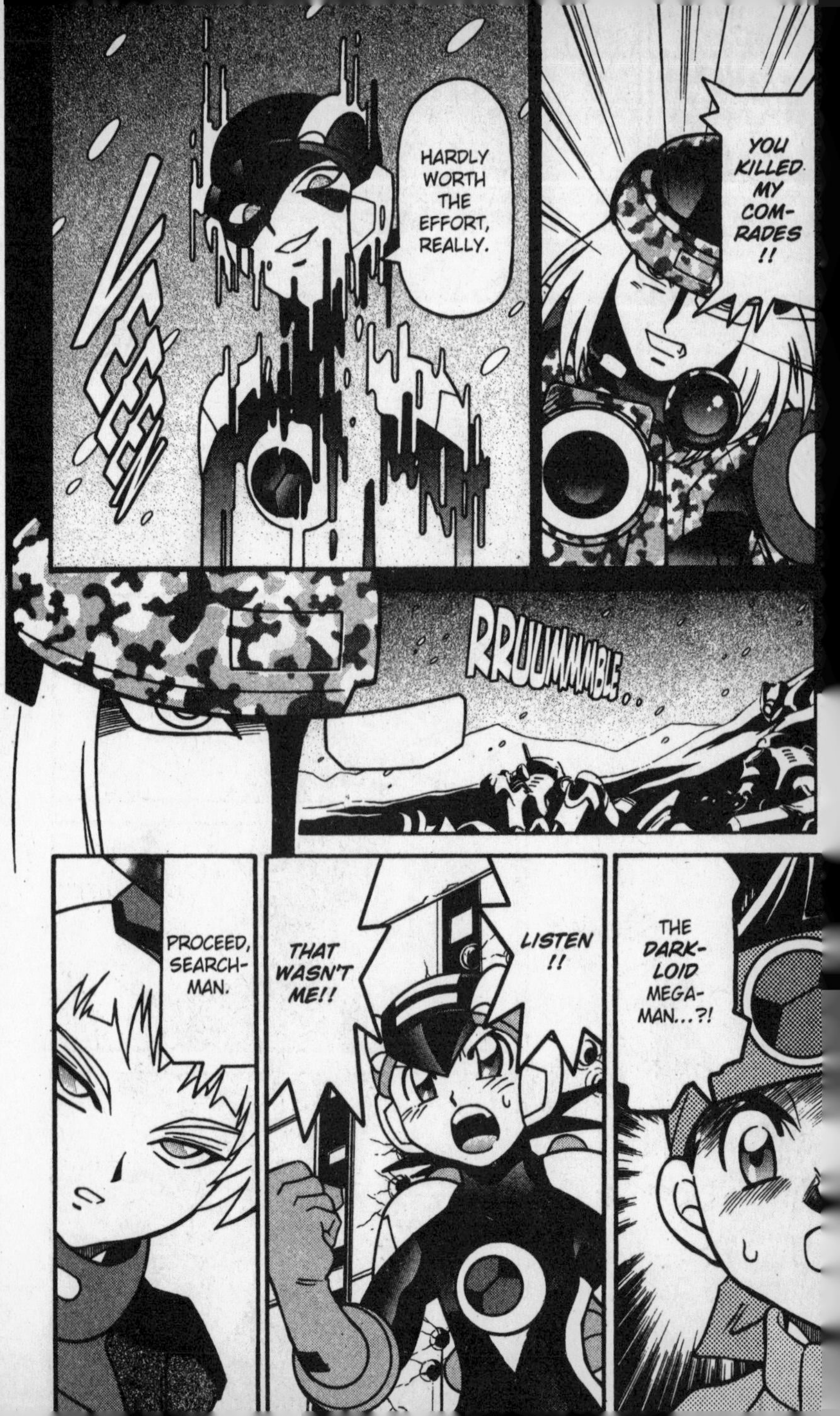
YOU KILLED MY COM-RADES!!
HARDLY WORTH THE EFFORT, REALLY.
RRUUMMMBLE...
THE DARK-LOID MEGA-MAN...?!
LISTEN!!
THAT WASN'T ME!!
PROCEED, SEARCH-MAN.

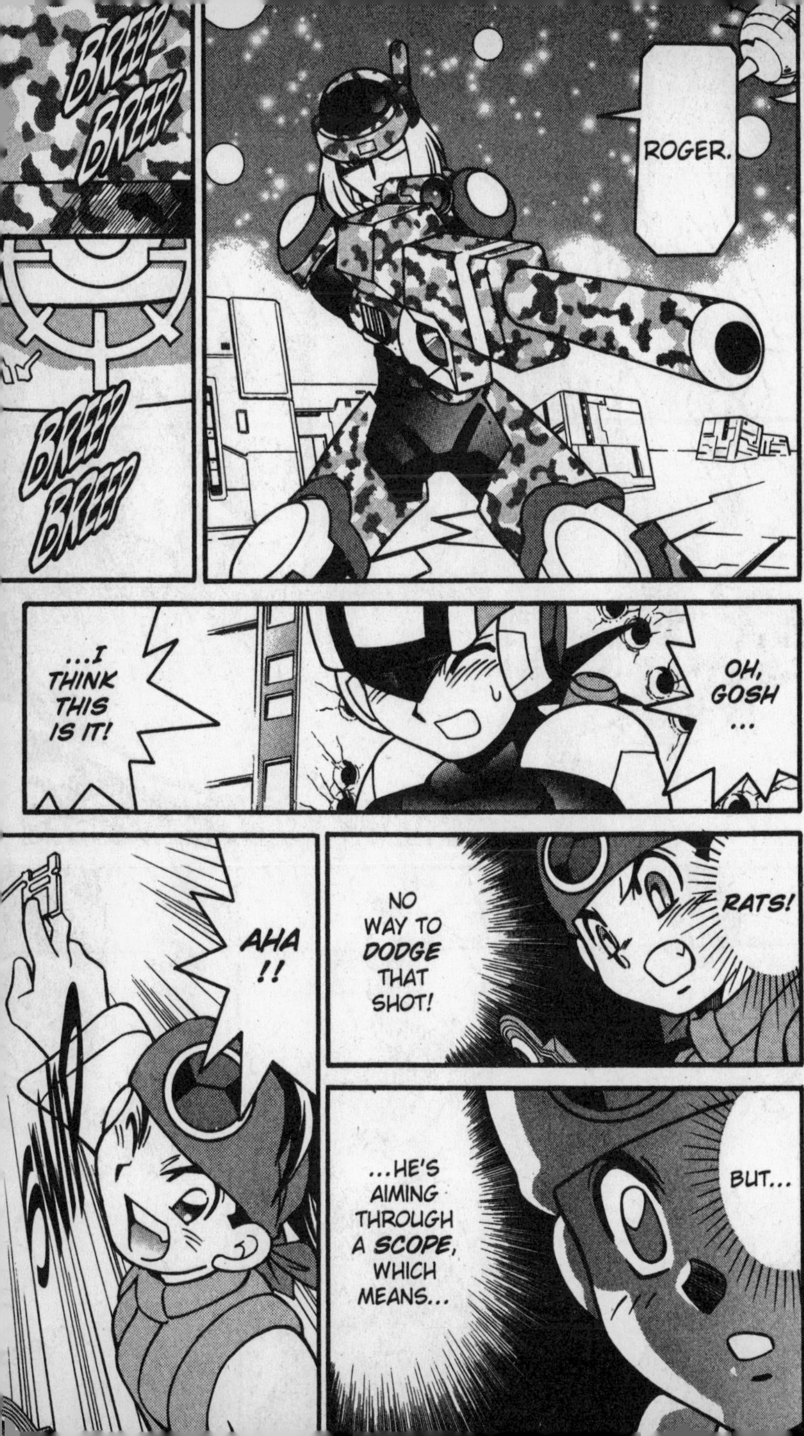
ROGER.
BREEP BREEP
BREEP BREEP
OH, GOSH...
...I THINK THIS IS IT!
RATS!
NO WAY TO DODGE THAT SHOT!
BUT...
...HE'S AIMING THROUGH A SCOPE, WHICH MEANS...
AHA!!

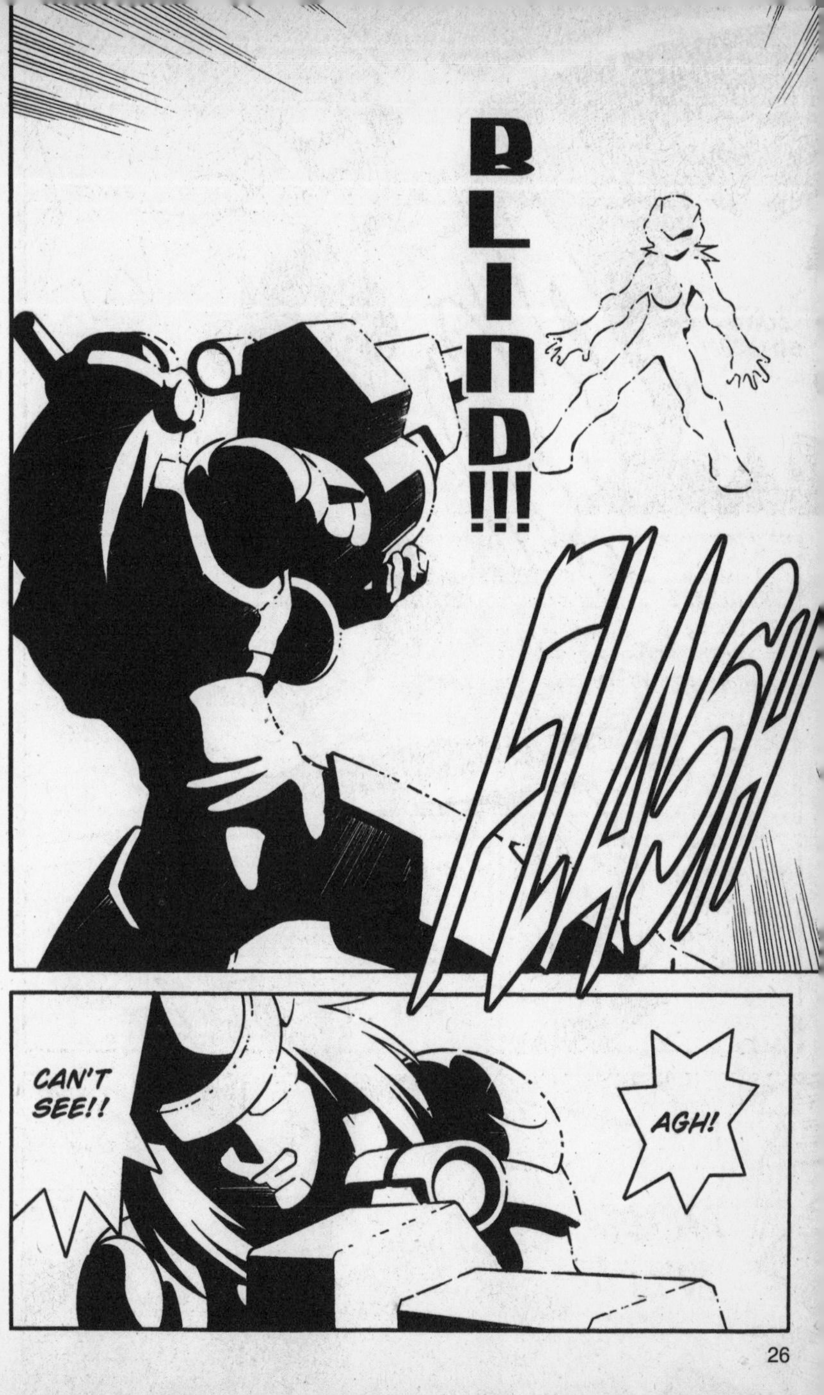
BLIND!!!
AGH!
CAN'T SEE!!

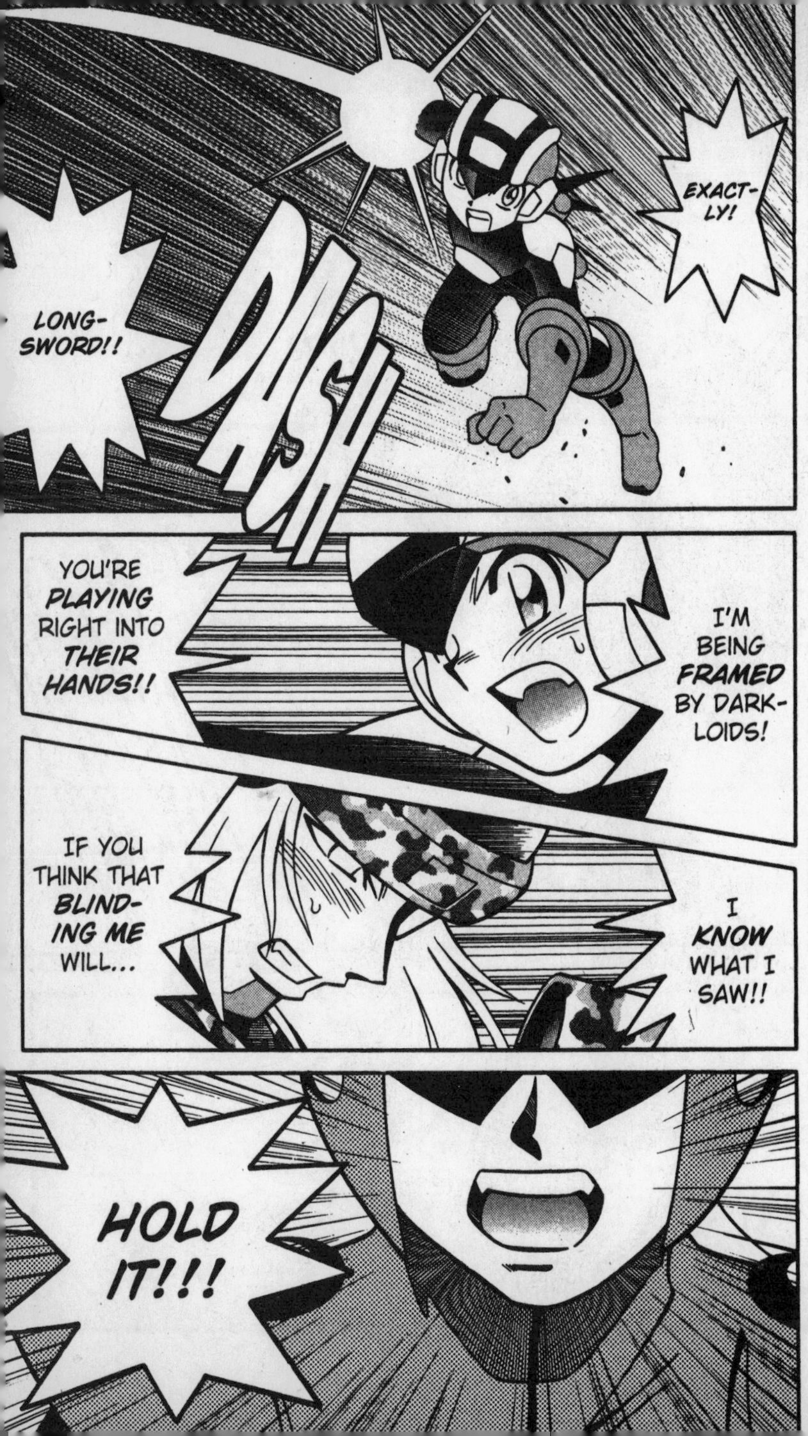
EXACT-LY!
DASH
LONG-SWORD!!
I'M BEING FRAMED BY DARK-LOIDS!
YOU'RE PLAYING RIGHT INTO THEIR HANDS!!
I KNOW WHAT I SAW!!
IF YOU THINK THAT BLIND-ING ME WILL...
HOLD IT!!!

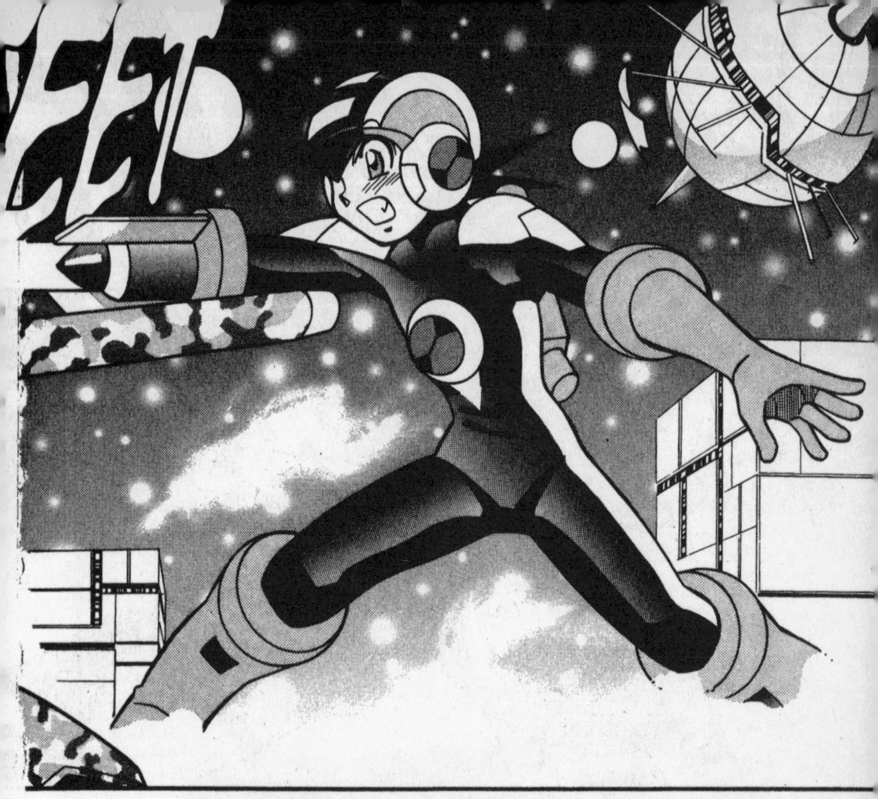

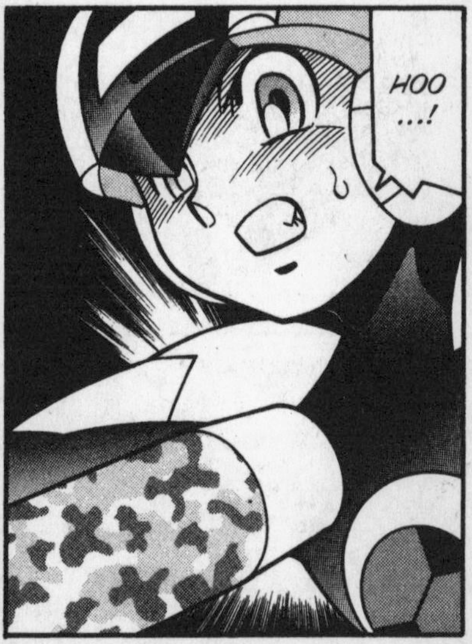
HOO
...!

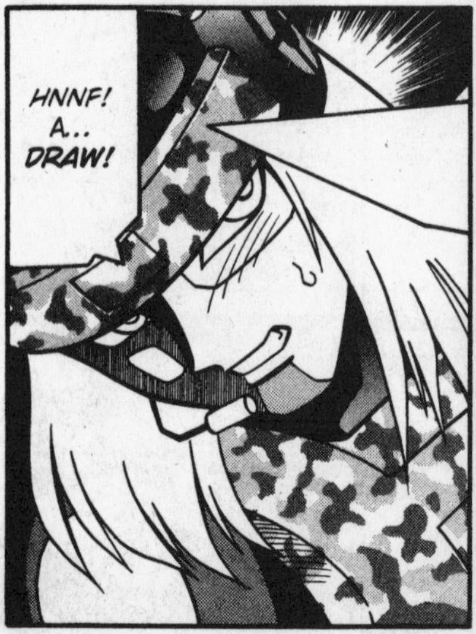
HNNF!
A...
DRAW!

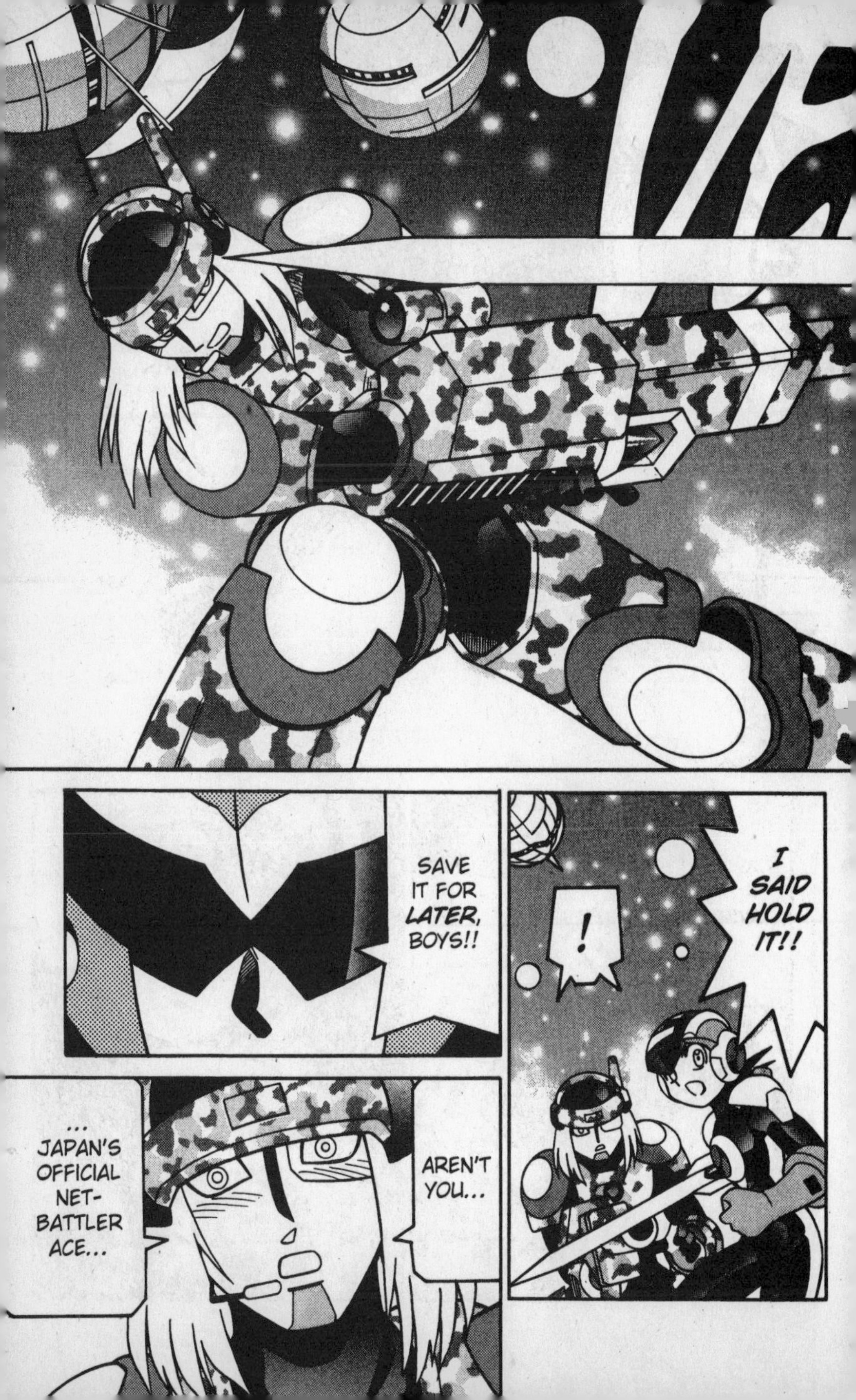
I SAID HOLD IT!!
!
SAVE IT FOR LATER, BOYS!!
AREN'T YOU...
...JAPAN'S OFFICIAL NET-BATTLER ACE...

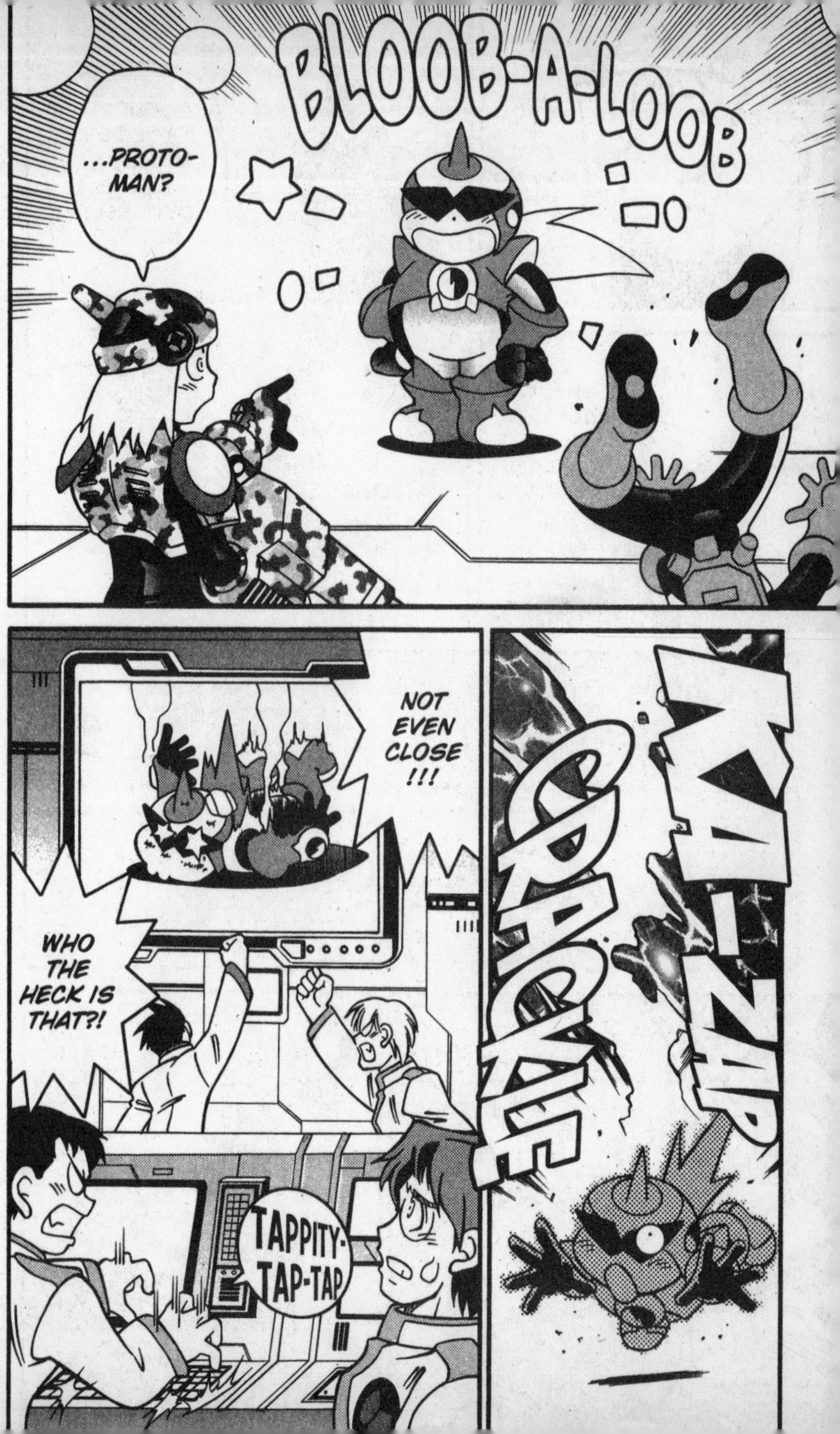
BLOOB-A-LOOB
...PROTO-MAN?
KA-ZAP
CRACKLE
NOT EVEN CLOSE !!!
WHO THE HECK IS THAT?!
TAPPITY-TAP-TAP

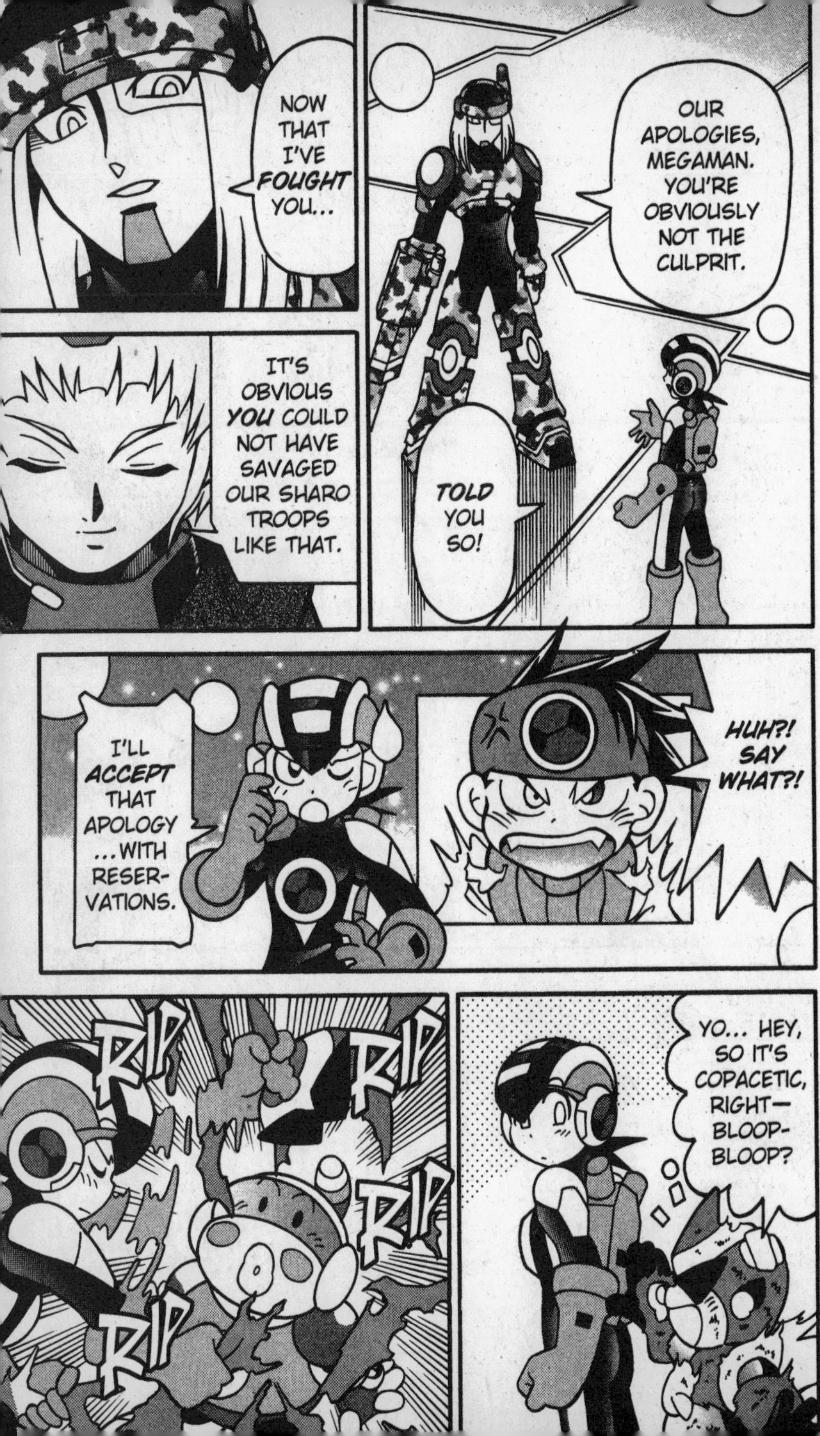
OUR APOLOGIES, MEGAMAN. YOU'RE OBVIOUSLY NOT THE CULPRIT.
TOLD YOU SO!
NOW THAT I'VE FOUGHT YOU...
IT'S OBVIOUS YOU COULD NOT HAVE SAVAGED OUR SHARO TROOPS LIKE THAT.
HUH?! SAY WHAT?!
I'LL ACCEPT THAT APOLOGY ...WITH RESERVATIONS.
YO... HEY, SO IT'S COPACETIC, RIGHT— BLOOP-BLOOP?
RIP
RIP
RIP
RIP

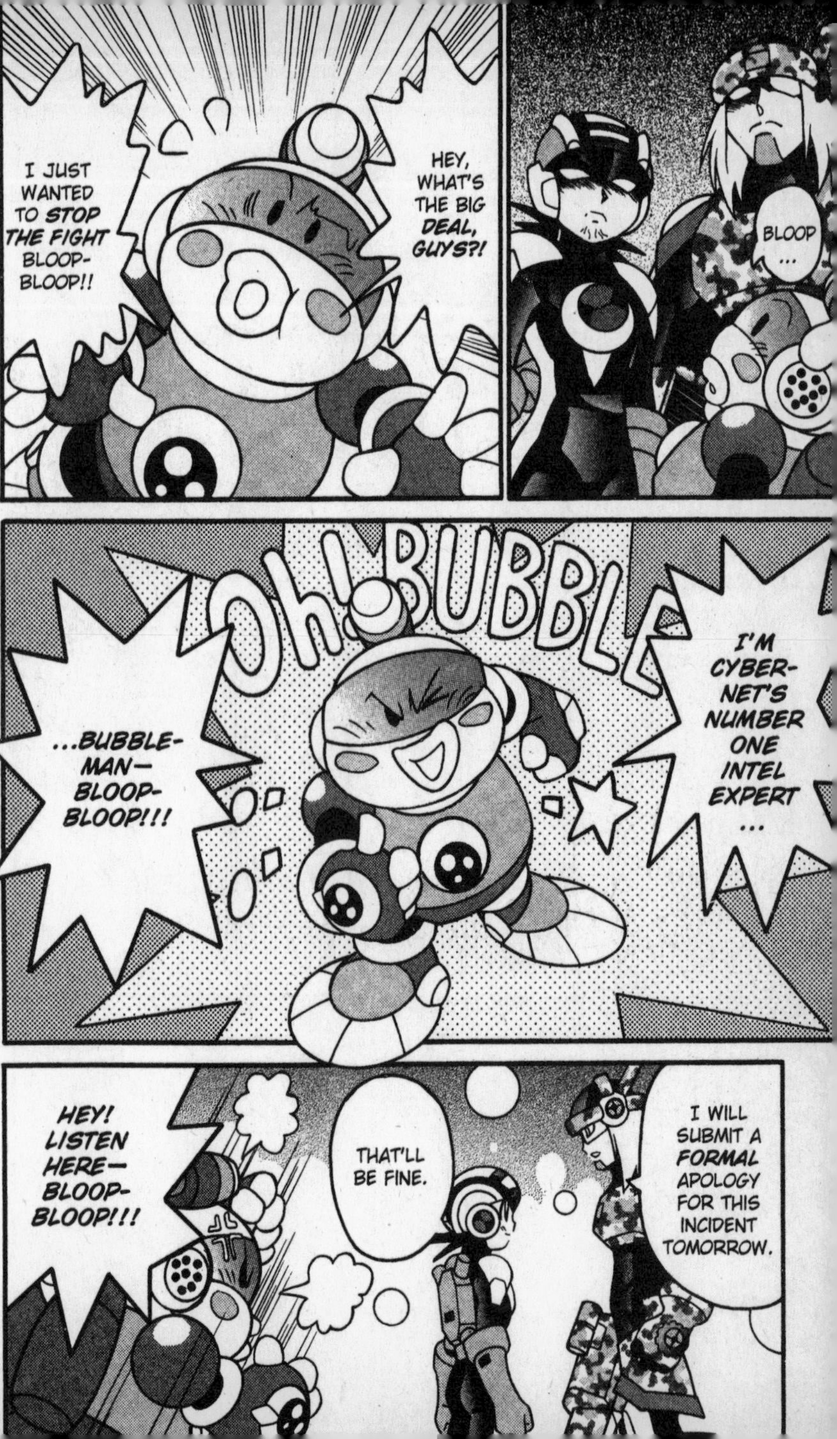
BLOOP ...
HEY, WHAT'S THE BIG DEAL, GUYS?!
I JUST WANTED TO STOP THE FIGHT BLOOP-BLOOP!!
Oh! BUBBLE
I'M CYBER-NET'S NUMBER ONE INTEL EXPERT ...
...BUBBLE-MAN—BLOOP-BLOOP!!!
I WILL SUBMIT A FORMAL APOLOGY FOR THIS INCIDENT TOMORROW.
THAT'LL BE FINE.
HEY! LISTEN HERE—BLOOP-BLOOP!!!

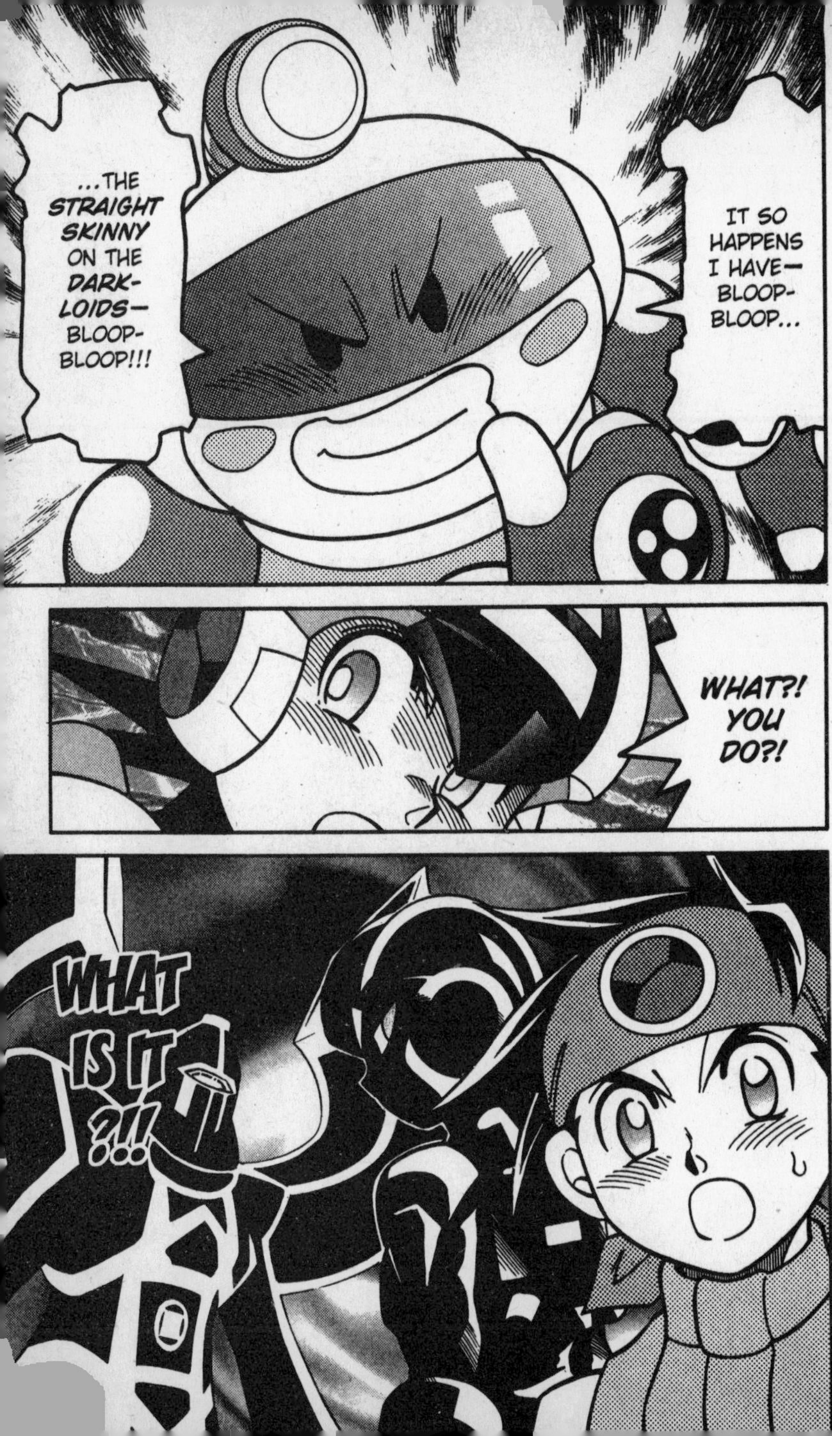
IT SO HAPPENS I HAVE— BLOOP-BLOOP...
...THE STRAIGHT SKINNY ON THE DARK-LOIDS— BLOOP-BLOOP!!!
WHAT?! YOU DO?!
WHAT IS IT ?!!

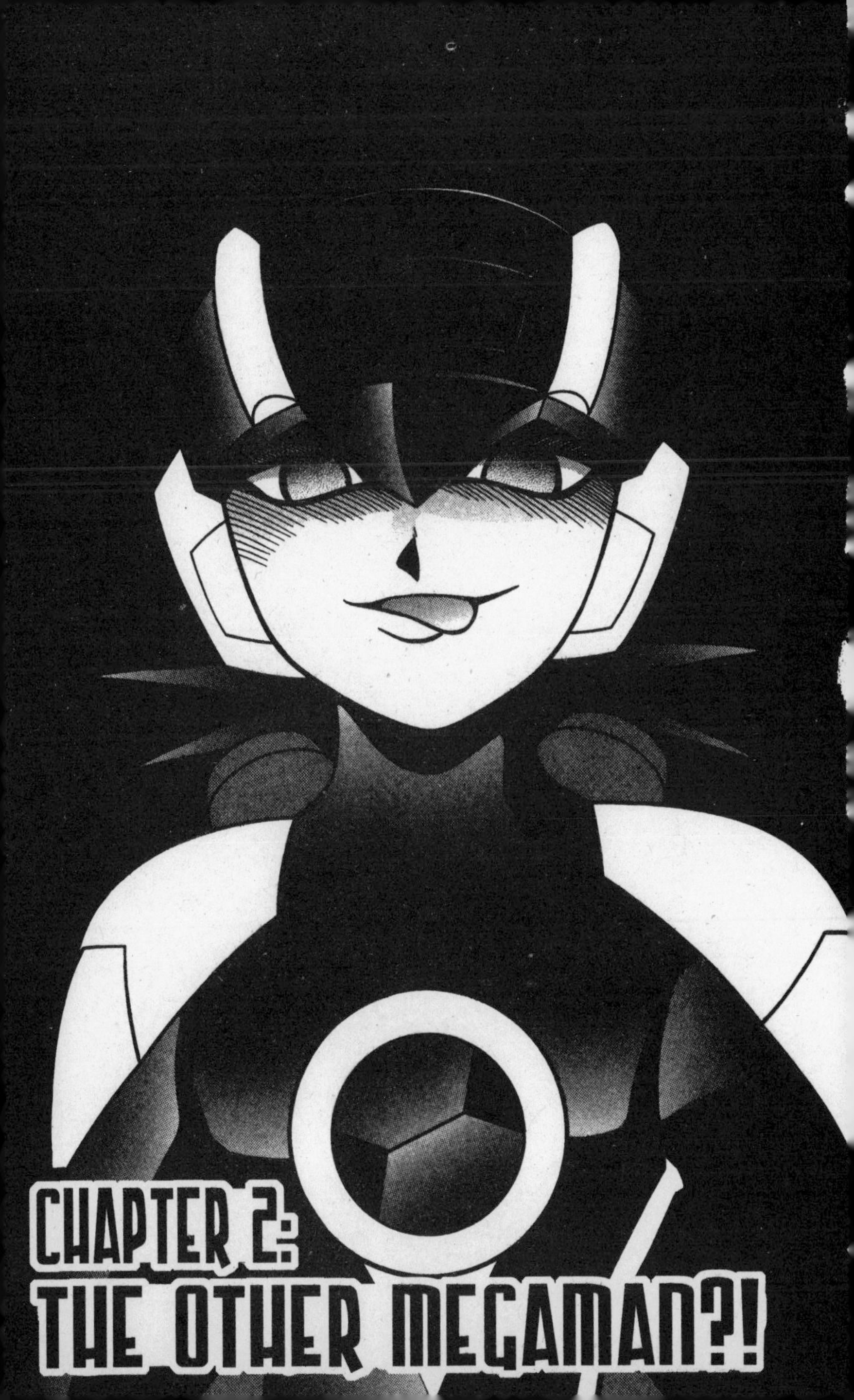
CHAPTER 2:
THE OTHER MEGAMAN?!

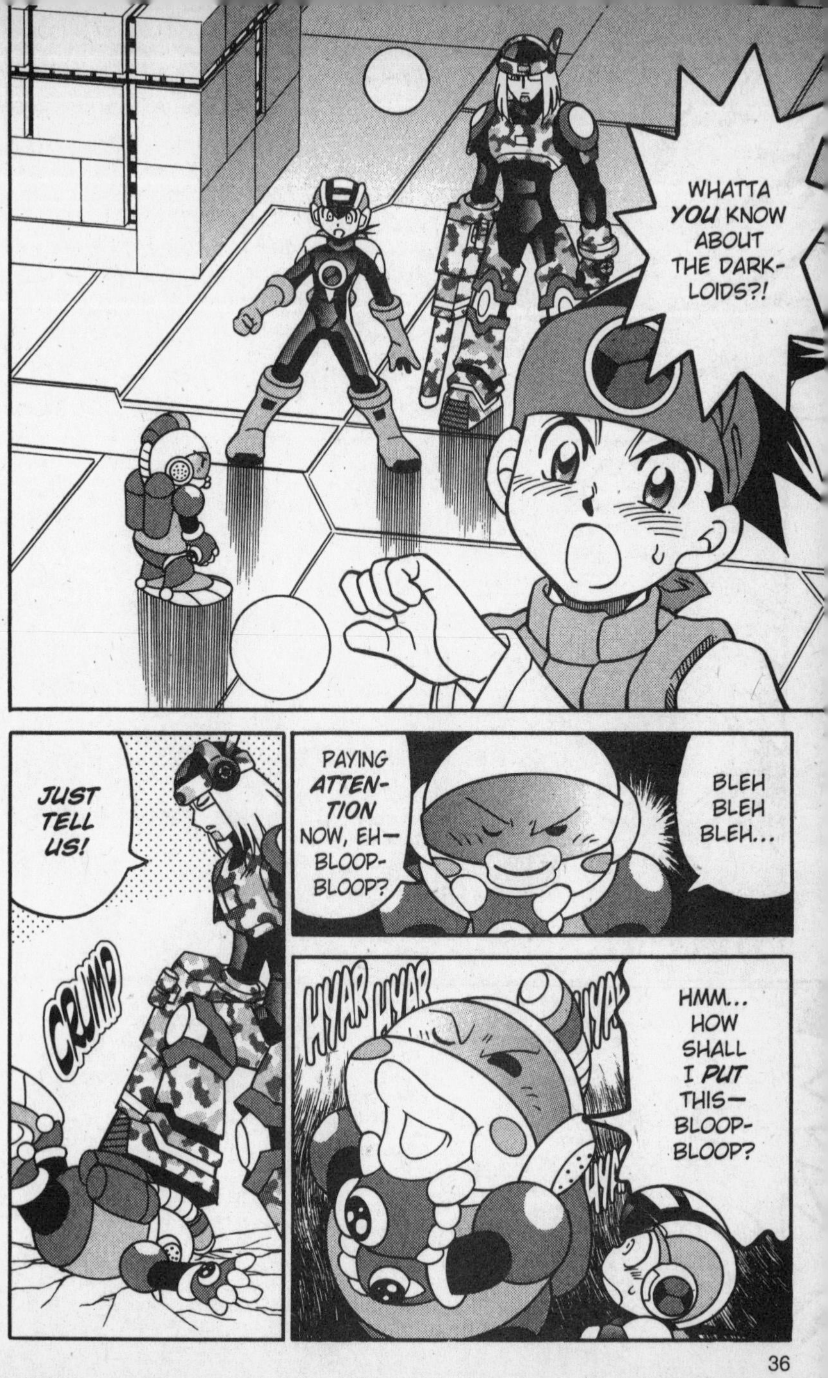
WHATTA *YOU* KNOW ABOUT THE DARK-LOIDS?!
BLEH BLEH BLEH...
PAYING *ATTEN-TION* NOW, EH—BLOOP-BLOOP?
HMM... HOW SHALL I *PUT* THIS—BLOOP-BLOOP?
HYAR HYAR
JUST TELL US!
CRUMP

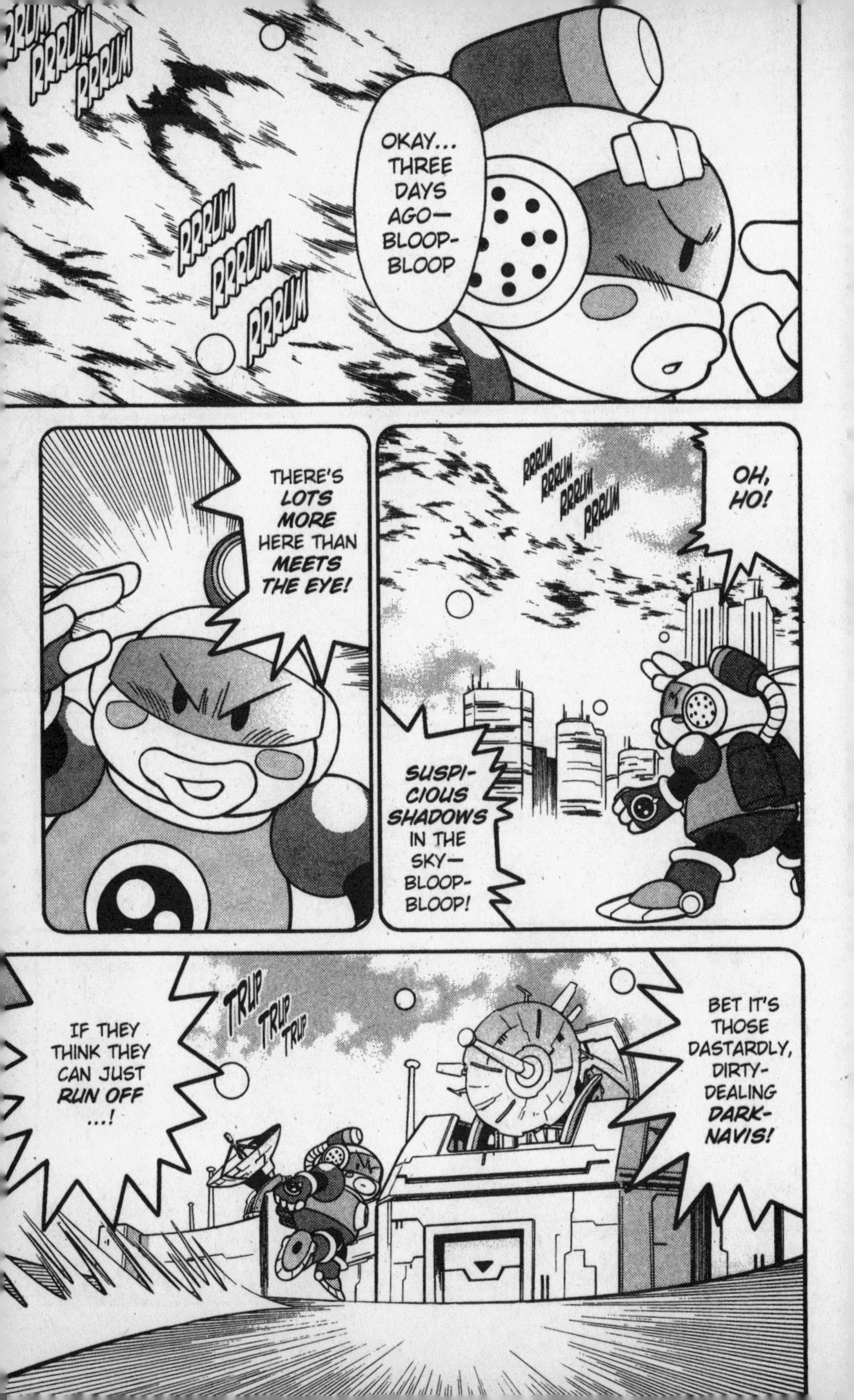
RRRUM RRRUM RRRUM
OKAY... THREE DAYS AGO—BLOOP-BLOOP
RRRUM RRRUM RRRUM
OH, HO!
RRRUM RRRUM RRRUM RRRUM
SUSPICIOUS SHADOWS IN THE SKY—BLOOP-BLOOP!
THERE'S LOTS MORE HERE THAN MEETS THE EYE!
BET IT'S THOSE DASTARDLY, DIRTY-DEALING DARK-NAVIS!
TRUP TRUP TRUP
IF THEY THINK THEY CAN JUST RUN OFF ...!

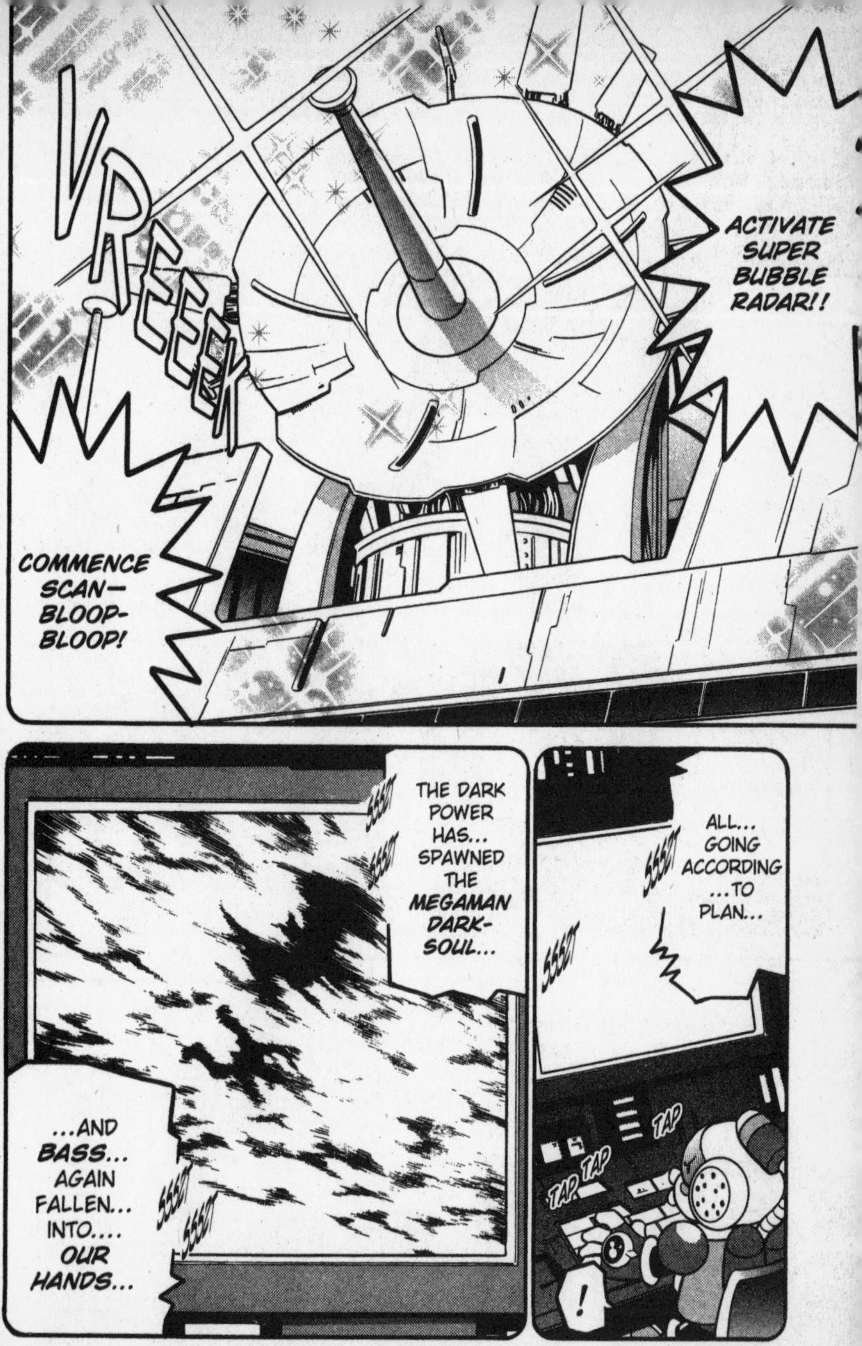
ACTIVATE SUPER BUBBLE RADAR!!
VREEEK
COMMENCE SCAN—BLOOP-BLOOP!
SSSZT
ALL... GOING ACCORDING ...TO PLAN...
SSSZT
TAP TAP TAP
!
SSSZT SSSZT
THE DARK POWER HAS... SPAWNED THE ***MEGAMAN DARK-SOUL***...
...AND ***BASS***... AGAIN FALLEN... INTO.... ***OUR HANDS***...
SSSZT SSSZT

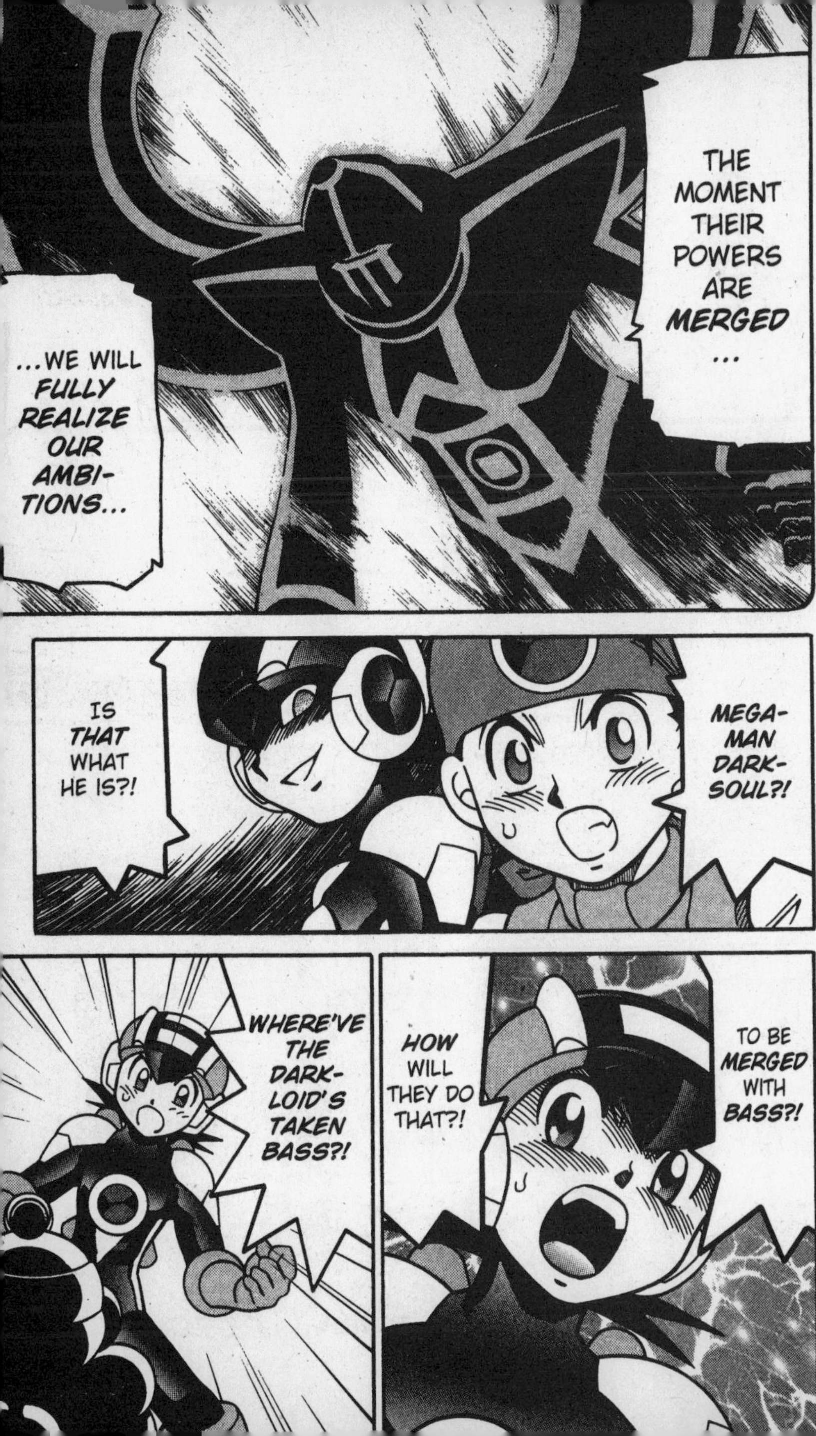
THE MOMENT THEIR POWERS ARE MERGED...
...WE WILL FULLY REALIZE OUR AMBITIONS...
MEGA-MAN DARK-SOUL?!
IS THAT WHAT HE IS?!
TO BE MERGED WITH BASS?!
HOW WILL THEY DO THAT?!
WHERE'VE THE DARK-LOID'S TAKEN BASS?!

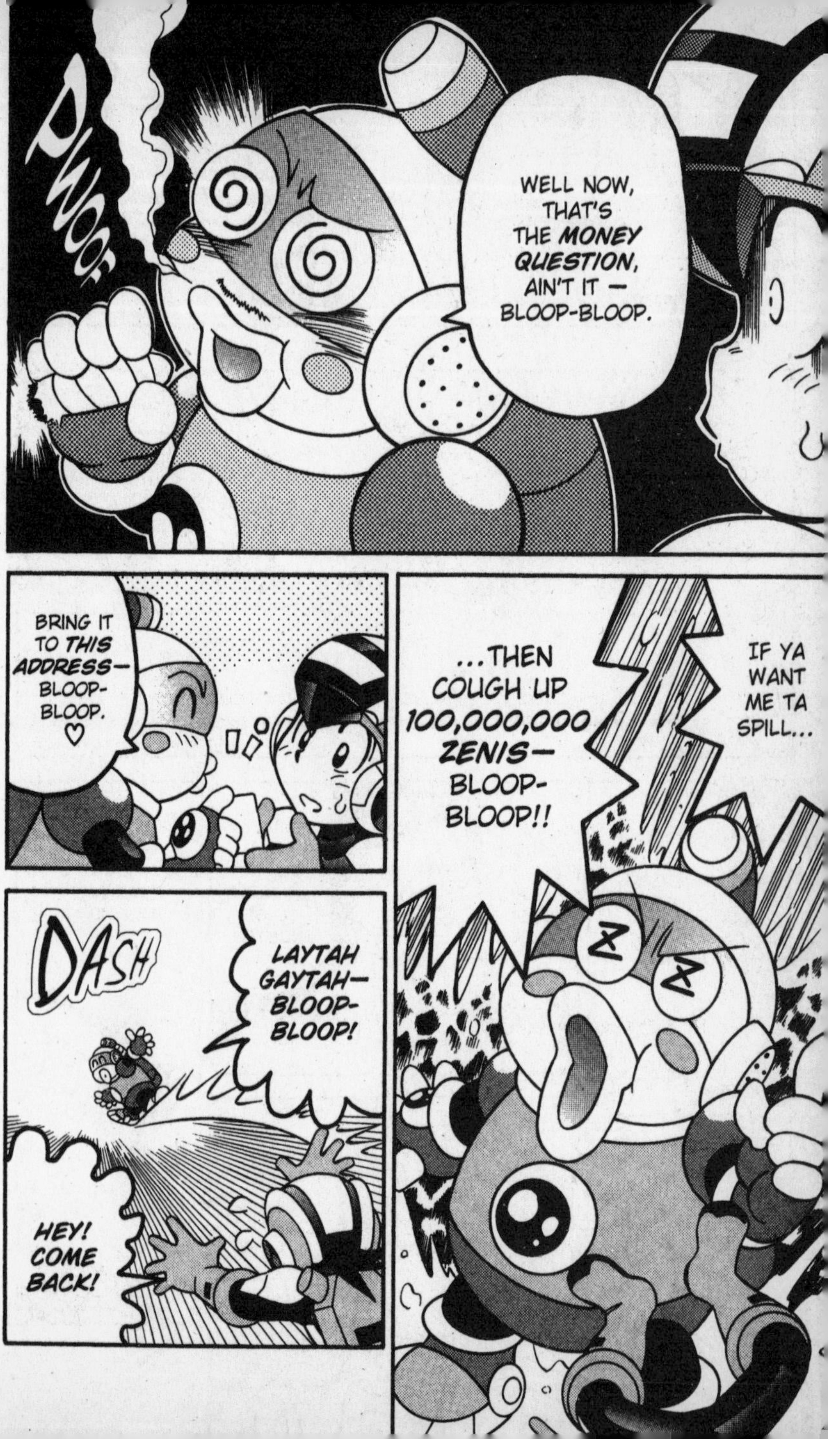
WELL NOW, THAT'S THE MONEY QUESTION, AIN'T IT — BLOOP-BLOOP.
PWOOF
IF YA WANT ME TA SPILL...
...THEN COUGH UP 100,000,000 ZENIS— BLOOP-BLOOP!!
BRING IT TO THIS ADDRESS— BLOOP-BLOOP. ♡
LAYTAH GAYTAH— BLOOP-BLOOP!
DASH
HEY! COME BACK!

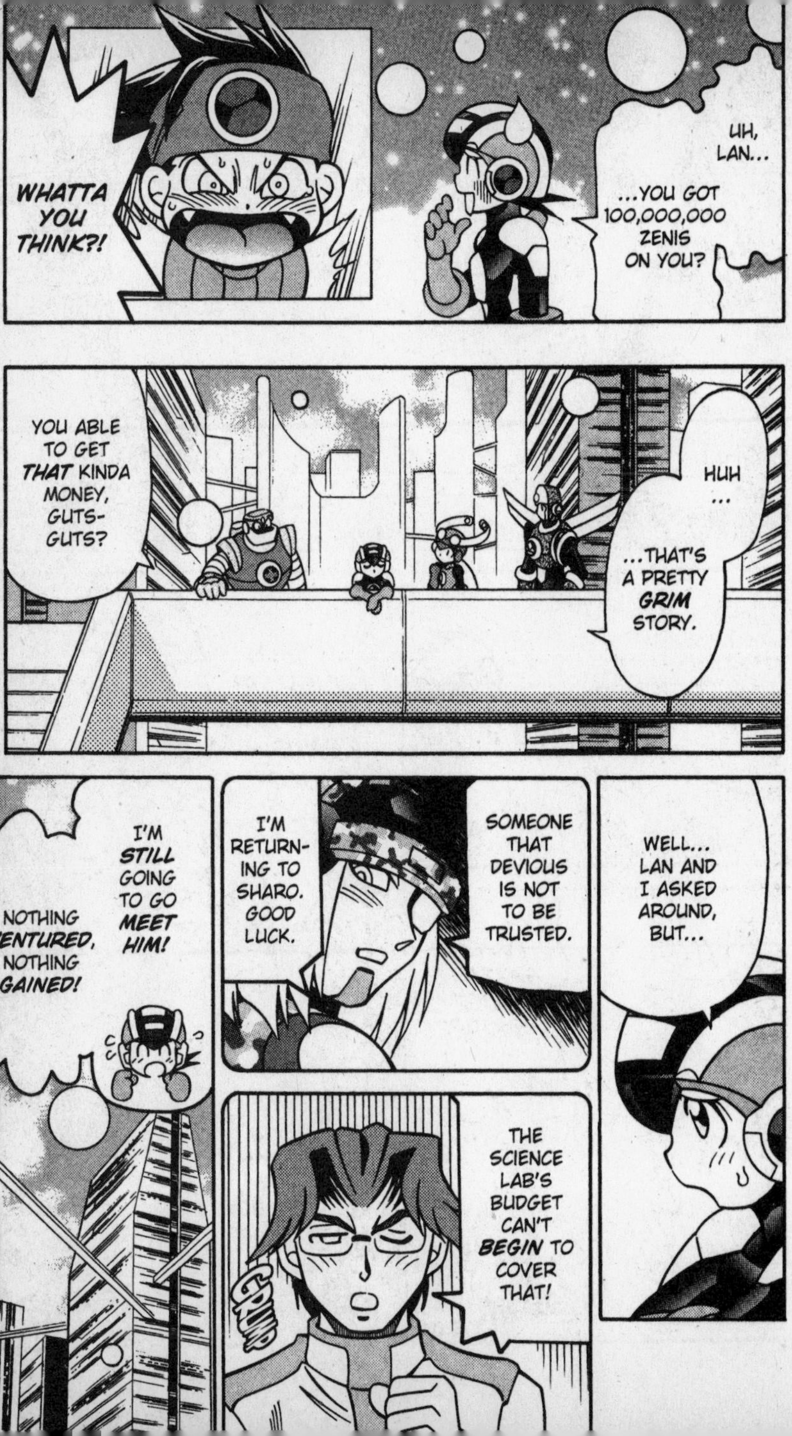
UH, LAN...
...YOU GOT 100,000,000 ZENIS ON YOU?
WHATTA YOU THINK?!
HUH... ...THAT'S A PRETTY GRIM STORY.
YOU ABLE TO GET THAT KINDA MONEY, GUTS-GUTS?
WELL... LAN AND I ASKED AROUND, BUT...
SOMEONE THAT DEVIOUS IS NOT TO BE TRUSTED.
I'M RETURNING TO SHARO. GOOD LUCK.
THE SCIENCE LAB'S BUDGET CAN'T BEGIN TO COVER THAT!
I'M STILL GOING TO GO MEET HIM!
NOTHING VENTURED, NOTHING GAINED!

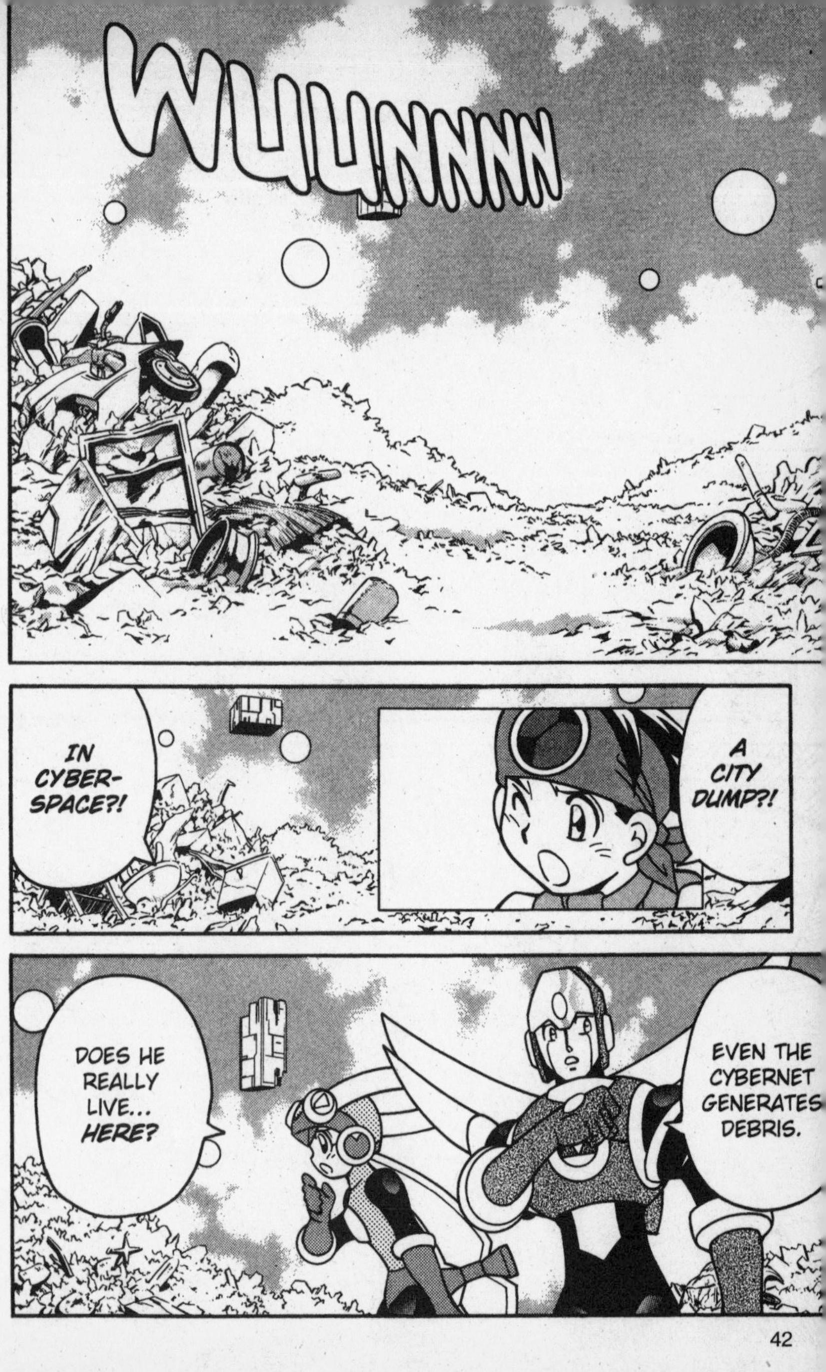
WUUNNNN
A CITY DUMP?!
IN CYBER-SPACE?!
EVEN THE CYBERNET GENERATES DEBRIS.
DOES HE REALLY LIVE... HERE?

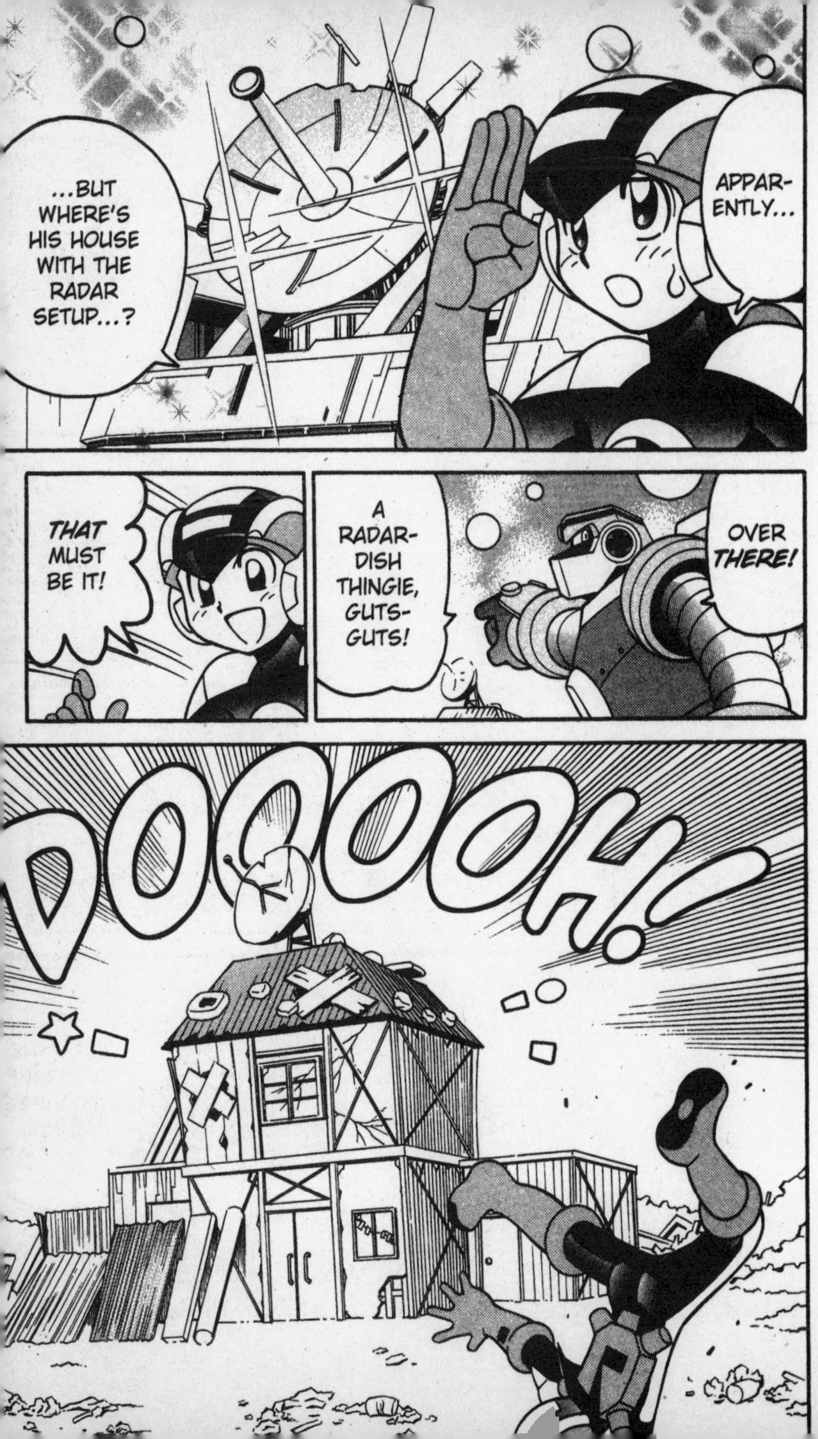
APPAR-ENTLY...
...BUT WHERE'S HIS HOUSE WITH THE RADAR SETUP...?
OVER *THERE!*
A RADAR-DISH THINGIE, GUTS-GUTS!
THAT MUST BE IT!
DOOOOH!!

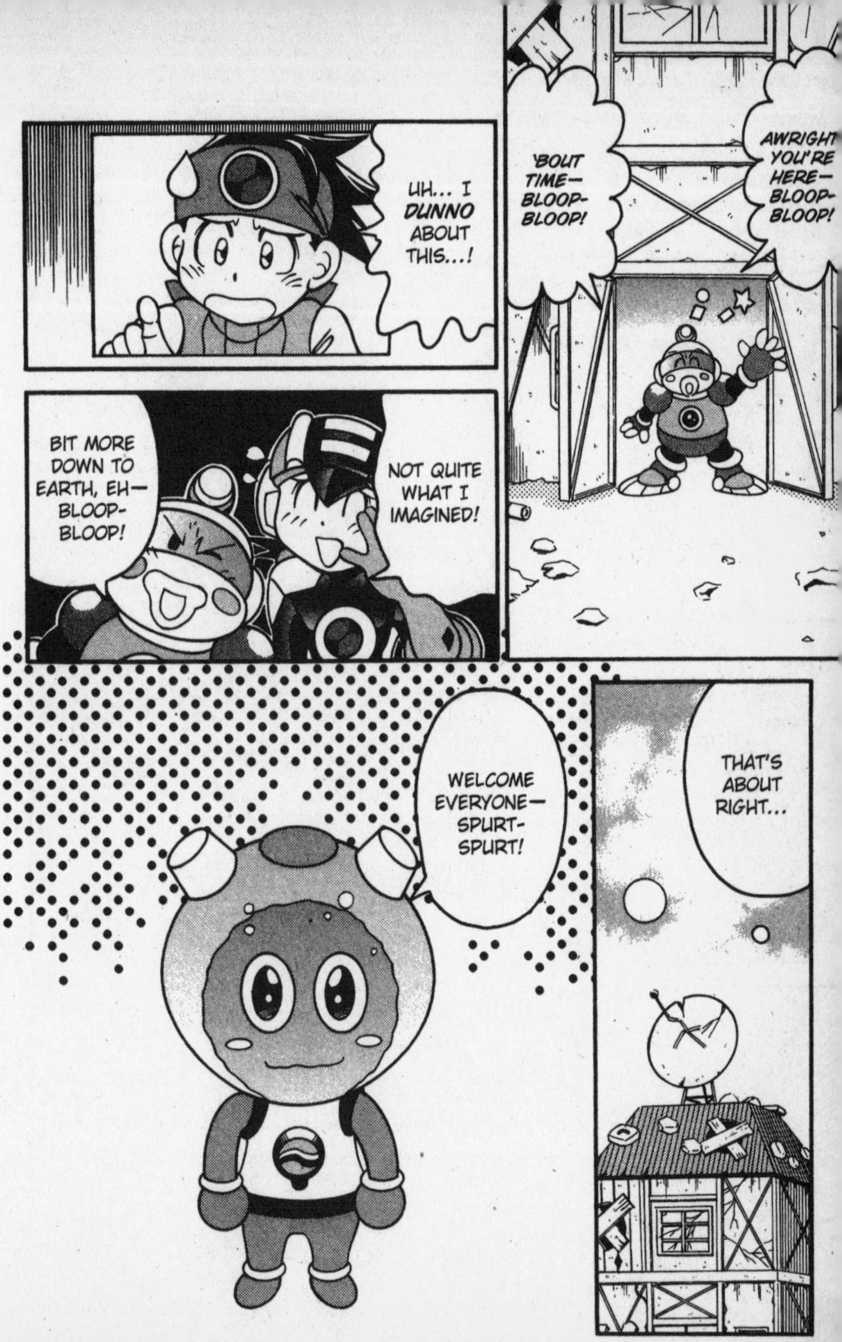
AWRIGHT YOU'RE HERE—BLOOP-BLOOP!
'BOUT TIME—BLOOP-BLOOP!
UH... I DUNNO ABOUT THIS...!
NOT QUITE WHAT I IMAGINED!
BIT MORE DOWN TO EARTH, EH—BLOOP-BLOOP!
THAT'S ABOUT RIGHT...
WELCOME EVERYONE—SPURT-SPURT!

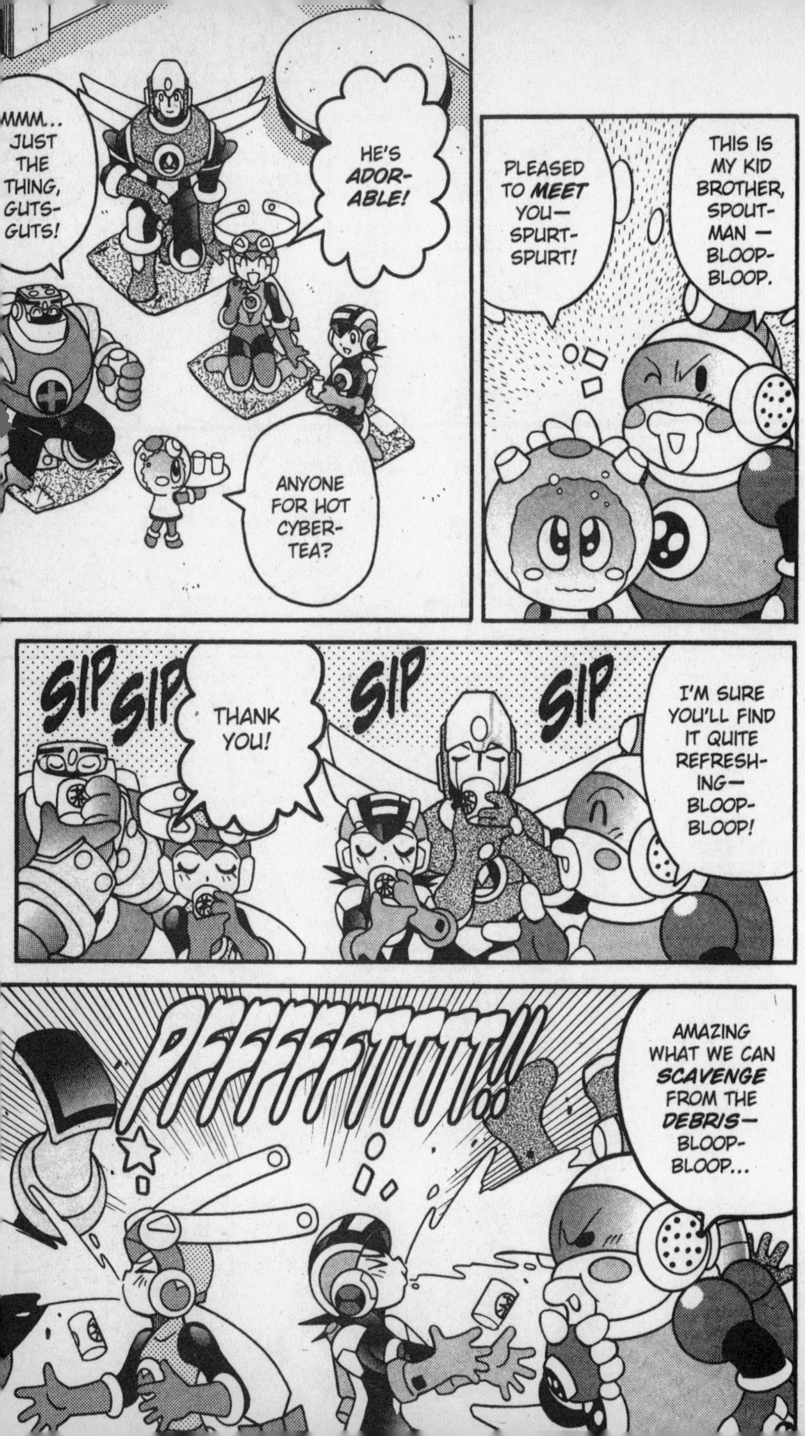
THIS IS MY KID BROTHER, SPOUTMAN — BLOOP-BLOOP.
PLEASED TO MEET YOU— SPURT-SPURT!
HE'S ADORABLE!
MMM... JUST THE THING, GUTS-GUTS!
ANYONE FOR HOT CYBER-TEA?
I'M SURE YOU'LL FIND IT QUITE REFRESHING— BLOOP-BLOOP!
SIP
SIP
THANK YOU!
SIP
SIP
AMAZING WHAT WE CAN SCAVENGE FROM THE DEBRIS— BLOOP-BLOOP...
PFFFFFTTTTT!!

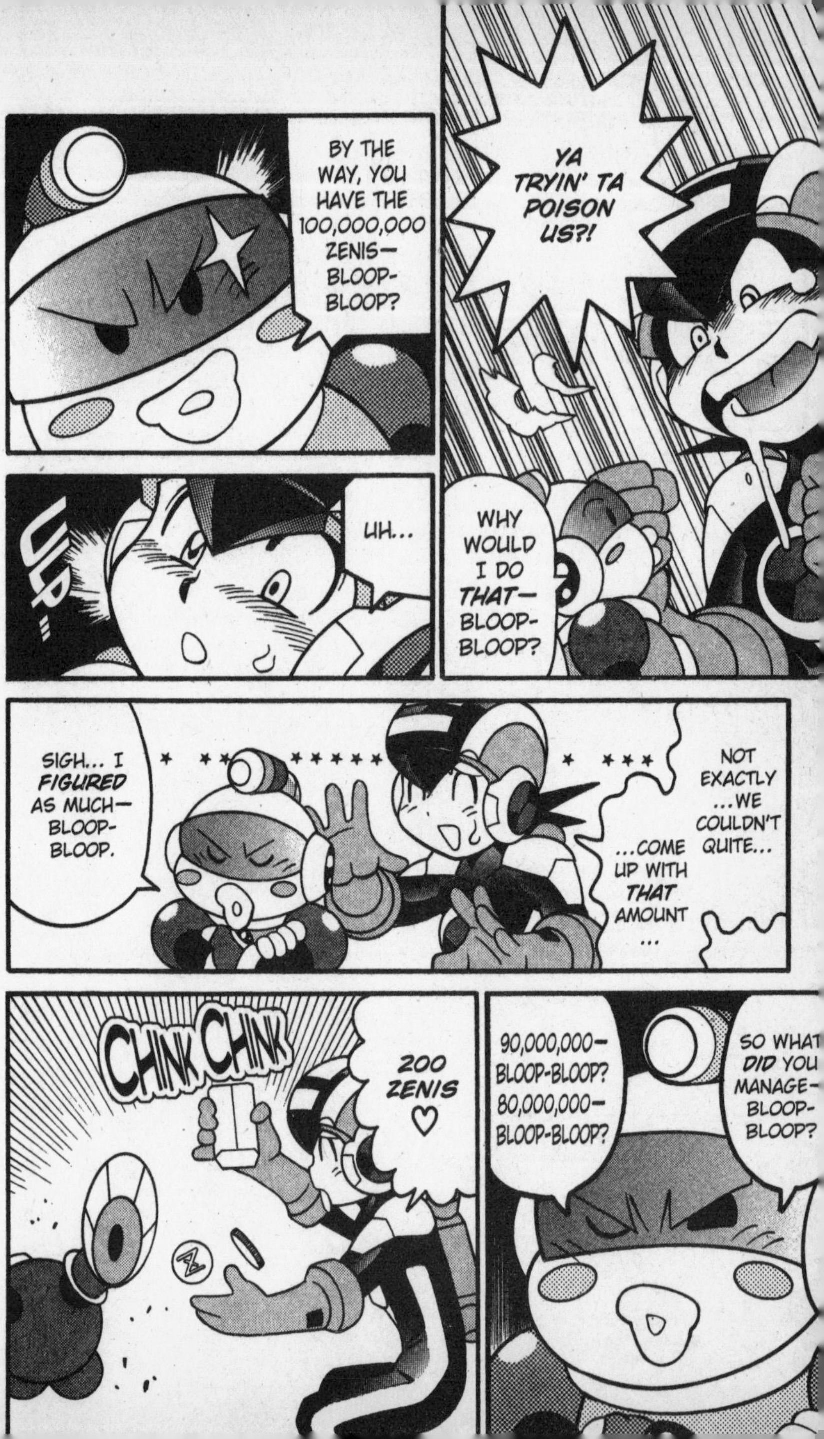
YA TRYIN' TA POISON US?!
WHY WOULD I DO THAT—BLOOP-BLOOP?
BY THE WAY, YOU HAVE THE 100,000,000 ZENIS—BLOOP-BLOOP?
ULP!!
UH...
NOT EXACTLY ...WE COULDN'T QUITE...
...COME UP WITH THAT AMOUNT ...
SIGH... I FIGURED AS MUCH—BLOOP-BLOOP.
SO WHAT DID YOU MANAGE—BLOOP-BLOOP?
90,000,000—BLOOP-BLOOP? 80,000,000—BLOOP-BLOOP?
200 ZENIS ♥
CHINK CHINK

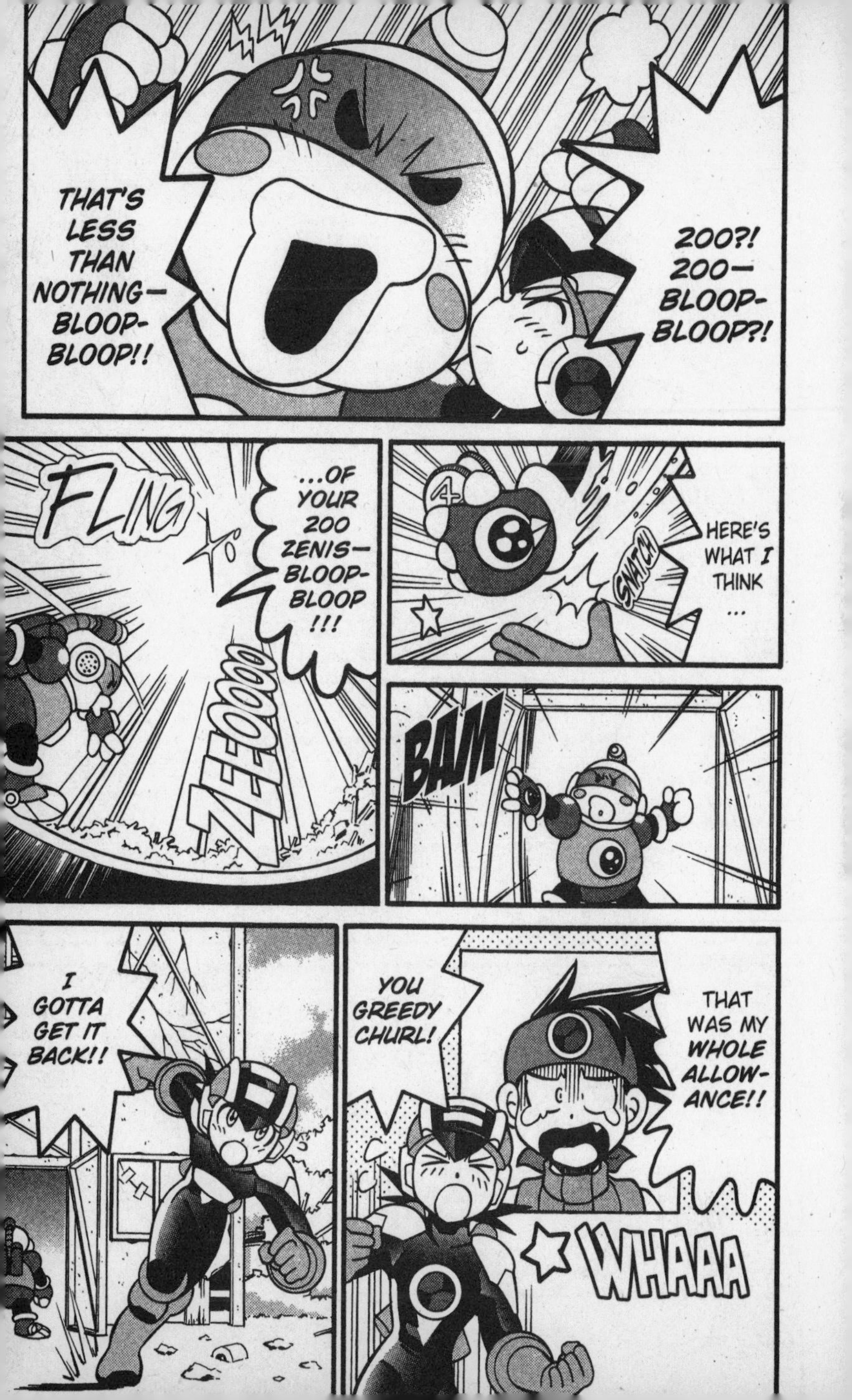
200?! 200—BLOOP-BLOOP?!
THAT'S LESS THAN NOTHING—BLOOP-BLOOP!!
HERE'S WHAT I THINK ...
SNATCH
BAM
FLING
...OF YOUR 200 ZENIS—BLOOP-BLOOP!!!
ZEEOOOO
THAT WAS MY WHOLE ALLOW-ANCE!!
YOU GREEDY CHURL!
WHAAA
I GOTTA GET IT BACK!!

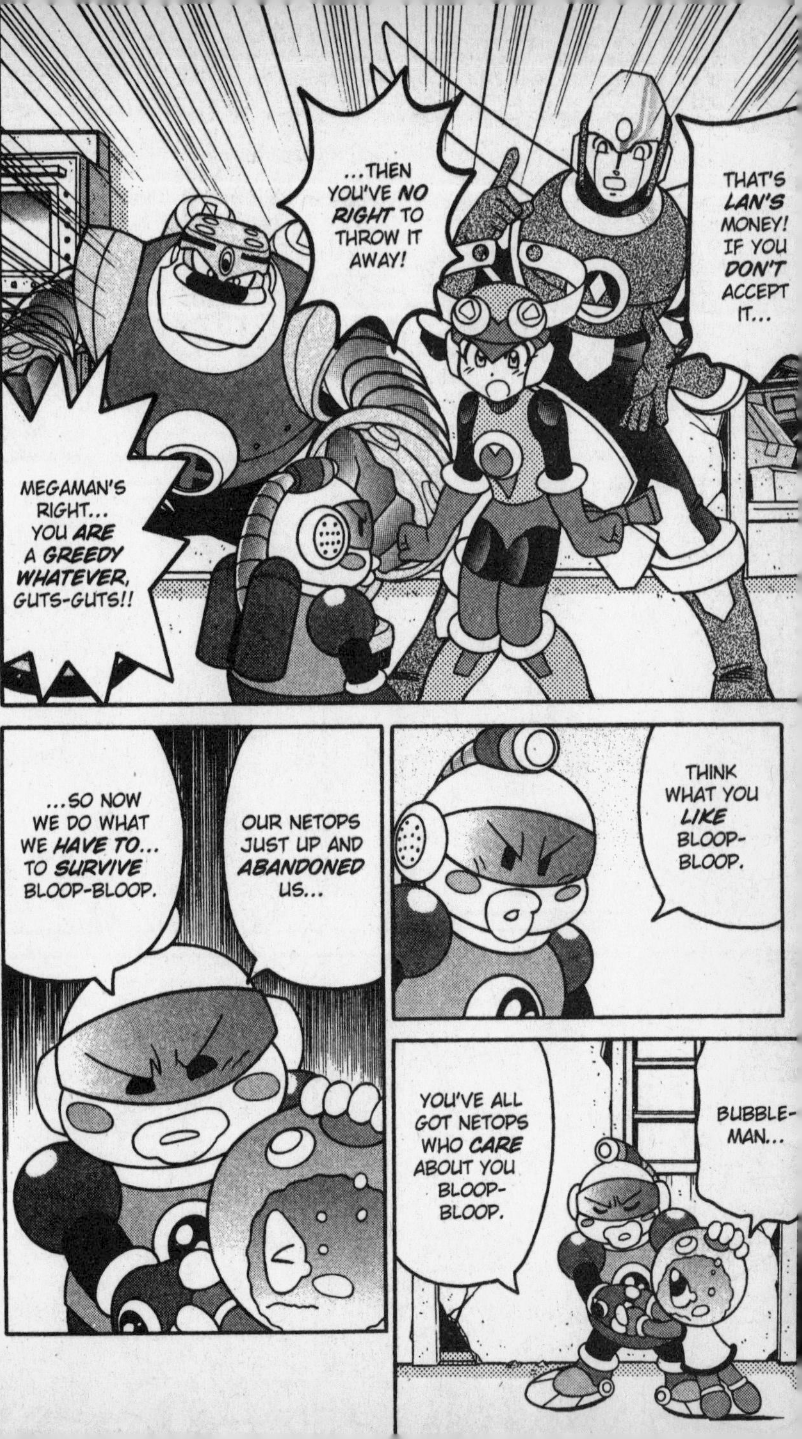
THAT'S LAN'S MONEY! IF YOU DON'T ACCEPT IT...
...THEN YOU'VE NO RIGHT TO THROW IT AWAY!
MEGAMAN'S RIGHT... YOU ARE A GREEDY WHATEVER, GUTS-GUTS!!
THINK WHAT YOU LIKE BLOOP-BLOOP.
BUBBLE-MAN...
YOU'VE ALL GOT NETOPS WHO CARE ABOUT YOU BLOOP-BLOOP.
OUR NETOPS JUST UP AND ABANDONED US...
...SO NOW WE DO WHAT WE HAVE TO... TO SURVIVE BLOOP-BLOOP.

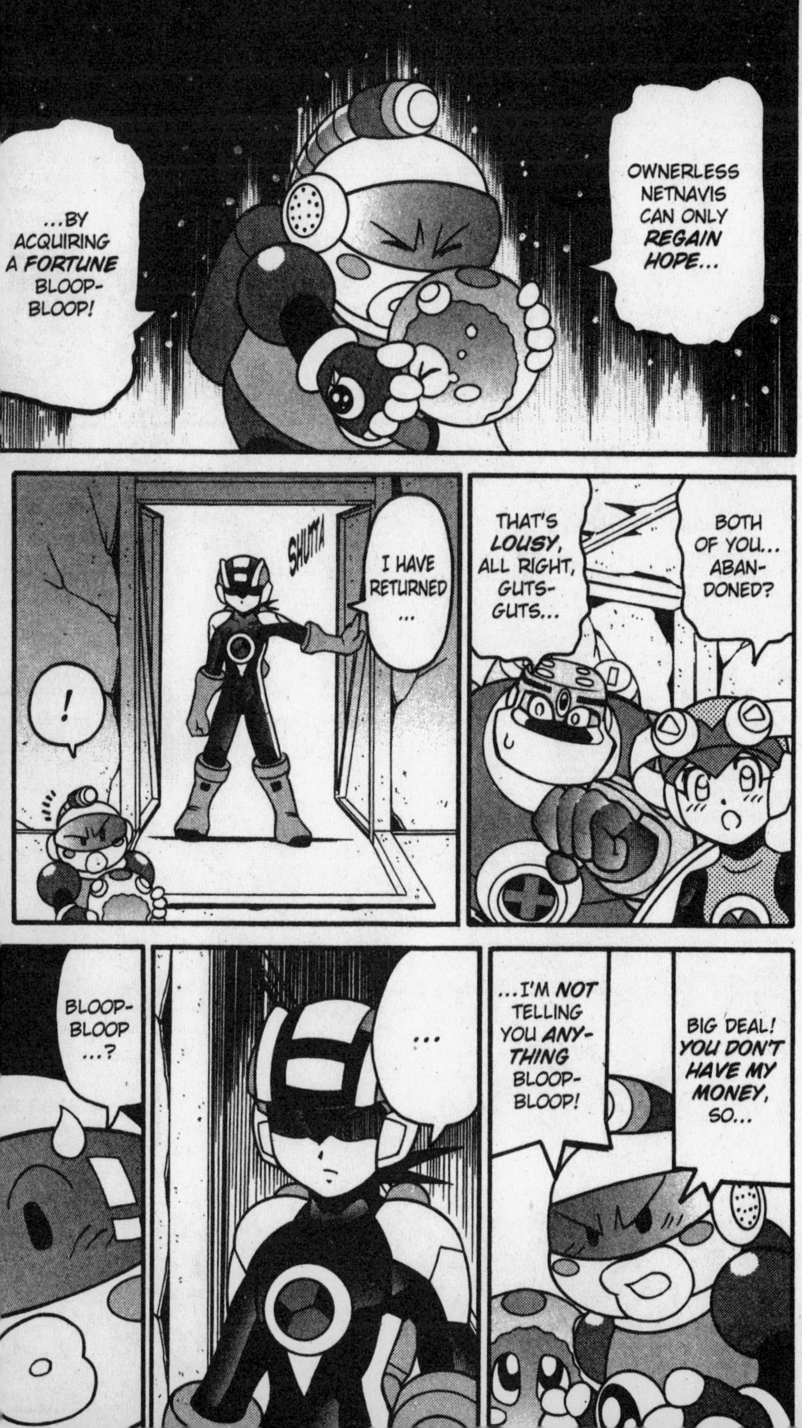
OWNERLESS NETNAVIS CAN ONLY **REGAIN HOPE...**
...BY ACQUIRING A ***FORTUNE*** BLOOP-BLOOP!
BOTH OF YOU... ABAN-DONED?
THAT'S ***LOUSY***, ALL RIGHT, GUTS-GUTS...
SHUTTA
I HAVE RETURNED ...
!
BIG DEAL! ***YOU DON'T HAVE MY MONEY***, SO...
...I'M ***NOT*** TELLING YOU ***ANY-THING*** BLOOP-BLOOP!
...
BLOOP-BLOOP ...?

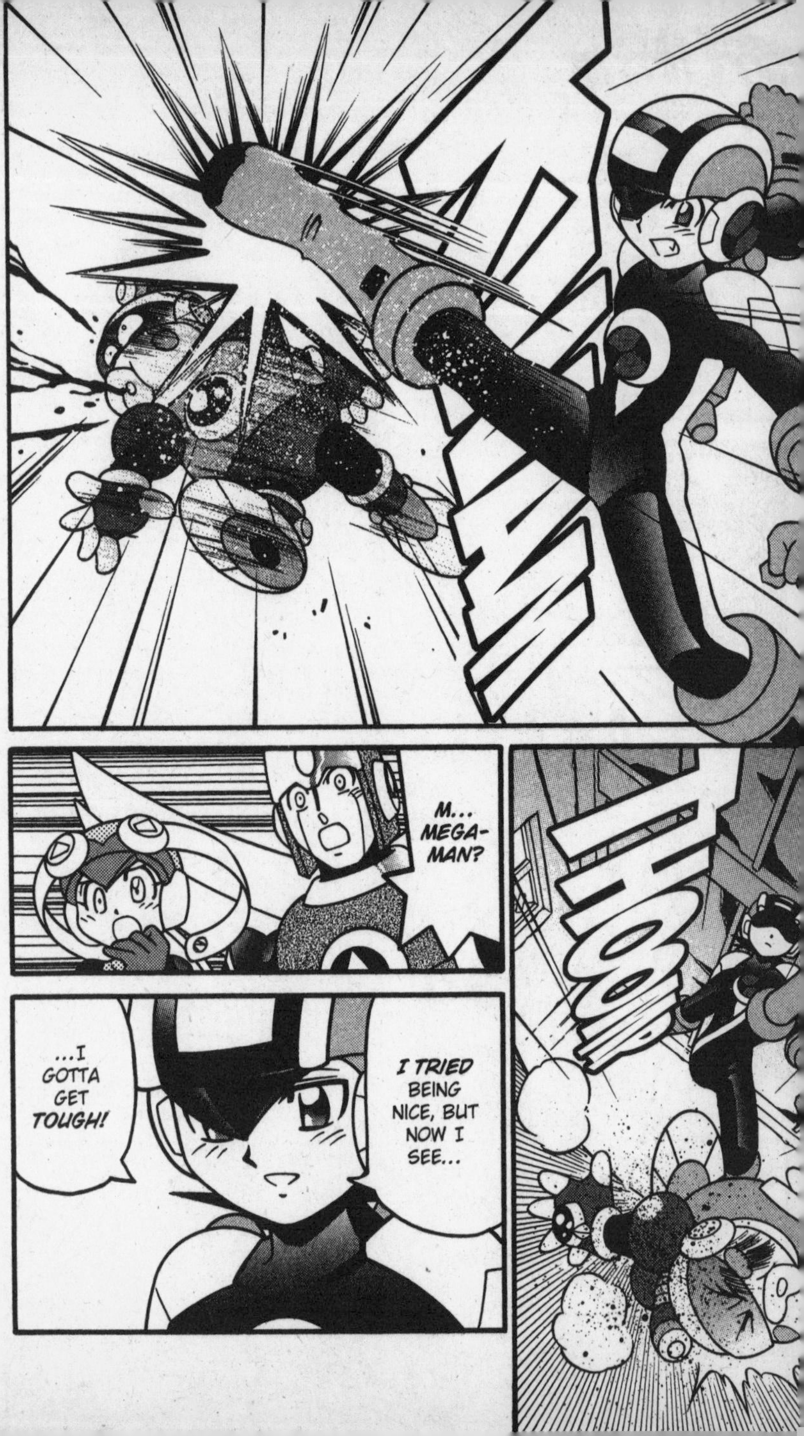
M... MEGA-MAN?
I TRIED BEING NICE, BUT NOW I SEE...
...I GOTTA GET TOUGH!

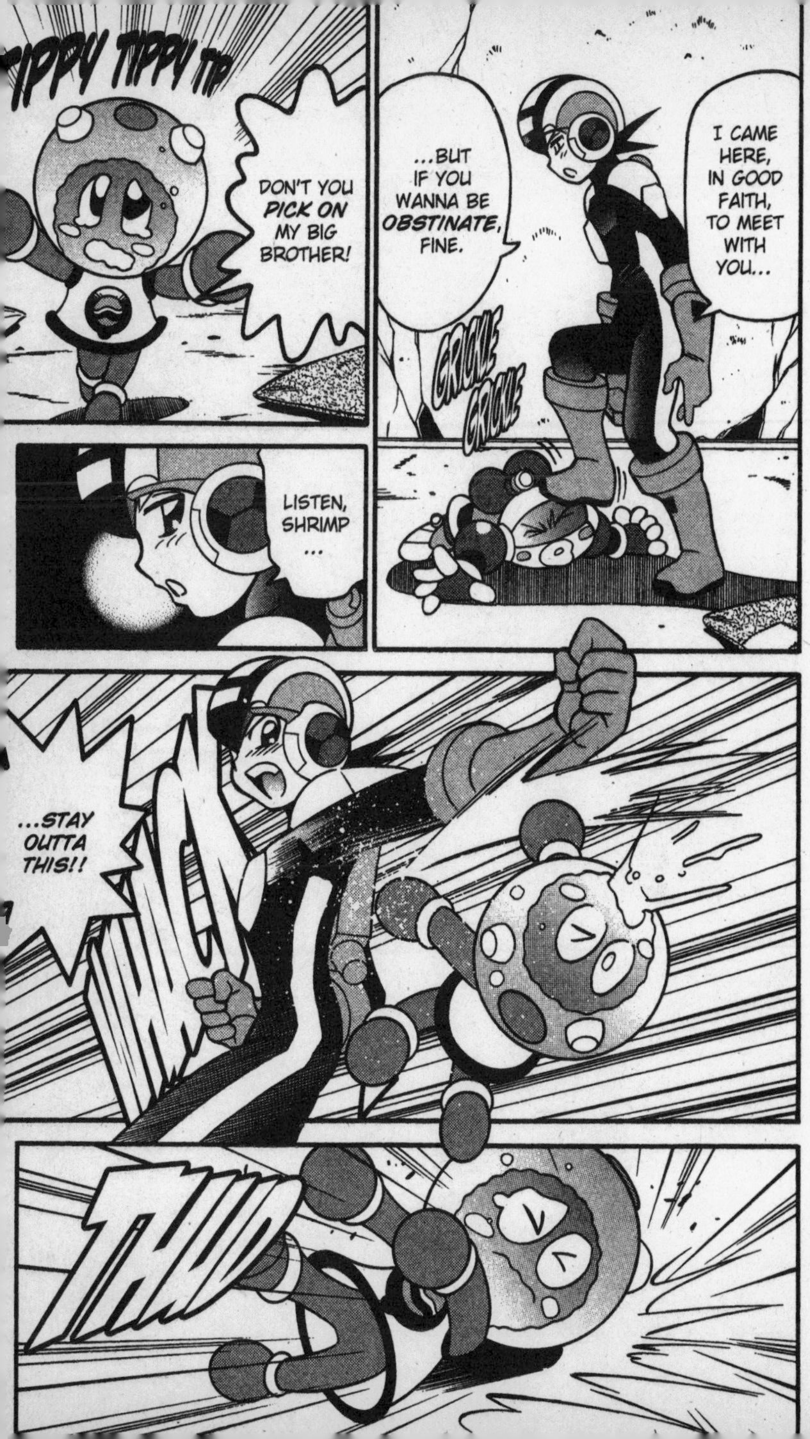
I CAME HERE, IN GOOD FAITH, TO MEET WITH YOU...
...BUT IF YOU WANNA BE OBSTINATE, FINE.
GRICKLE GRICKLE
TIPPY TIPPY TIP
DON'T YOU PICK ON MY BIG BROTHER!
LISTEN, SHRIMP ...
...STAY OUTTA THIS!!

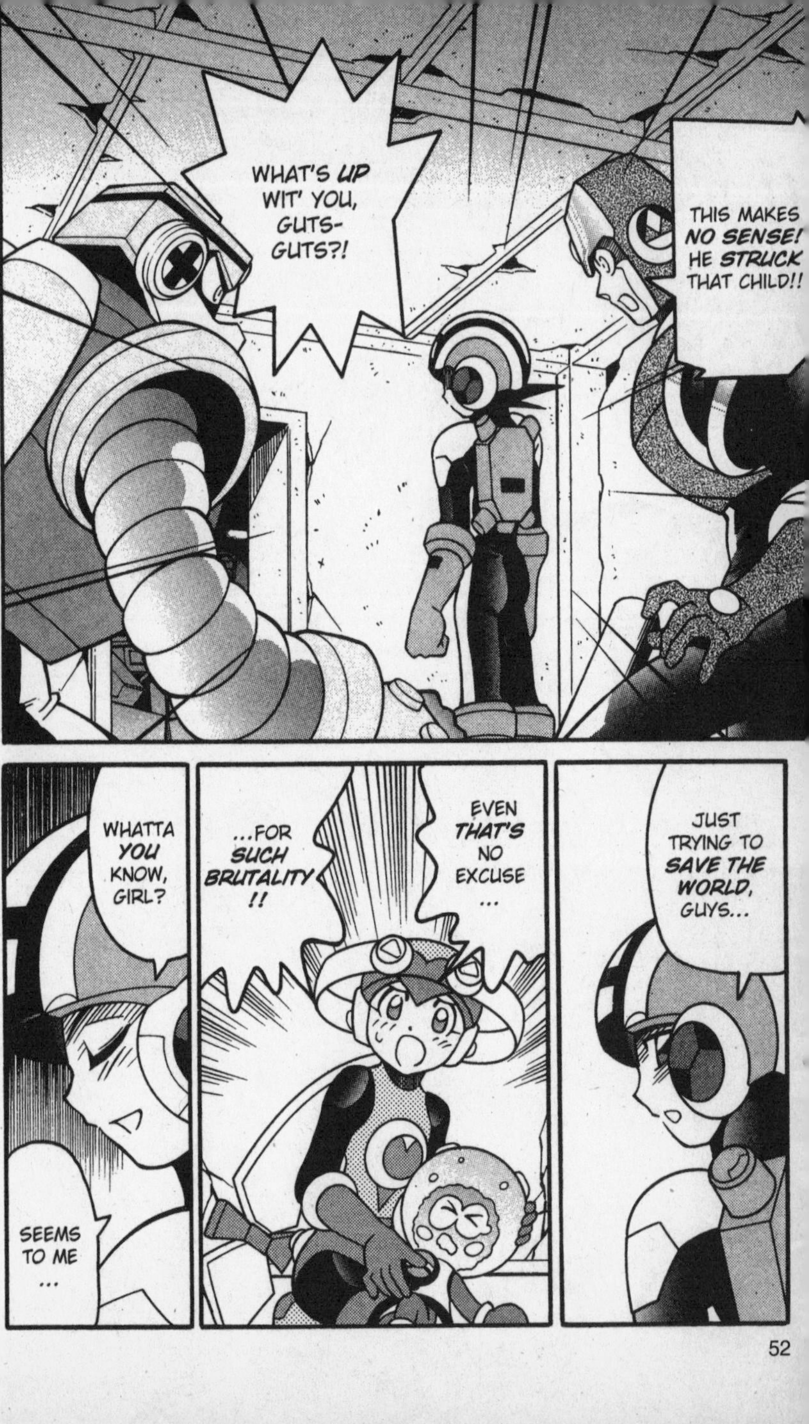
THIS MAKES NO SENSE! HE STRUCK THAT CHILD!!
WHAT'S UP WIT' YOU, GUTS-GUTS?!
JUST TRYING TO SAVE THE WORLD, GUYS...
EVEN THAT'S NO EXCUSE ...
...FOR SUCH BRUTALITY!!
WHATTA YOU KNOW, GIRL?
SEEMS TO ME ...

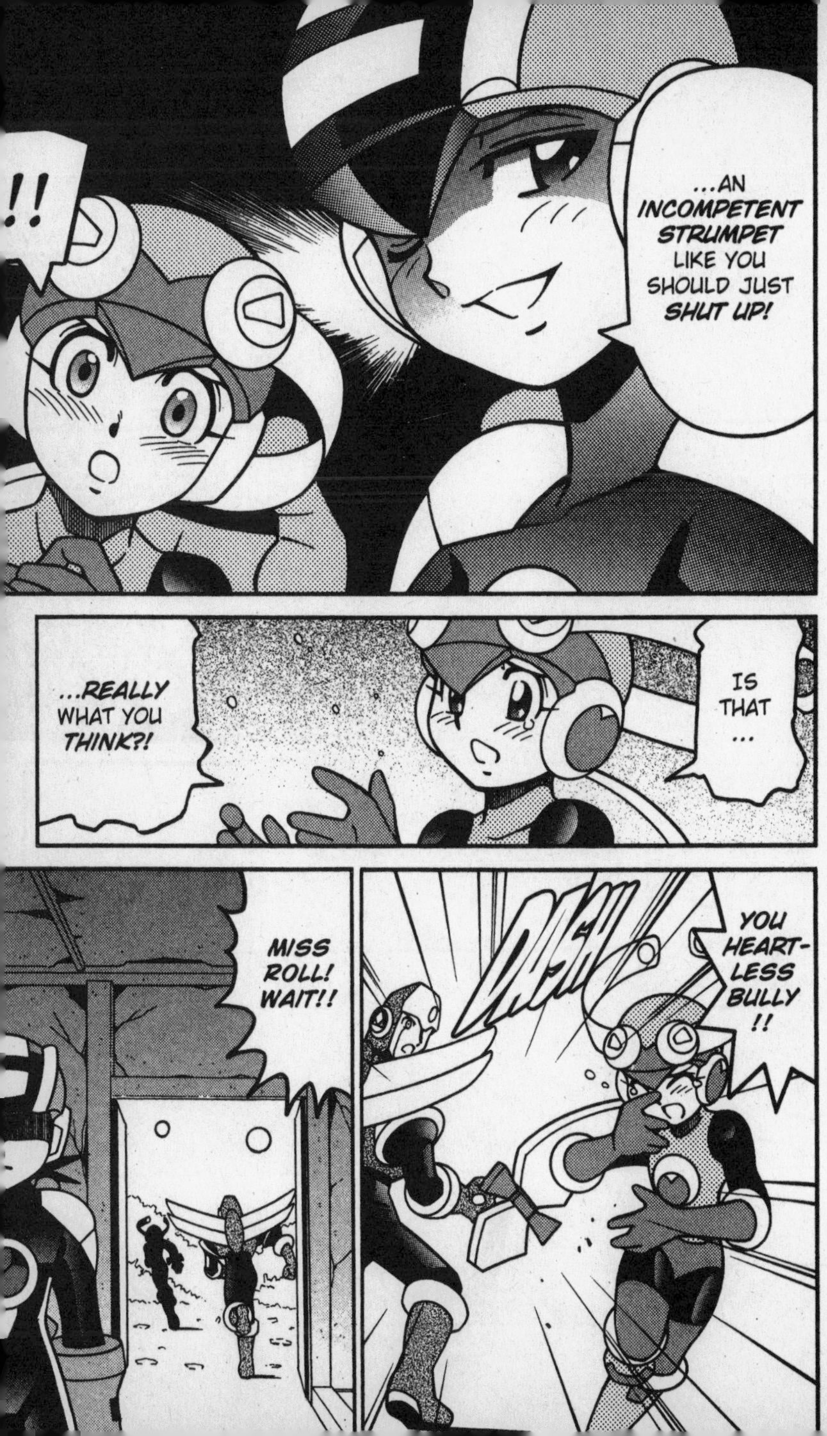

...AN INCOMPETENT STRUMPET LIKE YOU SHOULD JUST SHUT UP!
!!
IS THAT ...
...REALLY WHAT YOU THINK?!
YOU HEART-LESS BULLY !!
DASH
MISS ROLL! WAIT!!

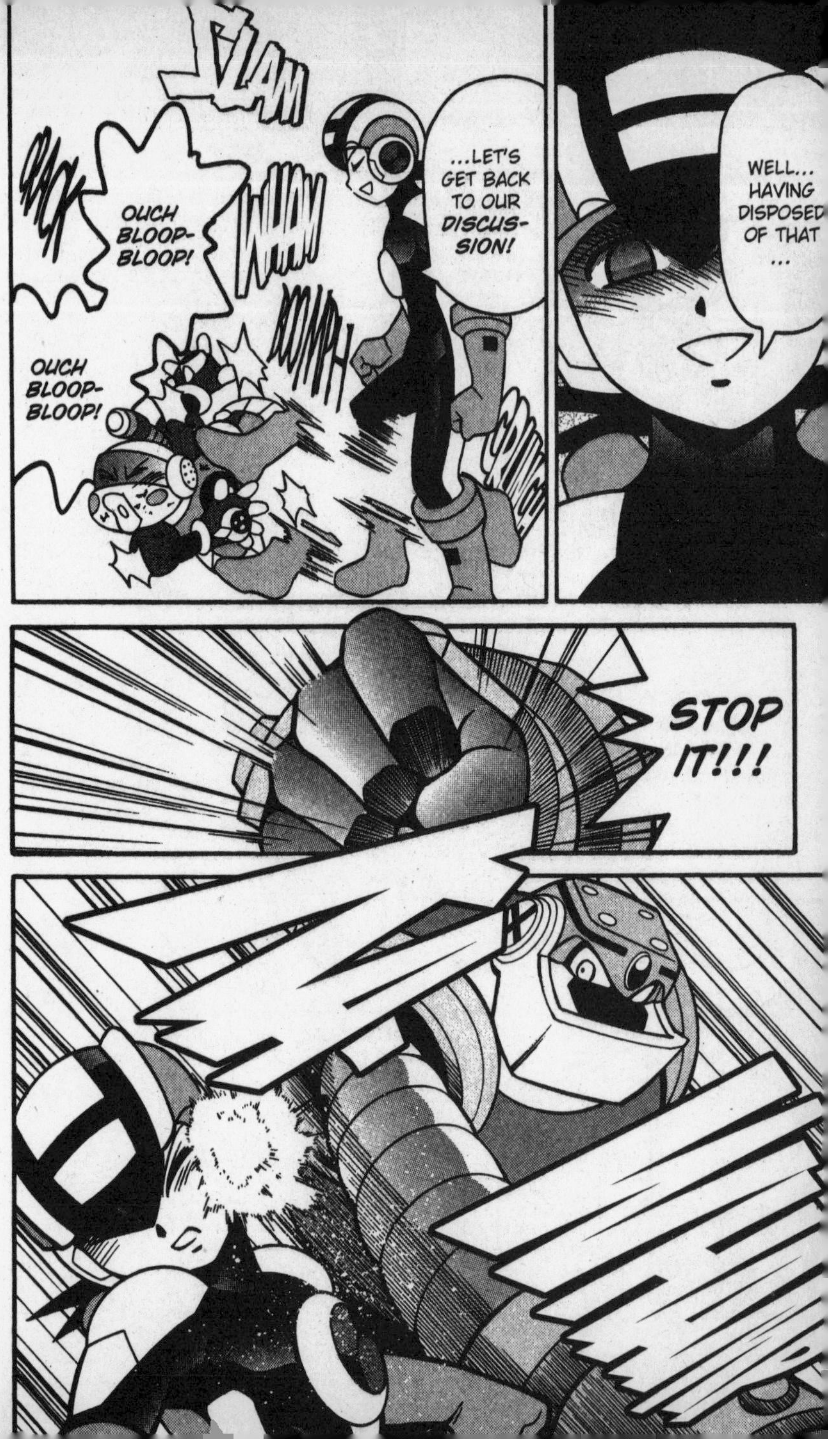
WELL... HAVING DISPOSED OF THAT ...
SLAM
...LET'S GET BACK TO OUR DISCUSSION!
WHAM
CRACK
OUCH BLOOP-BLOOP!
BOOMPH
OUCH BLOOP-BLOOP!
STOP IT!!!

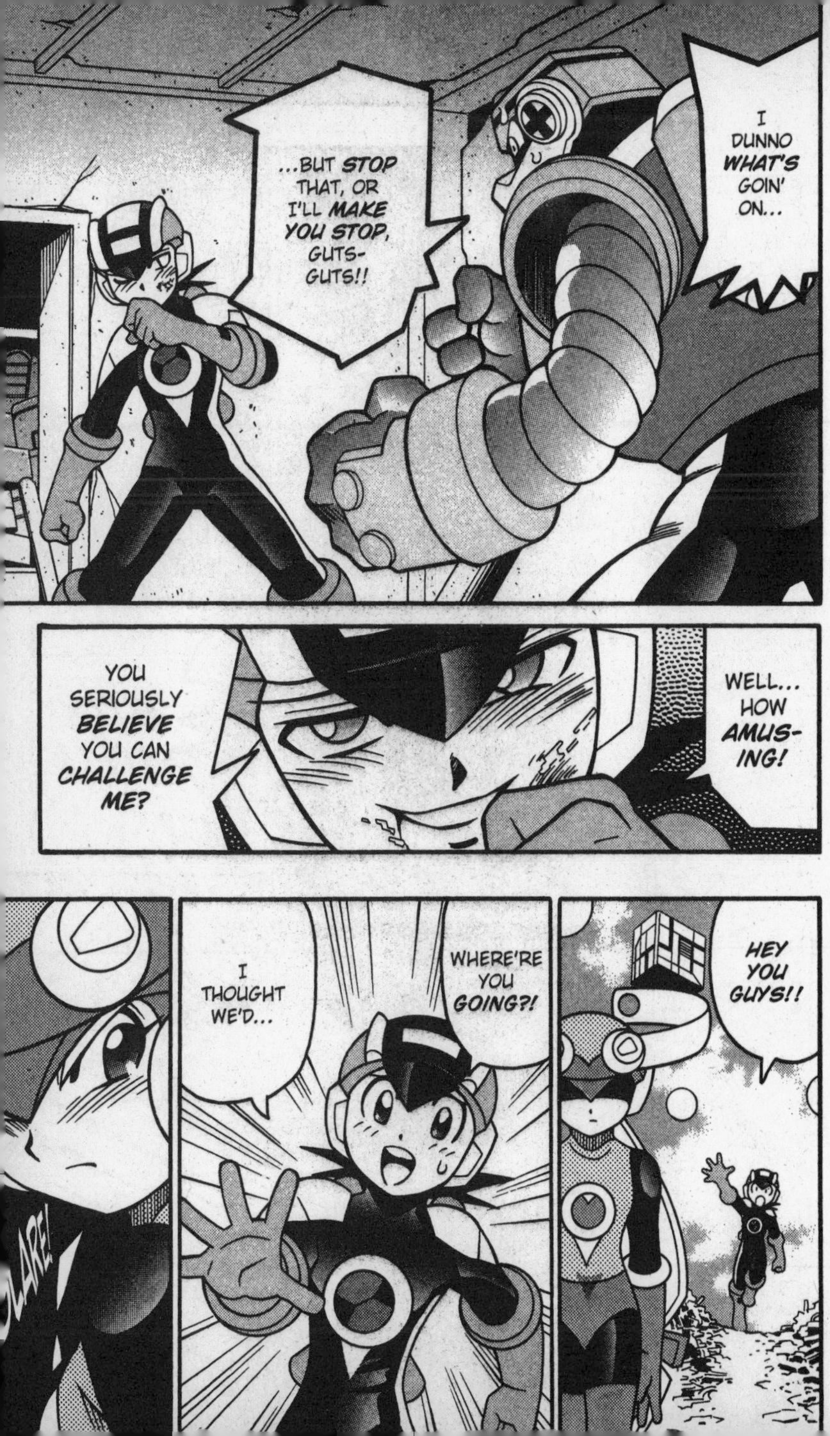
I DUNNO WHAT'S GOIN' ON...
...BUT STOP THAT, OR I'LL MAKE YOU STOP, GUTS-GUTS!!
WELL... HOW AMUSING!
YOU SERIOUSLY BELIEVE YOU CAN CHALLENGE ME?
HEY YOU GUYS!!
WHERE'RE YOU GOING?!
I THOUGHT WE'D...
LARE!

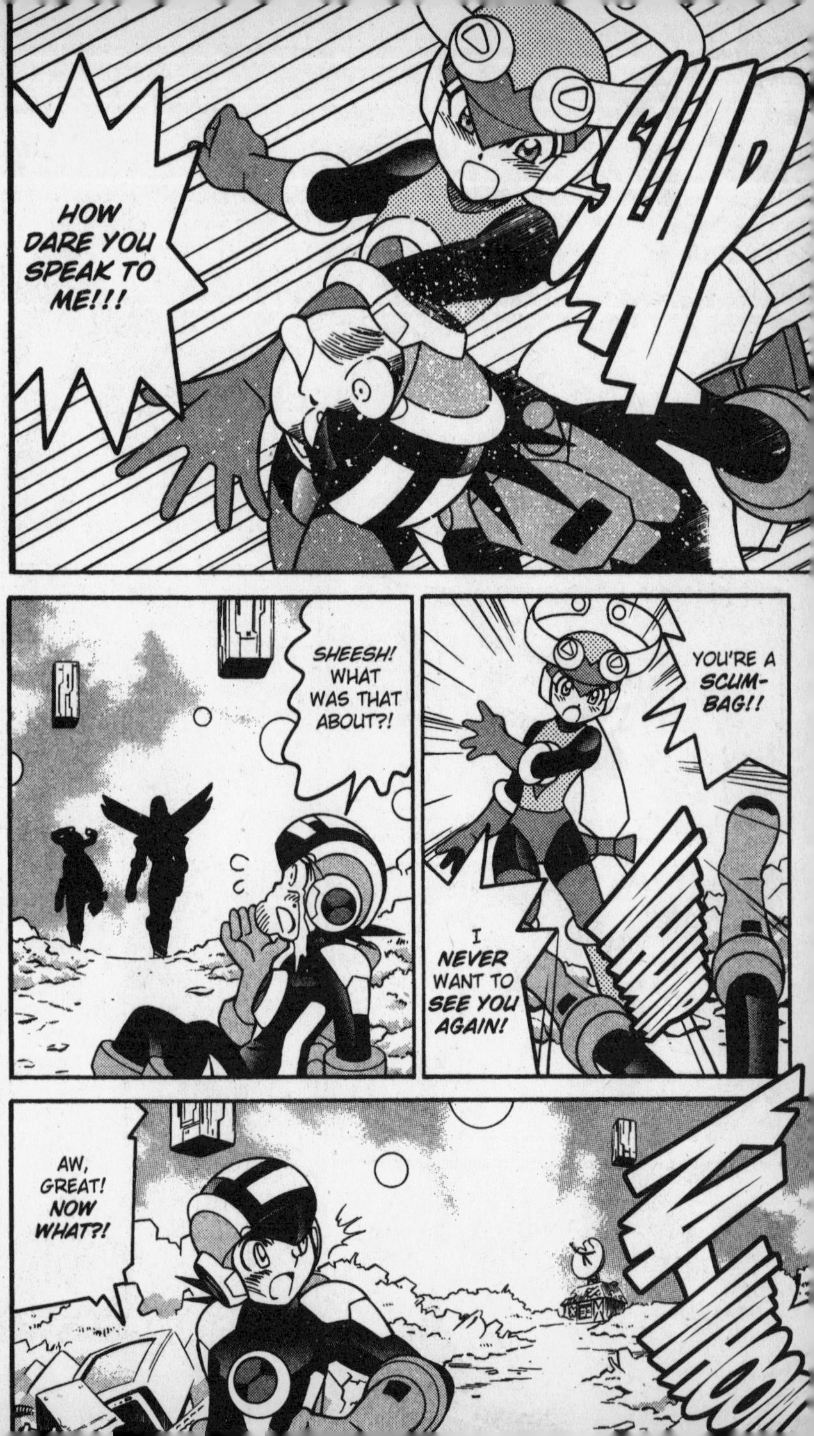
HOW DARE YOU SPEAK TO ME!!!
YOU'RE A SCUM-BAG!!
I NEVER WANT TO SEE YOU AGAIN!
SHEESH! WHAT WAS THAT ABOUT?!
AW, GREAT! NOW WHAT?!

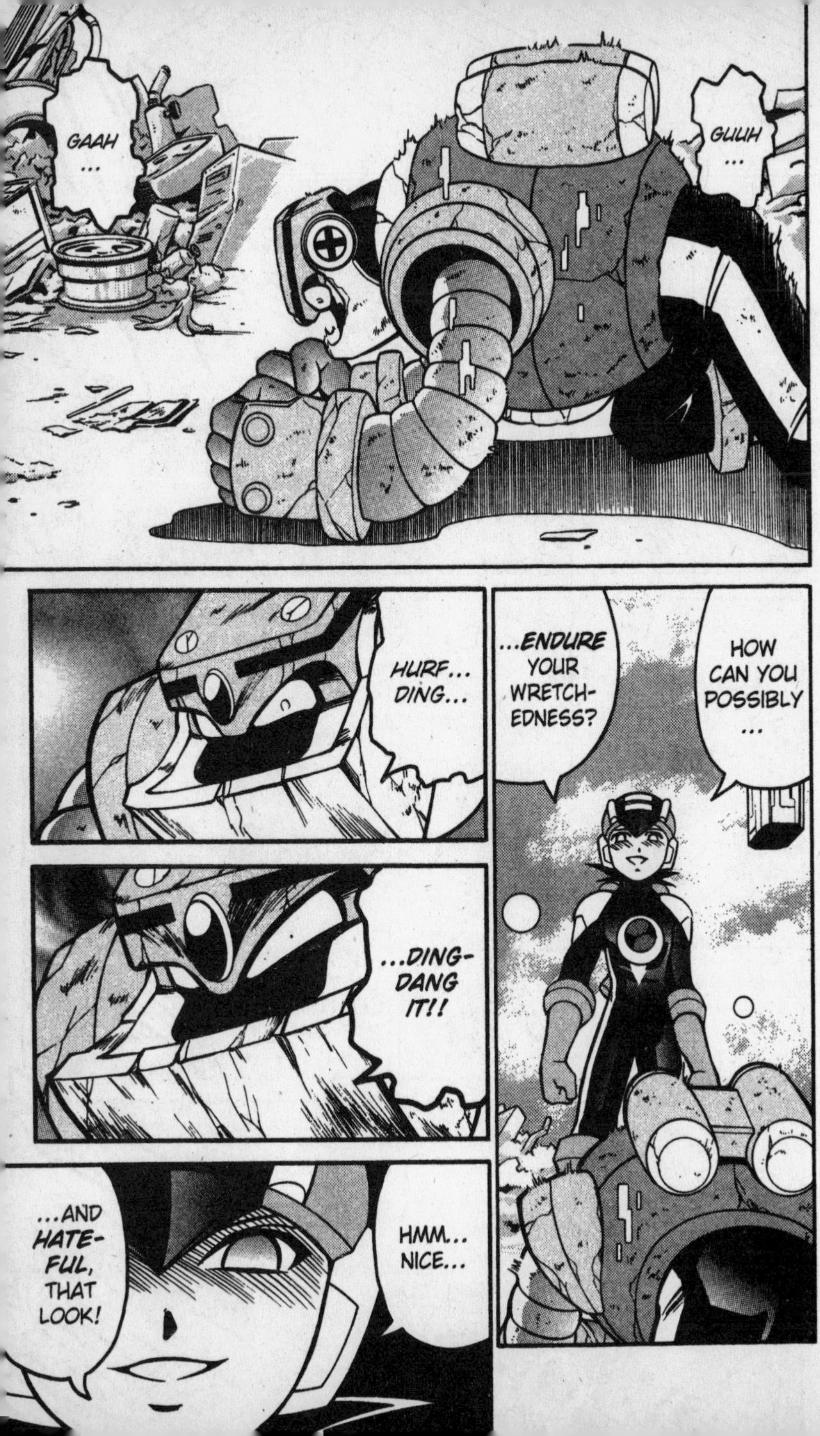
GUUH ...
GAAH ...
HOW CAN YOU POSSIBLY ...
...ENDURE YOUR WRETCH-EDNESS?
HURF... DING...
...DING-DANG IT!!
HMM... NICE...
...AND HATE-FUL, THAT LOOK!

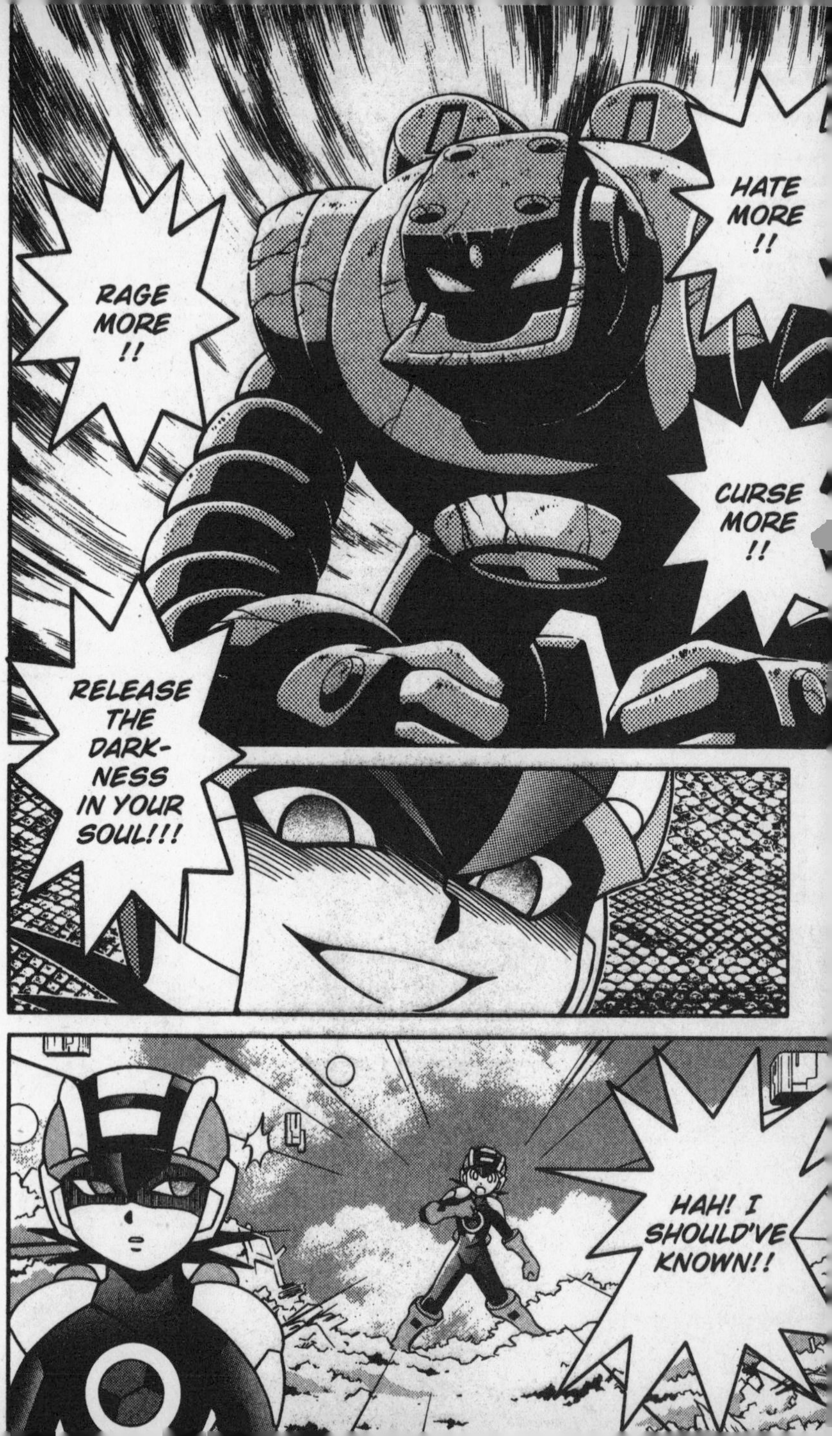
HATE MORE!!
CURSE MORE!!
RAGE MORE!!
RELEASE THE DARK-NESS IN YOUR SOUL!!!
HAH! I SHOULD'VE KNOWN!!

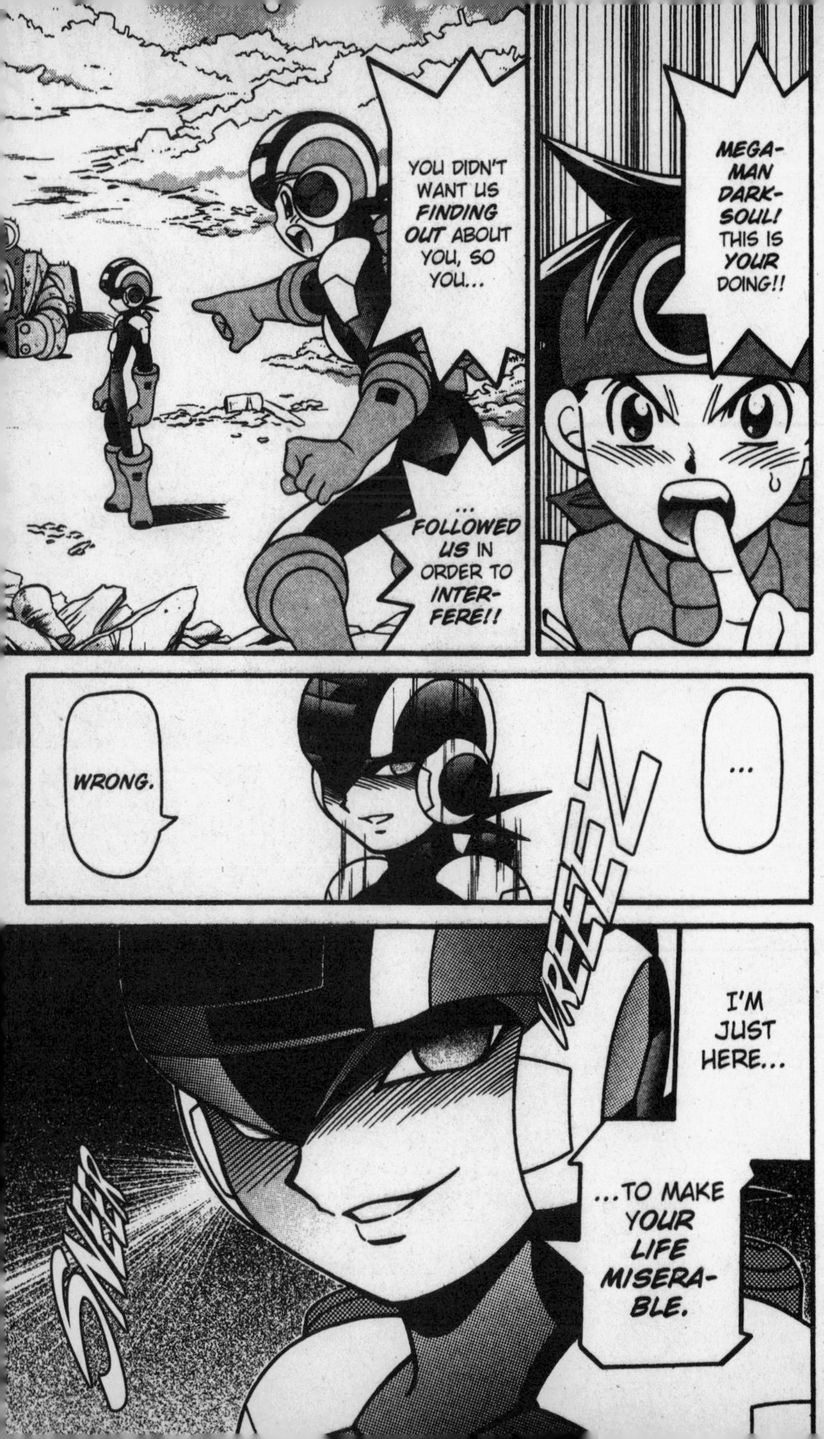
MEGA-MAN DARK-SOUL! THIS IS YOUR DOING!!
YOU DIDN'T WANT US FINDING OUT ABOUT YOU, SO YOU...
...FOLLOWED US IN ORDER TO INTER-FERE!!
...
WRONG.
VREEEZ
I'M JUST HERE...
...TO MAKE YOUR LIFE MISERA-BLE.
SNEER

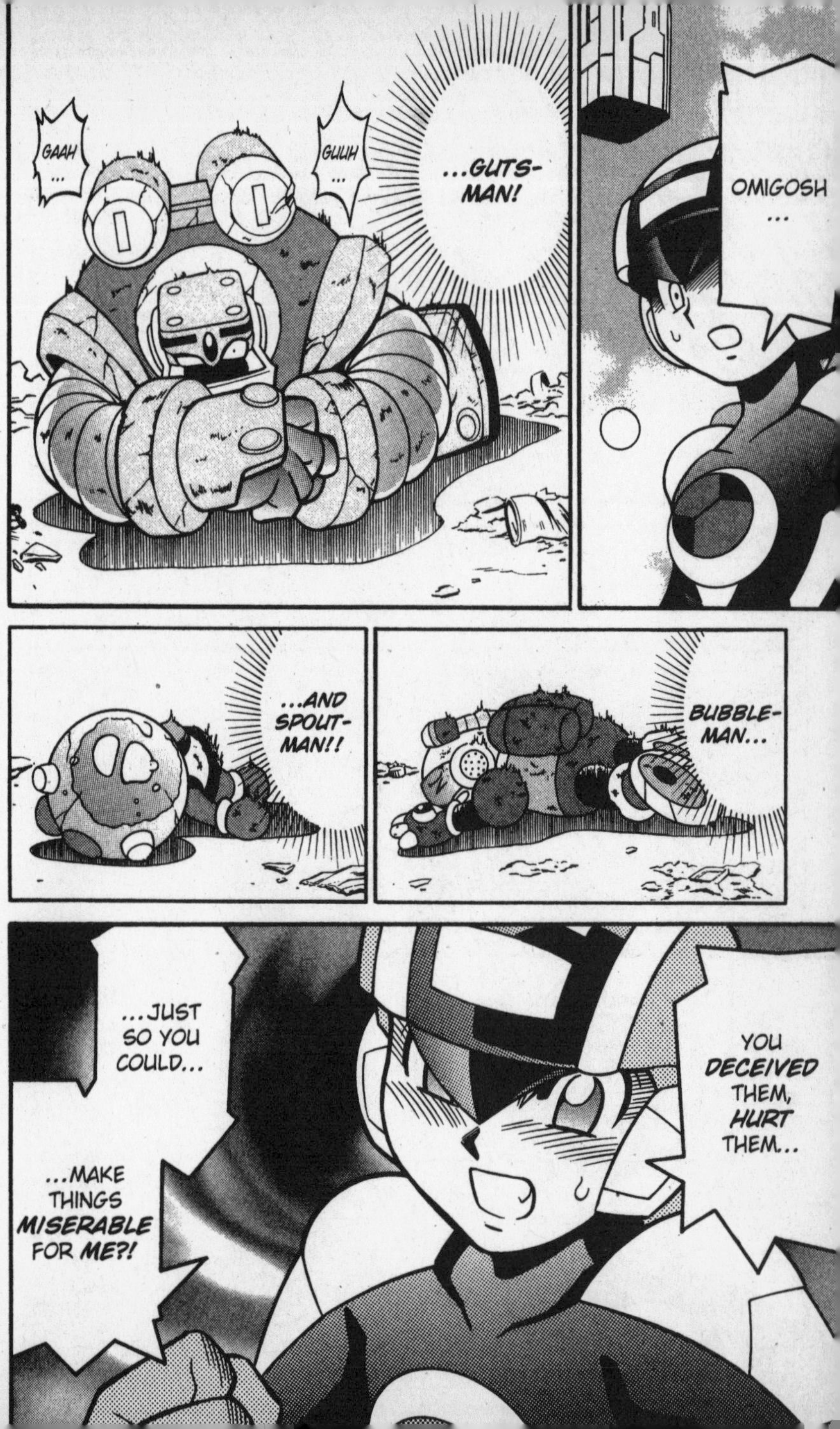
OMIGOSH ...
...GUTS-MAN!
GUUH ...
GAAH ...
BUBBLE-MAN...
...AND SPOUT-MAN!!
YOU DECEIVED THEM, HURT THEM...
...JUST SO YOU COULD...
...MAKE THINGS MISERABLE FOR ME?!

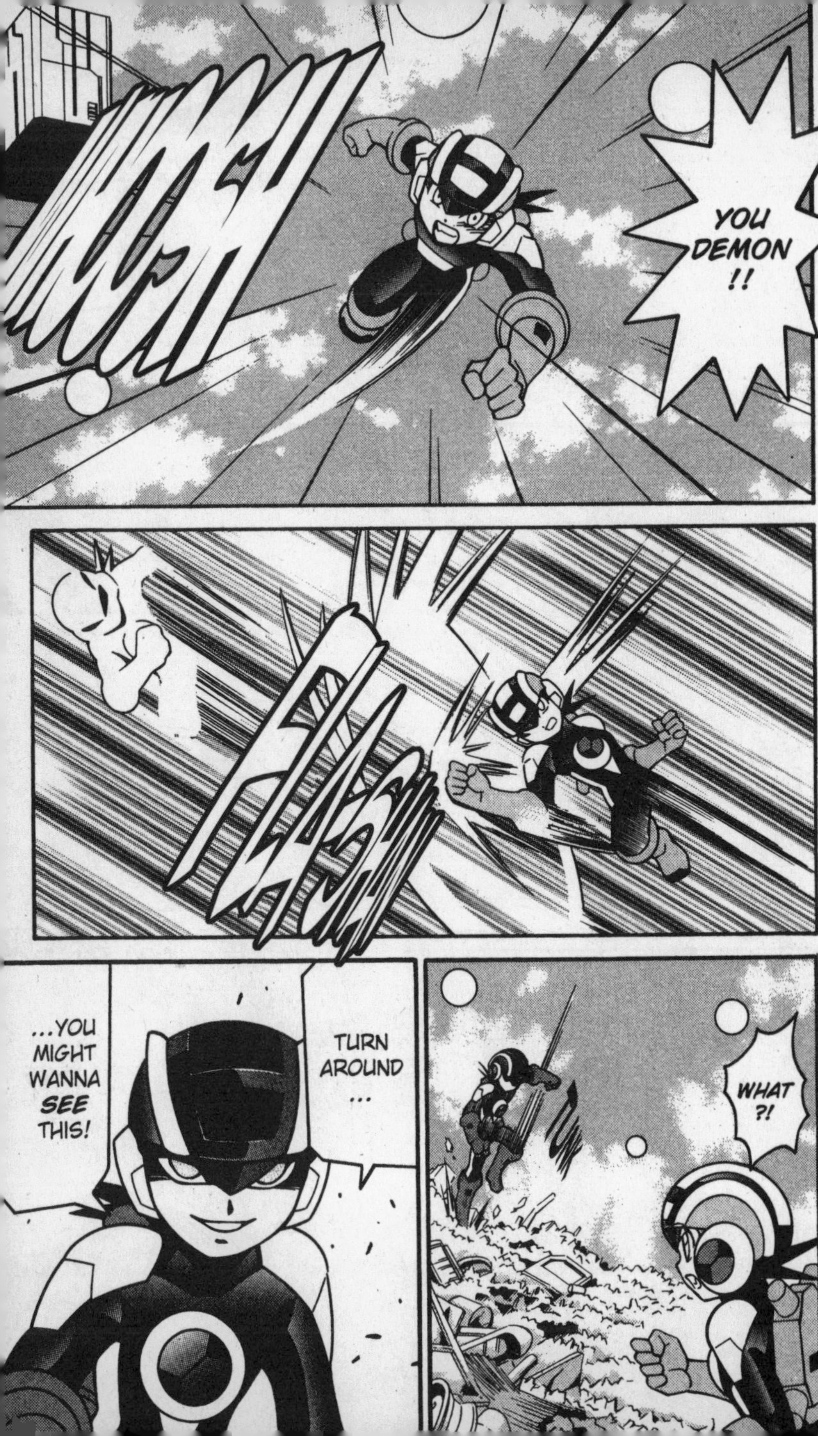
YOU DEMON !!
WHAT ?!
TURN AROUND ...
...YOU MIGHT WANNA SEE THIS!

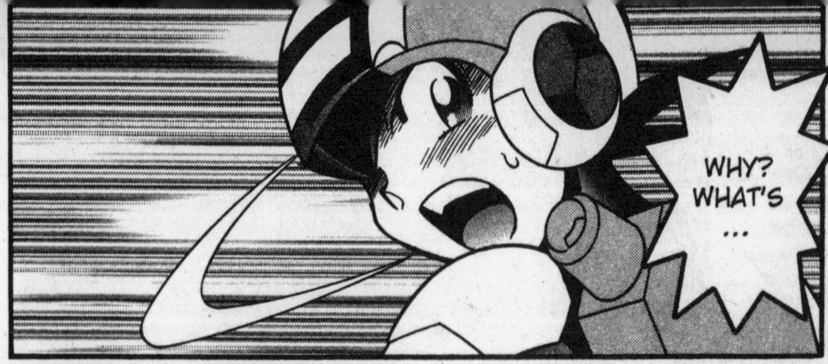
WHY? WHAT'S ...
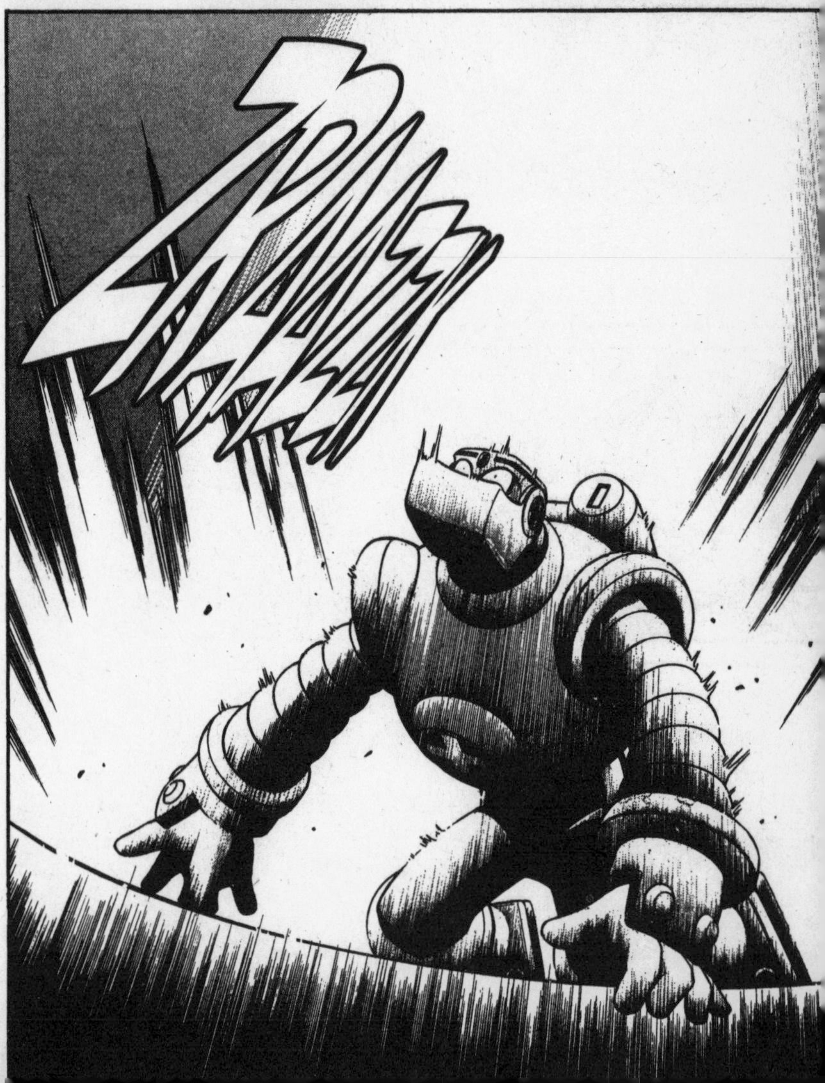

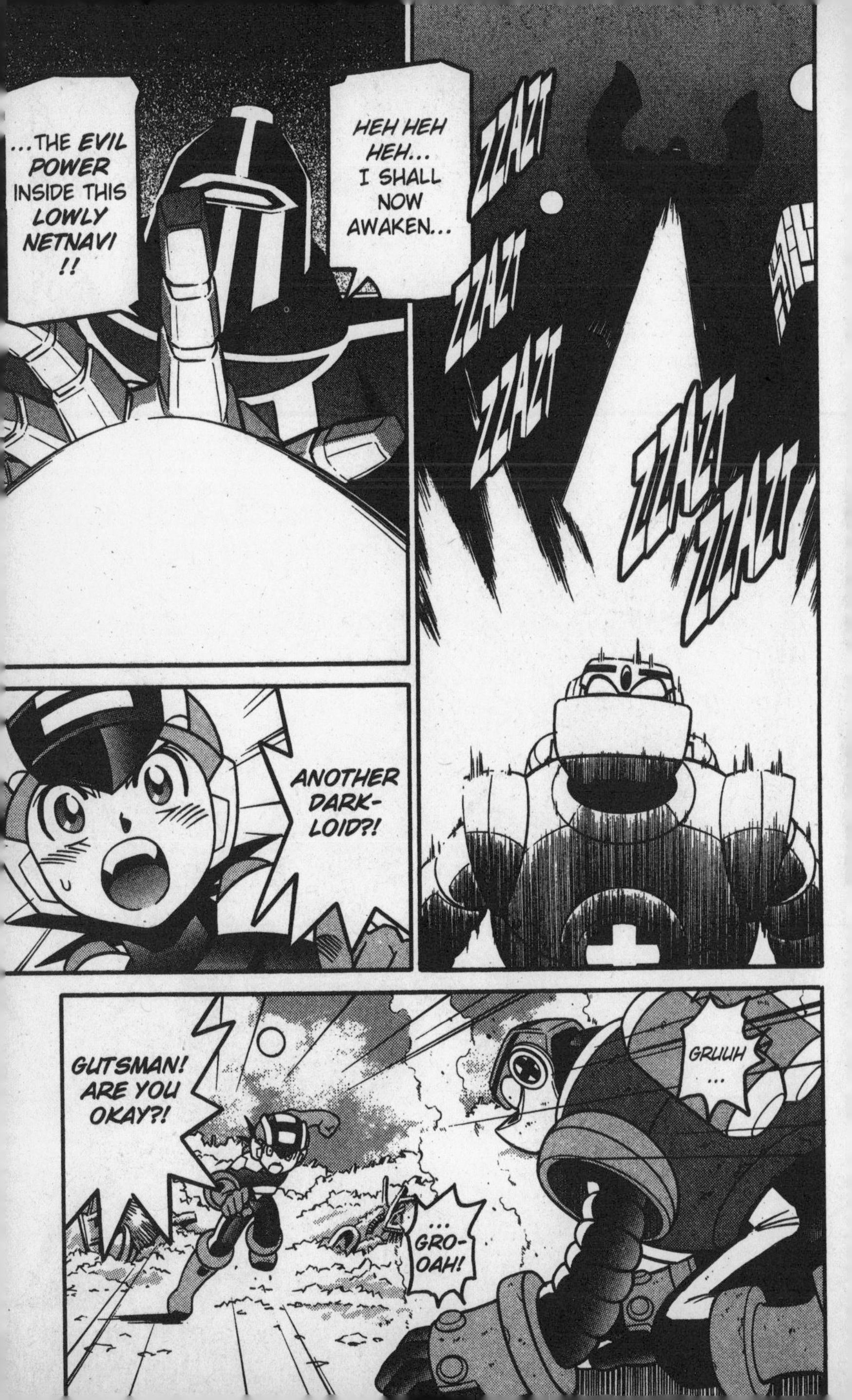
ZZAZT
ZZAZT
ZZAZT
ZZAZT
ZZAZT
HEH HEH HEH... I SHALL NOW AWAKEN...
...THE EVIL POWER INSIDE THIS LOWLY NETNAVI !!
ANOTHER DARK-LOID?!
GRUUH ...
... GRO-OAH!
GUTSMAN! ARE YOU OKAY?!

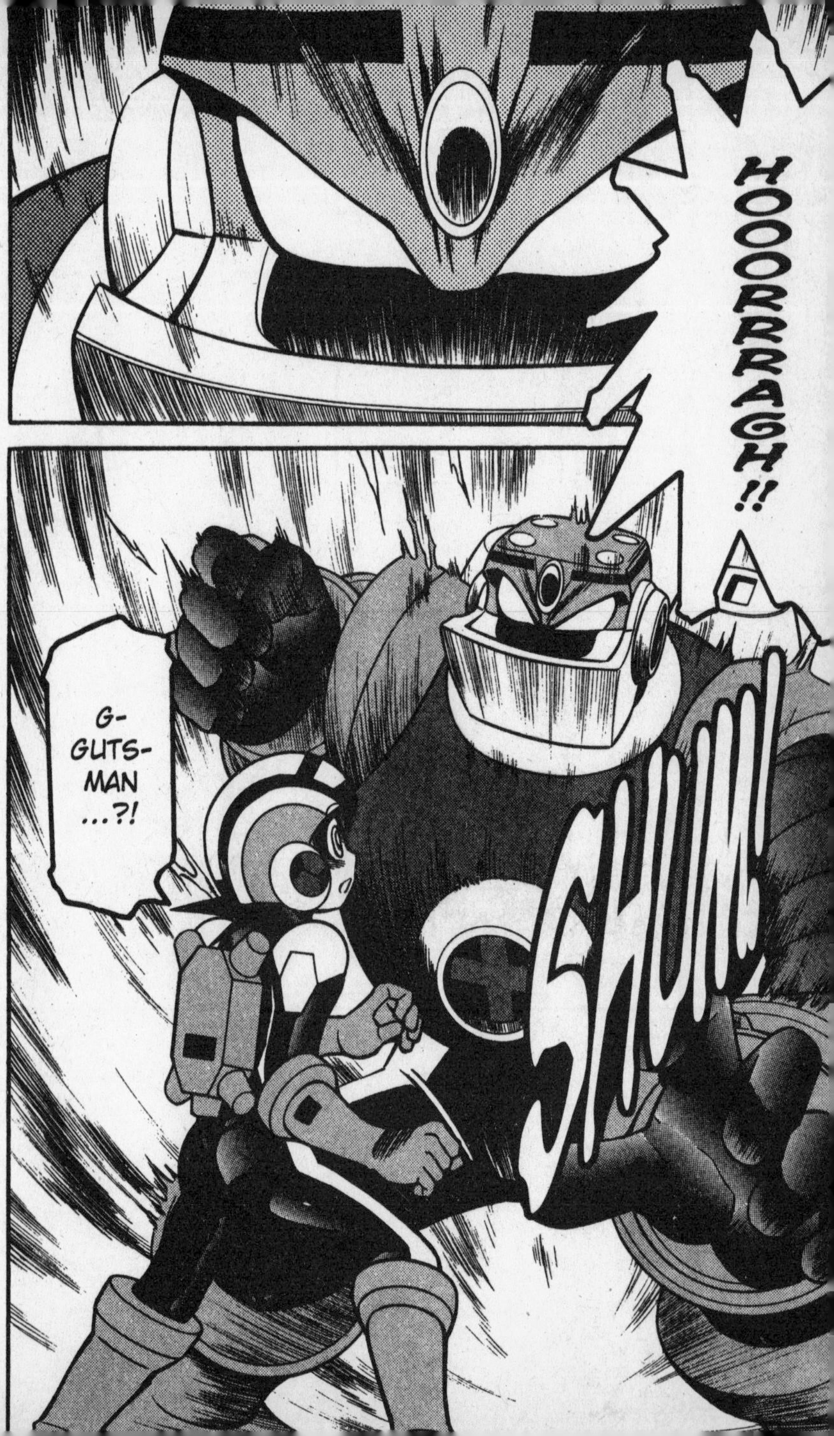
HOOORRRAGH!!
G-GUTS-MAN ...?!
SHUM!

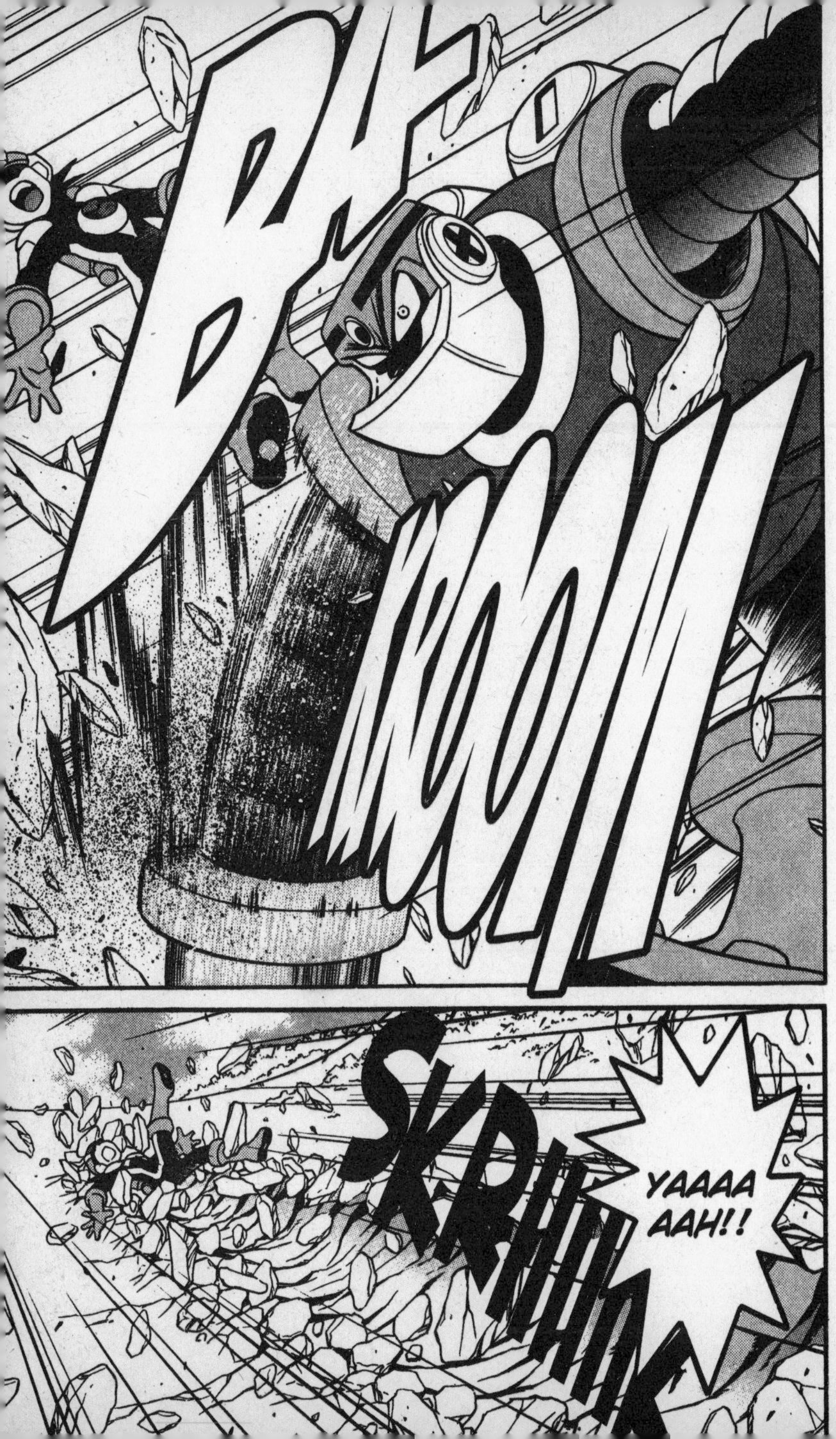
YAAAA
AAH!!

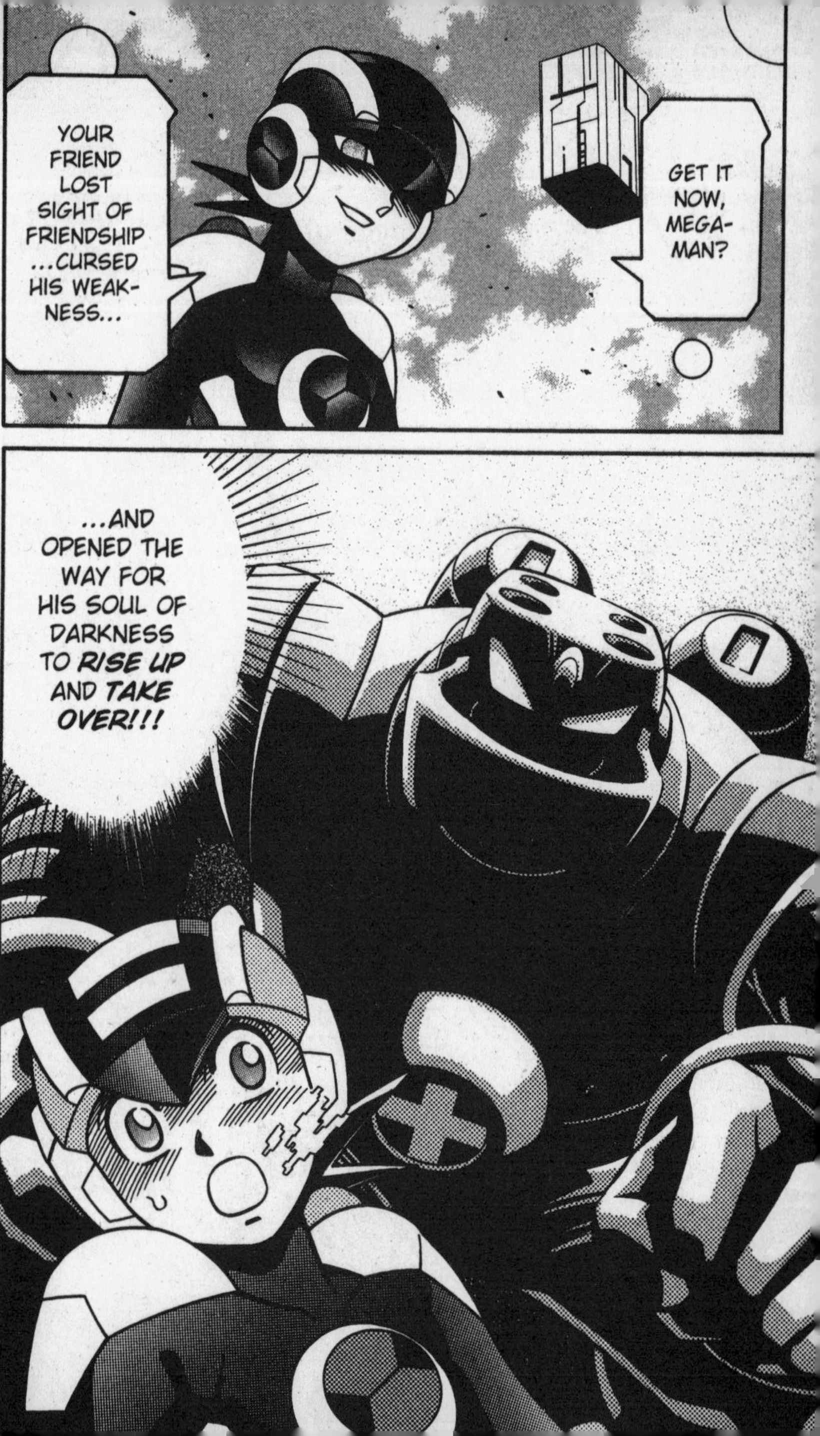
GET IT NOW, MEGA-MAN?
YOUR FRIEND LOST SIGHT OF FRIENDSHIP ...CURSED HIS WEAK-NESS...
...AND OPENED THE WAY FOR HIS SOUL OF DARKNESS TO *RISE UP* AND *TAKE OVER!!!*

CHAPTER 3: GUTSMAN, SWALLOWED BY DARKNESS!!

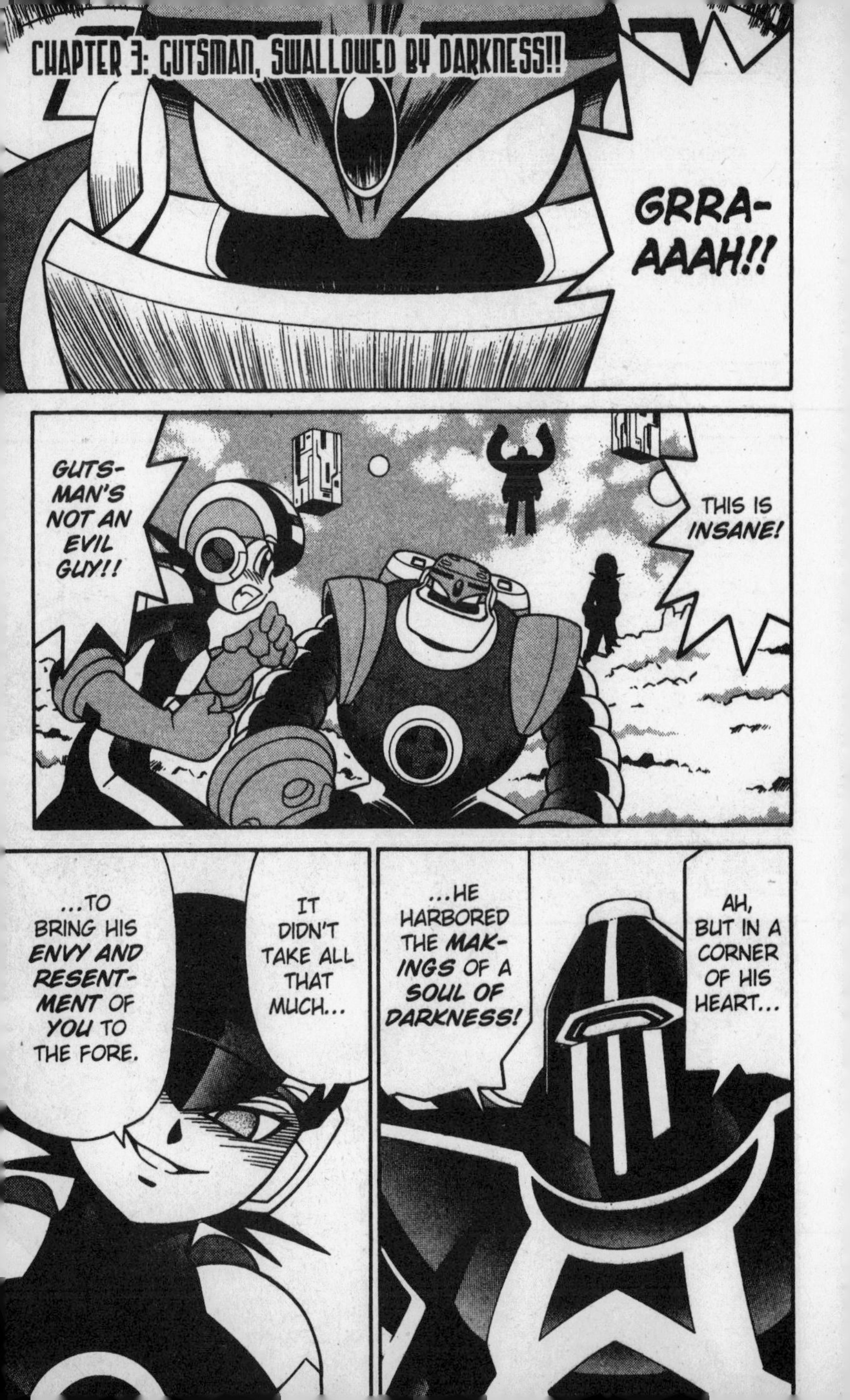
GRRA-AAAH!!
THIS IS INSANE!
GUTS-MAN'S NOT AN EVIL GUY!!
AH, BUT IN A CORNER OF HIS HEART...
...HE HARBORED THE *MAKINGS* OF A *SOUL OF DARKNESS!*
IT DIDN'T TAKE ALL THAT MUCH...
...TO BRING HIS *ENVY AND RESENTMENT* OF *YOU* TO THE FORE.

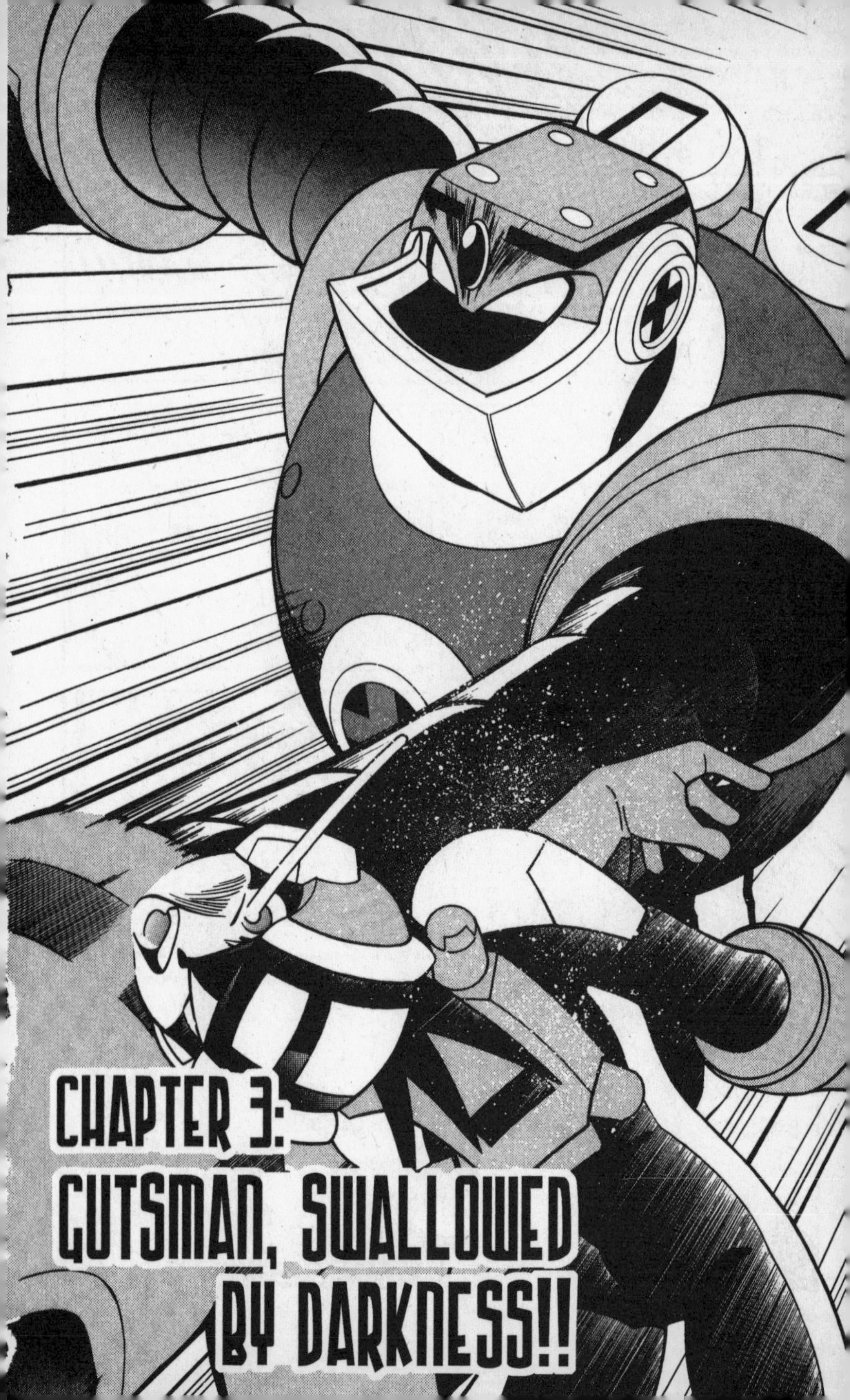
CHAPTER 3:
GUTSMAN, SWALLOWED BY DARKNESS!!

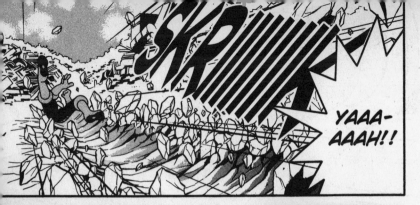

YAAA-AAAH!!

GRAAAAAH!!

WHAT POWER!!

WHOA!

DARK POWER!!

I'M NOT YOUR ENEMY! I'M...

WAIT, GUTS-MAN!!

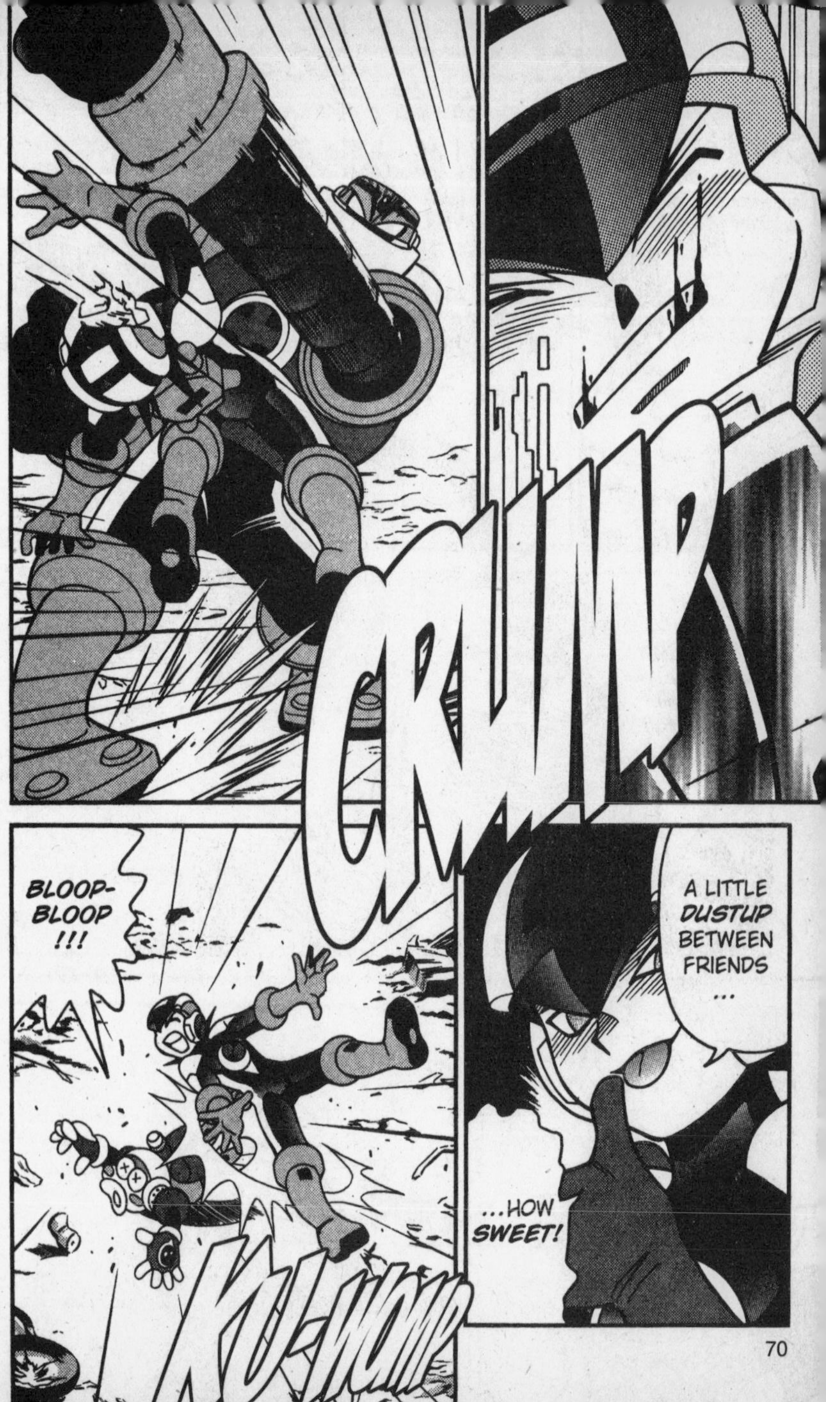
CRUMP
A LITTLE DUSTUP BETWEEN FRIENDS ...
...HOW SWEET!
BLOOP-BLOOP !!!

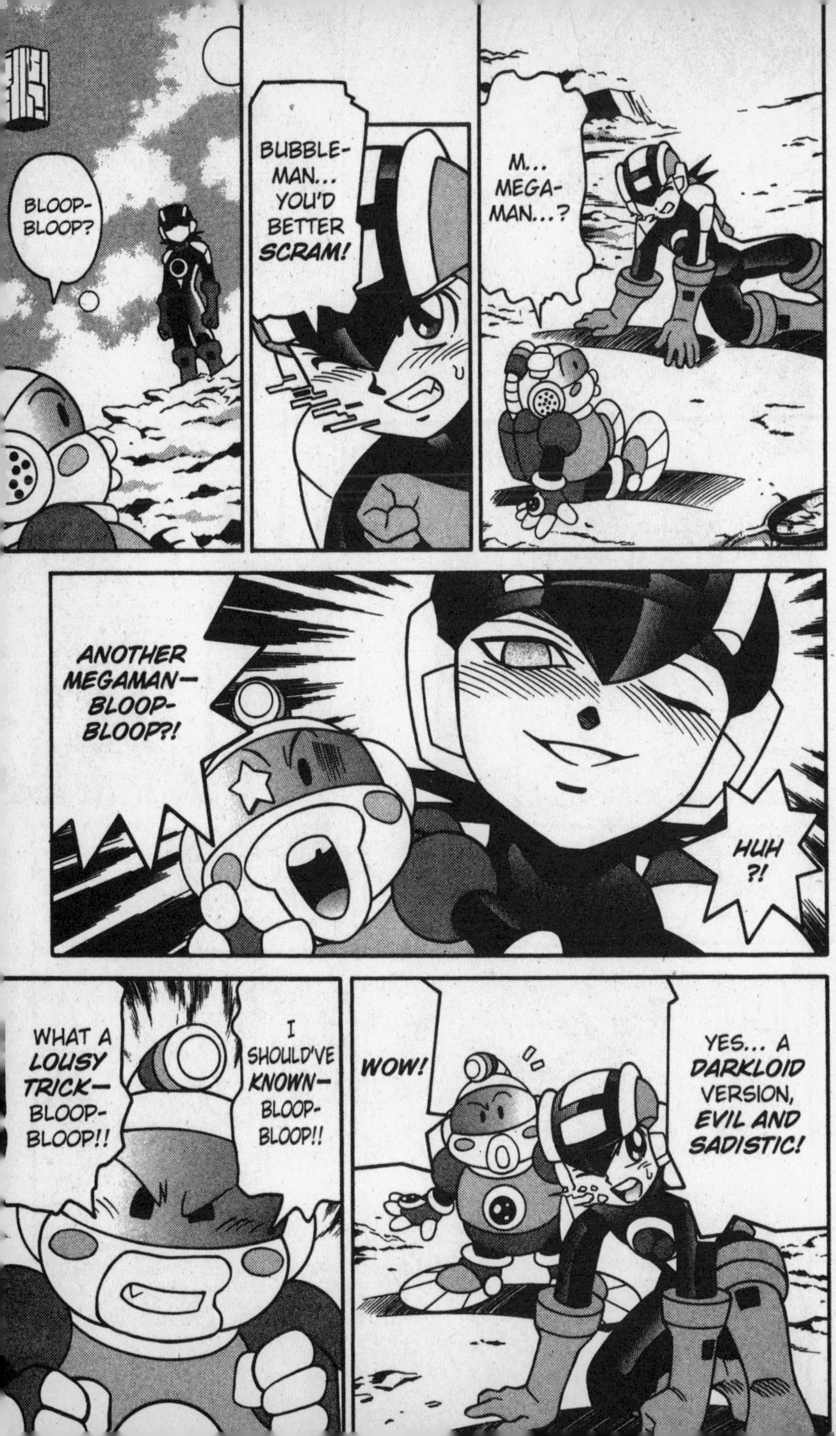
M... MEGA-MAN...?
BUBBLE-MAN... YOU'D BETTER SCRAM!
BLOOP-BLOOP?
ANOTHER MEGAMAN—BLOOP-BLOOP?!
HUH?!
YES... A DARKLOID VERSION, EVIL AND SADISTIC!
WOW!
I SHOULD'VE KNOWN—BLOOP-BLOOP!!
WHAT A LOUSY TRICK—BLOOP-BLOOP!!

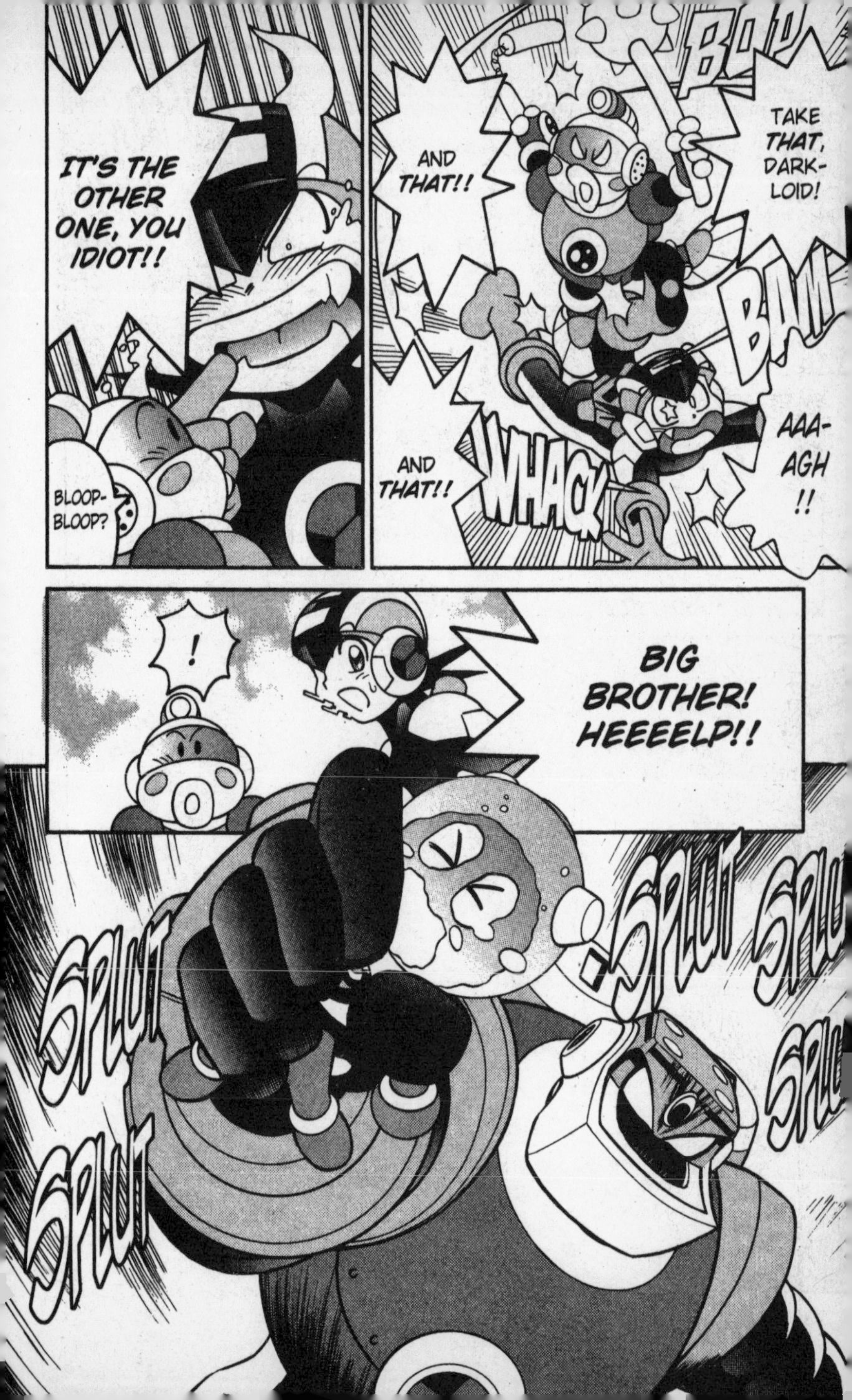
B-DP
TAKE THAT, DARK-LOID!
AND THAT!!
BAM
AAA-AGH!!
WHACK
AND THAT!!
IT'S THE OTHER ONE, YOU IDIOT!!
BLOOP-BLOOP?
BIG BROTHER! HEEEELP!!
!
SPLUT
SPLUT
SPLUT
SPLUT
SPLUT

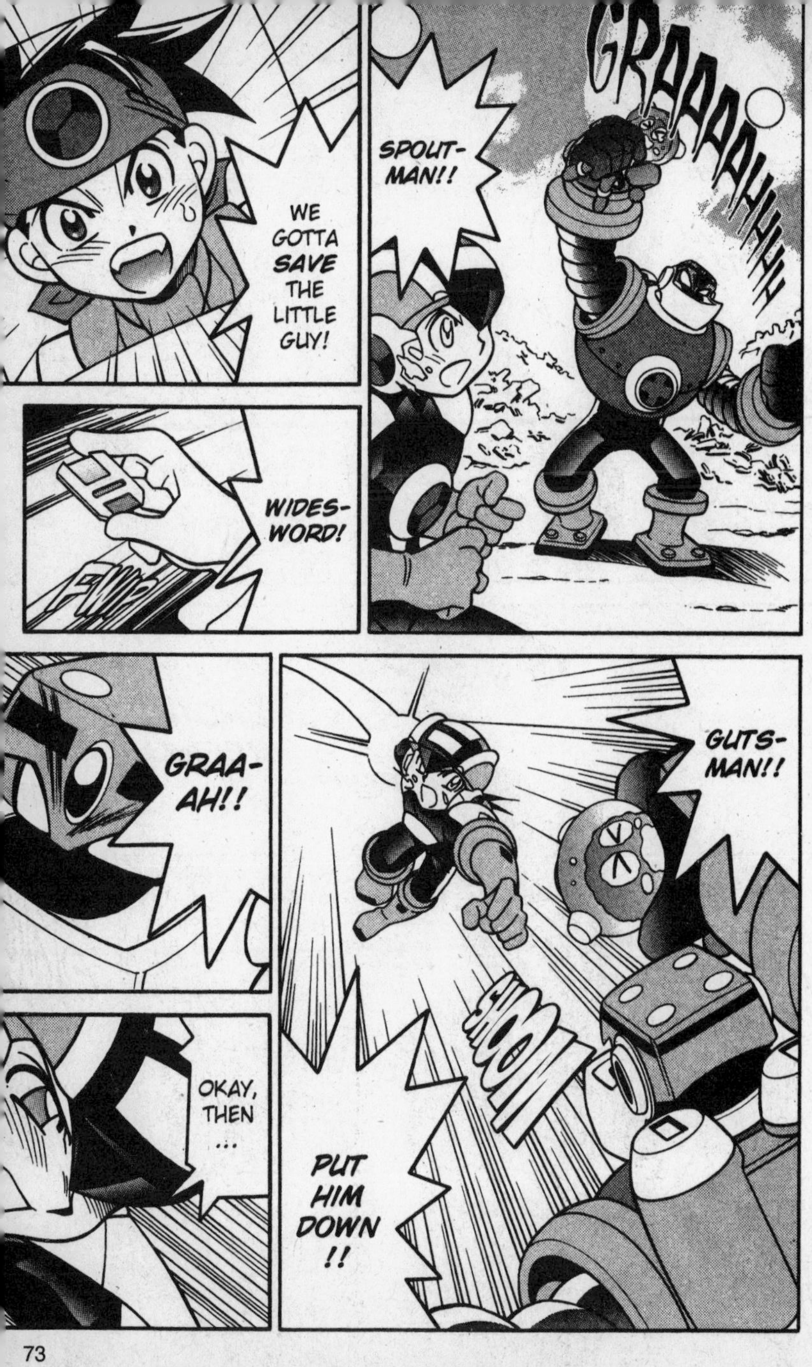
GRAAAAHHHH
SPOUT-MAN!!
WE GOTTA SAVE THE LITTLE GUY!
WIDES-WORD!
FWIP
GUTS-MAN!!
SHOOM
PUT HIM DOWN!!
GRAA-AH!!
OKAY, THEN ...

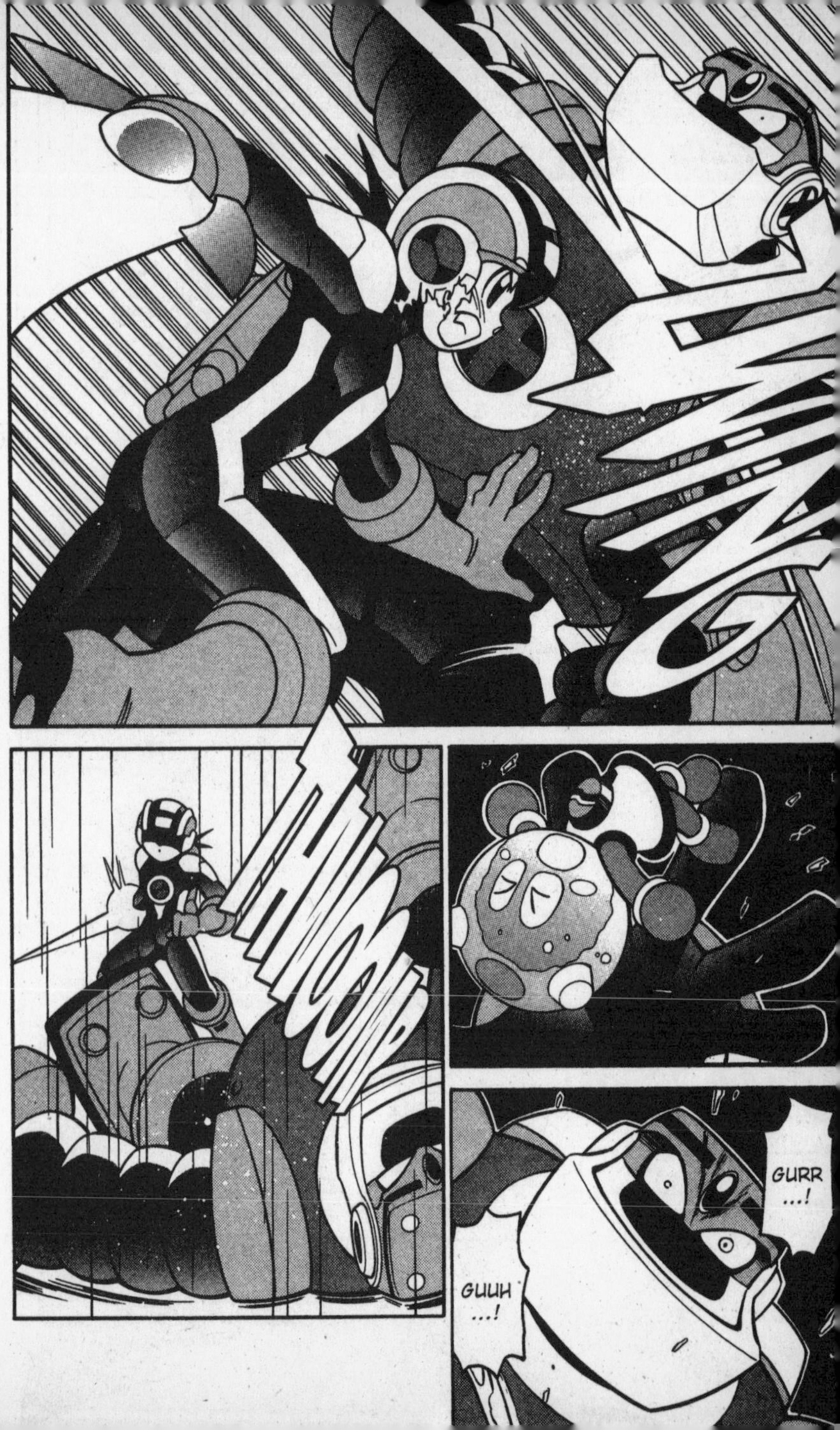
GURR ...!
GUUH ...!

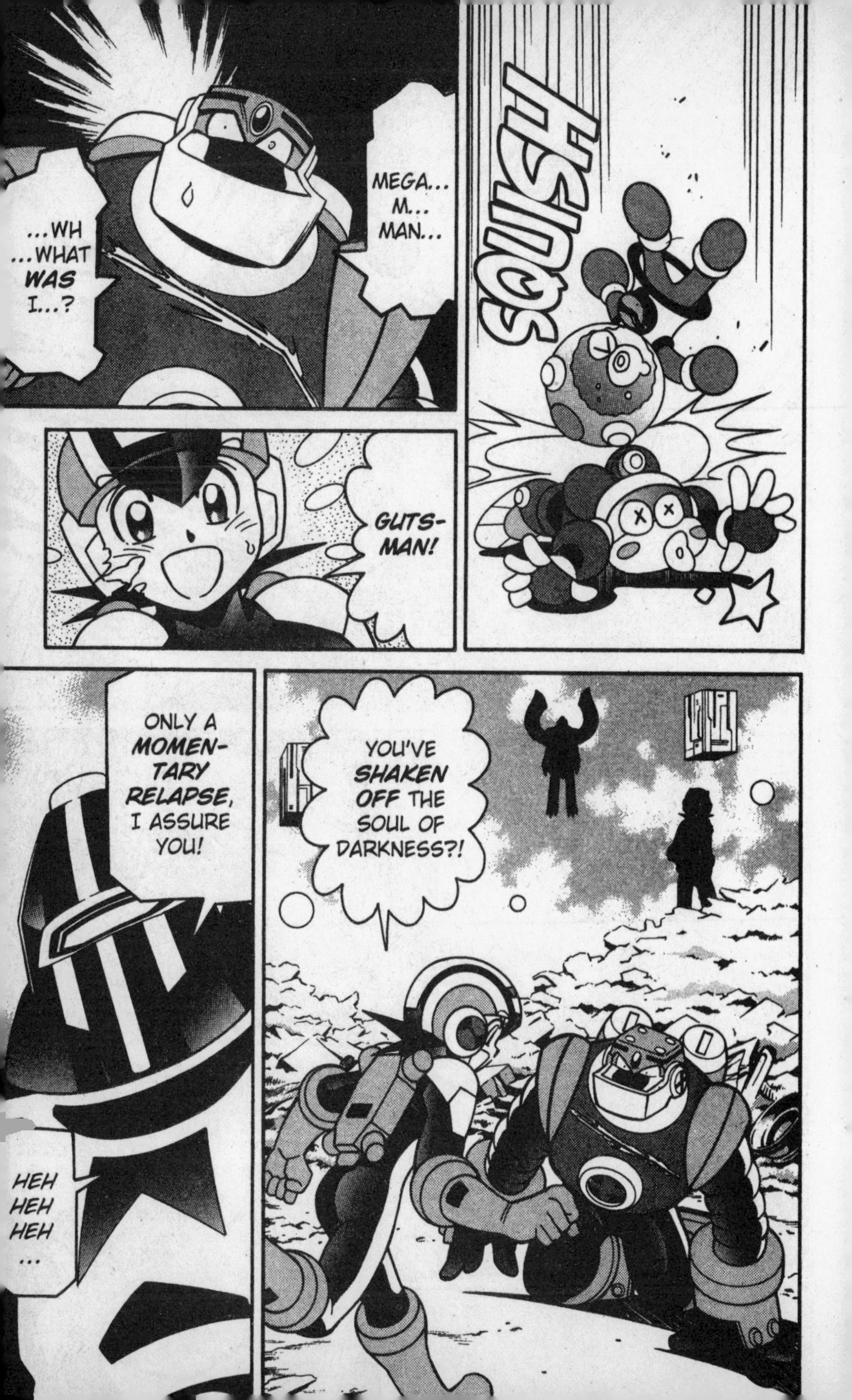
SQUISH
MEGA... M... MAN...
...WH ...WHAT WAS I...?
GUTS-MAN!
YOU'VE SHAKEN OFF THE SOUL OF DARKNESS?!
ONLY A MOMENTARY RELAPSE, I ASSURE YOU!
HEH HEH HEH ...

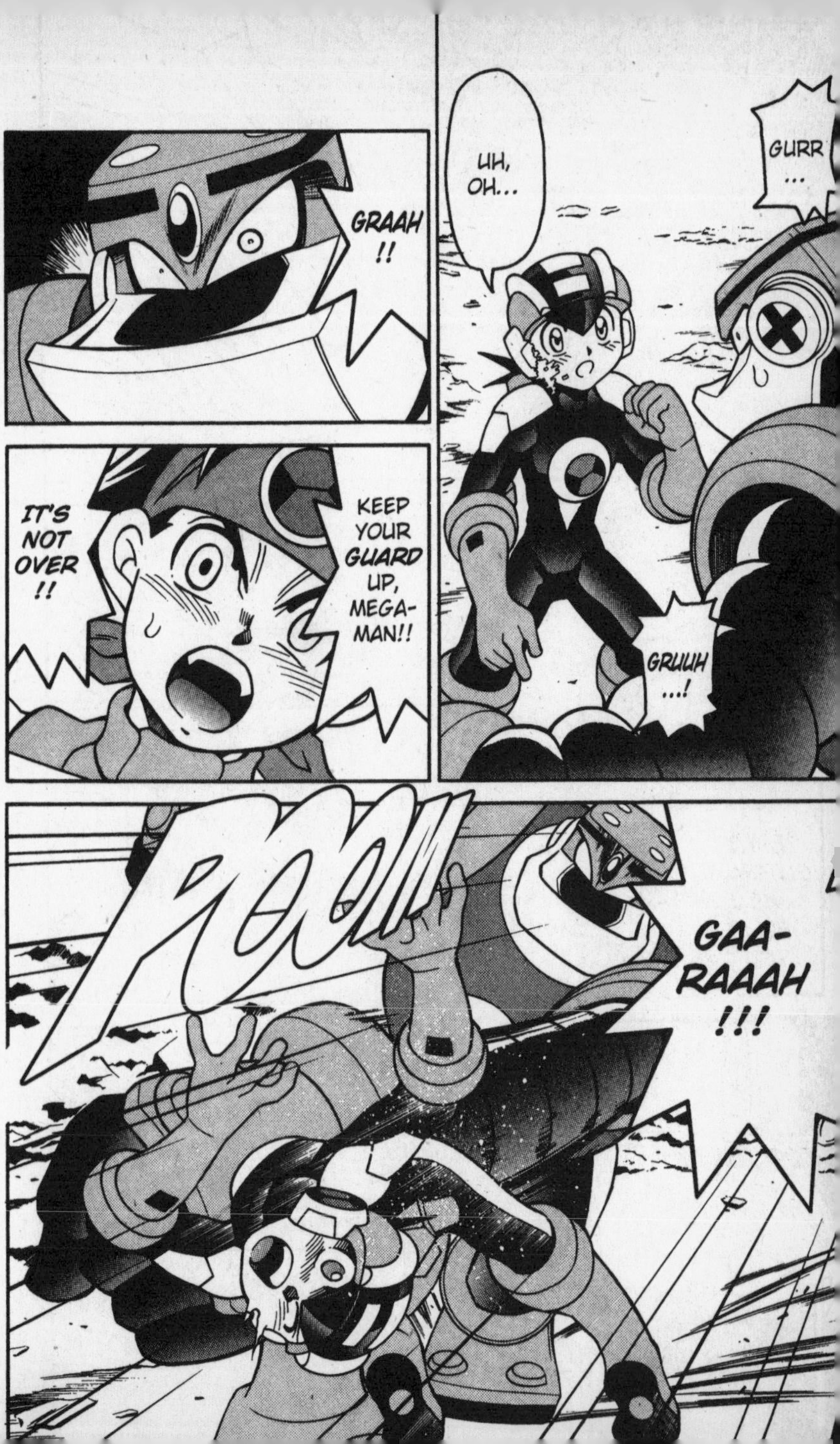
GURR...
UH, OH...
GRUUH...!
GRAAH!!
KEEP YOUR GUARD UP, MEGA-MAN!!
IT'S NOT OVER!!
GAA-RAAAH!!!

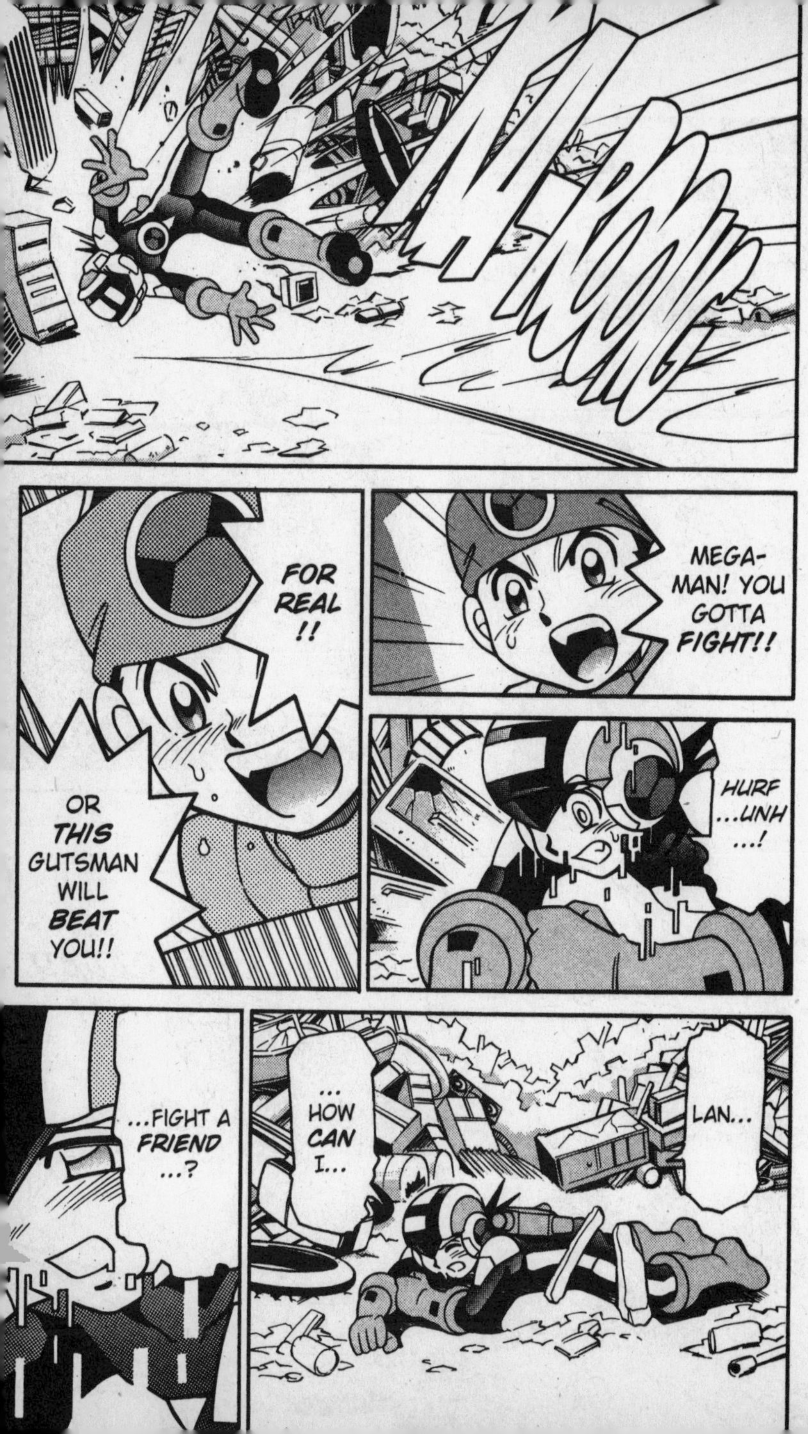
MEGA-MAN! YOU GOTTA FIGHT!!
HURF ...UNH ...!
FOR REAL!!
OR THIS GUTSMAN WILL BEAT YOU!!
LAN...
...HOW CAN I...
...FIGHT A FRIEND ...?

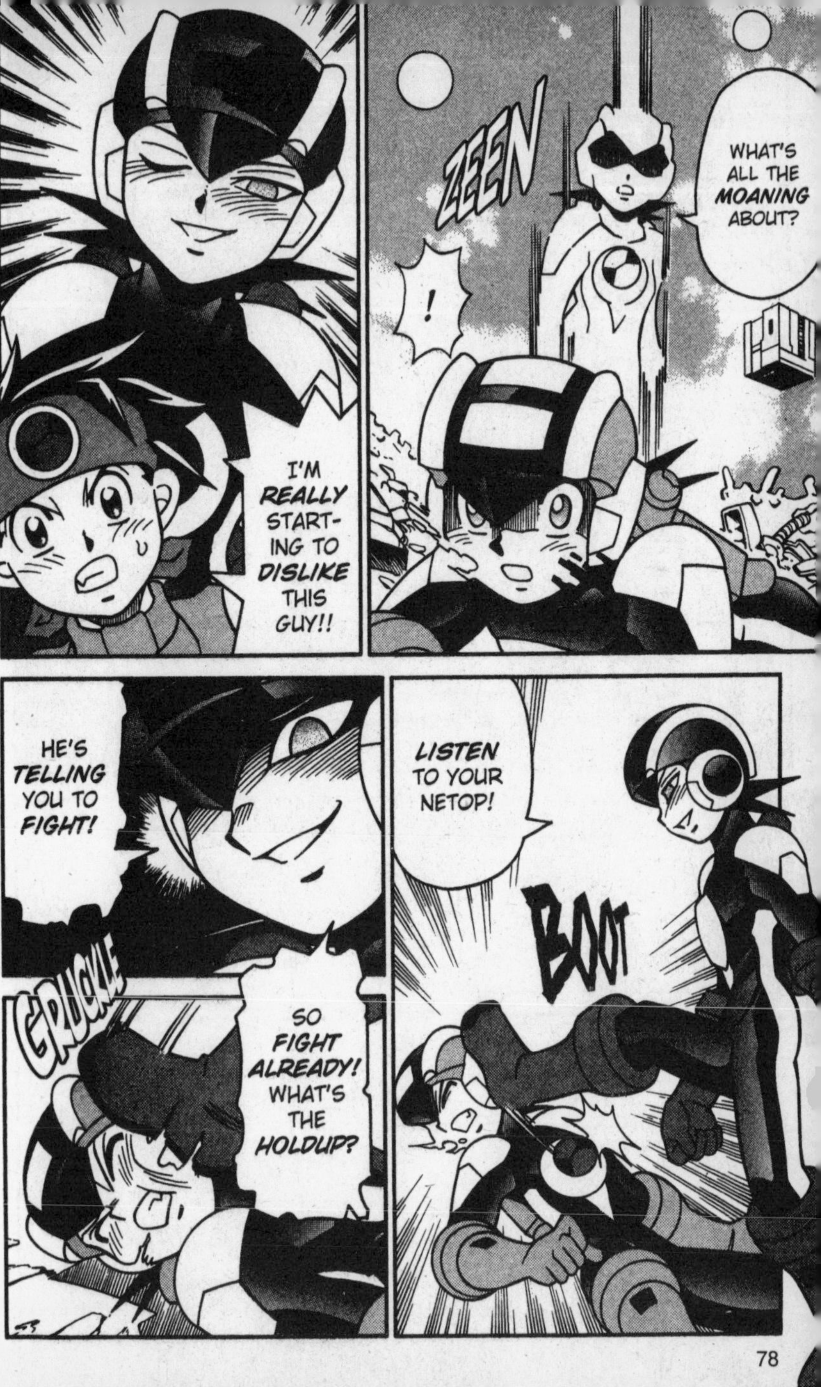
WHAT'S ALL THE MOANING ABOUT?
ZEEN
!
I'M REALLY STARTING TO DISLIKE THIS GUY!!
LISTEN TO YOUR NETOP!
BOOT
HE'S TELLING YOU TO FIGHT!
CRUCKLE
SO FIGHT ALREADY! WHAT'S THE HOLDUP?

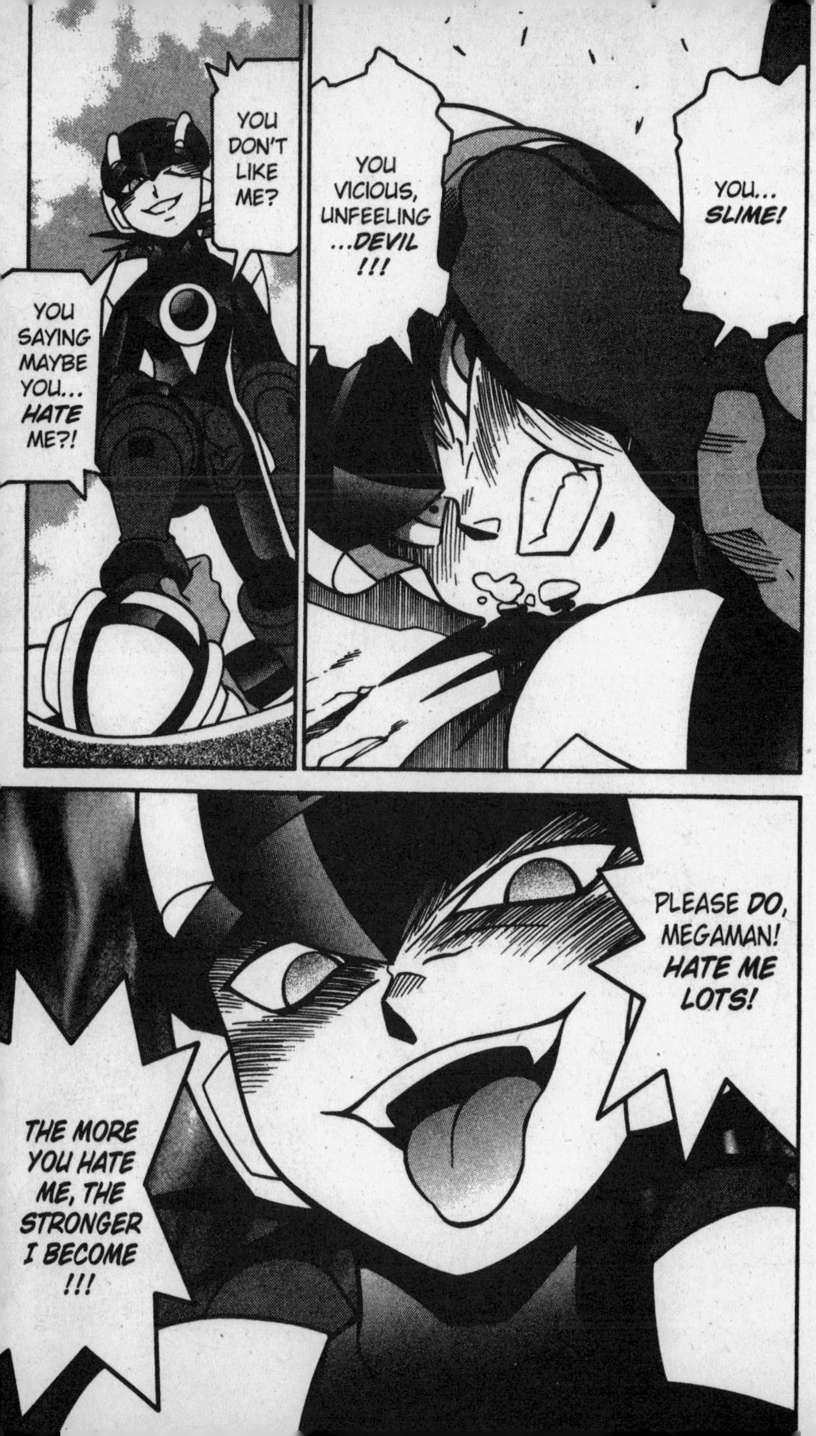
YOU... SLIME!
YOU VICIOUS, UNFEELING ...DEVIL !!!
YOU DON'T LIKE ME?
YOU SAYING MAYBE YOU... HATE ME?!
PLEASE DO, MEGAMAN! HATE ME LOTS!
THE MORE YOU HATE ME, THE STRONGER I BECOME !!!

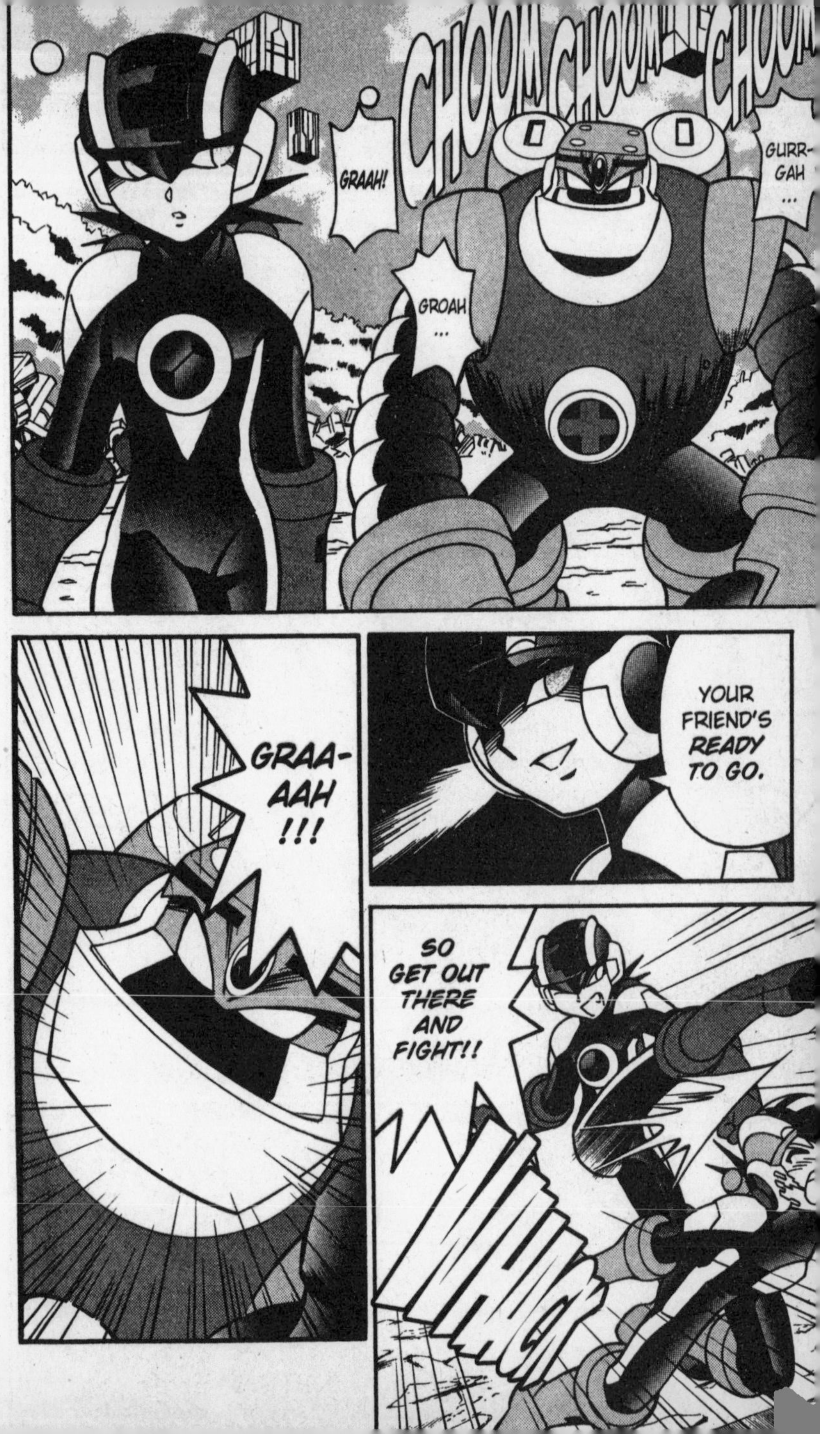
CHOOM CHOOM CHOOM
GURR-GAH ...
GRAAH!
GROAH ...
YOUR FRIEND'S READY TO GO.
SO GET OUT THERE AND FIGHT!!
WHACK
GRAA-AAH!!!

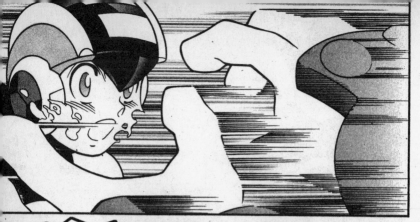

MEGA-
MAN
!!!

GLUK...
HUUUU...

SQUEEZE

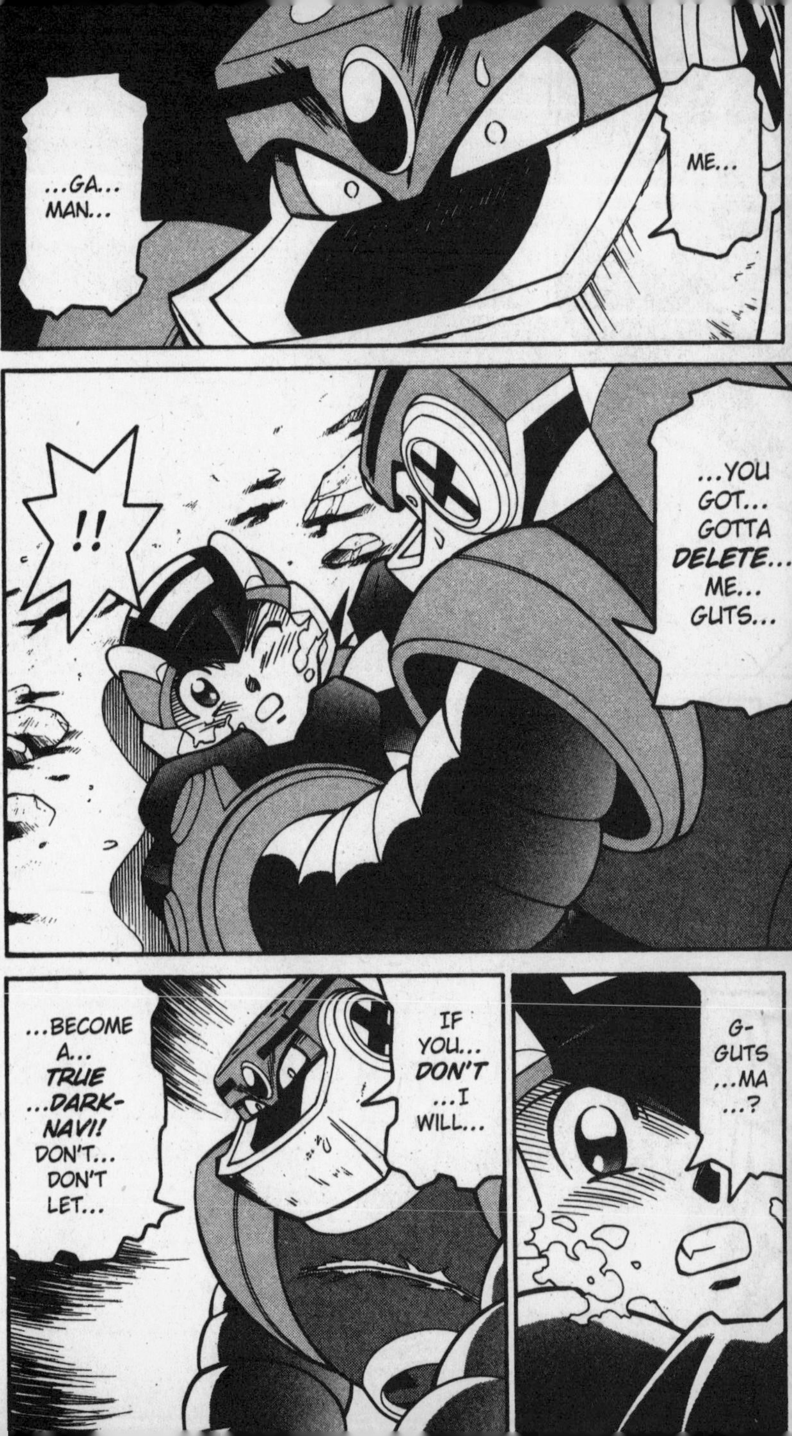
ME...
...GA... MAN...
...YOU GOT... GOTTA **DELETE...** ME... GUTS...
!!
G-GUTS ...MA ...?
IF YOU... **DON'T** ...I WILL...
...BECOME A... **TRUE ...DARK-NAVI!** DON'T... DON'T LET...

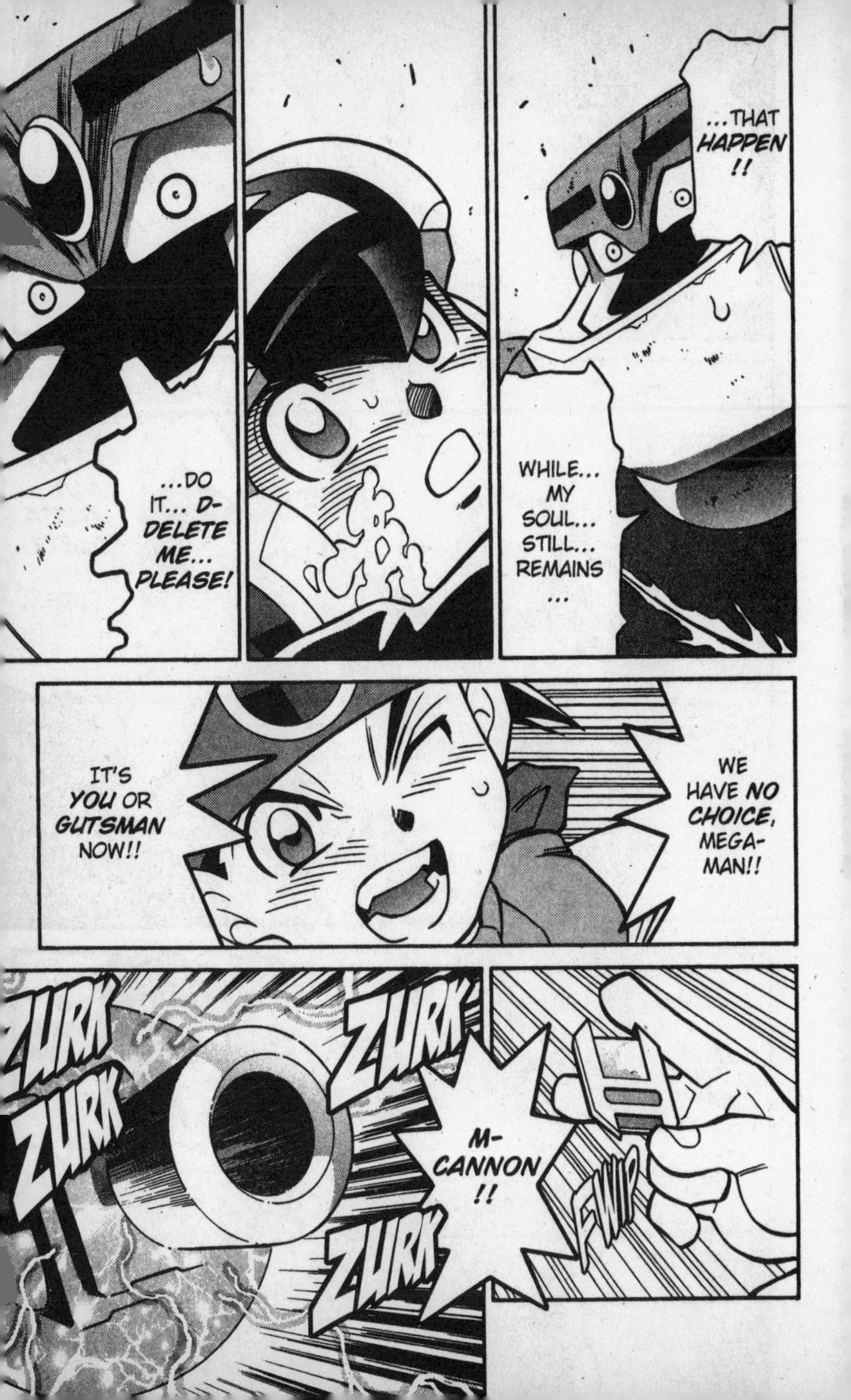
...THAT HAPPEN!!
WHILE... MY SOUL... STILL... REMAINS...
...DO IT... D-DELETE ME... PLEASE!
WE HAVE NO CHOICE, MEGA-MAN!!
IT'S YOU OR GUTSMAN NOW!!
FWIP
ZURK
ZURK
ZURK
M-CANNON!!
ZURK

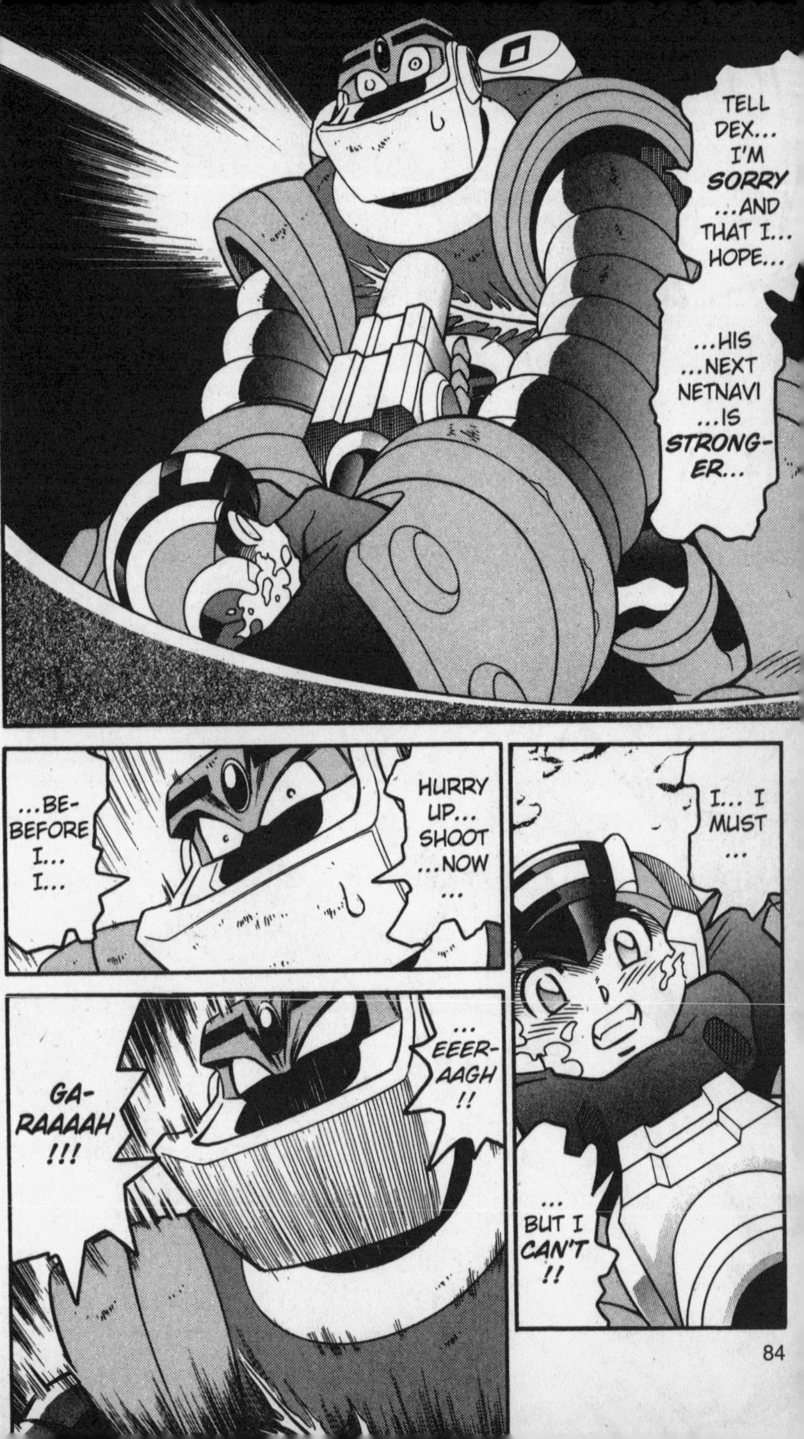
TELL DEX... I'M SORRY ...AND THAT I... HOPE...
...HIS ...NEXT NETNAVI ...IS STRONG-ER...
I... I MUST ...
... BUT I CAN'T !!
HURRY UP... SHOOT ...NOW ...
...BE- BEFORE I... I...
... EEER-AAGH !!
GA-RAAAAH !!!

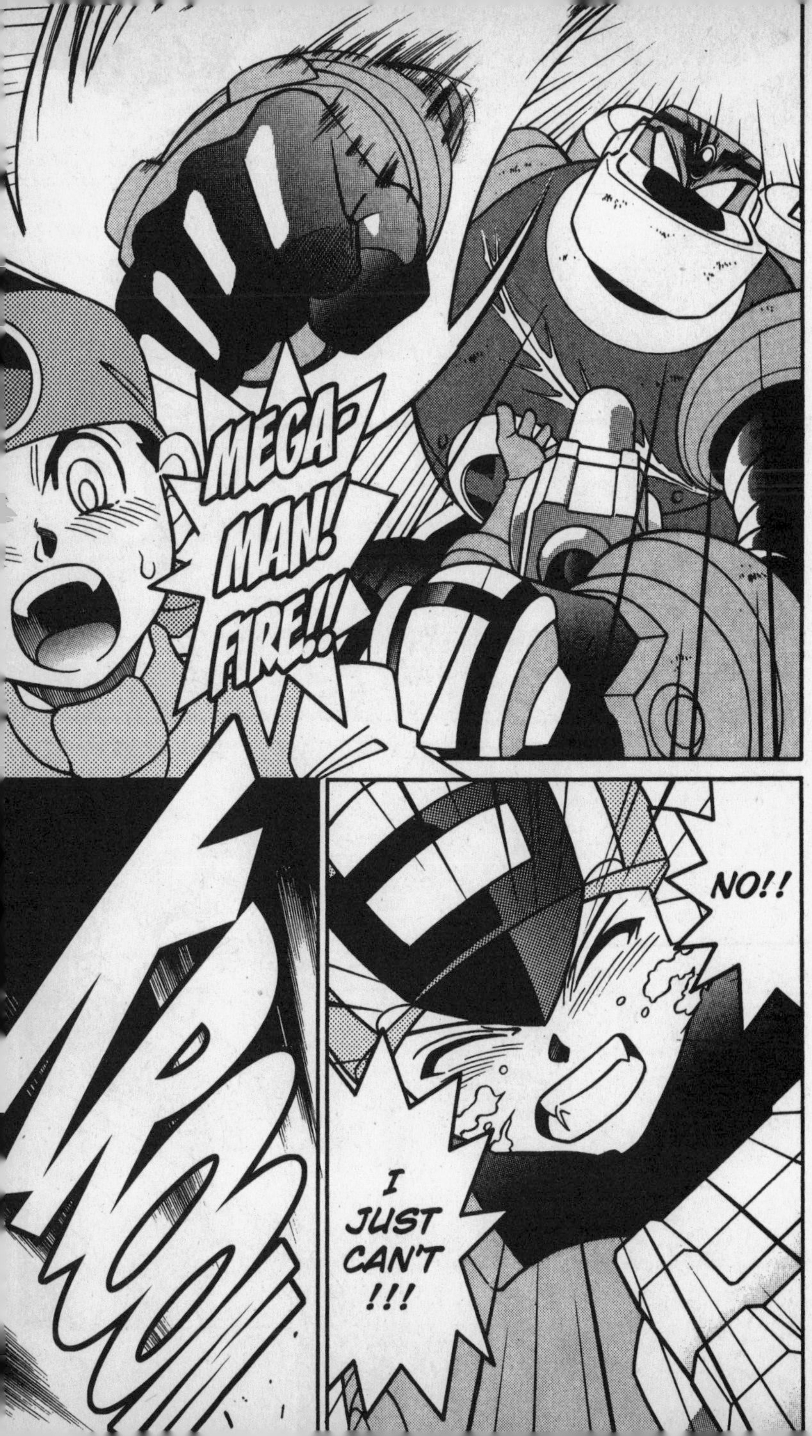
MEGA-MAN! FIRE!!
NO!!
I JUST CAN'T!!!

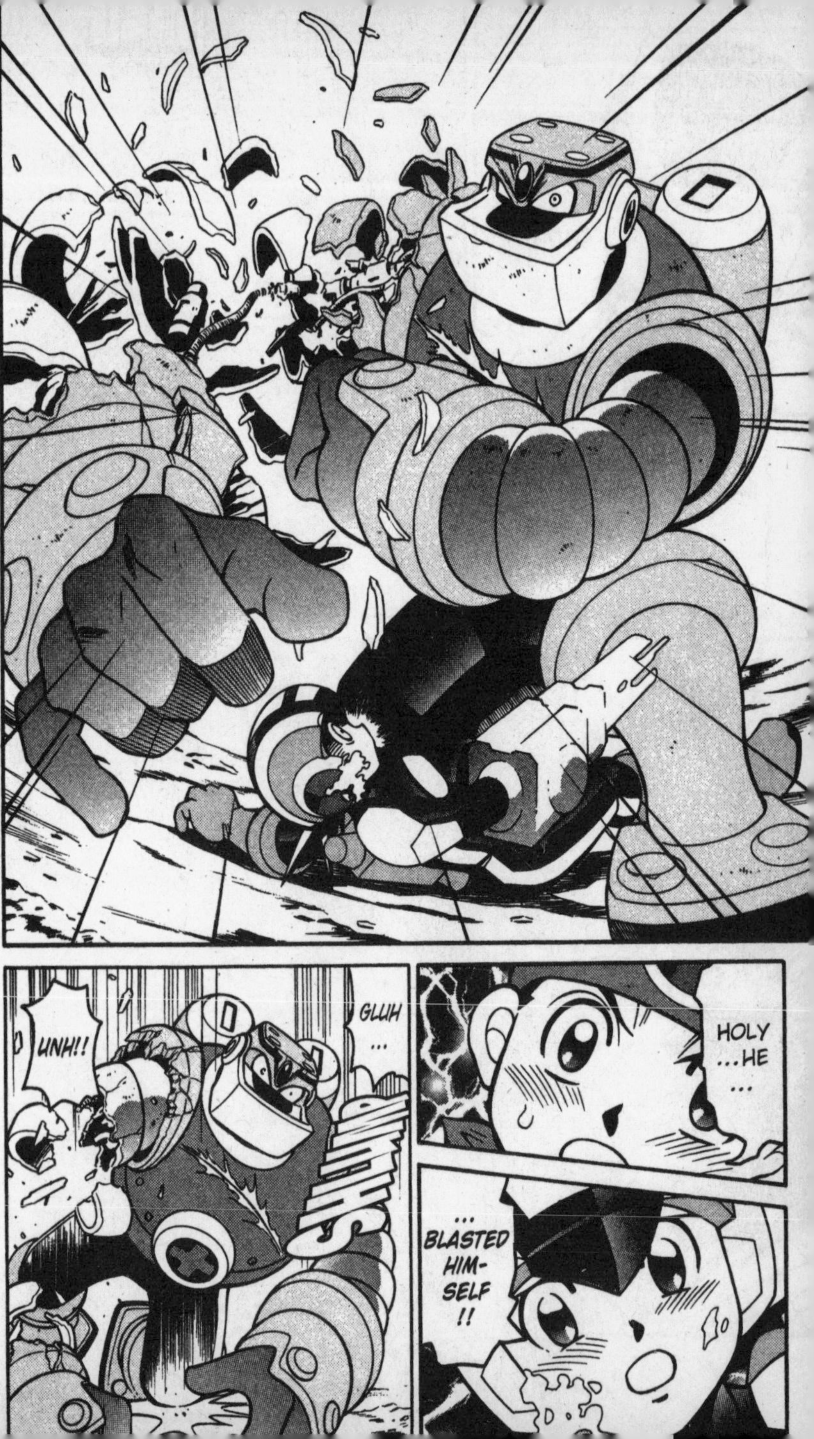
HOLY ...HE ...
... BLASTED HIM-SELF !!
UNH!!
GLUH ...

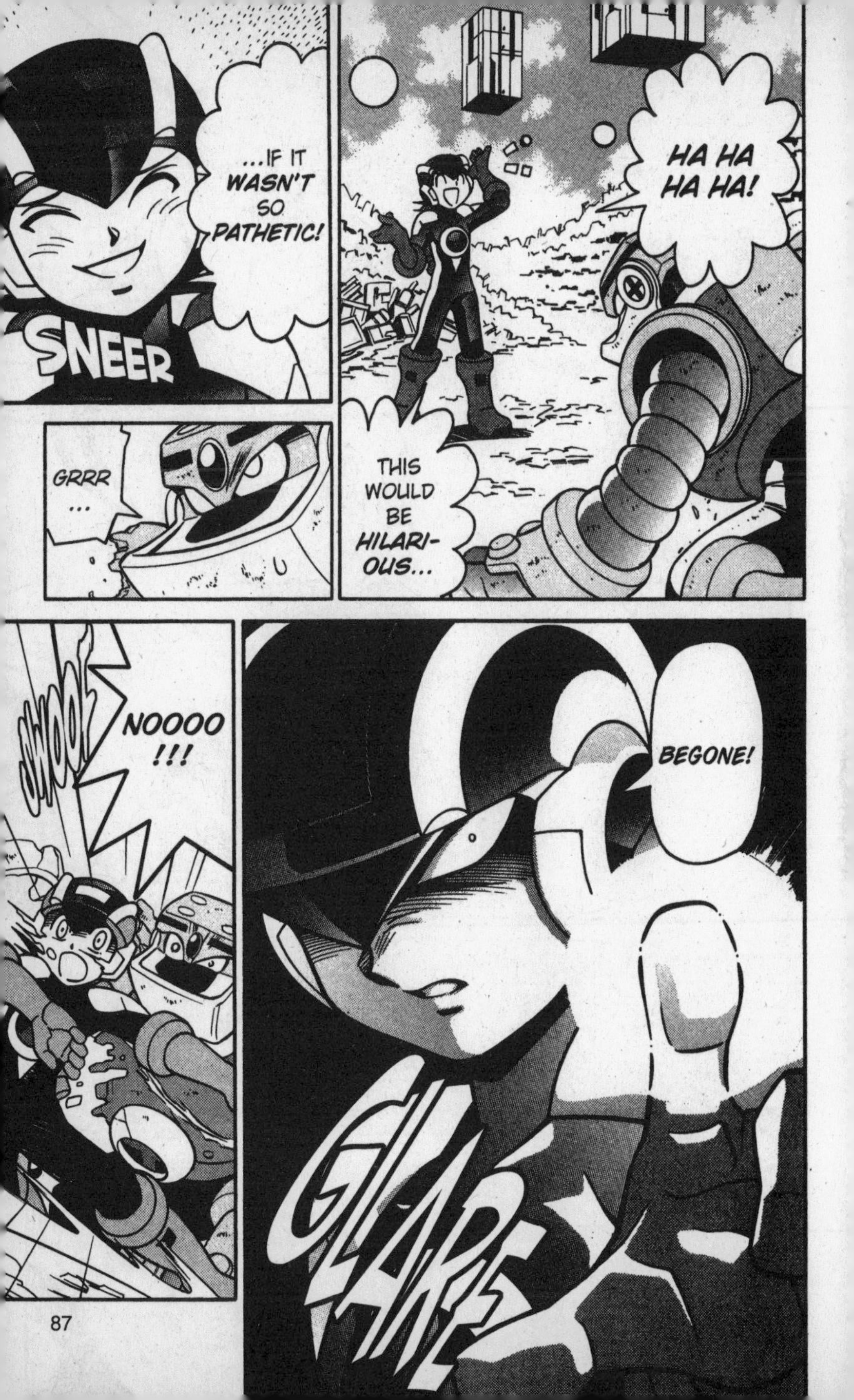
HA HA HA HA!
THIS WOULD BE HILARIOUS...
...IF IT WASN'T SO PATHETIC!
SNEER
GRRR ...
BEGONE!
GLARE
NOOOO !!!

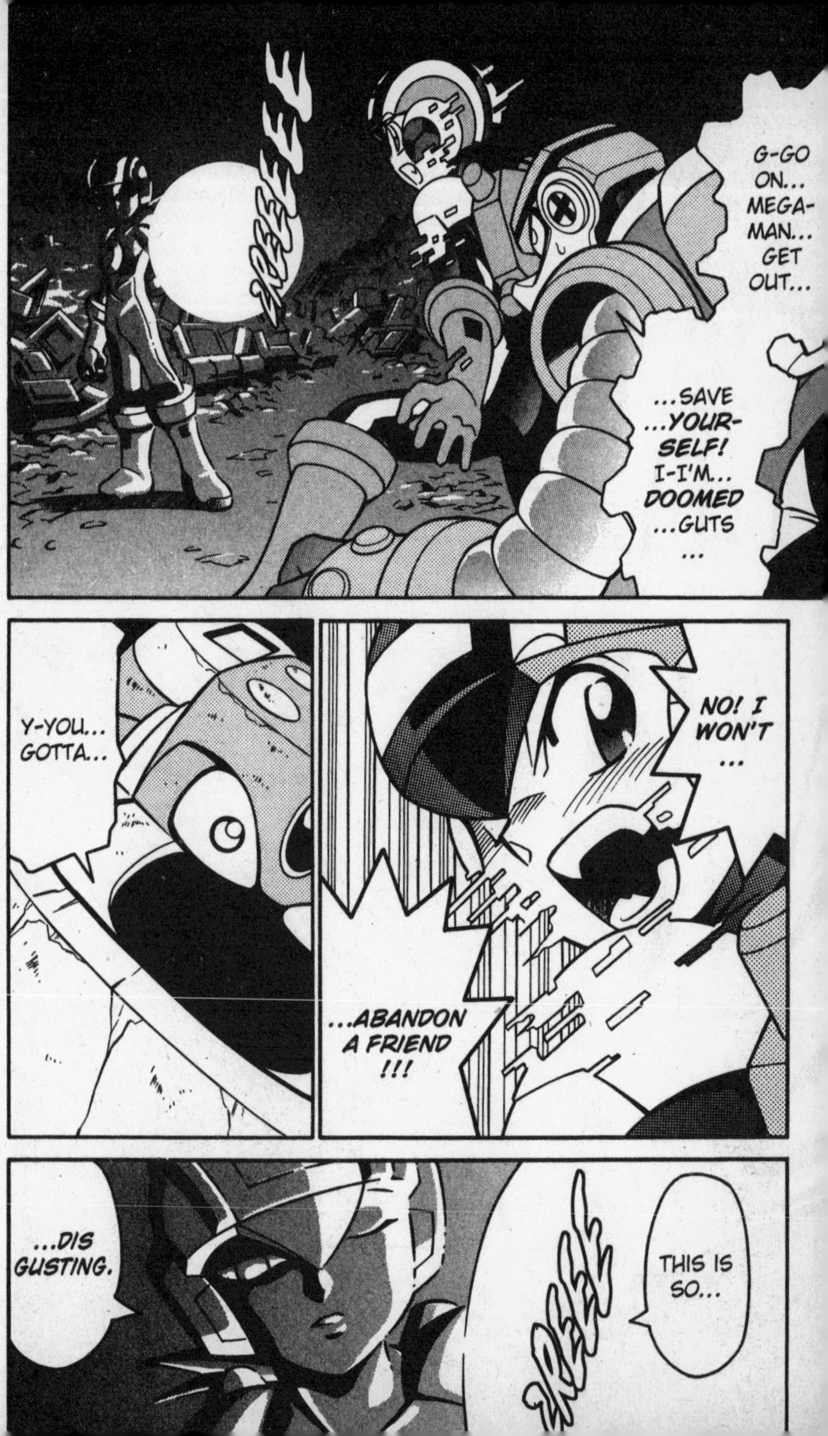
G-GO ON... MEGA-MAN... GET OUT...
...SAVE ...YOUR-SELF! I-I'M... DOOMED ...GUTS ...
NO! I WON'T ...
...ABANDON A FRIEND !!!
Y-YOU... GOTTA...
THIS IS SO...
...DIS GUSTING.

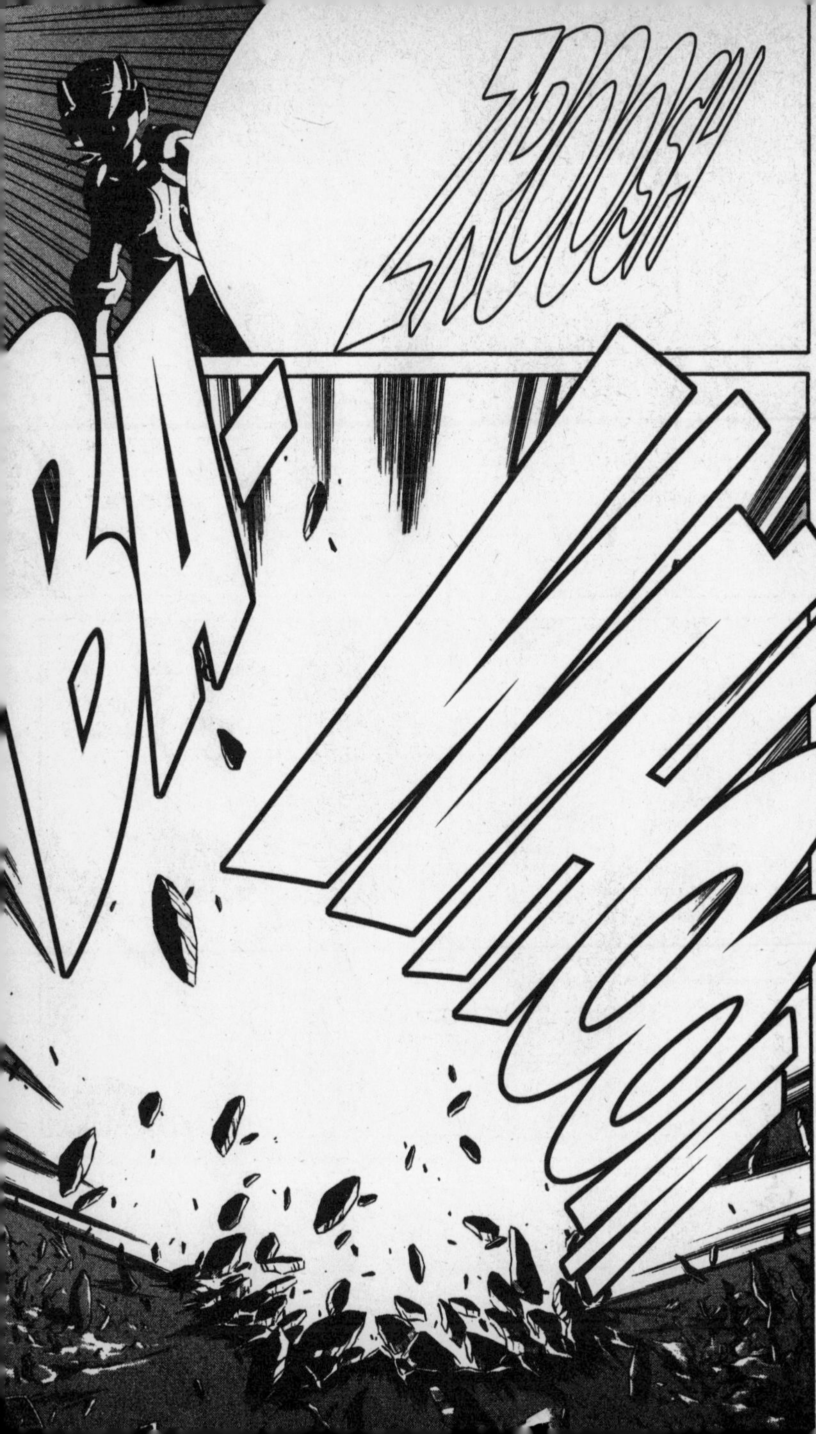
ZOOOSH

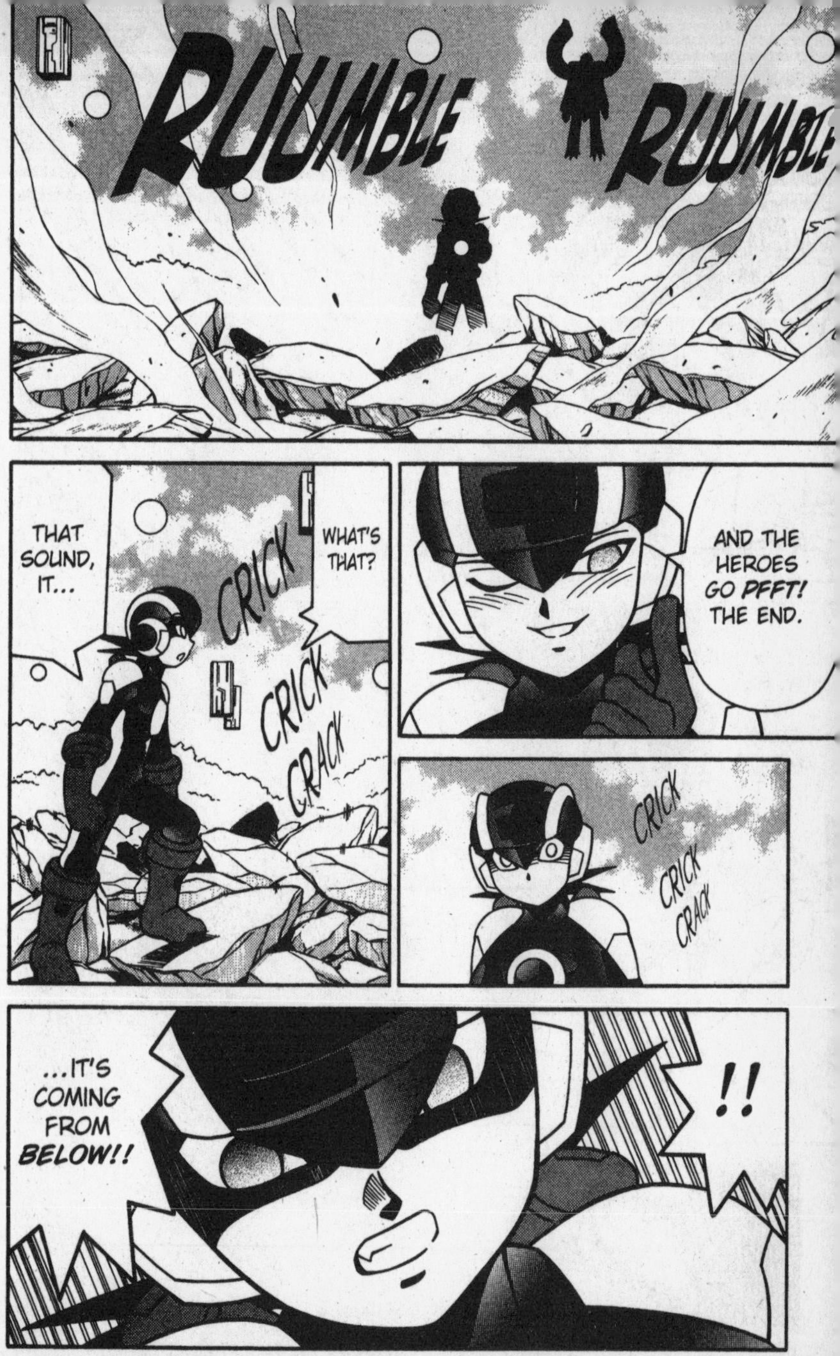
RUUMBLE
RUUMBLE
AND THE HEROES GO PFFT! THE END.
CRICK
CRICK
CRACK
WHAT'S THAT?
THAT SOUND, IT...
CRICK
CRICK
CRACK
!!
...IT'S COMING FROM BELOW!!

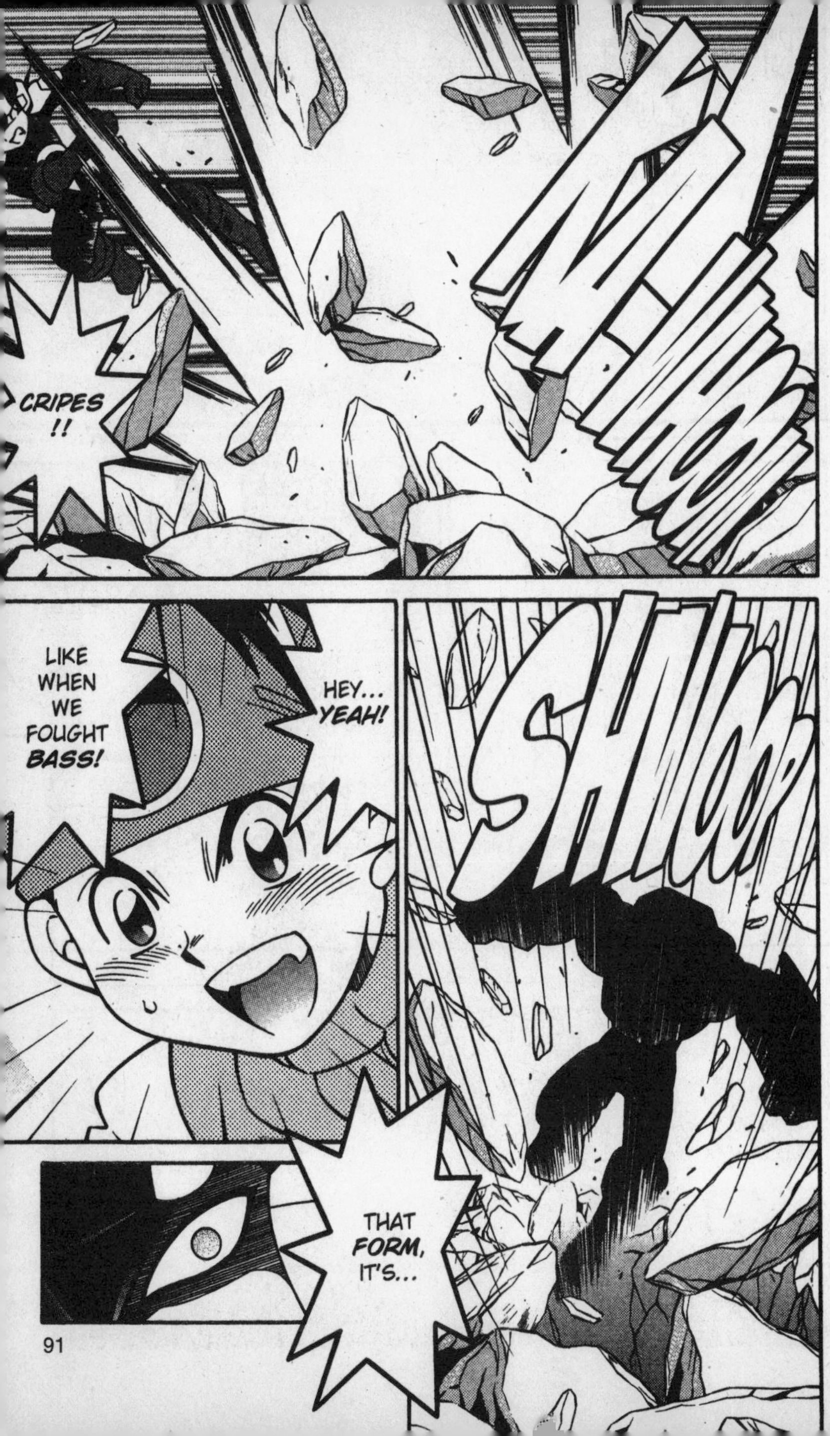
CRIPES !!
HEY... YEAH!
LIKE WHEN WE FOUGHT BASS!
THAT FORM, IT'S...

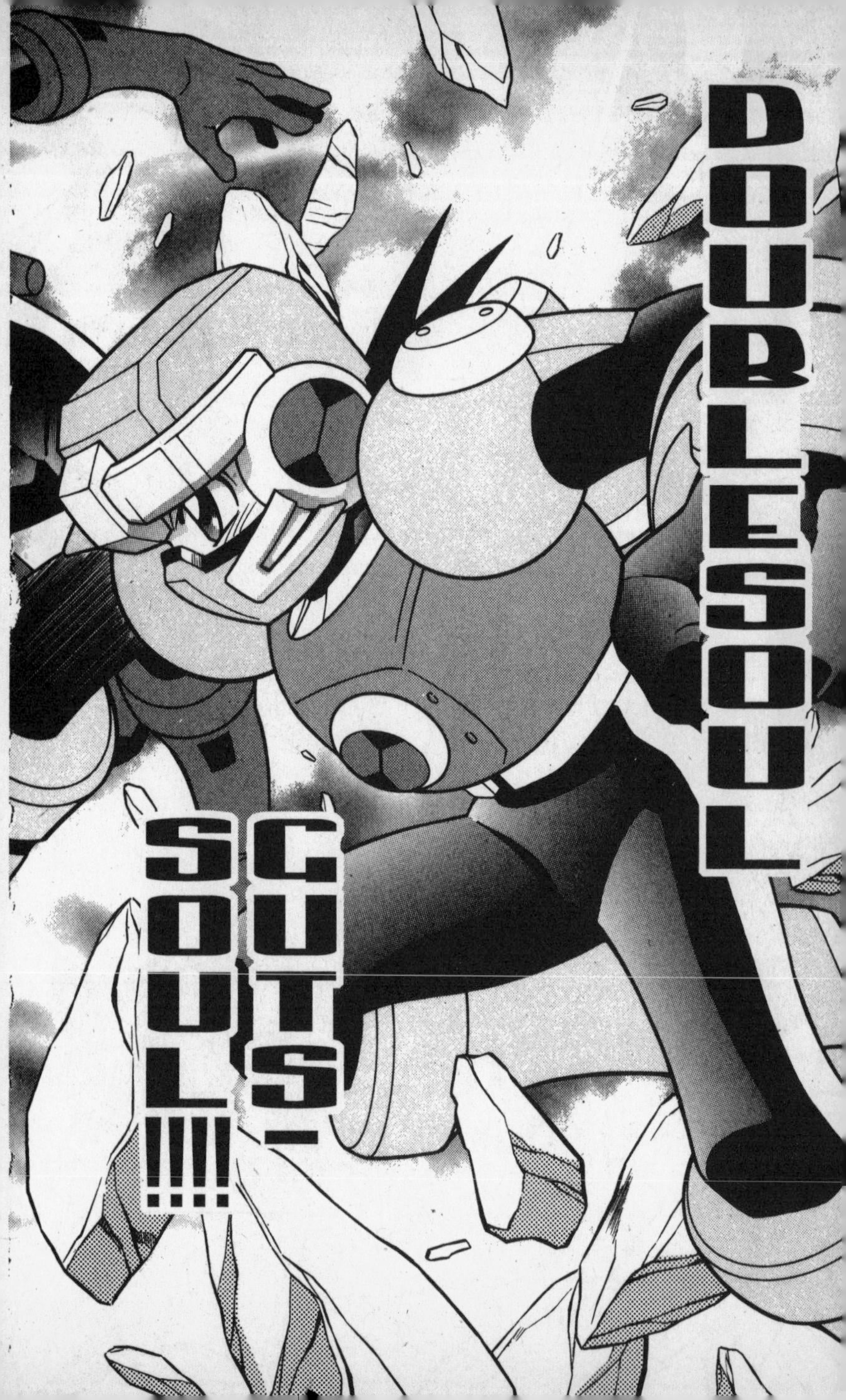
DOUBLE SOUL
SCOUTS-
SOUL!!!!

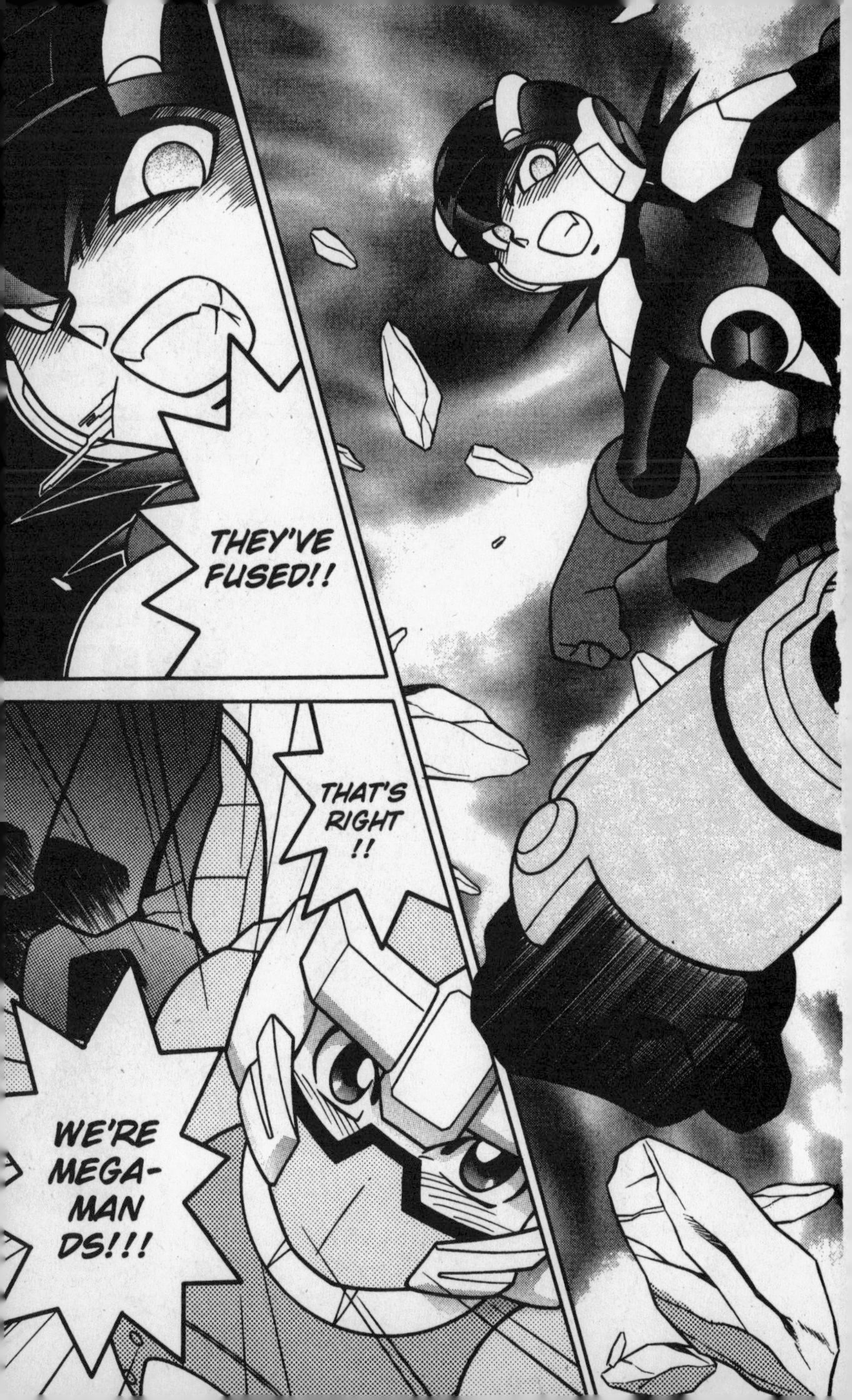
THEY'VE FUSED!!
THAT'S RIGHT!!
WE'RE MEGA-MAN DS!!!

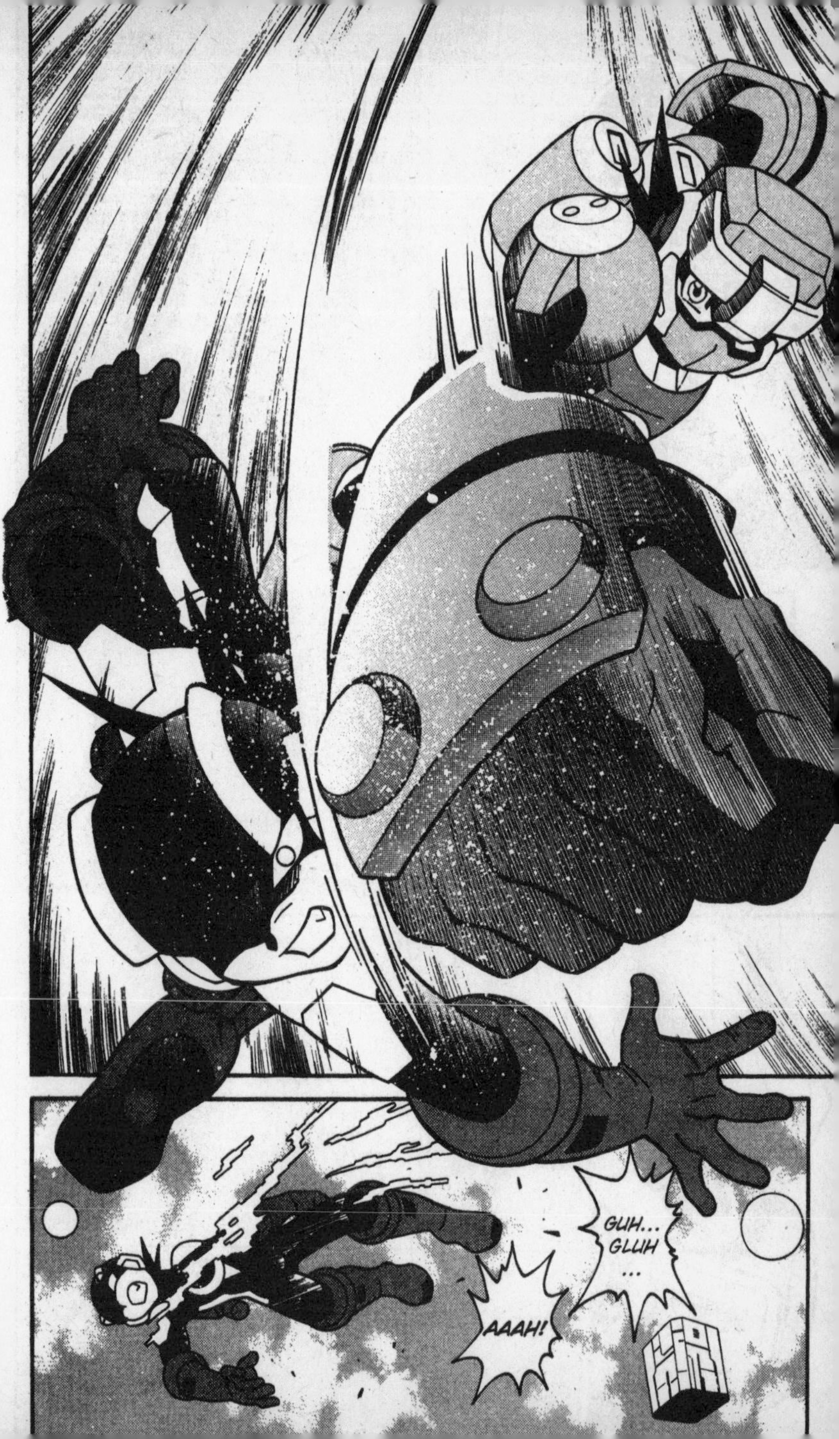
GUH... GLUH ...
AAAH!

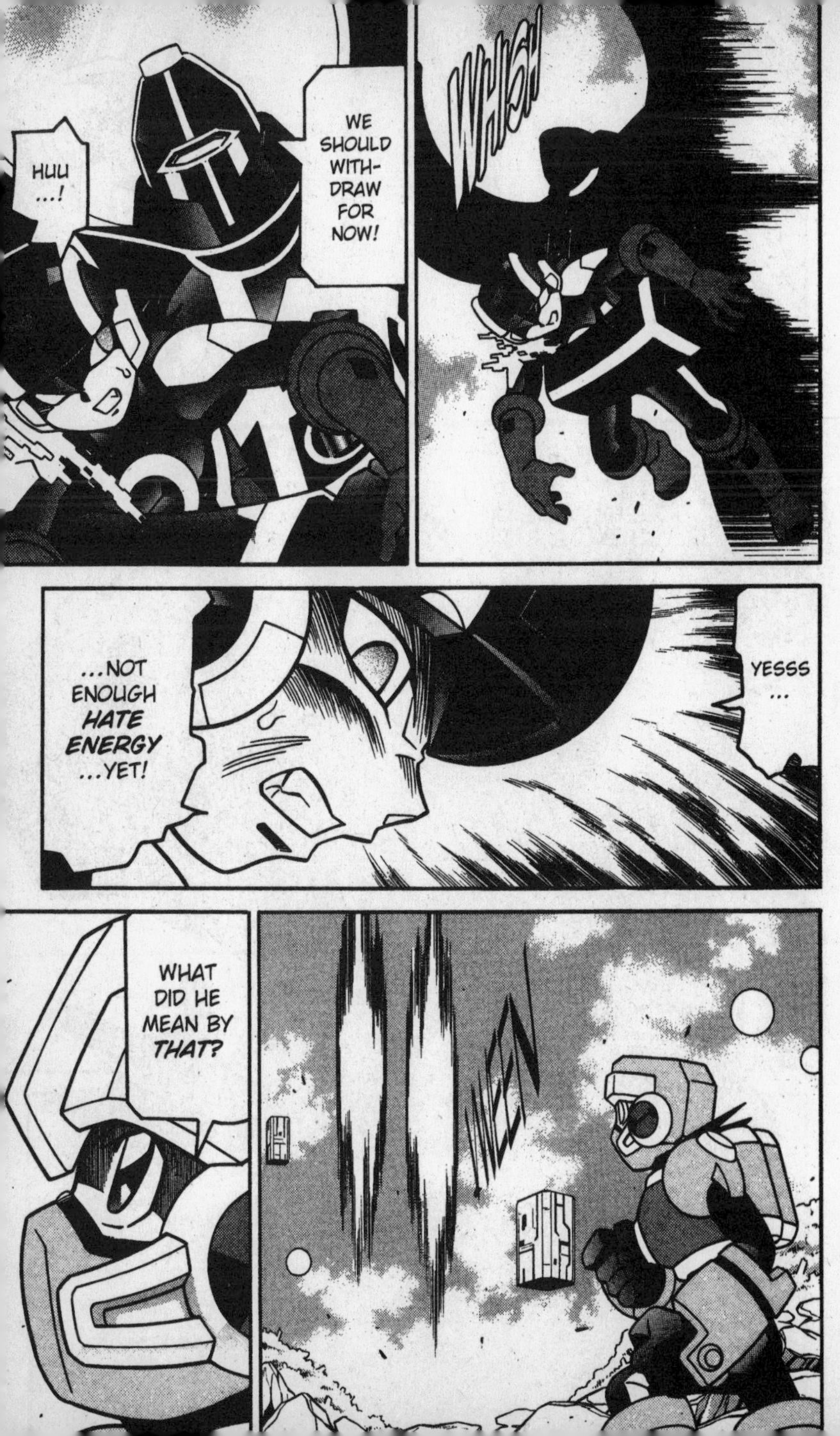
WHISH
WE SHOULD WITH-DRAW FOR NOW!
HUU ...!
YESSS ...
...NOT ENOUGH *HATE ENERGY* ...YET!
WHAT DID HE MEAN BY *THAT?*

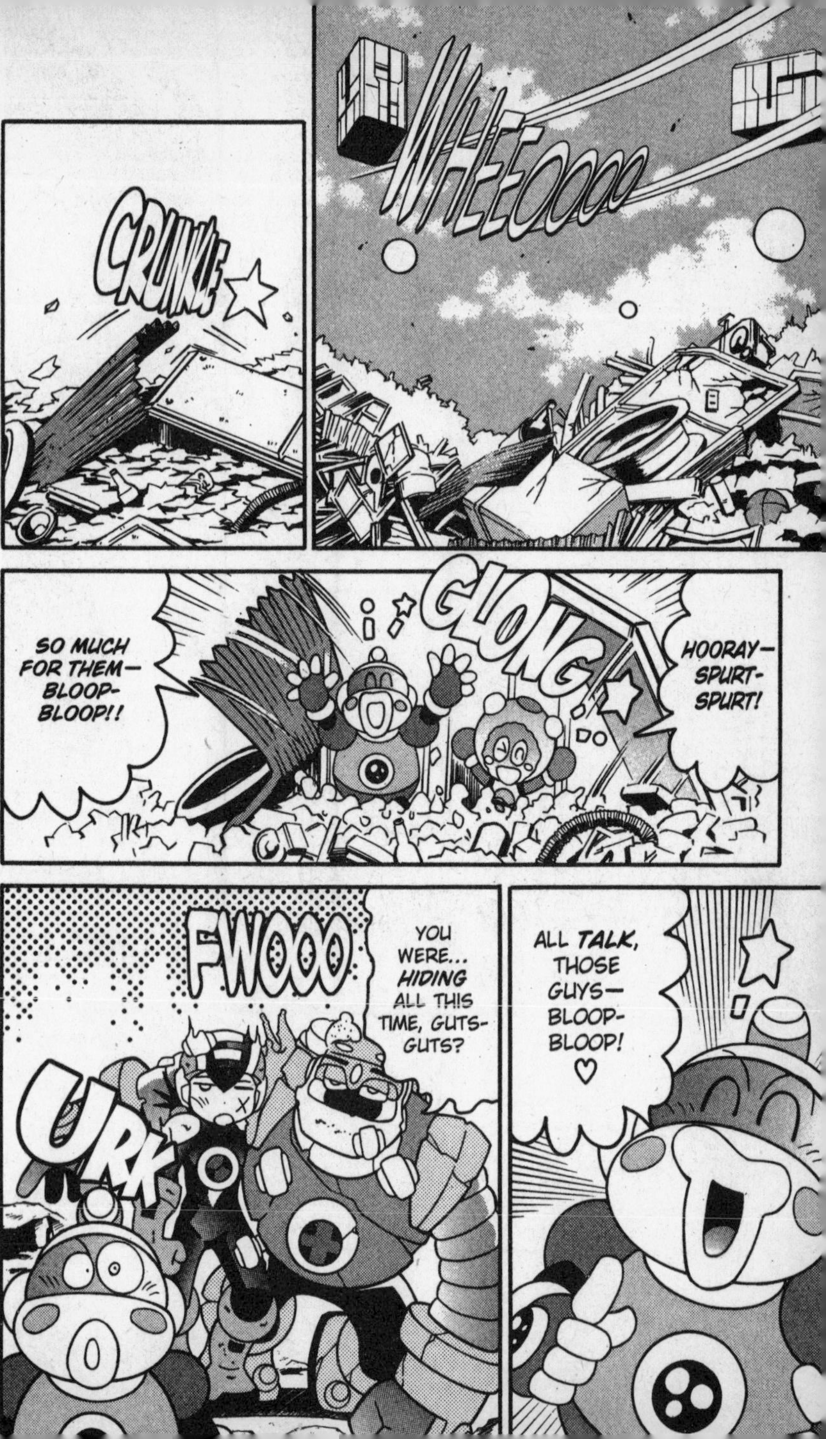
WHEEOOOO
CRUNKLE
HOORAY—SPURT-SPURT!
GLONG
SO MUCH FOR THEM—BLOOP-BLOOP!!
ALL TALK, THOSE GUYS—BLOOP-BLOOP!
YOU WERE... HIDING ALL THIS TIME, GUTS-GUTS?
FWOOO
URK

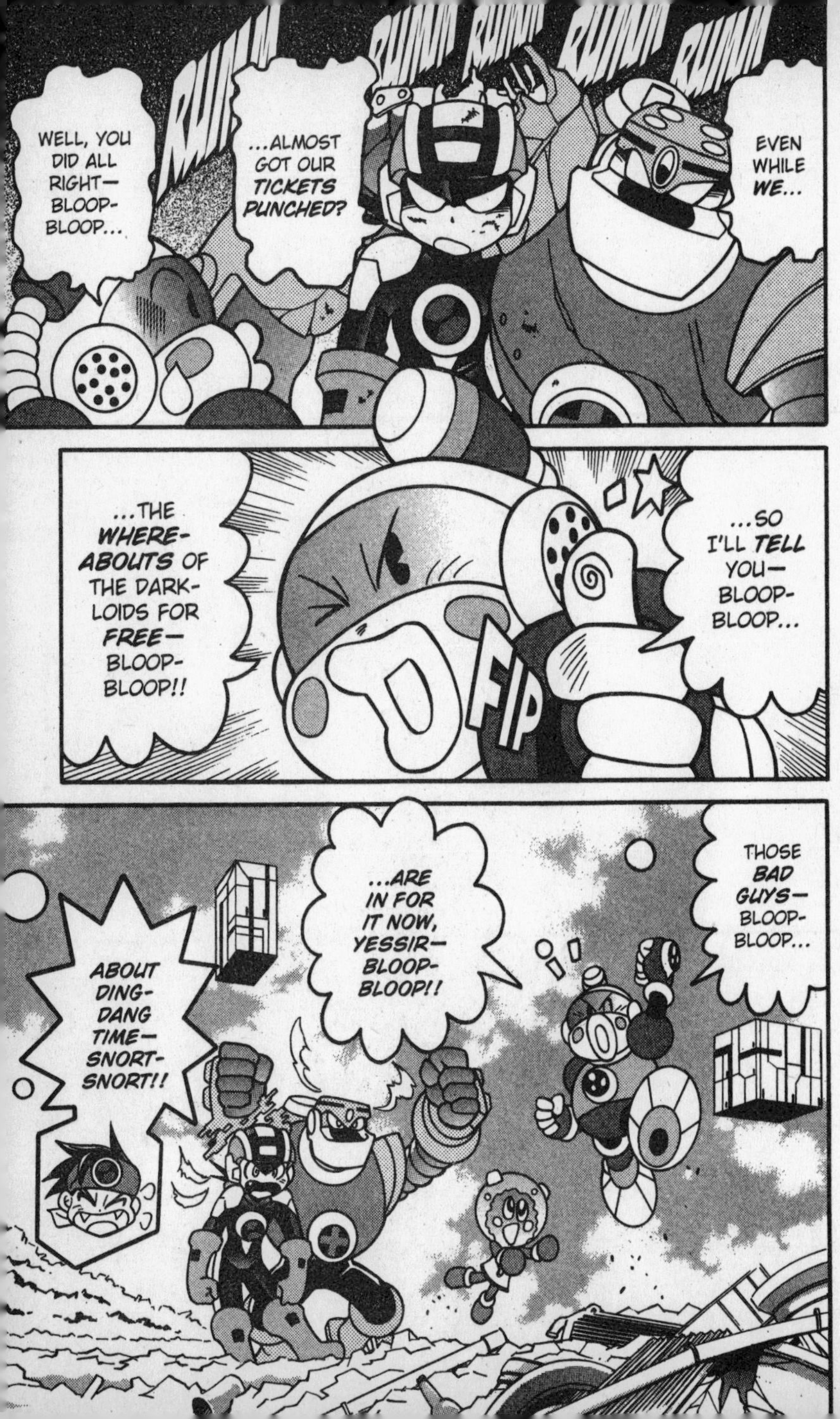
RUMM RUMM RUMM RUMM RUMM
WELL, YOU DID ALL RIGHT—BLOOP-BLOOP...
...ALMOST GOT OUR TICKETS PUNCHED?
EVEN WHILE WE...
...THE WHEREABOUTS OF THE DARK-LOIDS FOR FREE—BLOOP-BLOOP!!
...SO I'LL TELL YOU—BLOOP-BLOOP...
FIP
THOSE BAD GUYS—BLOOP-BLOOP...
...ARE IN FOR IT NOW, YESSIR—BLOOP-BLOOP!!
ABOUT DING-DANG TIME—SNORT-SNORT!!

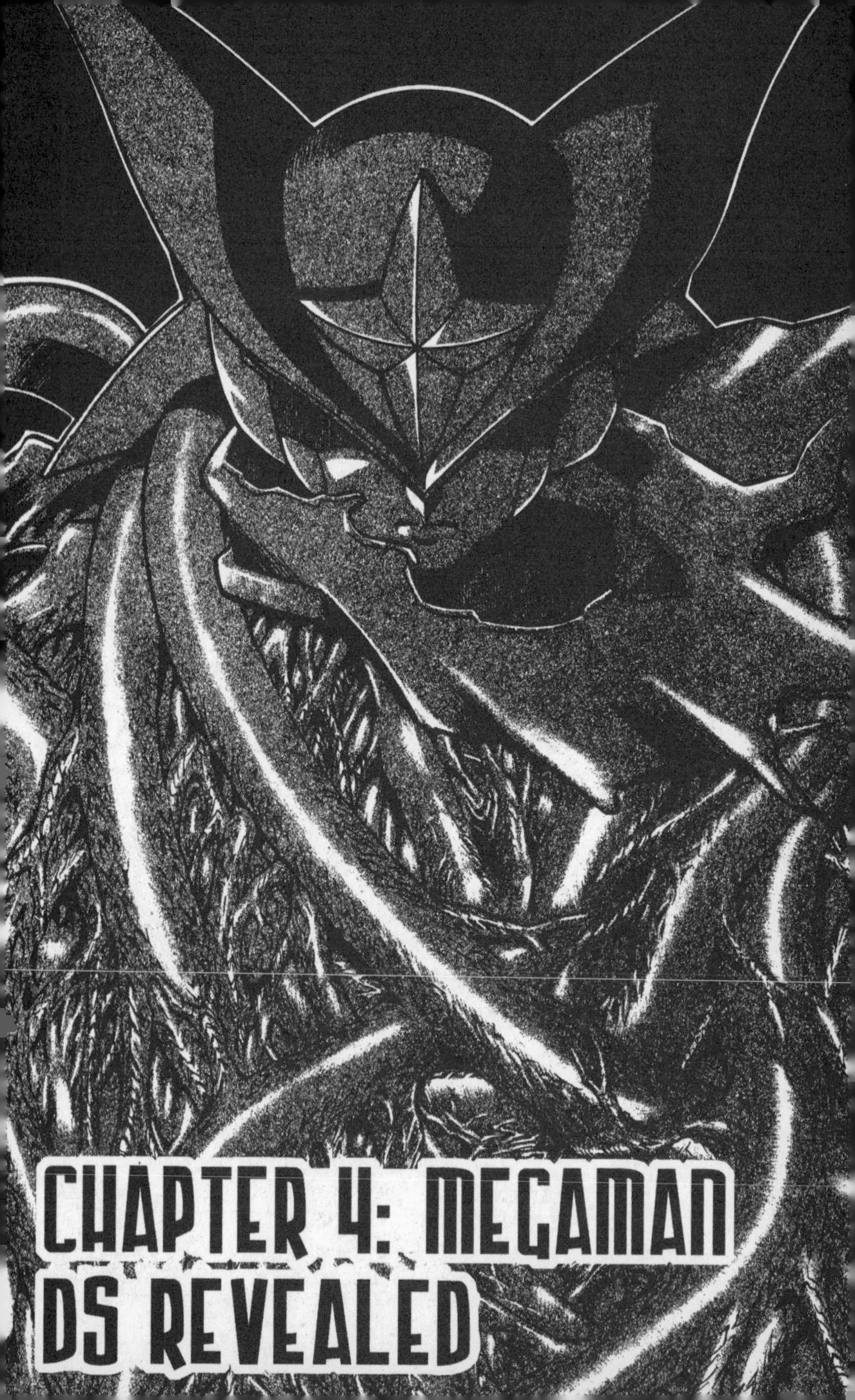
CHAPTER 4: MEGAMAN DS REVEALED

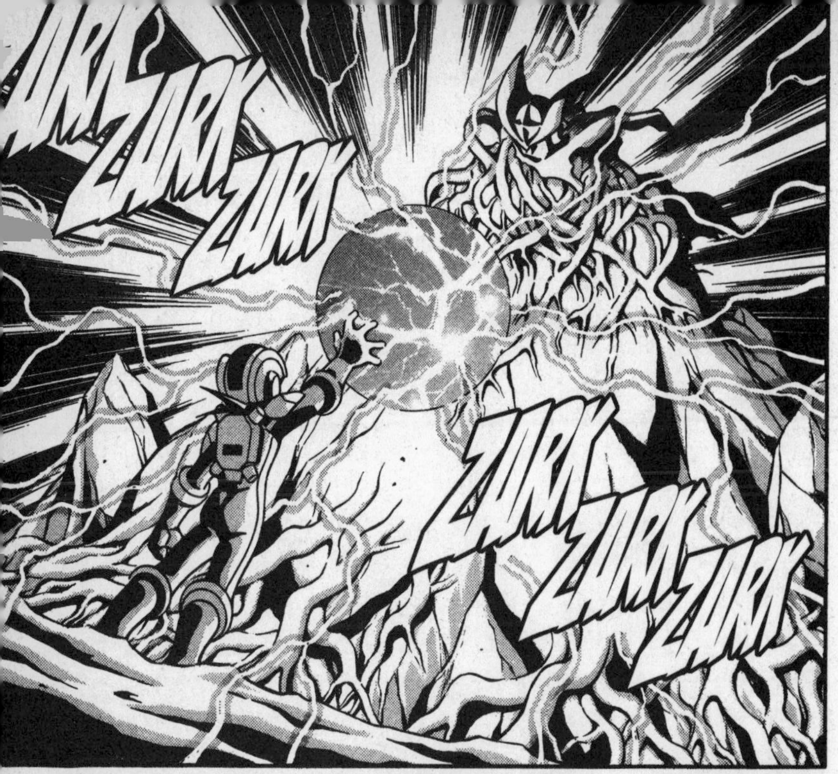
ZARK ZARK ZARK
ZARK ZARK ZARK
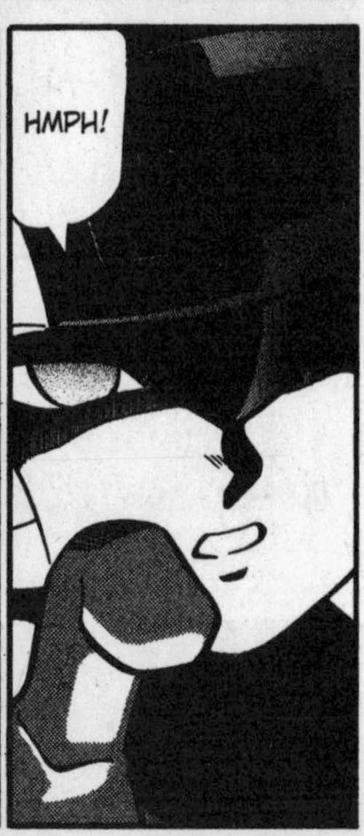
HMPH!
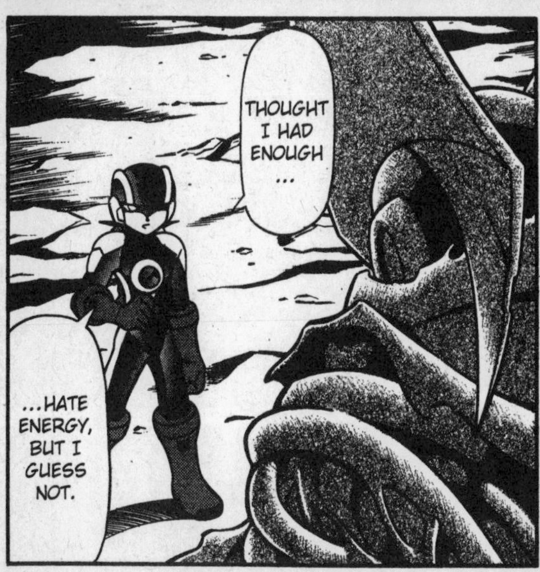
THOUGHT I HAD ENOUGH ...
...HATE ENERGY, BUT I GUESS NOT.

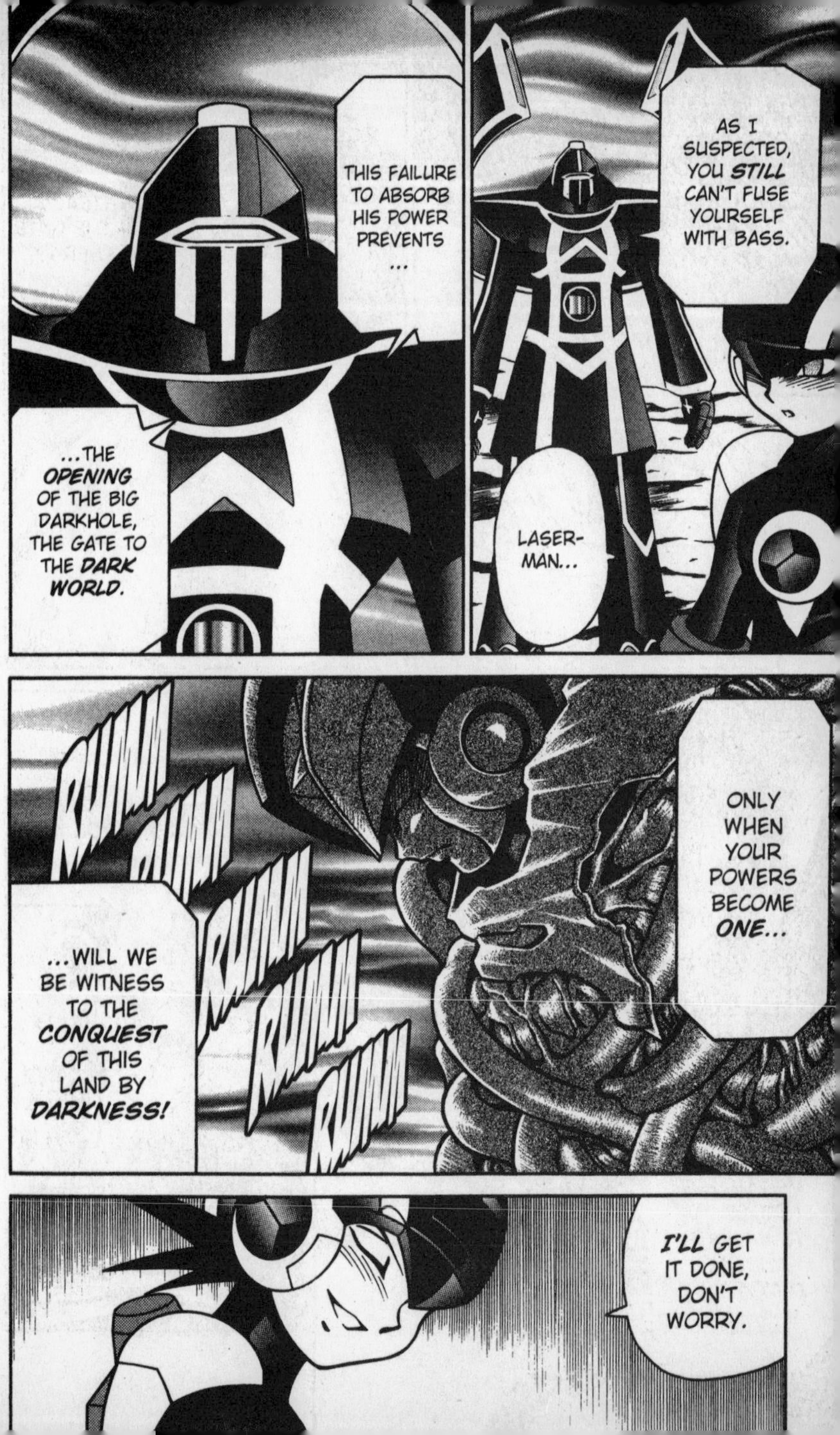
AS I SUSPECTED, YOU *STILL* CAN'T FUSE YOURSELF WITH BASS.
LASER-MAN...
THIS FAILURE TO ABSORB HIS POWER PREVENTS ...
...THE *OPENING* OF THE BIG DARKHOLE, THE GATE TO THE *DARK WORLD*.
ONLY WHEN YOUR POWERS BECOME *ONE*...
RUMM RUMM RUMM RUMM RUMM
...WILL WE BE WITNESS TO THE *CONQUEST* OF THIS LAND BY *DARKNESS!*
I'LL GET IT DONE, DON'T WORRY.

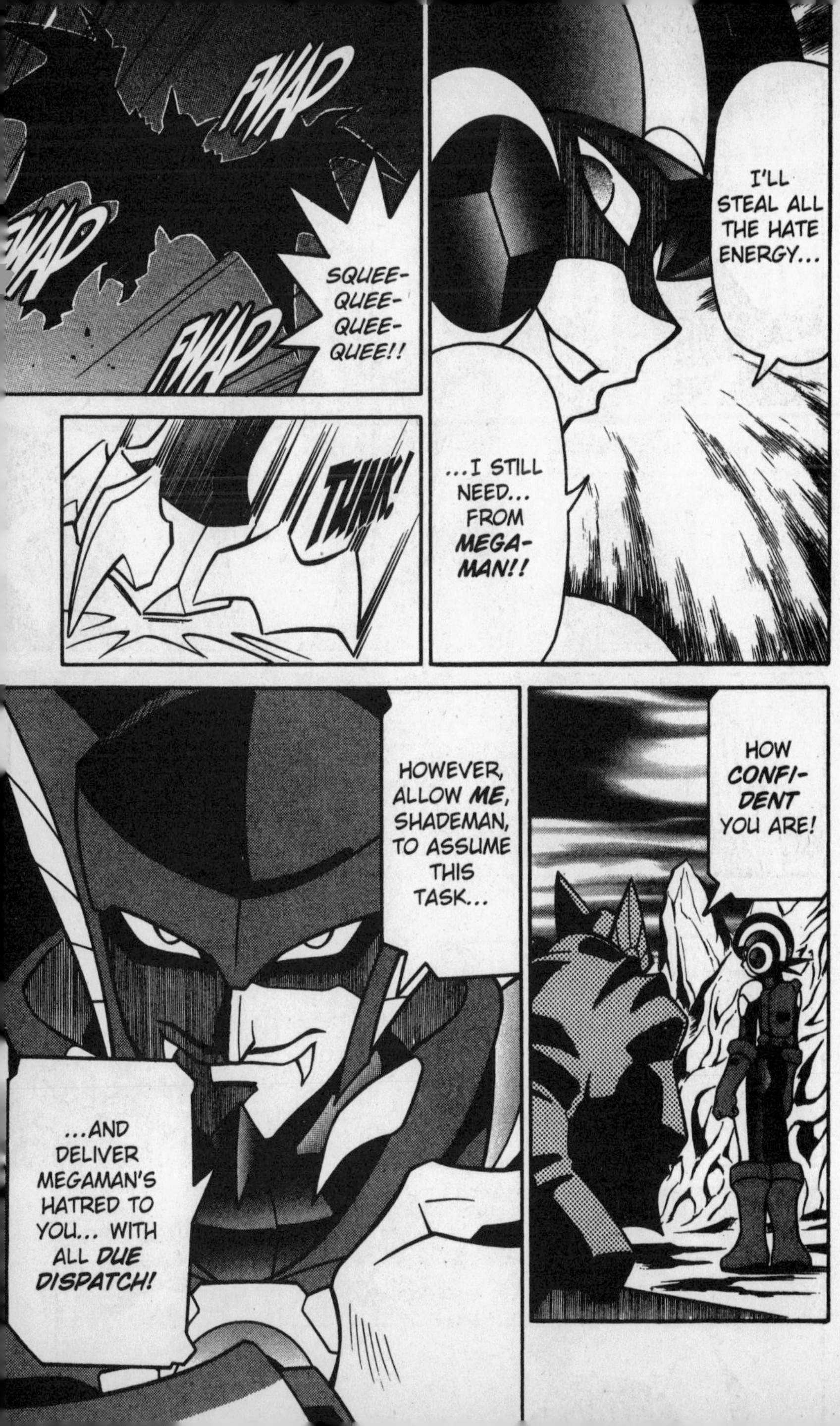
I'LL STEAL ALL THE HATE ENERGY...
...I STILL NEED... FROM MEGA-MAN!!
FWAP
FWAP
FWAP
SQUEE-QUEE-QUEE-QUEE!!
TUNK!
HOW CONFIDENT YOU ARE!
HOWEVER, ALLOW ME, SHADEMAN, TO ASSUME THIS TASK...
...AND DELIVER MEGAMAN'S HATRED TO YOU... WITH ALL DUE DISPATCH!

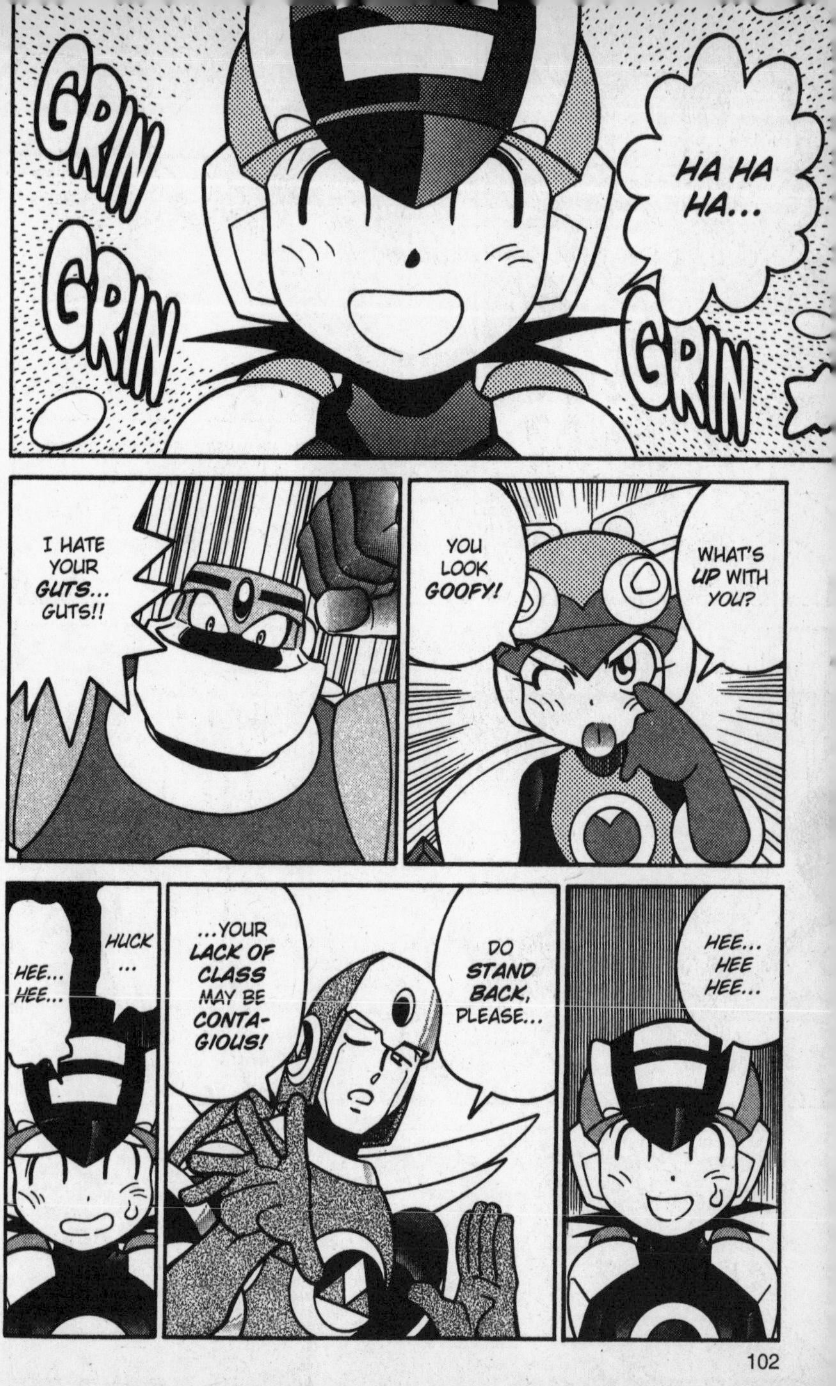
HA HA HA...
GRIN
GRIN
GRIN
WHAT'S UP WITH YOU?
YOU LOOK GOOFY!
I HATE YOUR GUTS... GUTS!!
HEE... HEE HEE...
DO STAND BACK, PLEASE...
...YOUR LACK OF CLASS MAY BE CONTA-GIOUS!
HUCK...
HEE... HEE...

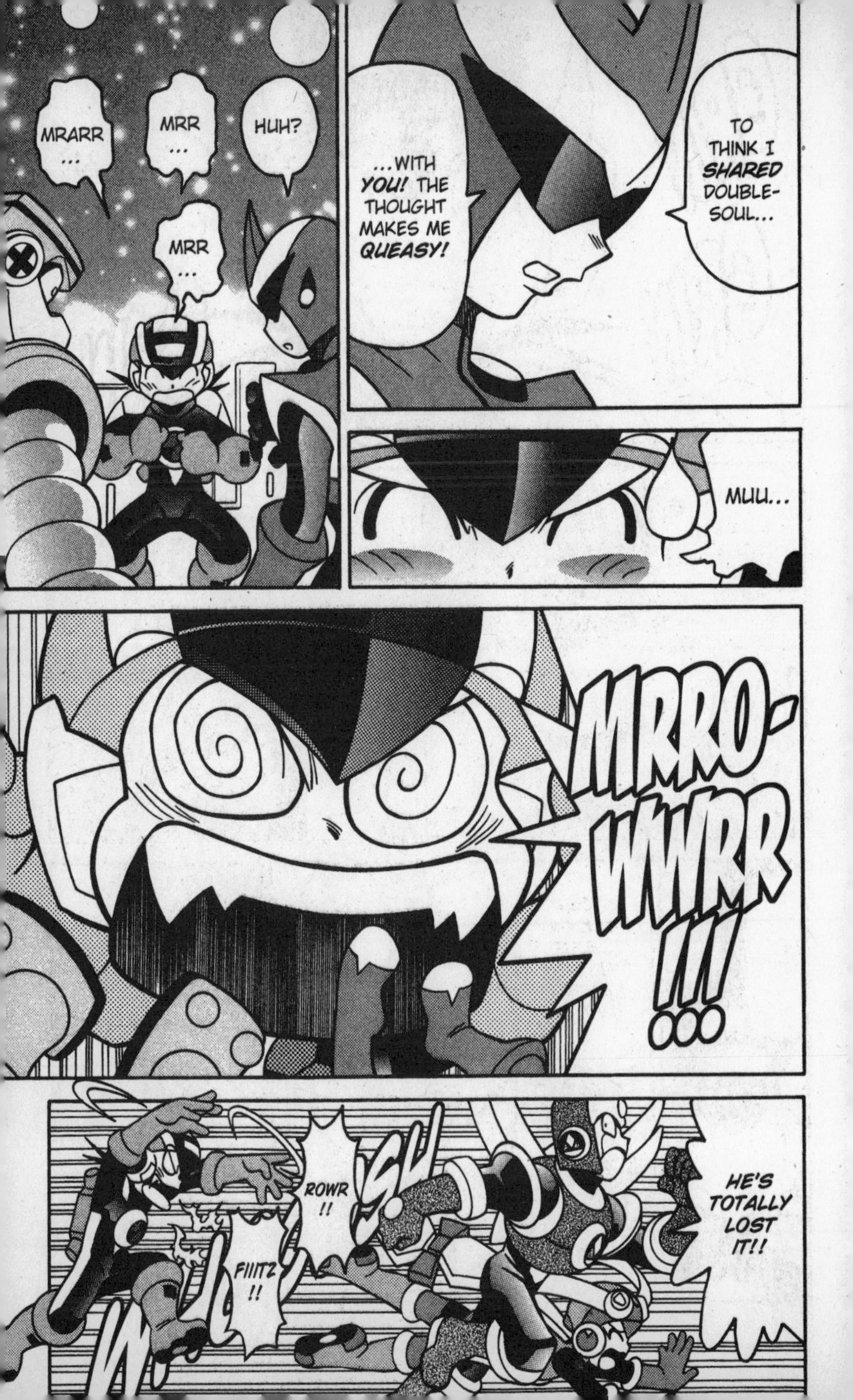
TO THINK I SHARED DOUBLE-SOUL...
...WITH YOU! THE THOUGHT MAKES ME QUEASY!
MUU...
HUH?
MRR ...
MRARR ...
MRR ...
MRRO-WWRR !!!...
HE'S TOTALLY LOST IT!!
ROWR !!
FIIITZ !!

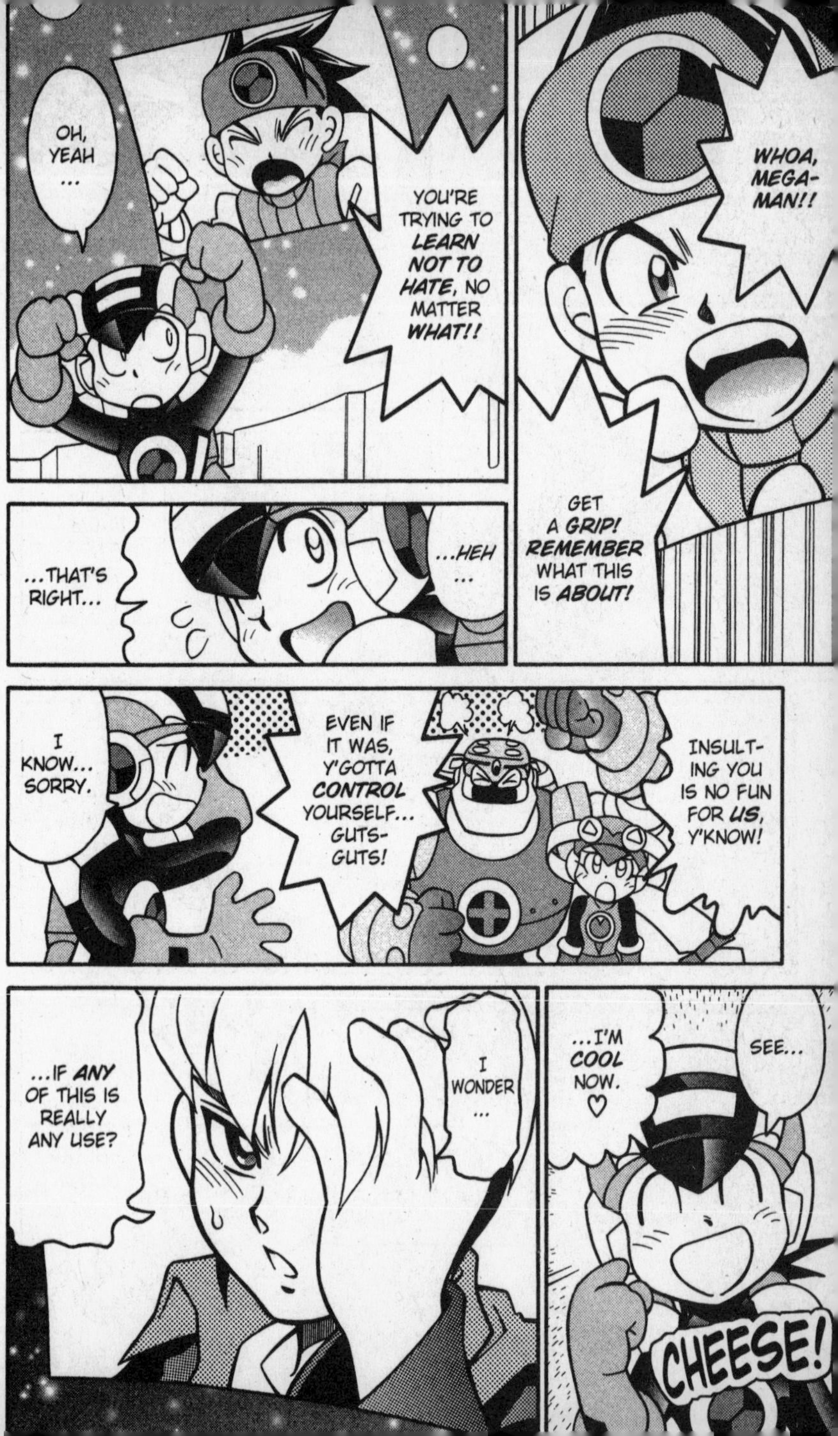
WHOA, MEGA-MAN!!
GET A GRIP! REMEMBER WHAT THIS IS ABOUT!
YOU'RE TRYING TO LEARN NOT TO HATE, NO MATTER WHAT!!
OH, YEAH ...
...HEH ...
...THAT'S RIGHT...
INSULT-ING YOU IS NO FUN FOR US, Y'KNOW!
EVEN IF IT WAS, Y'GOTTA CONTROL YOURSELF... GUTS-GUTS!
I KNOW... SORRY.
SEE...
...I'M COOL NOW. ♡
CHEESE!
I WONDER ...
...IF ANY OF THIS IS REALLY ANY USE?

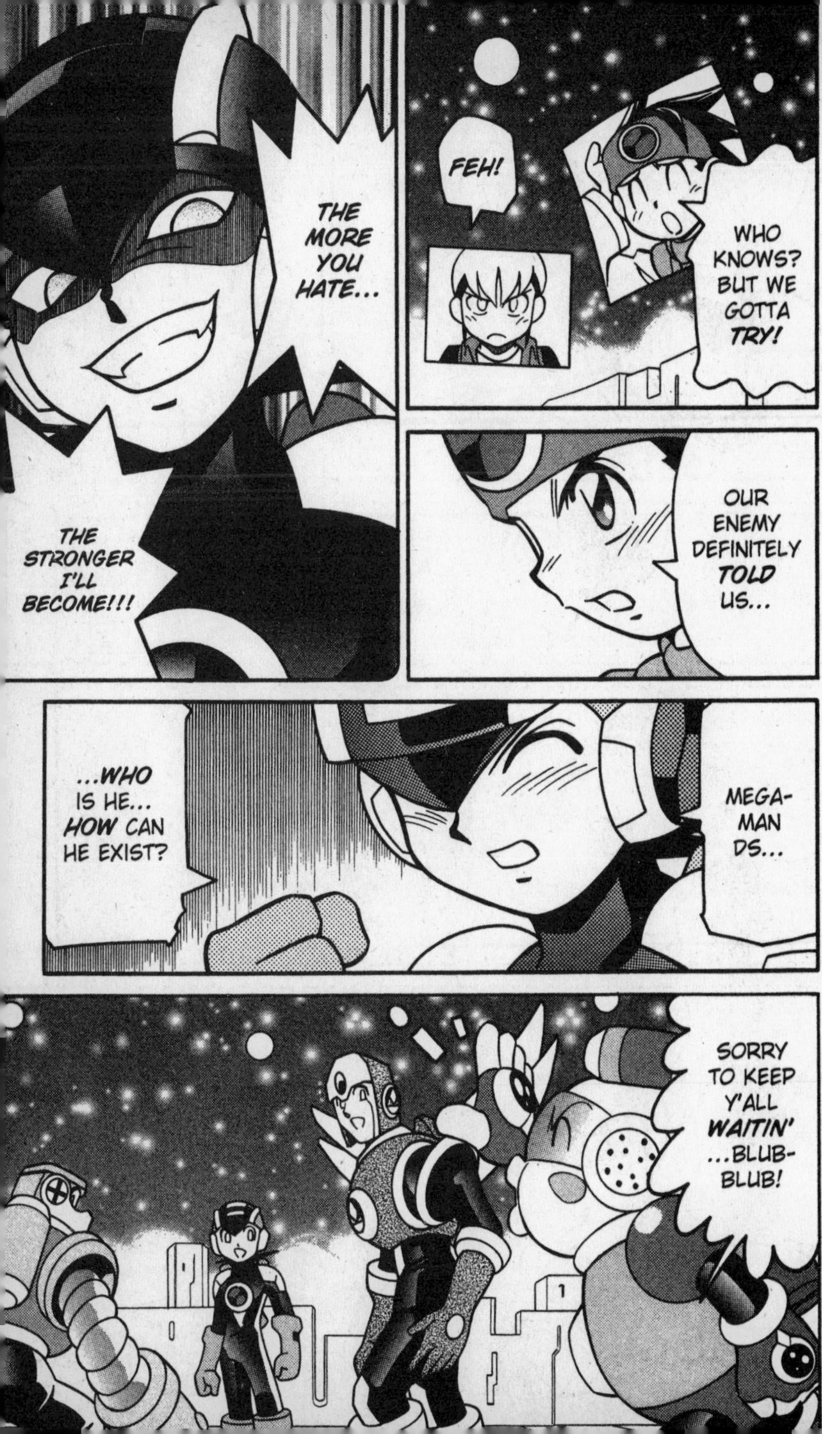
WHO KNOWS? BUT WE GOTTA TRY!
FEH!
OUR ENEMY DEFINITELY TOLD US...
THE MORE YOU HATE...
THE STRONGER I'LL BECOME!!!
MEGA-MAN DS...
...WHO IS HE... HOW CAN HE EXIST?
SORRY TO KEEP Y'ALL WAITIN' ...BLUB-BLUB!

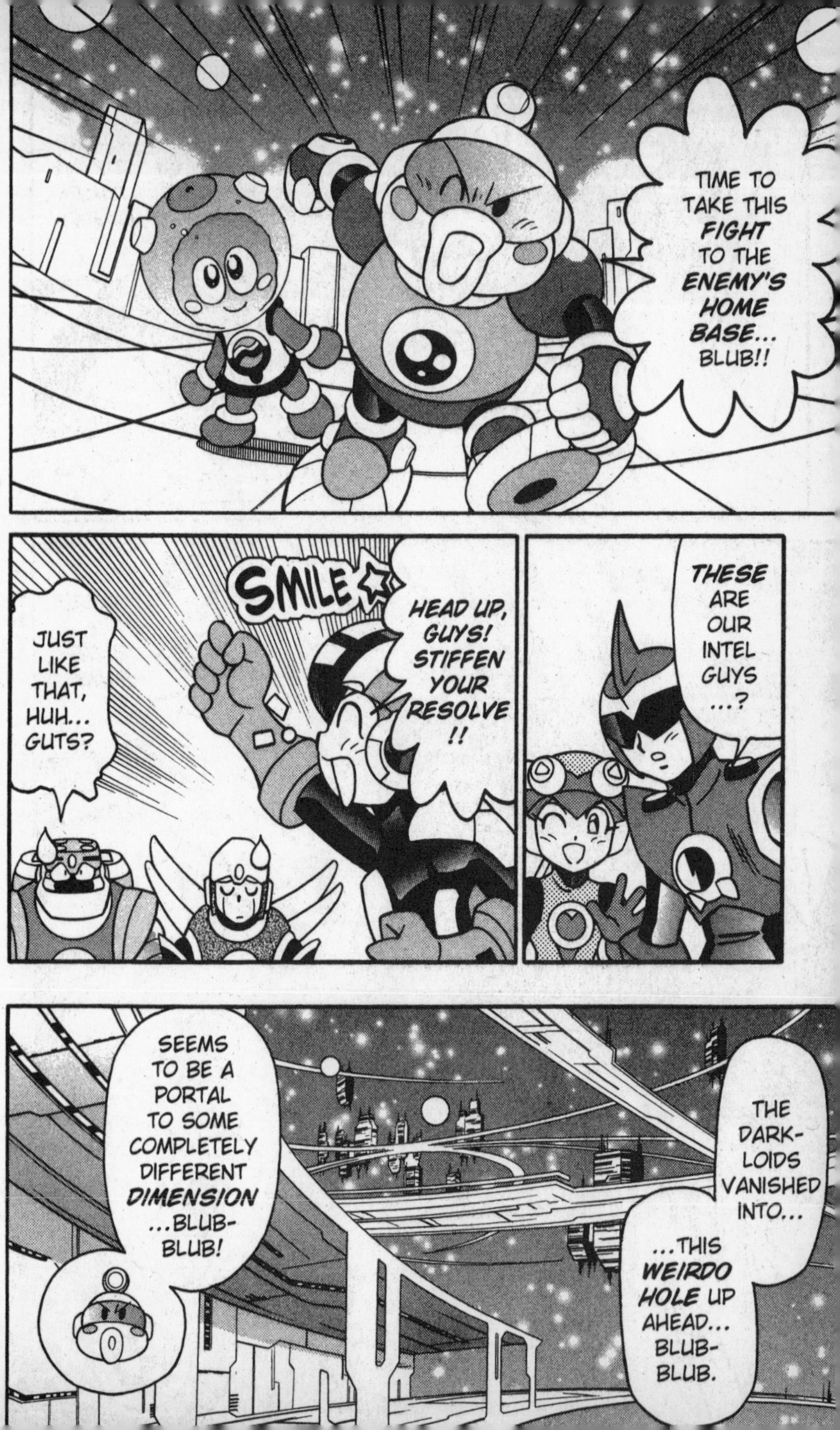

TIME TO TAKE THIS FIGHT TO THE ENEMY'S HOME BASE... BLUB!!
THESE ARE OUR INTEL GUYS ...?
SMILE
HEAD UP, GUYS! STIFFEN YOUR RESOLVE !!
JUST LIKE THAT, HUH... GUTS?
THE DARK-LOIDS VANISHED INTO...
...THIS WEIRDO HOLE UP AHEAD... BLUB-BLUB.
SEEMS TO BE A PORTAL TO SOME COMPLETELY DIFFERENT DIMENSION ...BLUB-BLUB!

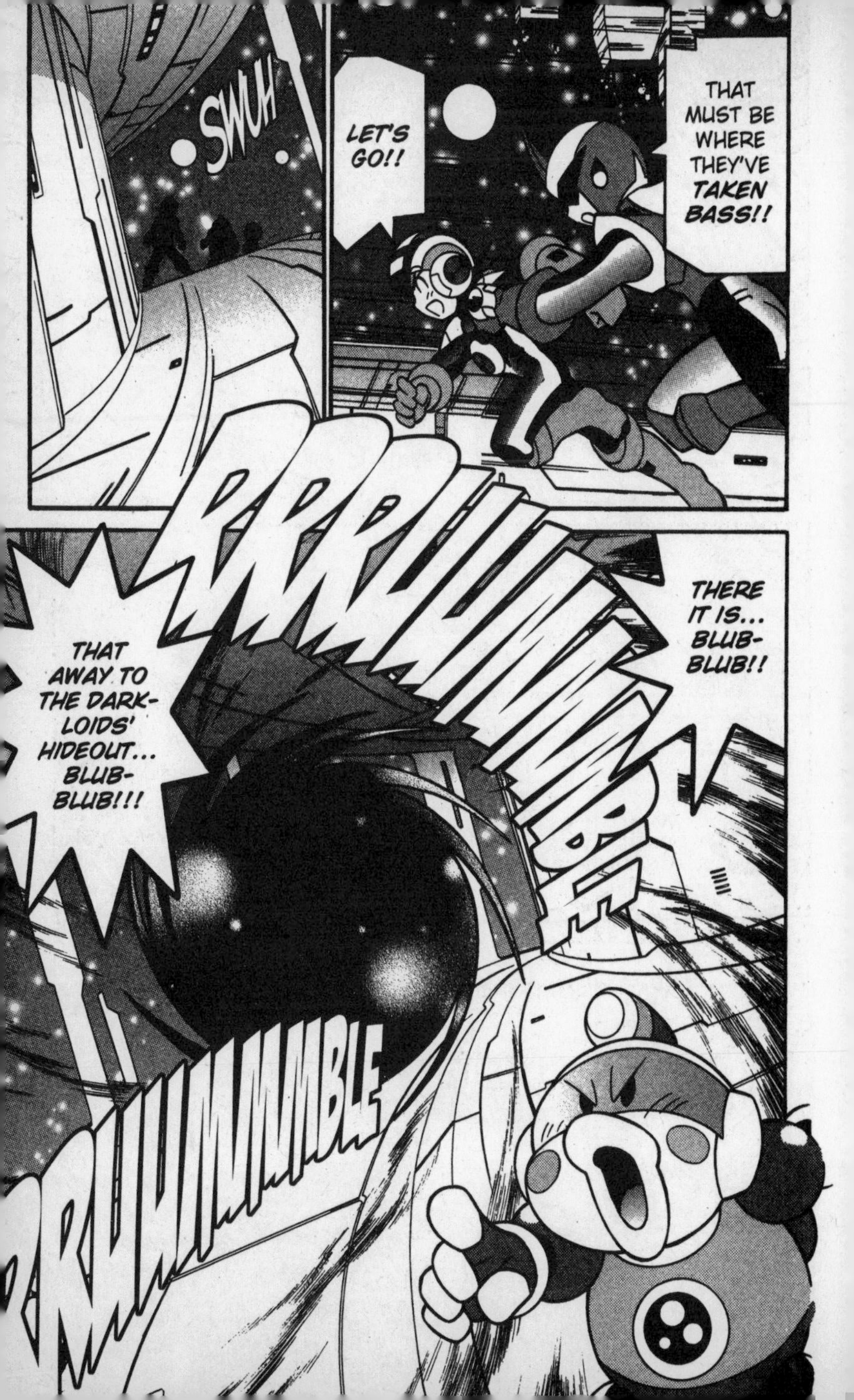
THAT MUST BE WHERE THEY'VE TAKEN BASS!!
LET'S GO!!
SWUH
BRRUMMMMBLE
THERE IT IS... BLUB-BLUB!!
THAT AWAY TO THE DARK-LOIDS' HIDEOUT... BLUB-BLUB!!!
BRUMMMMBLE

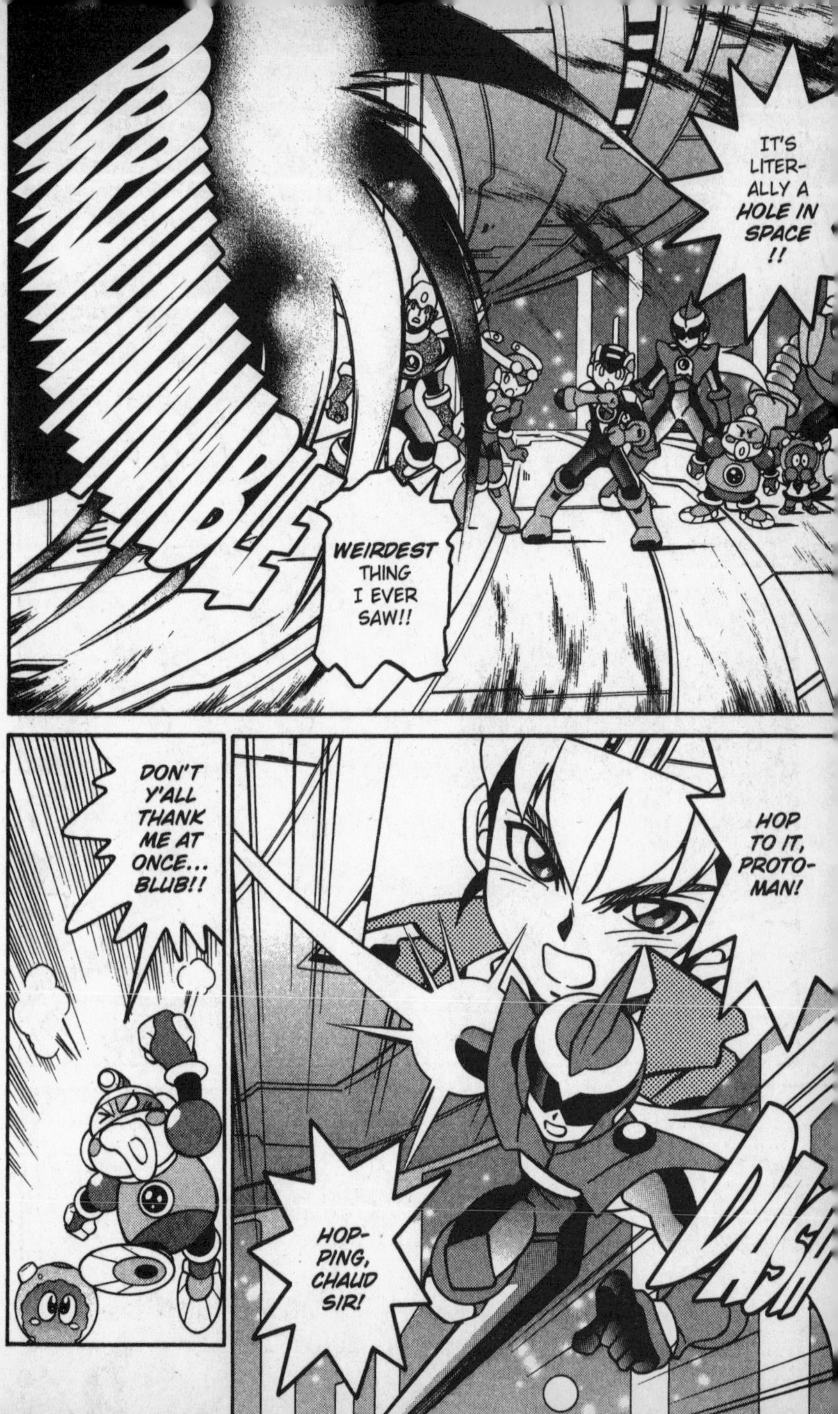
IT'S LITERALLY A HOLE IN SPACE !!
WEIRDEST THING I EVER SAW!!
HOP TO IT, PROTOMAN!
HOPPING, CHAUD SIR!
DASH
DON'T Y'ALL THANK ME AT ONCE... BLUB!!

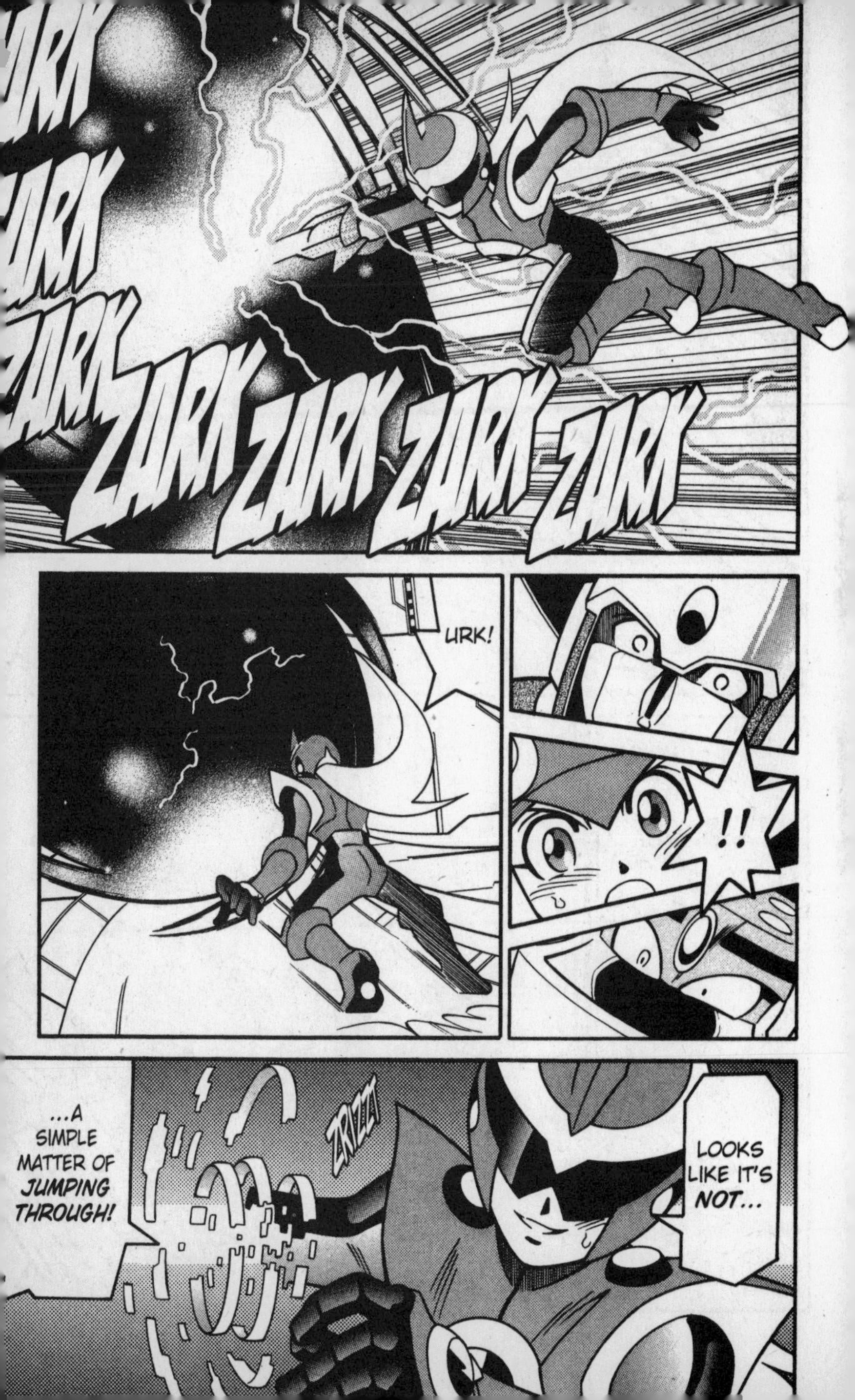
ZARK ZARK ZARK ZARK
!!
URK!
LOOKS LIKE IT'S *NOT*...
...A SIMPLE MATTER OF *JUMPING THROUGH!*

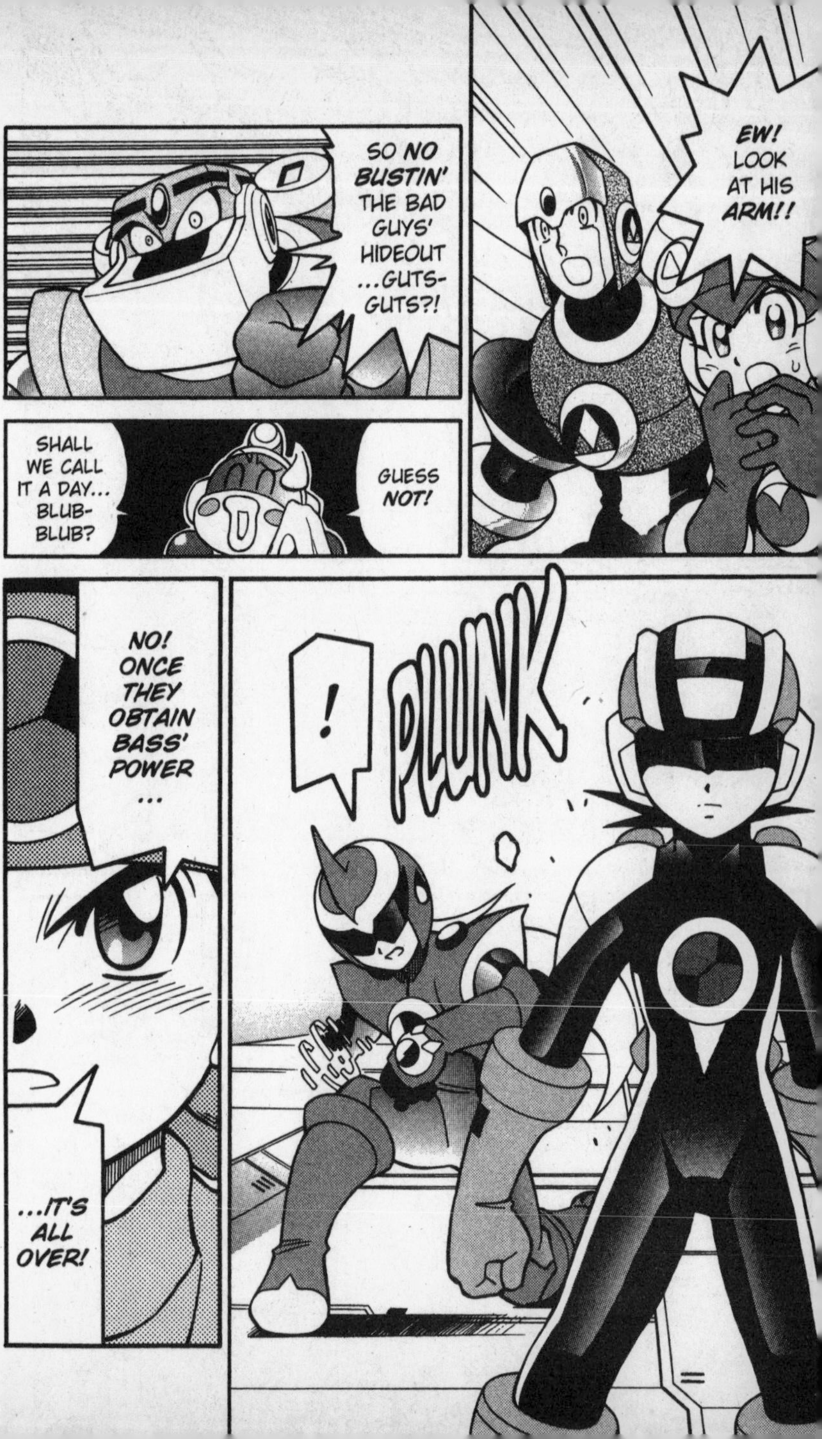
EW! LOOK AT HIS ARM!!
SO NO BUSTIN' THE BAD GUYS' HIDEOUT ...GUTS-GUTS?!
SHALL WE CALL IT A DAY... BLUB-BLUB?
GUESS NOT!
!
PLUNK
NO! ONCE THEY OBTAIN BASS' POWER ...
...IT'S ALL OVER!

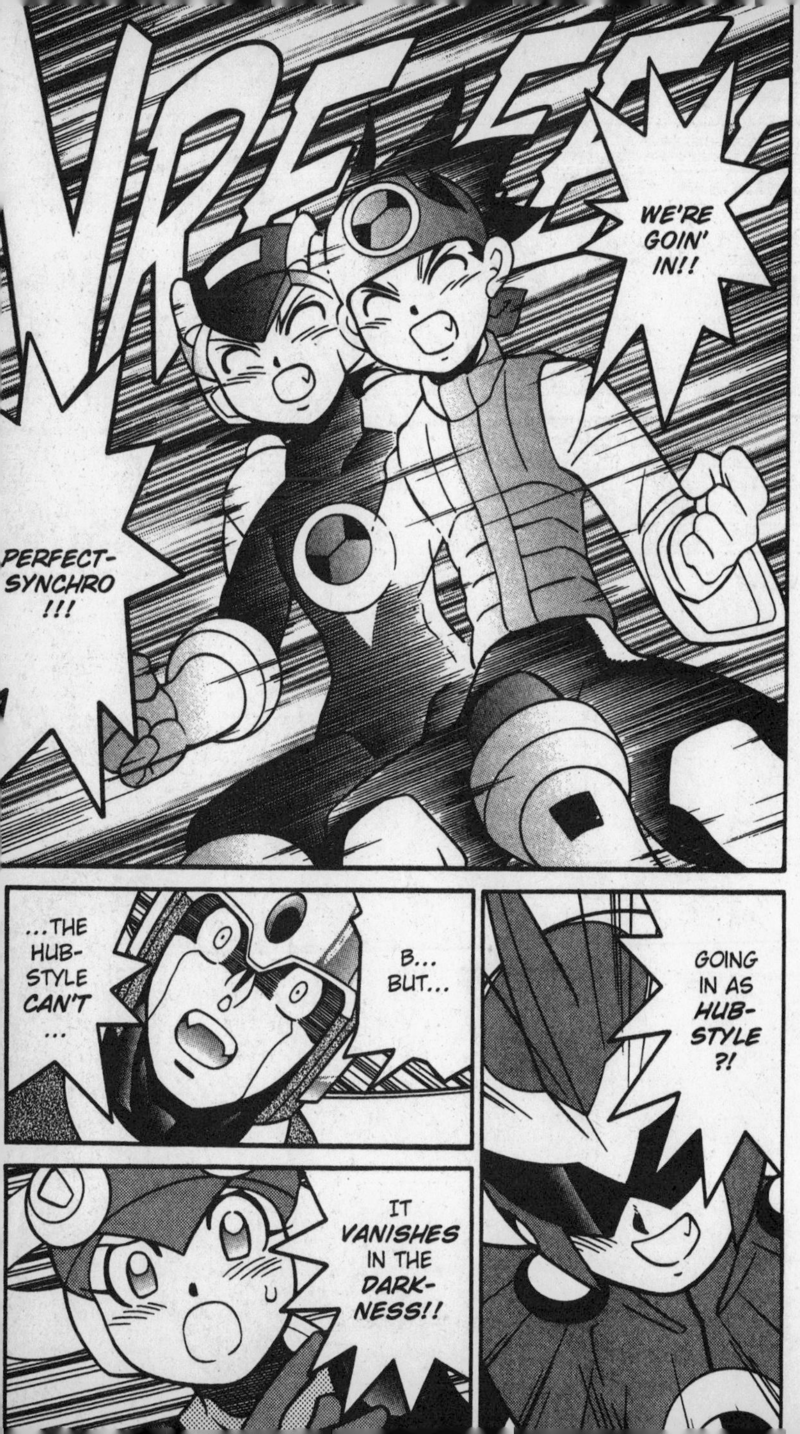
WE'RE GOIN' IN!!
PERFECT-SYNCHRO!!!
GOING IN AS HUB-STYLE?!
B... BUT...
...THE HUB-STYLE CAN'T ...
IT VANISHES IN THE DARKNESS!!

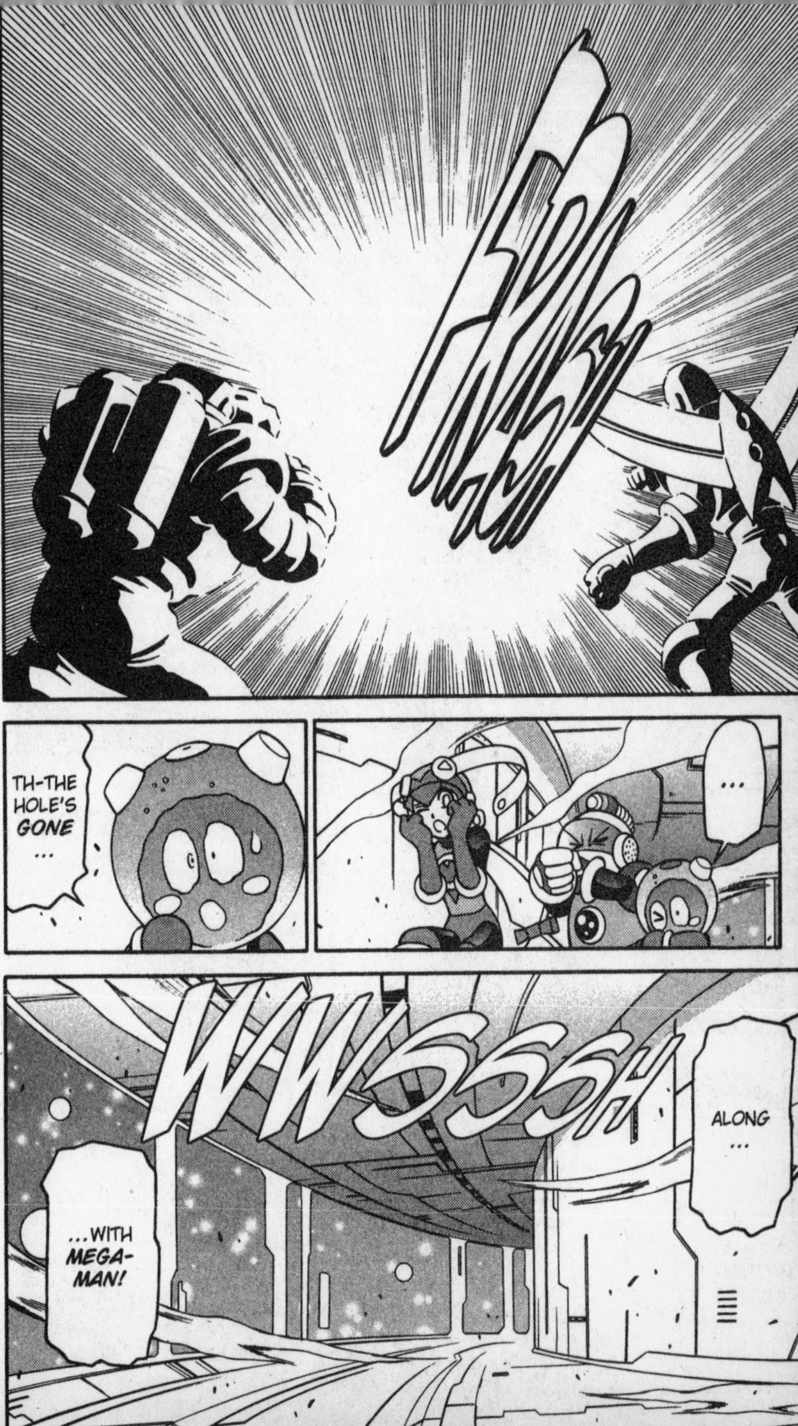
...
TH-THE HOLE'S GONE ...
WWSSSH
ALONG ...
...WITH MEGA-MAN!

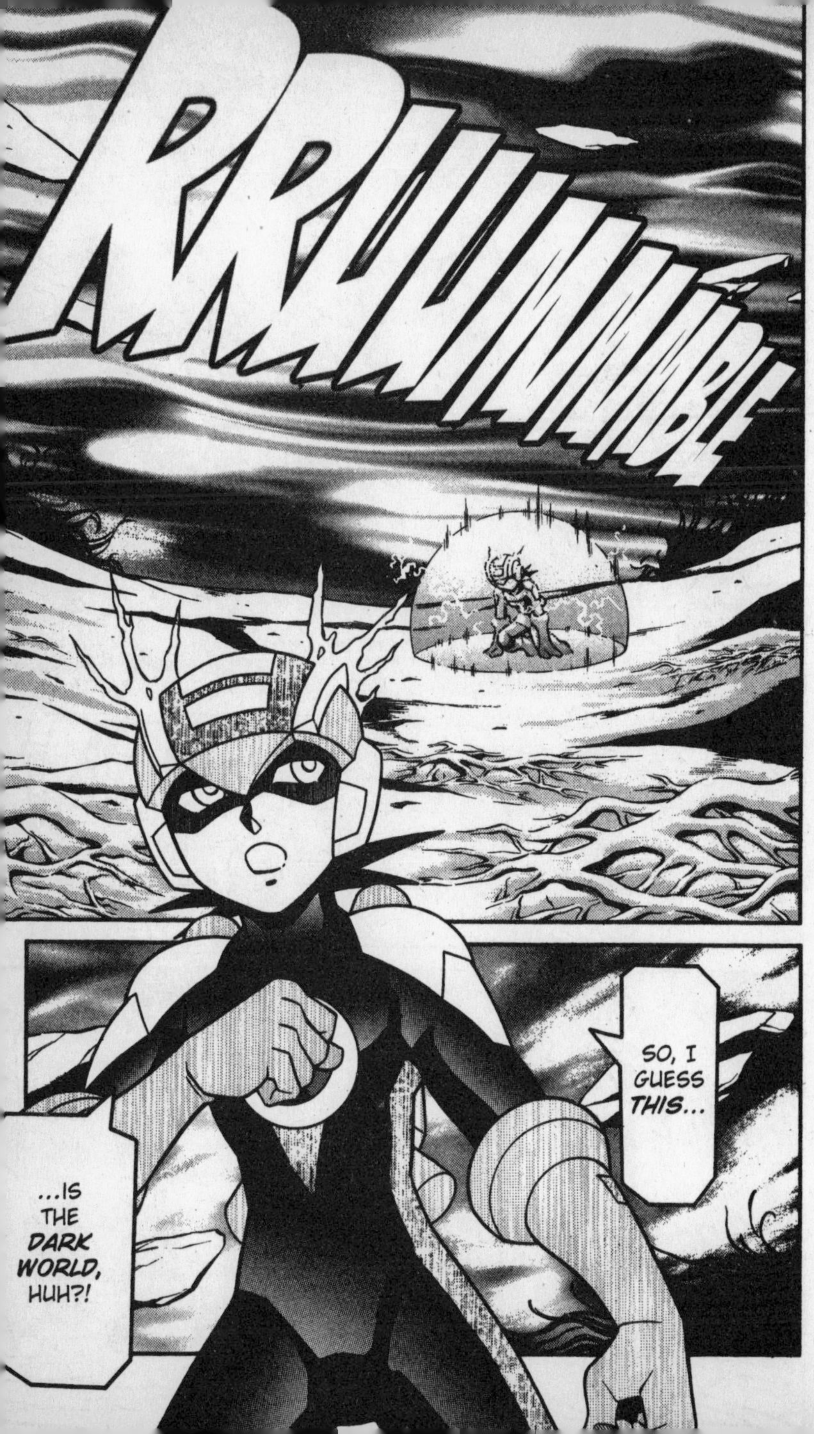
RRUMMMBLE
SO, I GUESS *THIS*...
...IS THE *DARK WORLD*, HUH?!

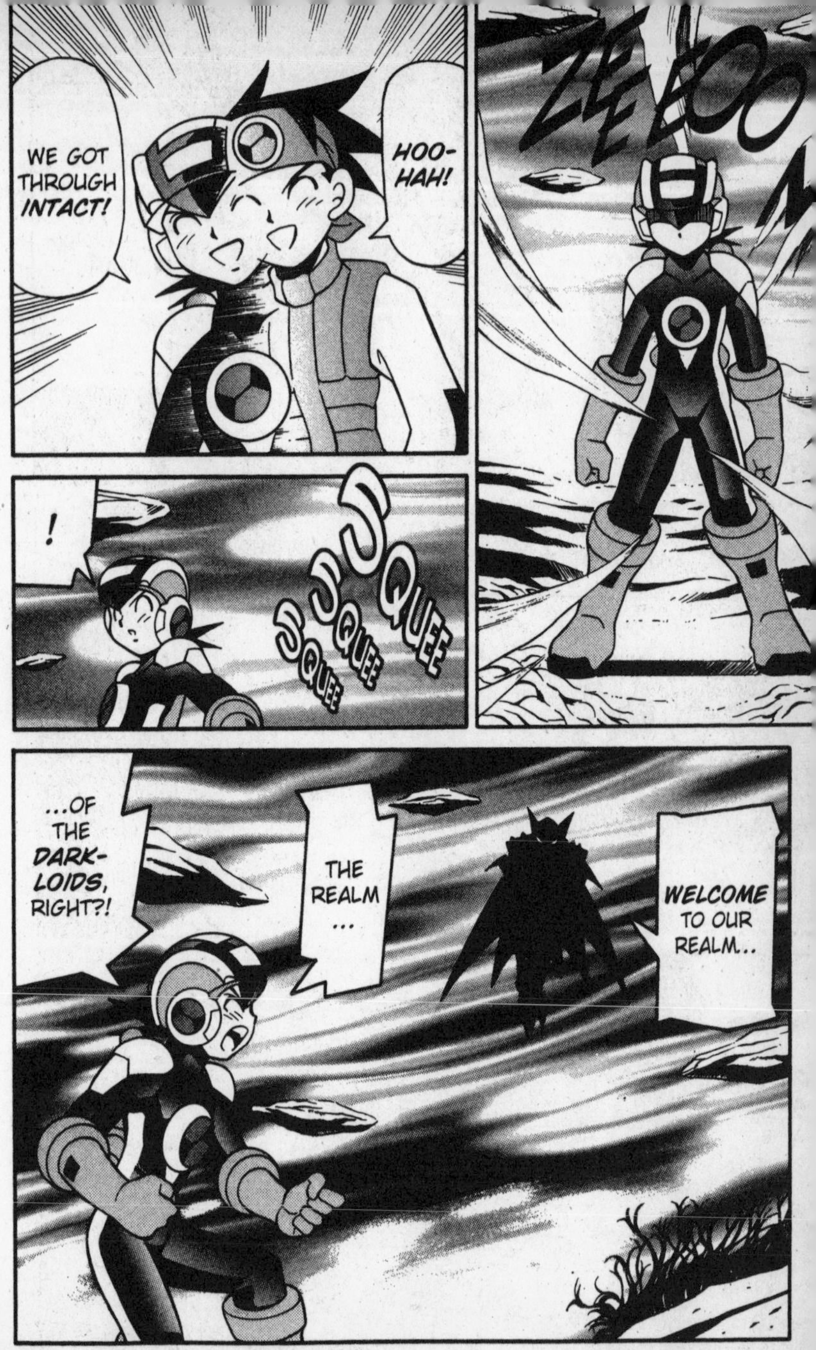
ZEEBOOM
HOO-HAH!
WE GOT THROUGH INTACT!
!
SQUEE SQUEE SQUEE
WELCOME TO OUR REALM...
THE REALM ...
...OF THE DARK-LOIDS, RIGHT?!

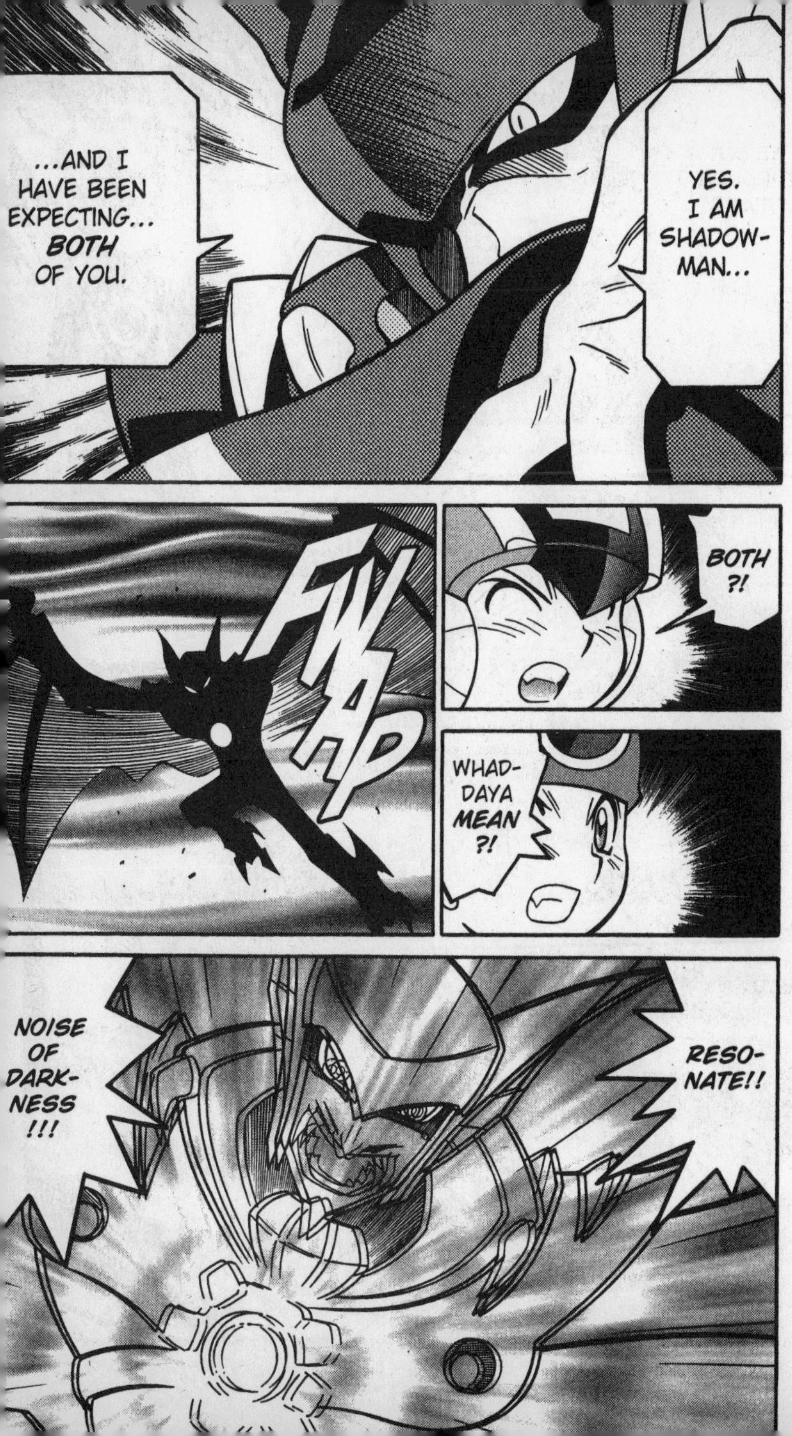
YES. I AM SHADOW-MAN...
...AND I HAVE BEEN EXPECTING... BOTH OF YOU.
BOTH ?!
WHAD-DAYA MEAN ?!
FWAP
NOISE OF DARK-NESS !!!
RESO-NATE!!

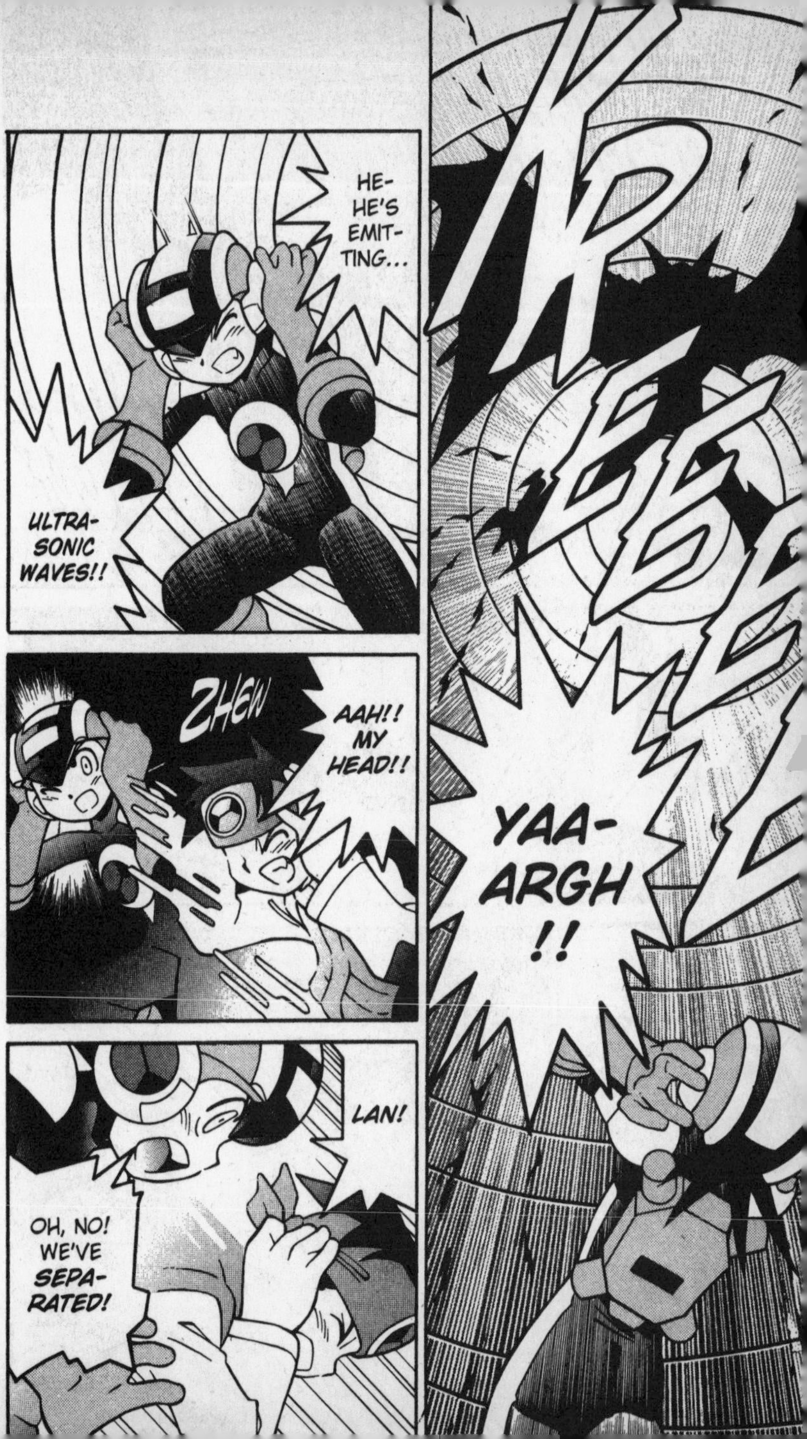
YAA-ARGH!!
HE-HE'S EMITTING...
ULTRA-SONIC WAVES!!
AAH!! MY HEAD!!
ZHEW
LAN!
OH, NO! WE'VE SEPARATED!

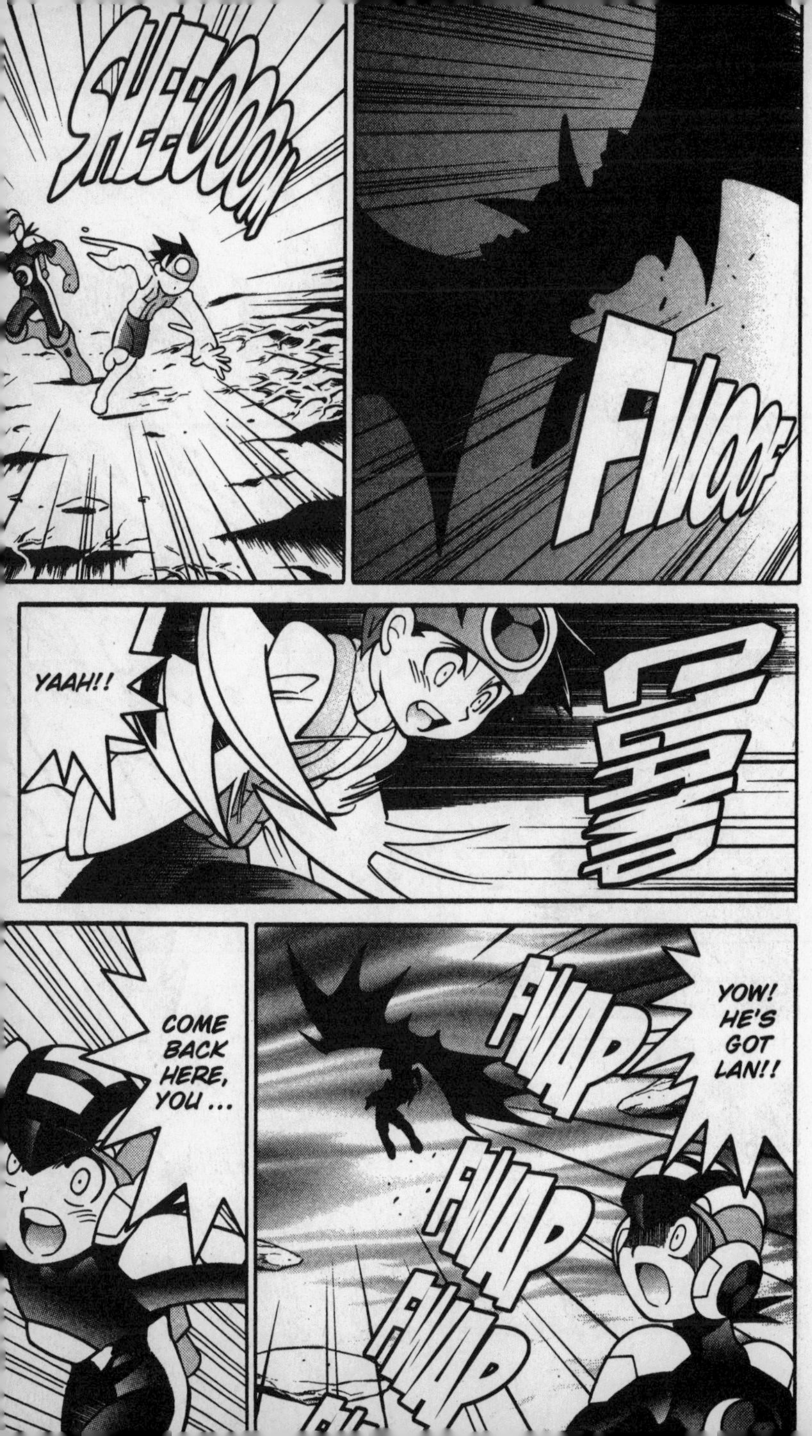
FWOOF
SHEEOOON
YAAH!!
YOW! HE'S GOT LAN!!
FWAP
FWAP
FWAP
FWAP
COME BACK HERE, YOU ...

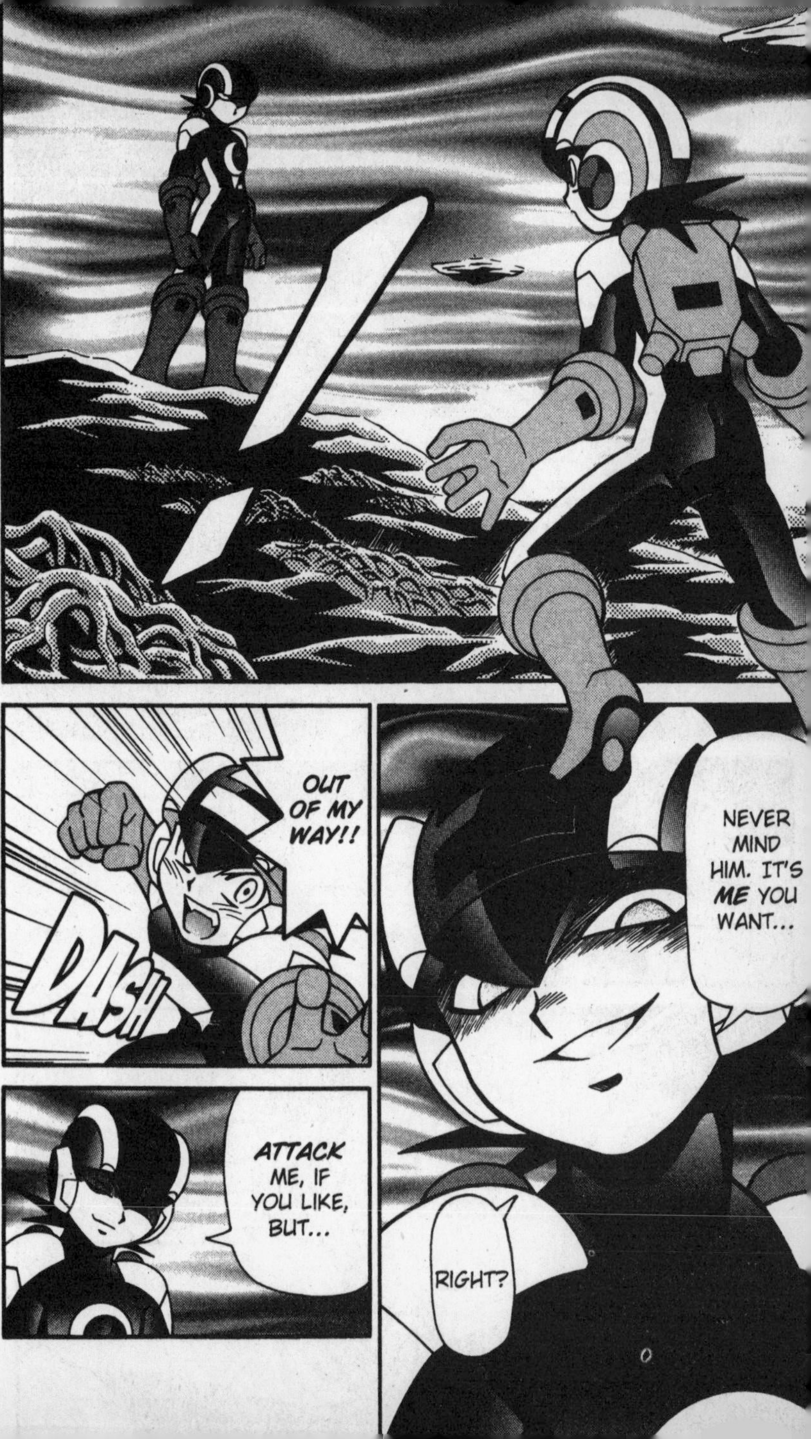
OUT OF MY WAY!!
DASH
NEVER MIND HIM. IT'S ME YOU WANT...
ATTACK ME, IF YOU LIKE, BUT...
RIGHT?

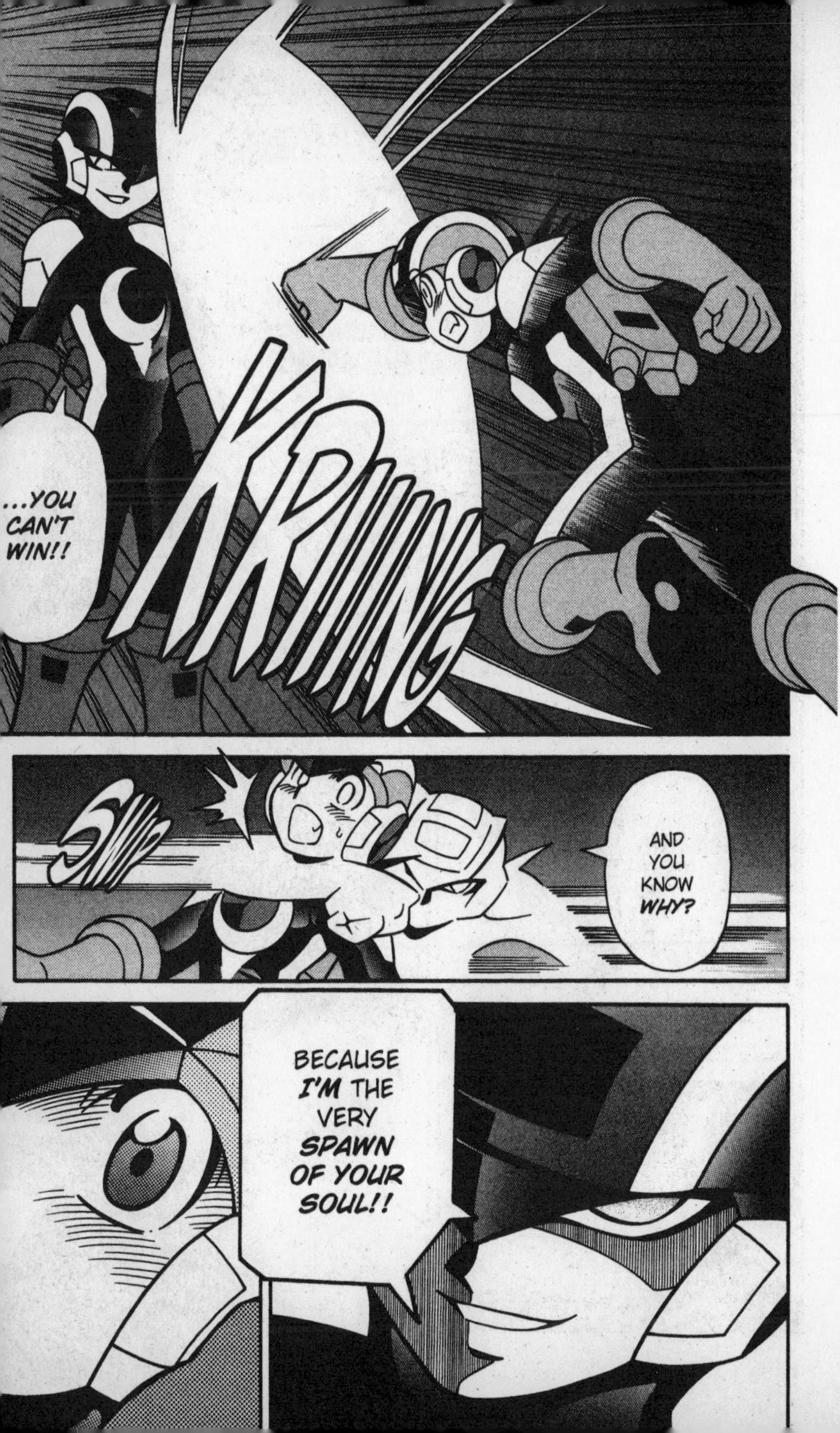
...YOU CAN'T WIN!!
AND YOU KNOW *WHY?*
BECAUSE *I'M* THE VERY *SPAWN OF YOUR SOUL!!*

LIKE AN *IDIOT*, YOU CHASED AFTER *ULTIMATE STRENGTH*, NEVER THINKING...

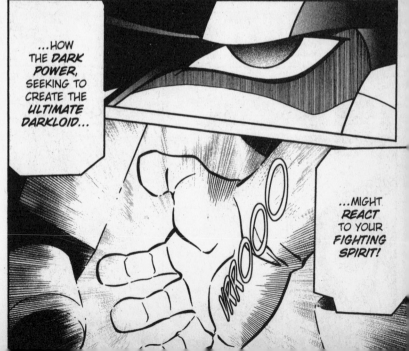

...HOW THE *DARK POWER*, SEEKING TO CREATE THE *ULTIMATE DARKLOID*...

...MIGHT *REACT* TO YOUR *FIGHTING SPIRIT!*

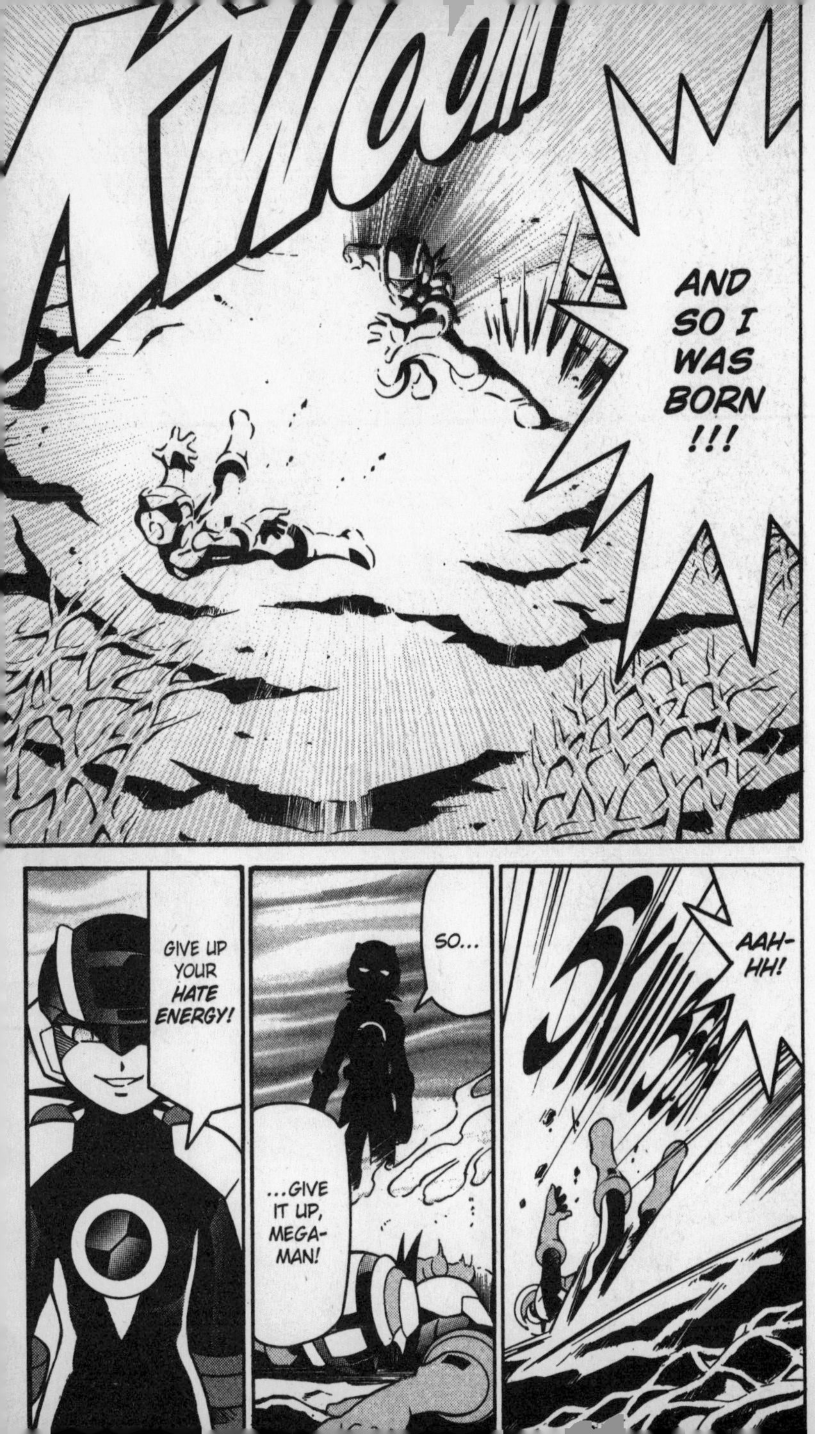
AND SO I WAS BORN!!!
AAH-HH!
SO...
...GIVE IT UP, MEGA-MAN!
GIVE UP YOUR HATE ENERGY!

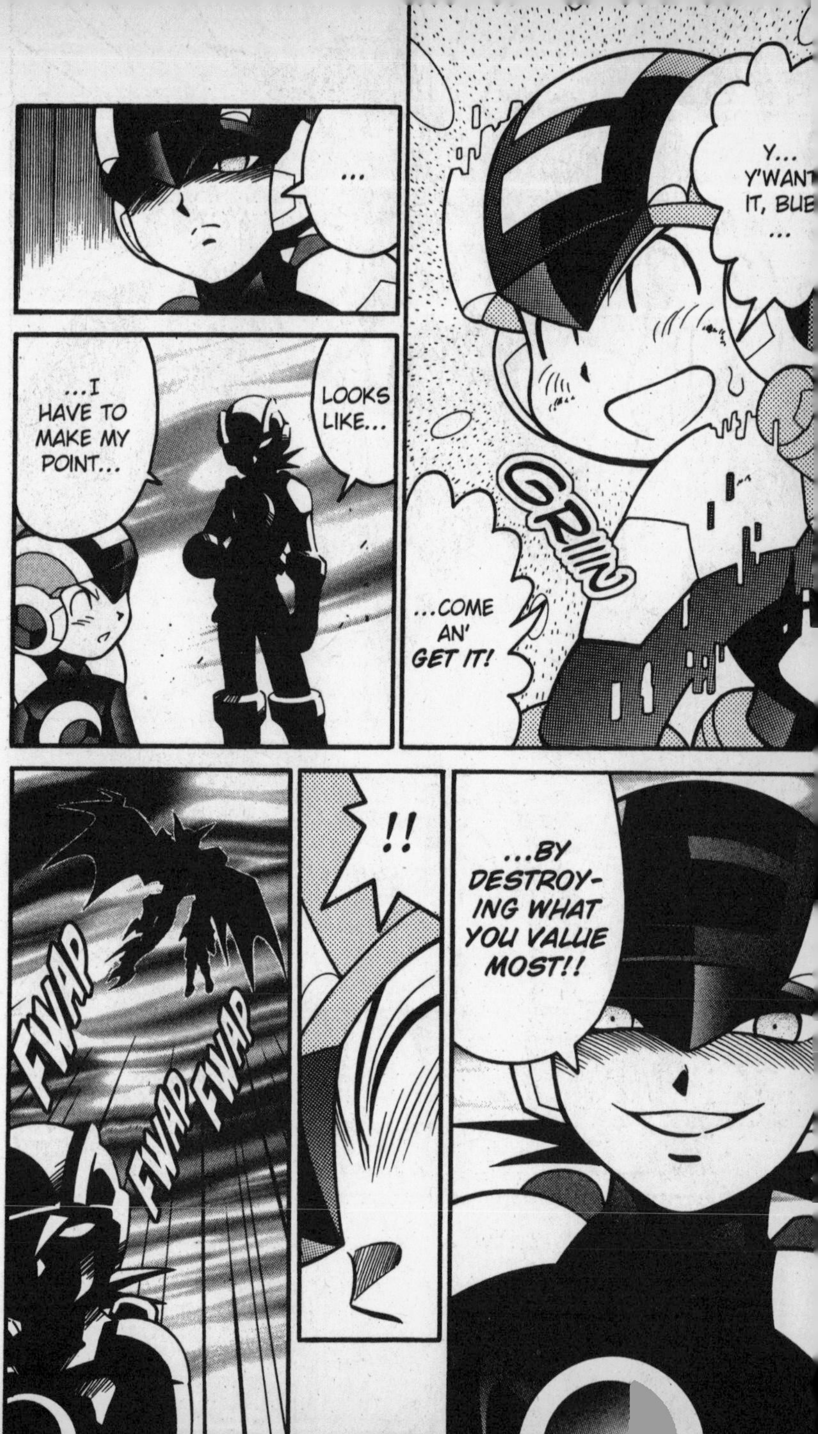
Y... Y'WANT IT, BUB ...
GRIN
...COME AN' GET IT!
...
LOOKS LIKE...
...I HAVE TO MAKE MY POINT...
...BY DESTROYING WHAT YOU VALUE MOST!!
!!
FWAP
FWAP FWAP

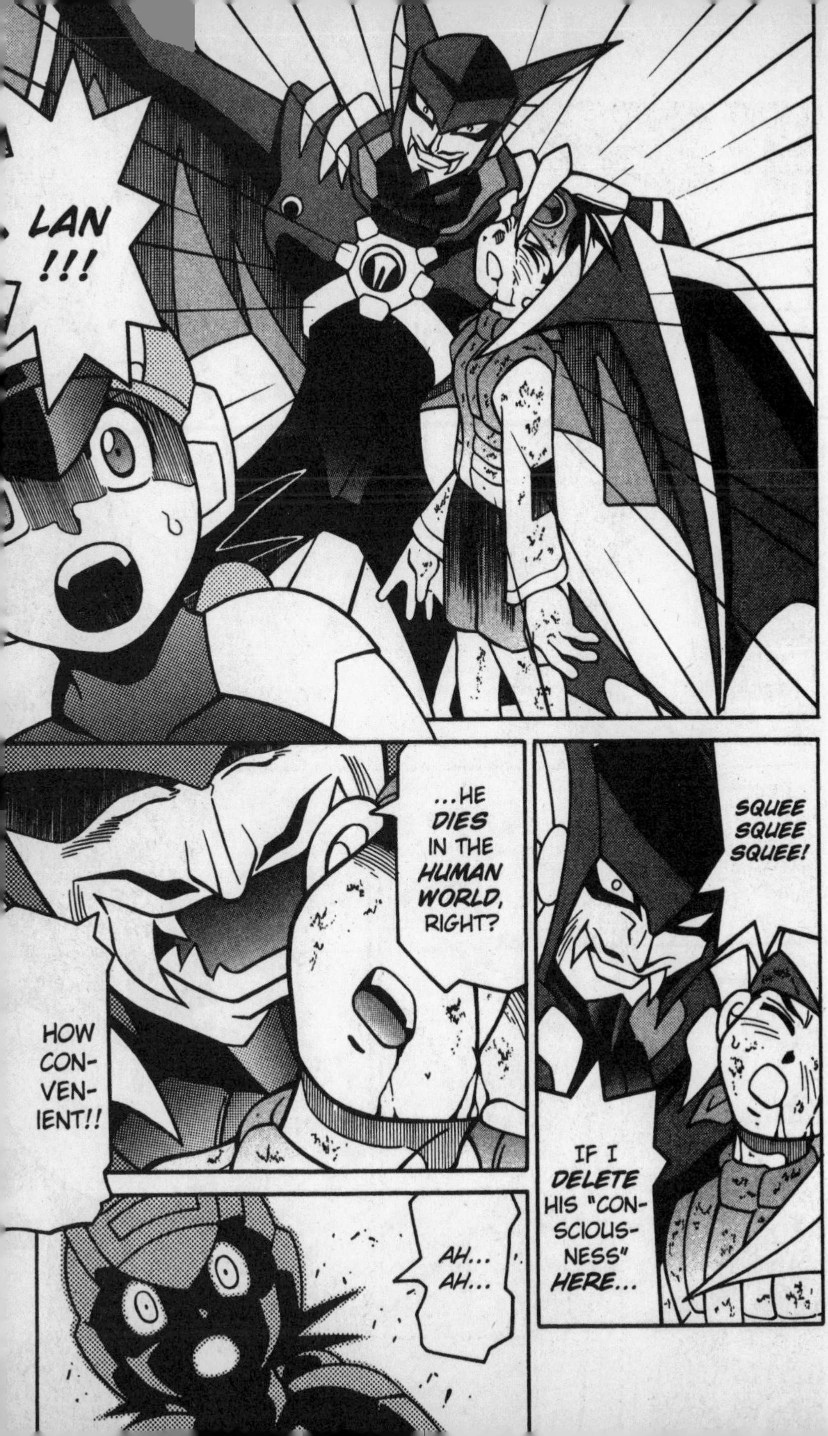
LAN !!!
SQUEE SQUEE SQUEE!
IF I DELETE HIS "CONSCIOUSNESS" HERE...
...HE DIES IN THE HUMAN WORLD, RIGHT?
HOW CONVENIENT!!
AH... AH...

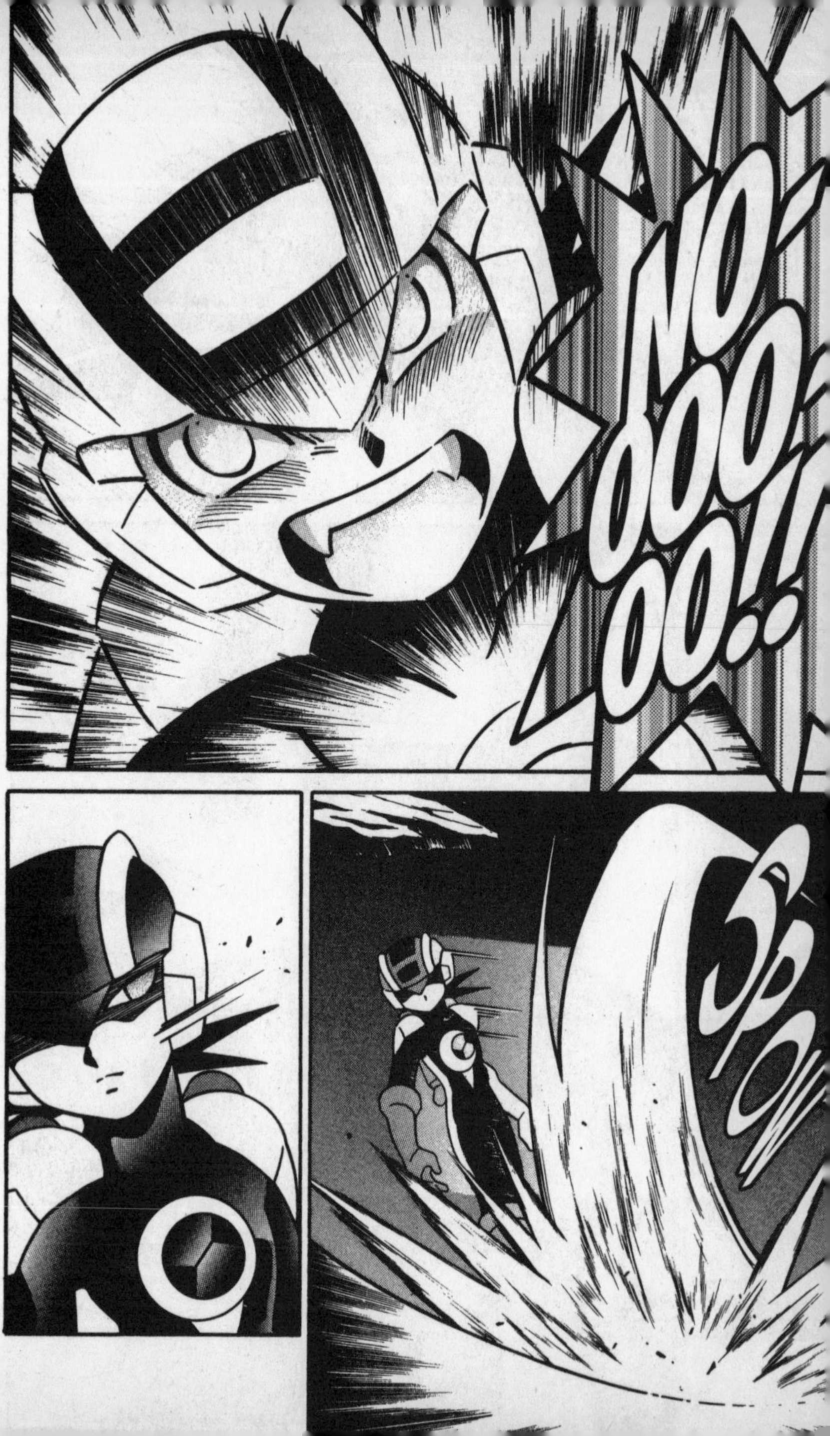
NO-OOO-OO!!

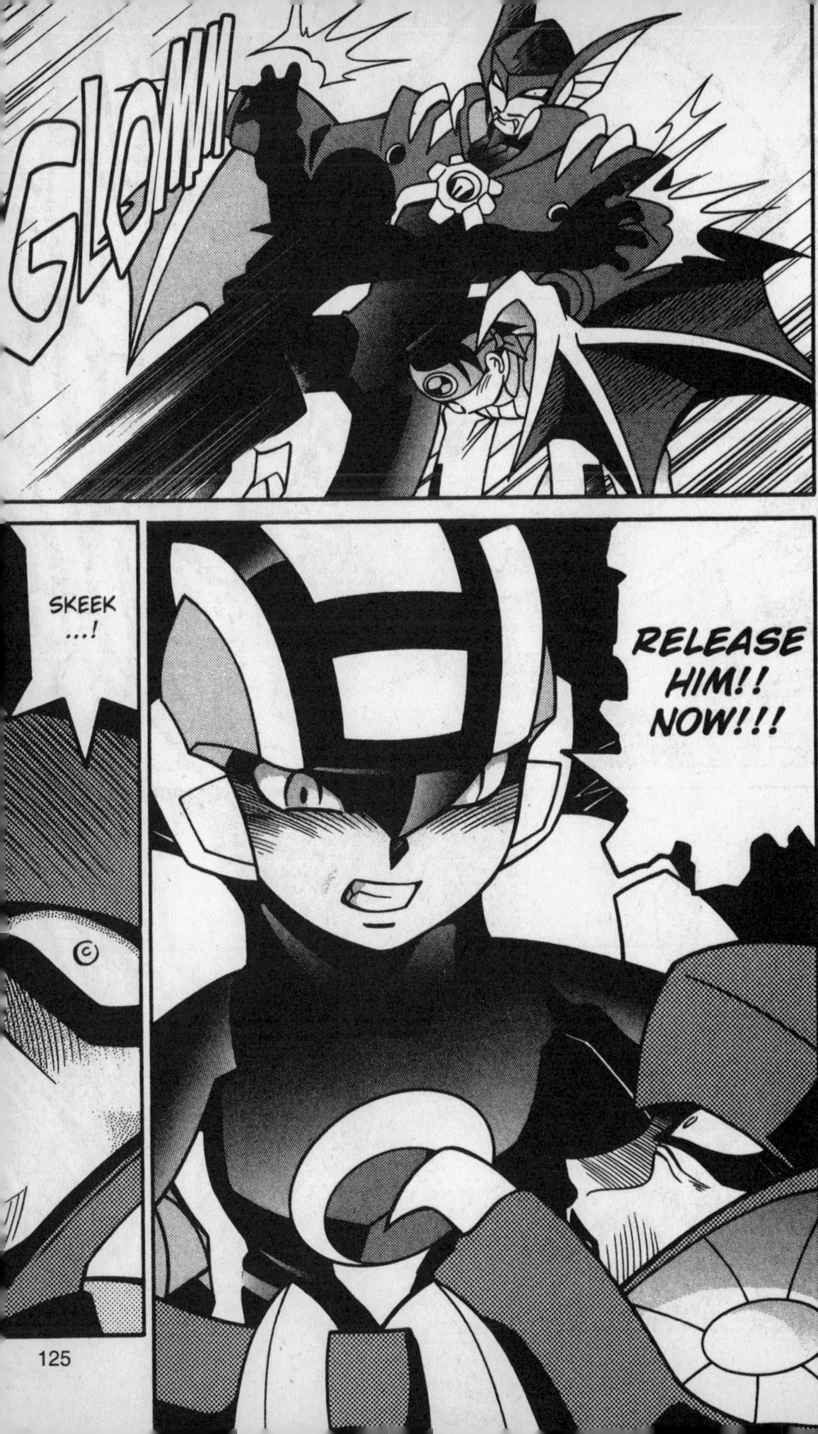
GLOMM
RELEASE HIM!! NOW!!!
SKEEK ...!

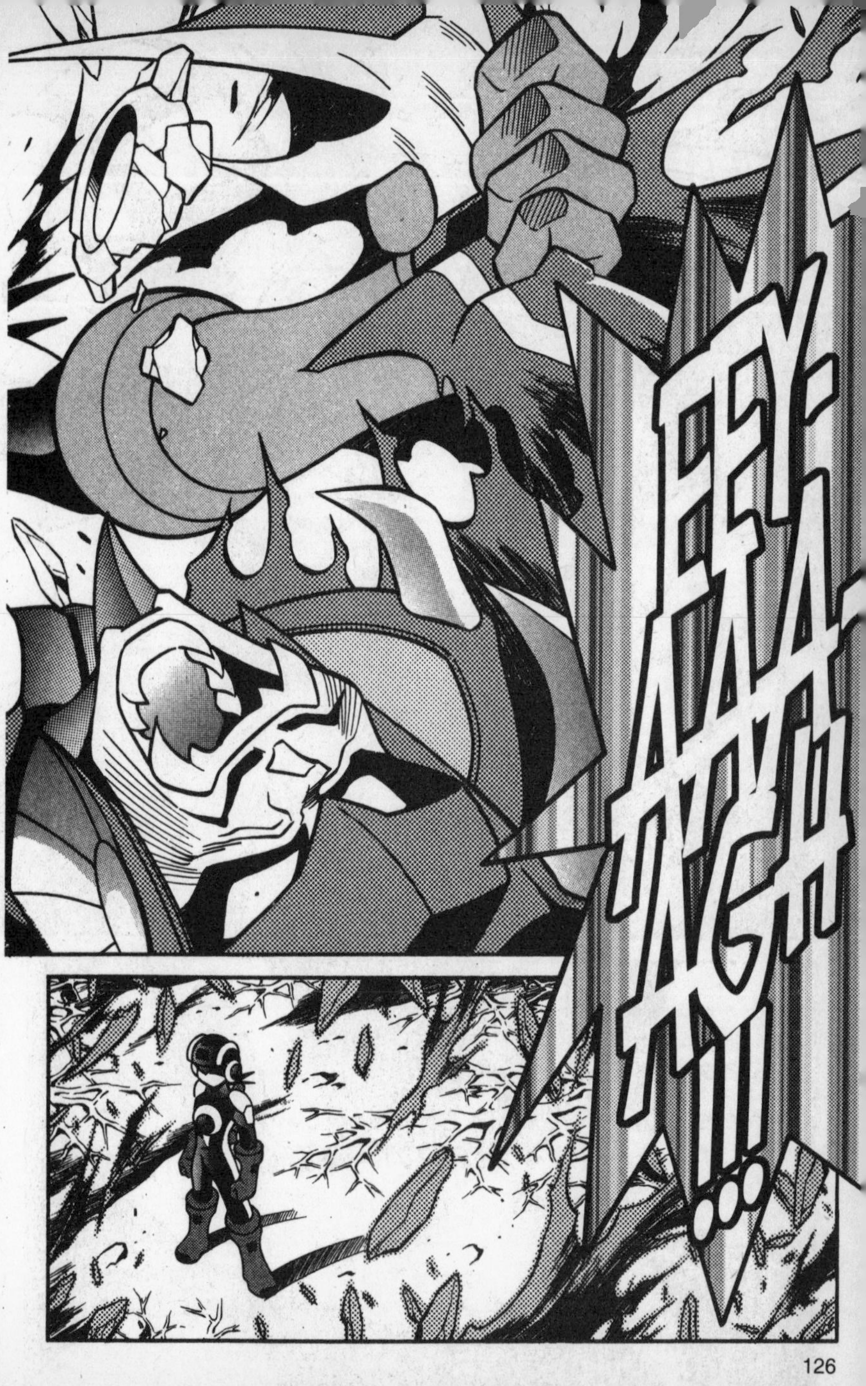
EEY-AAA-AAGH!!!...

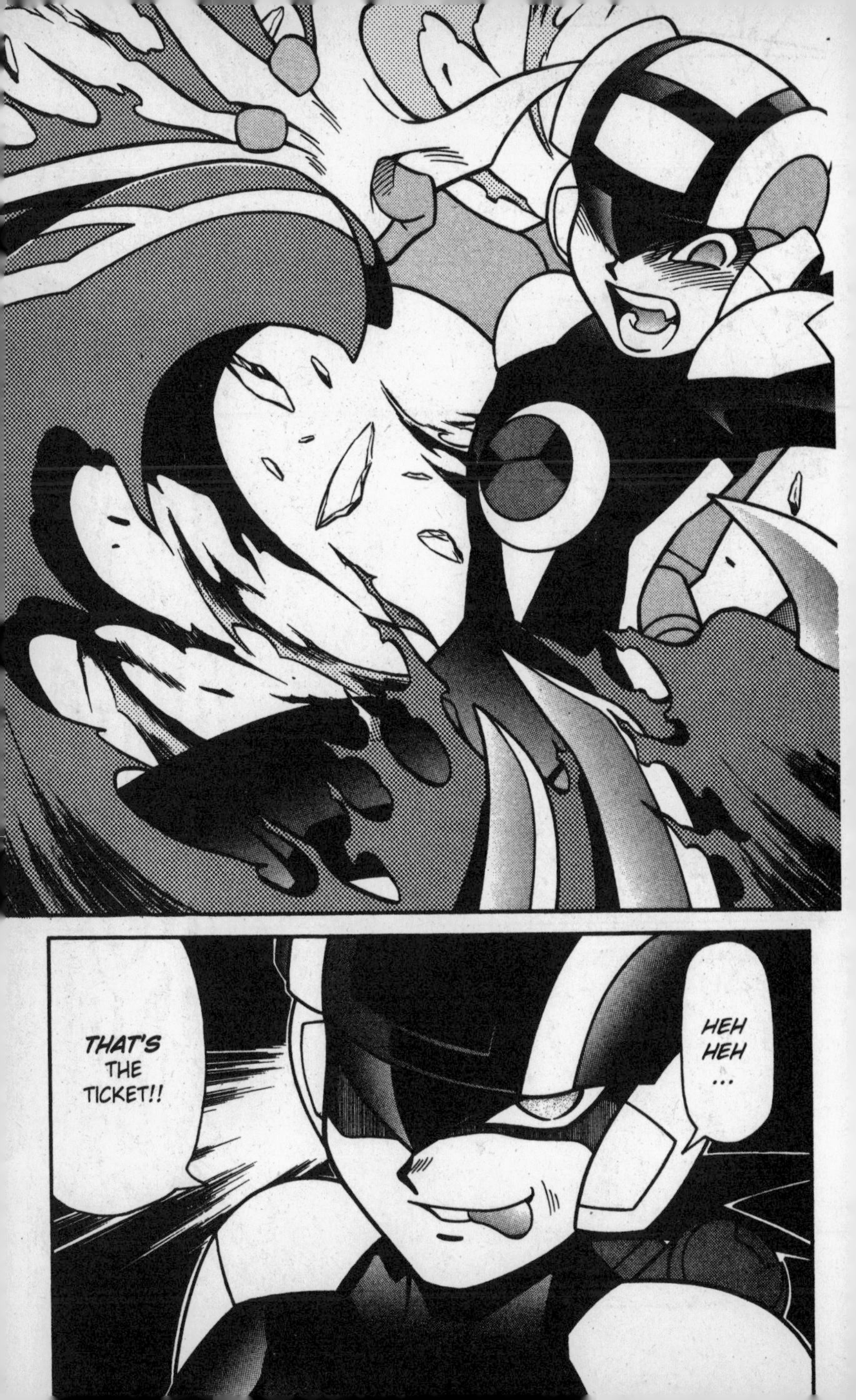
HEH HEH ...
THAT'S THE TICKET!!

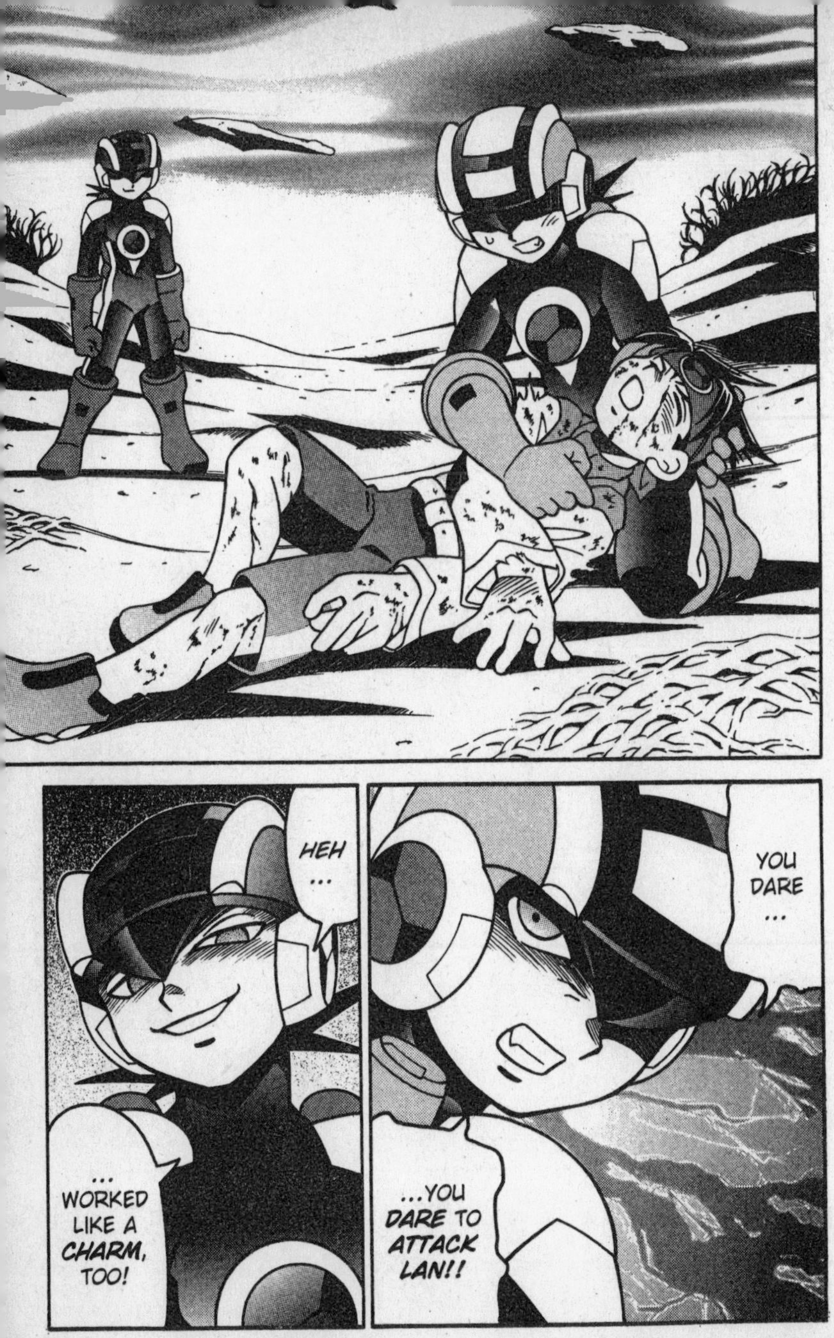
YOU DARE ...
...YOU DARE TO ATTACK LAN!!
HEH ...
... WORKED LIKE A CHARM, TOO!

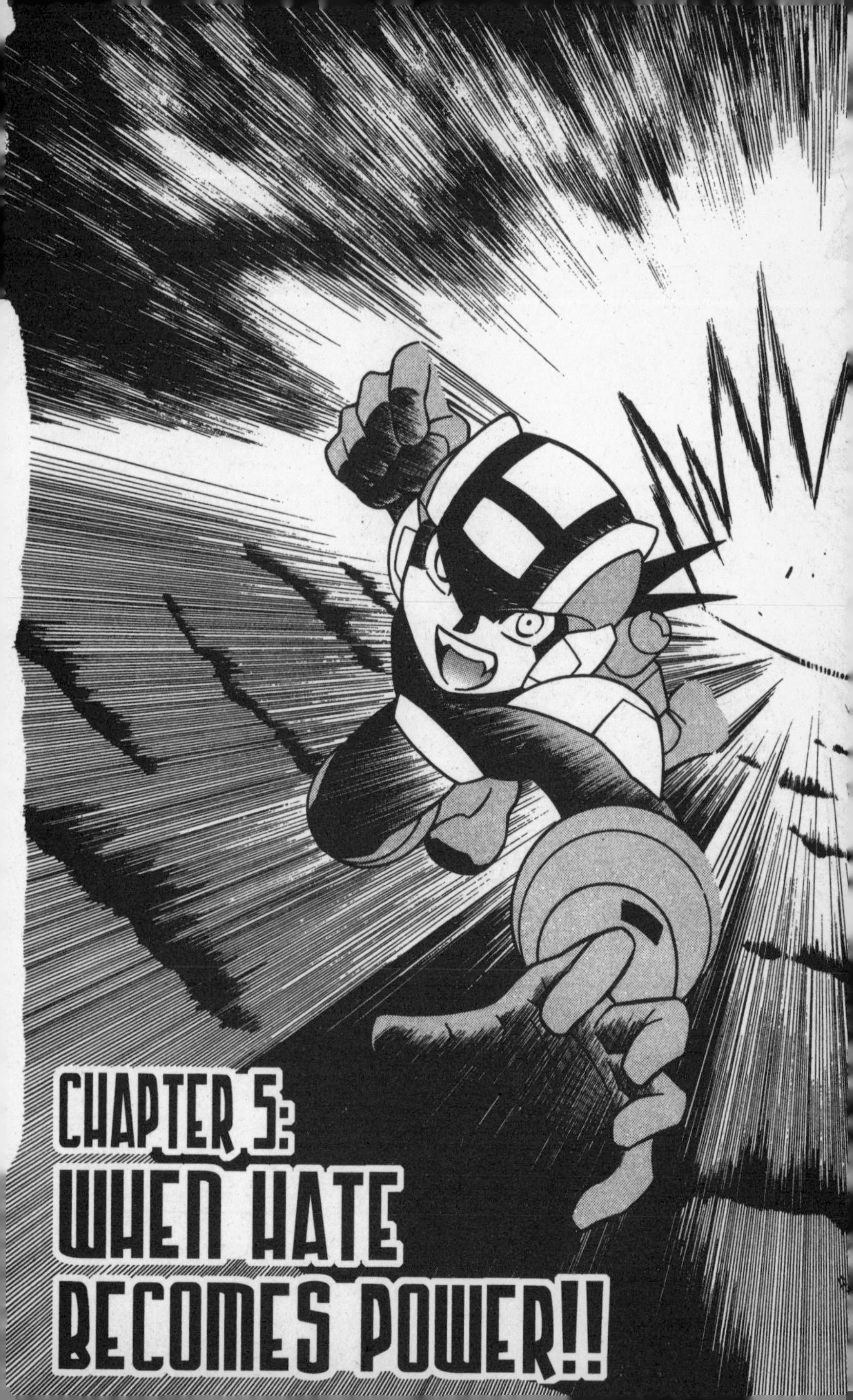
CHAPTER 5:
WHEN HATE
BECOMES POWER!!

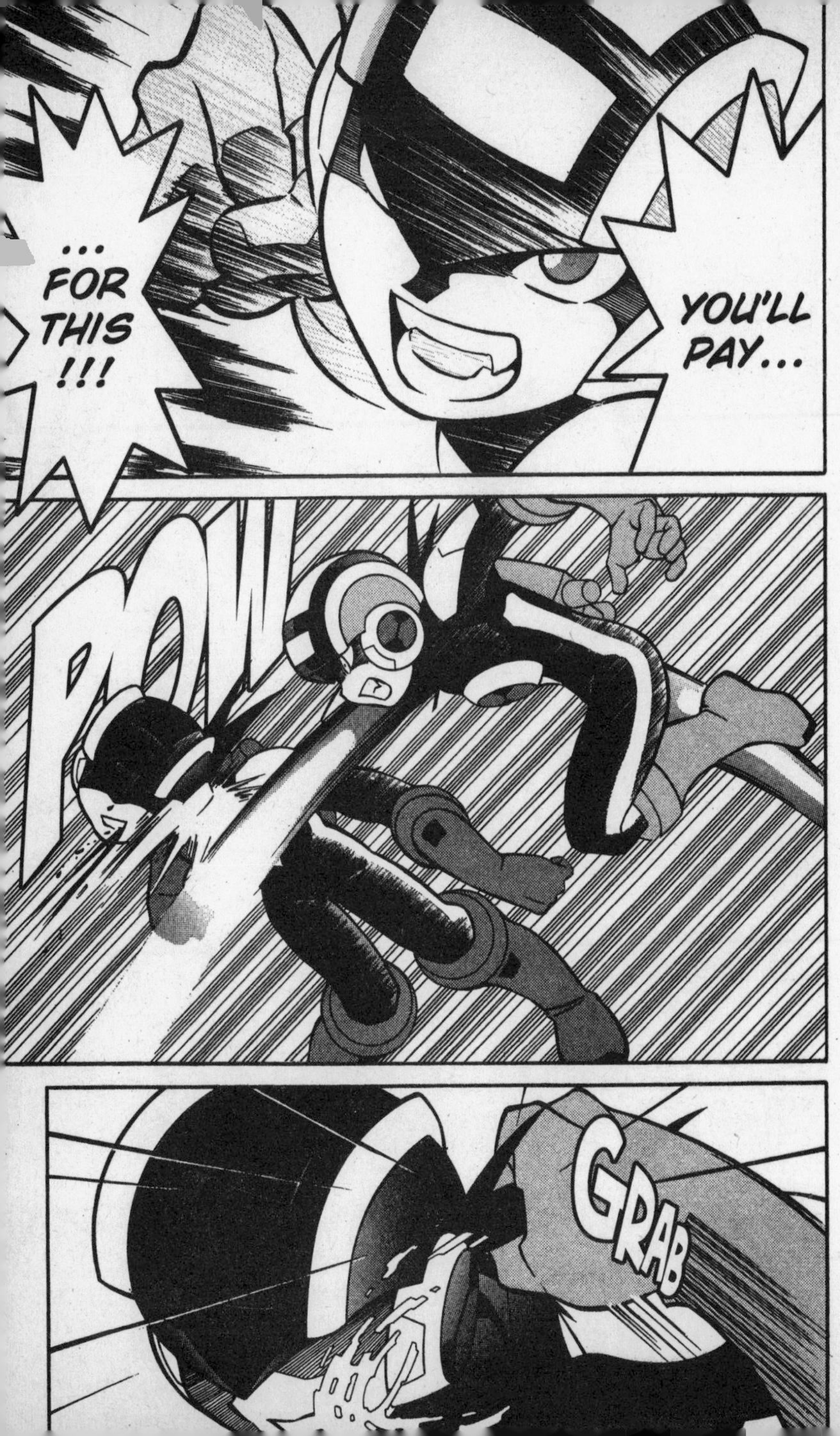
YOU'LL PAY...
...FOR THIS!!!
POW
GRAB

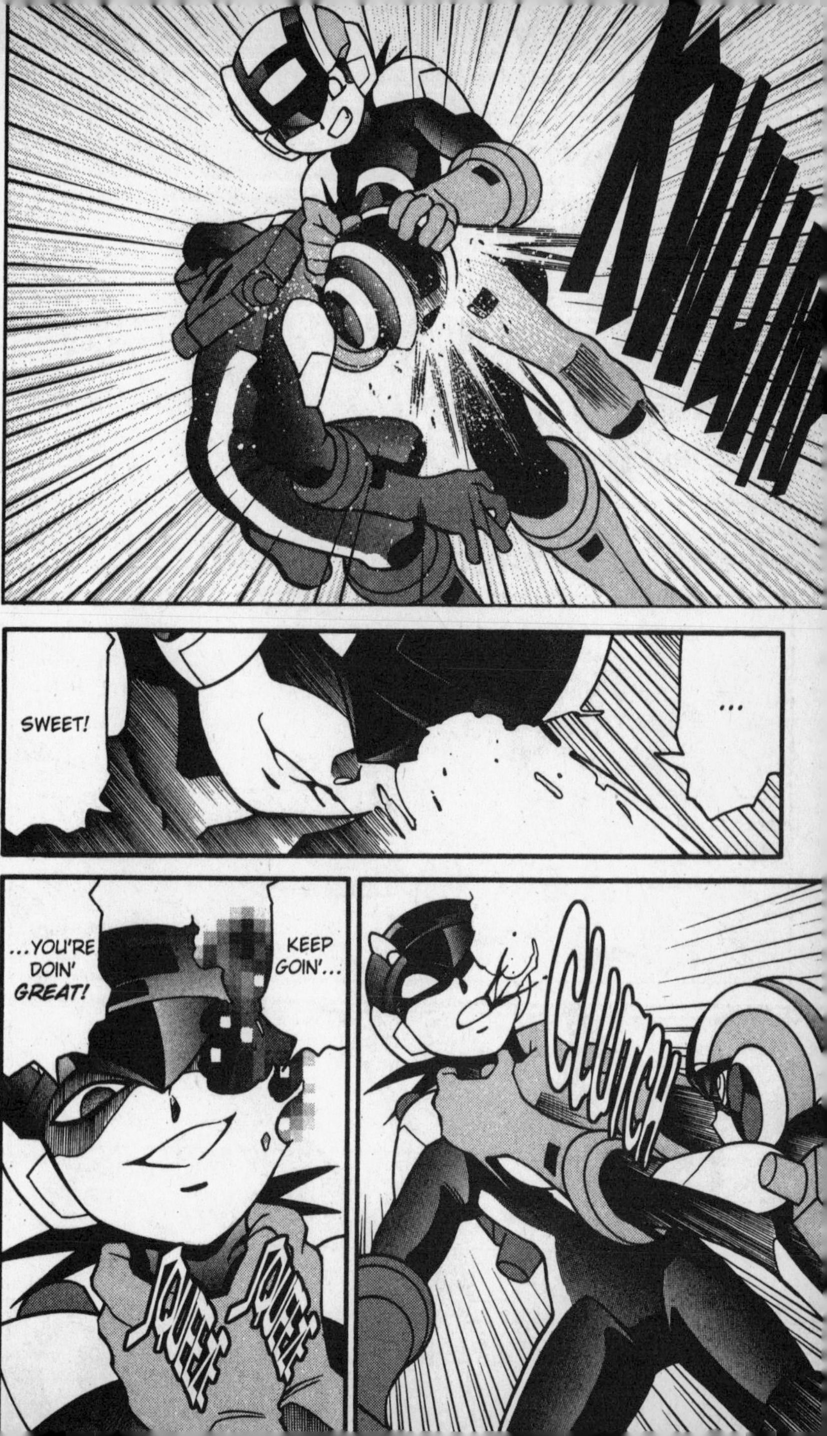
...
SWEET!
CLENCH
KEEP GOIN'...
...YOU'RE DOIN' GREAT!
SQUEEZE
SQUEEZE

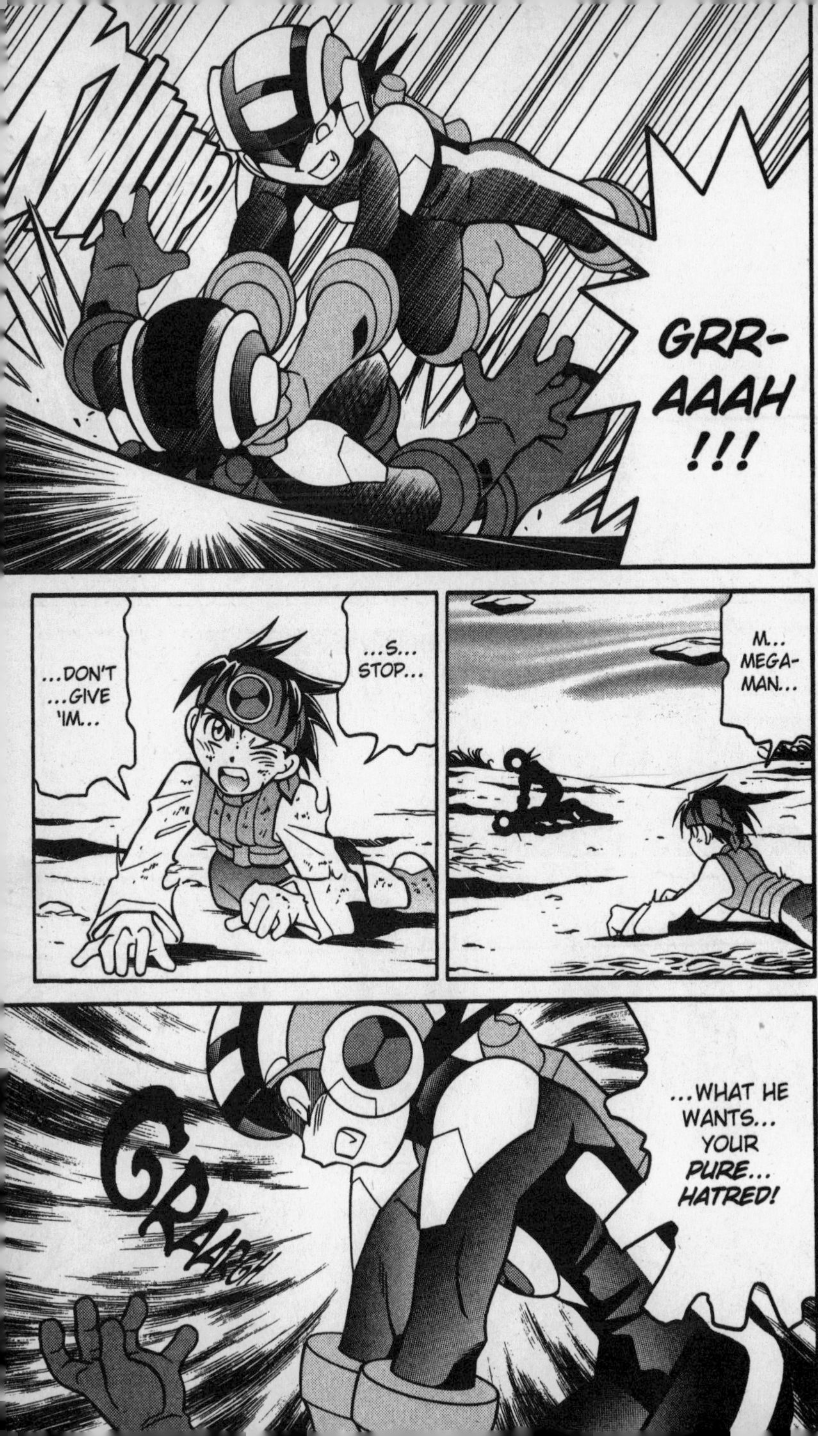
GRR-AAAH!!!
M... MEGA-MAN...
...S... STOP...
...DON'T ...GIVE 'IM...
...WHAT HE WANTS... YOUR PURE... HATRED!
GRAARGH

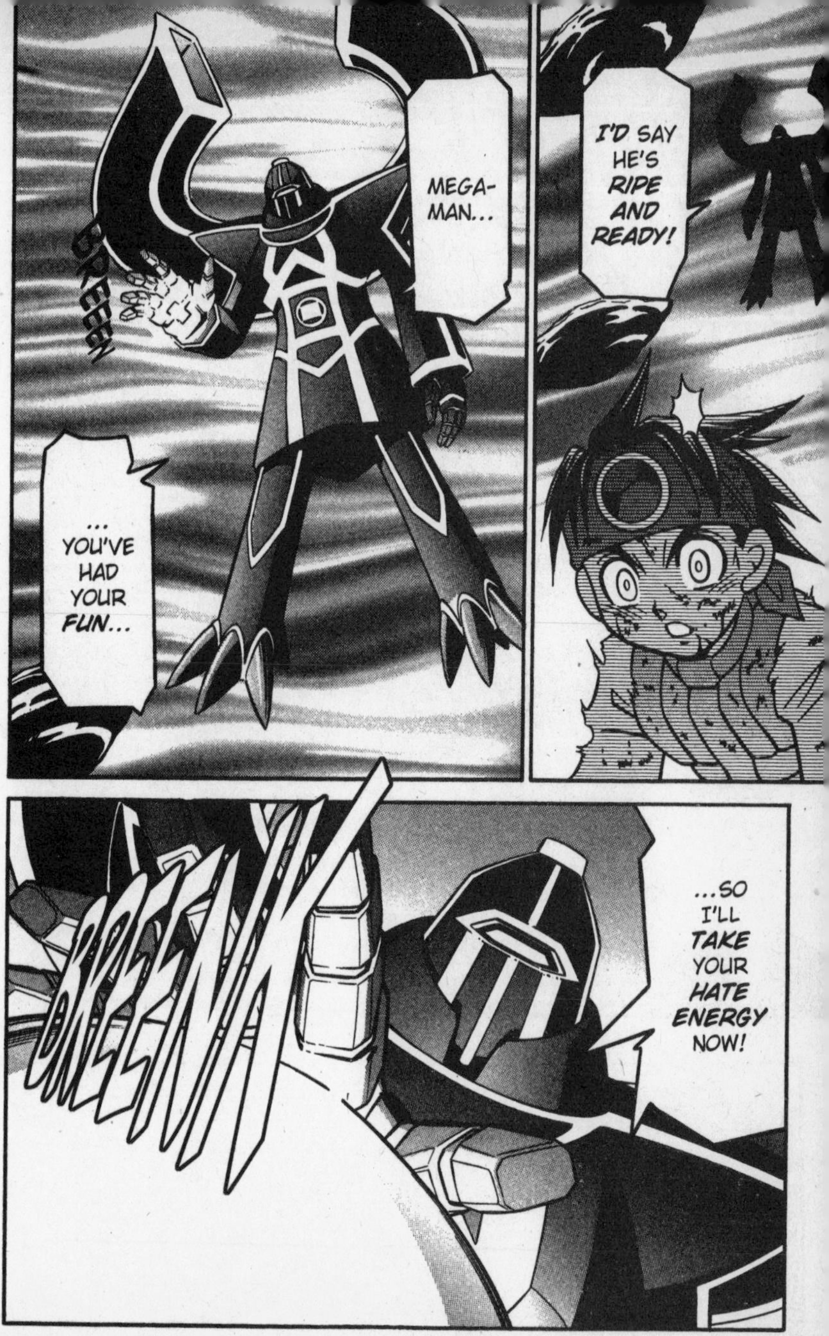
I'D SAY HE'S RIPE AND READY!
MEGA-MAN...
...YOU'VE HAD YOUR FUN...
...SO I'LL TAKE YOUR HATE ENERGY NOW!

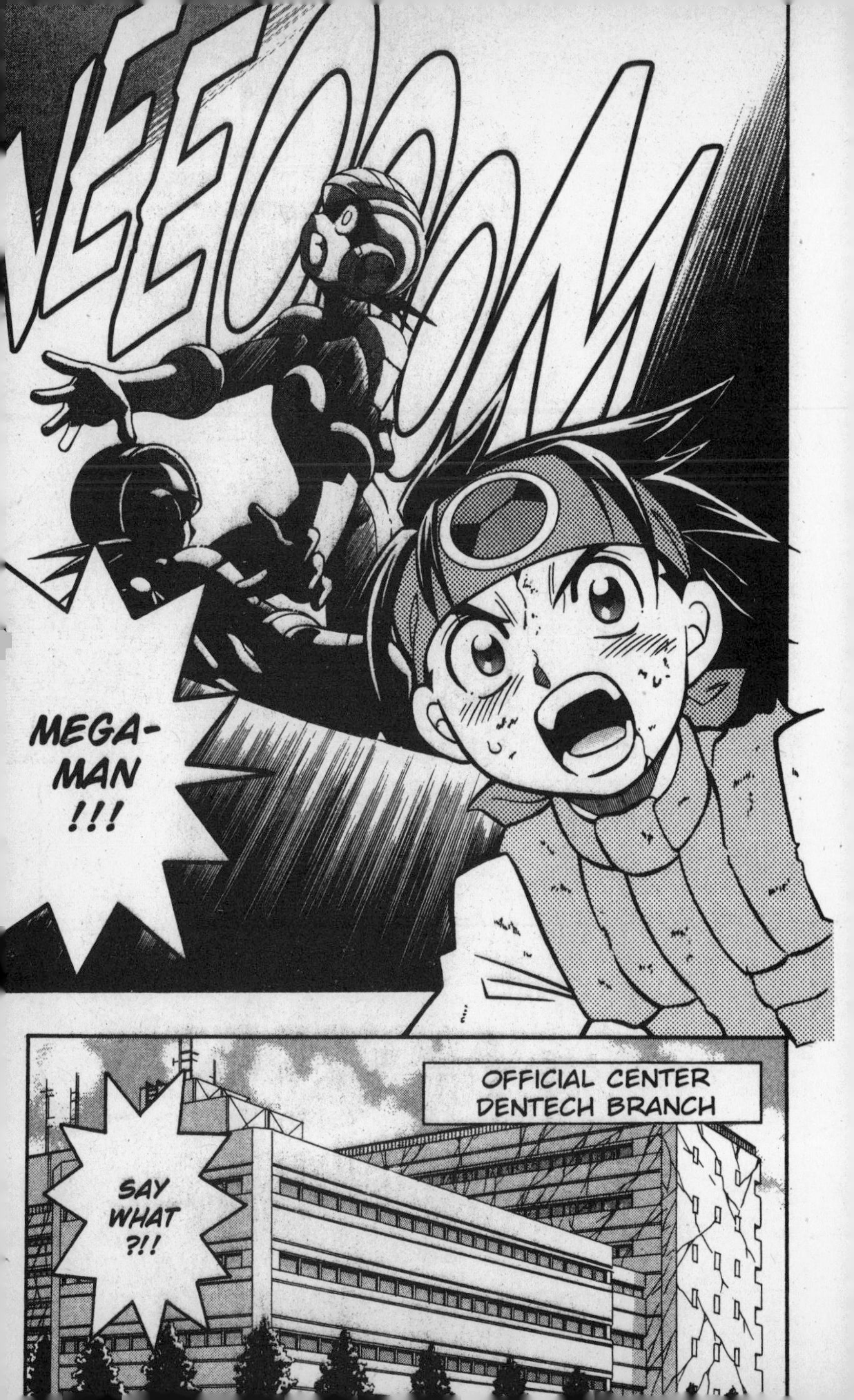
VEEOOOM
MEGA-MAN!!!
OFFICIAL CENTER DENTECH BRANCH
SAY WHAT?!!

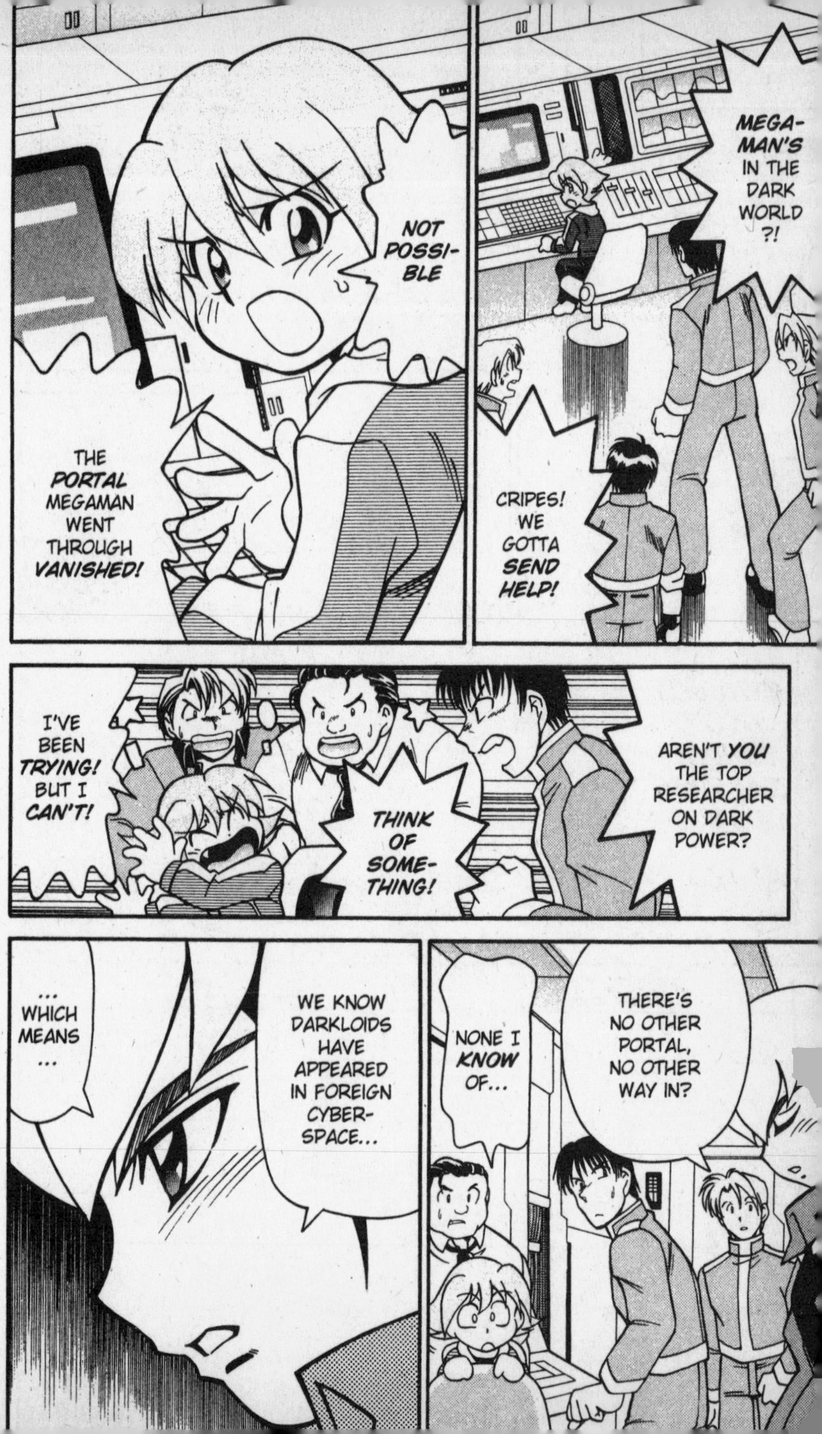
MEGA-MAN'S IN THE DARK WORLD ?!
CRIPES! WE GOTTA SEND HELP!
NOT POSSI-BLE
THE PORTAL MEGAMAN WENT THROUGH VANISHED!
AREN'T YOU THE TOP RESEARCHER ON DARK POWER?
THINK OF SOME-THING!
I'VE BEEN TRYING! BUT I CAN'T!
THERE'S NO OTHER PORTAL, NO OTHER WAY IN?
NONE I KNOW OF...
WE KNOW DARKLOIDS HAVE APPEARED IN FOREIGN CYBER-SPACE...
... WHICH MEANS ...

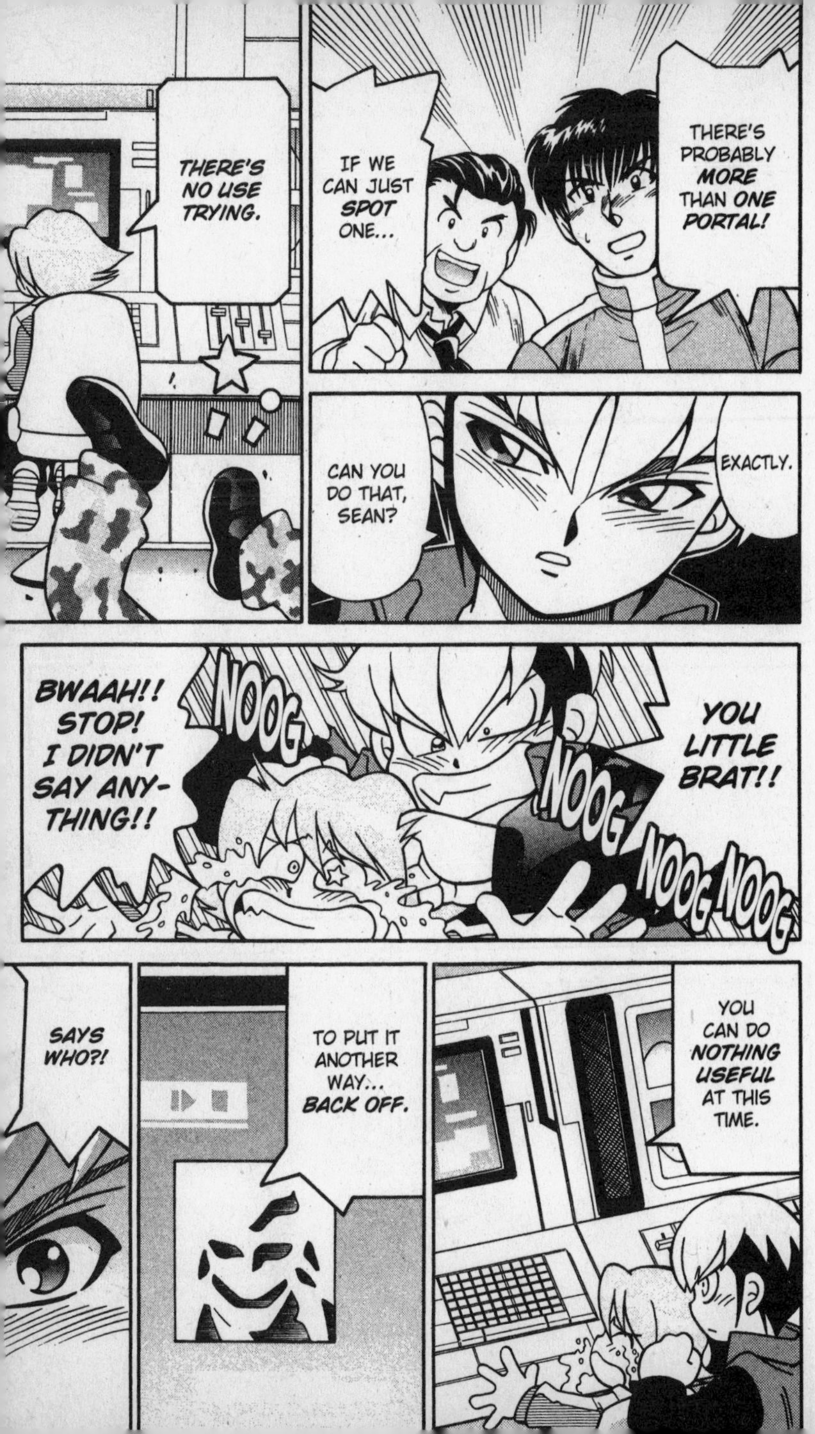

THERE'S PROBABLY MORE THAN ONE PORTAL!
IF WE CAN JUST SPOT ONE...
EXACTLY.
CAN YOU DO THAT, SEAN?
THERE'S NO USE TRYING.
YOU LITTLE BRAT!!
NOOG NOOG NOOG NOOG NOOG
BWAAH!! STOP! I DIDN'T SAY ANY-THING!!
YOU CAN DO NOTHING USEFUL AT THIS TIME.
TO PUT IT ANOTHER WAY... BACK OFF.
SAYS WHO?!

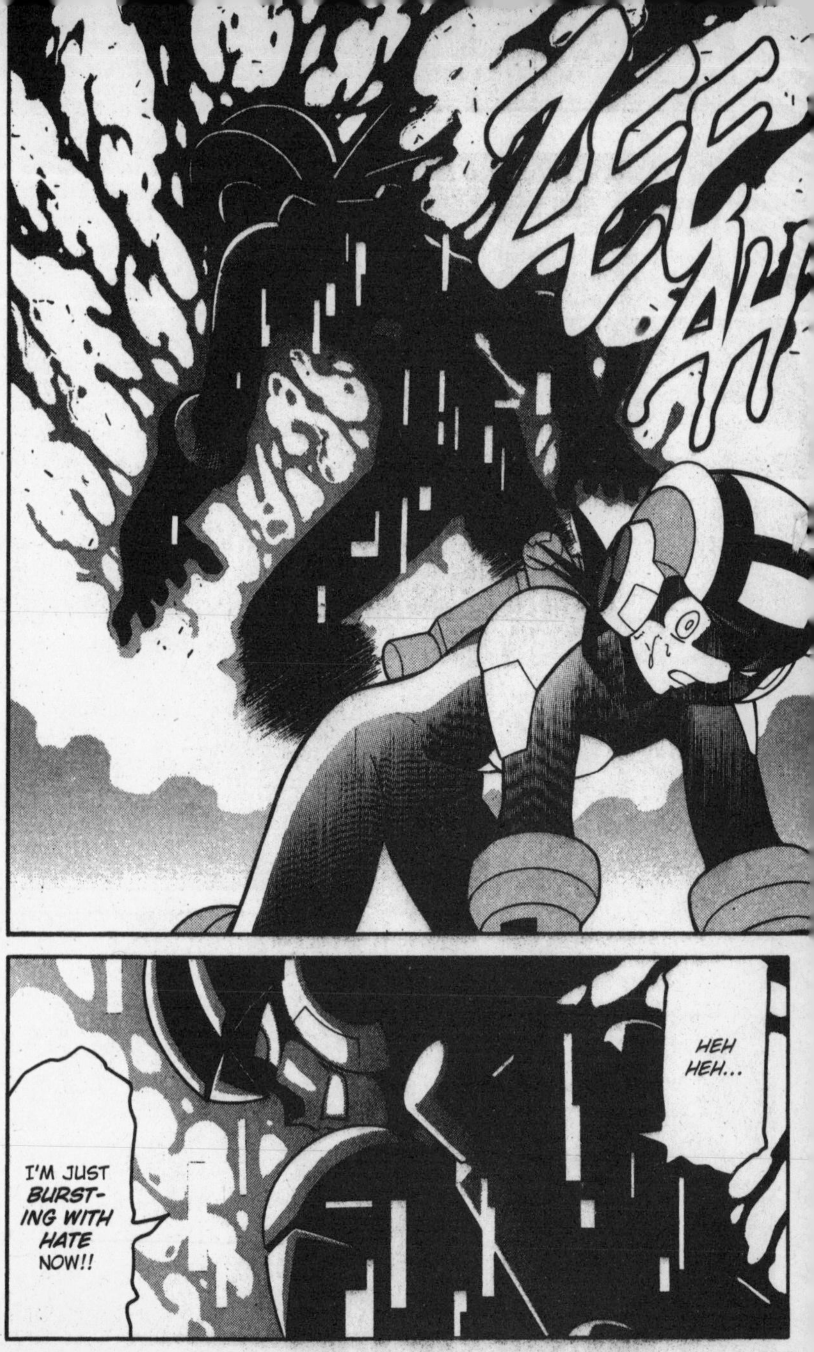
ZEEAH
HEH HEH...
I'M JUST BURSTING WITH HATE NOW!!

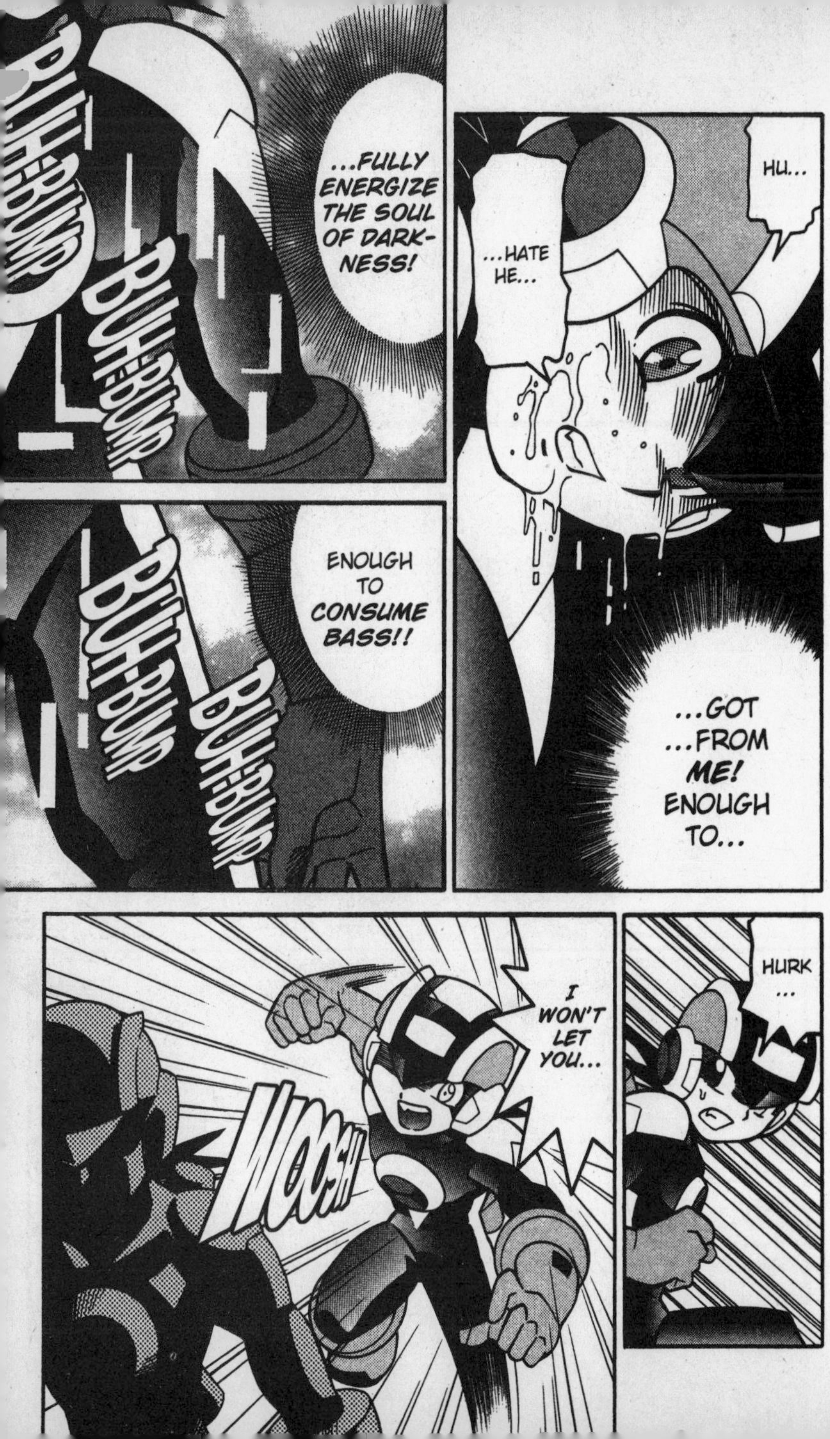
HU...
...HATE HE...
...GOT ...FROM ME! ENOUGH TO...
BUH-BUMP
BUH-BUMP
...FULLY ENERGIZE THE SOUL OF DARK-NESS!
BUH-BUMP
BUH-BUMP
BUH-BUMP
ENOUGH TO CONSUME BASS!!
HURK ...
I WON'T LET YOU...
WOOSH

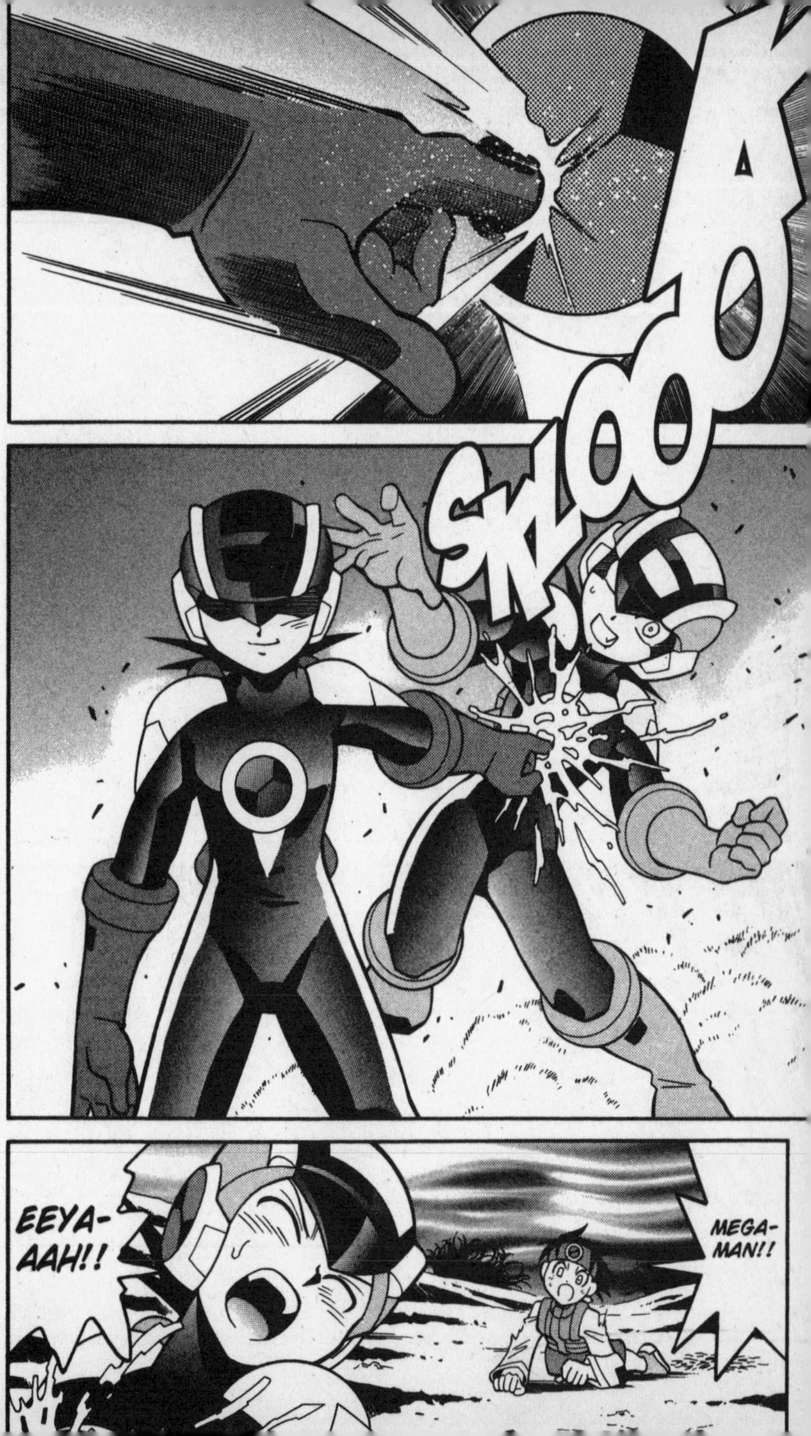
SKLOOOOOA!
MEGA-MAN!!
EEYA-AAH!!

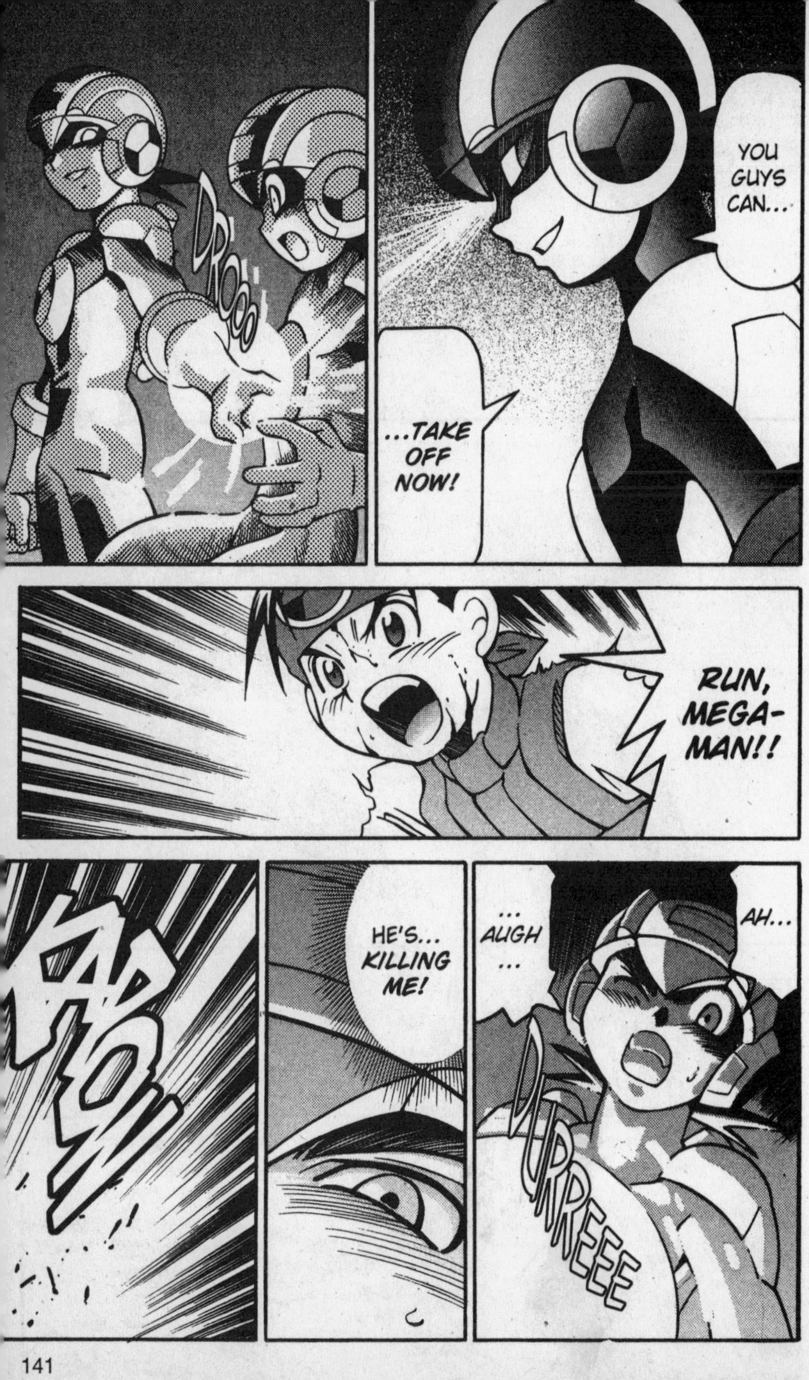
YOU GUYS CAN...
...TAKE OFF NOW!
DROOO
RUN, MEGA-MAN!!
AH...
...AUGH...
DURREEE
HE'S... KILLING ME!

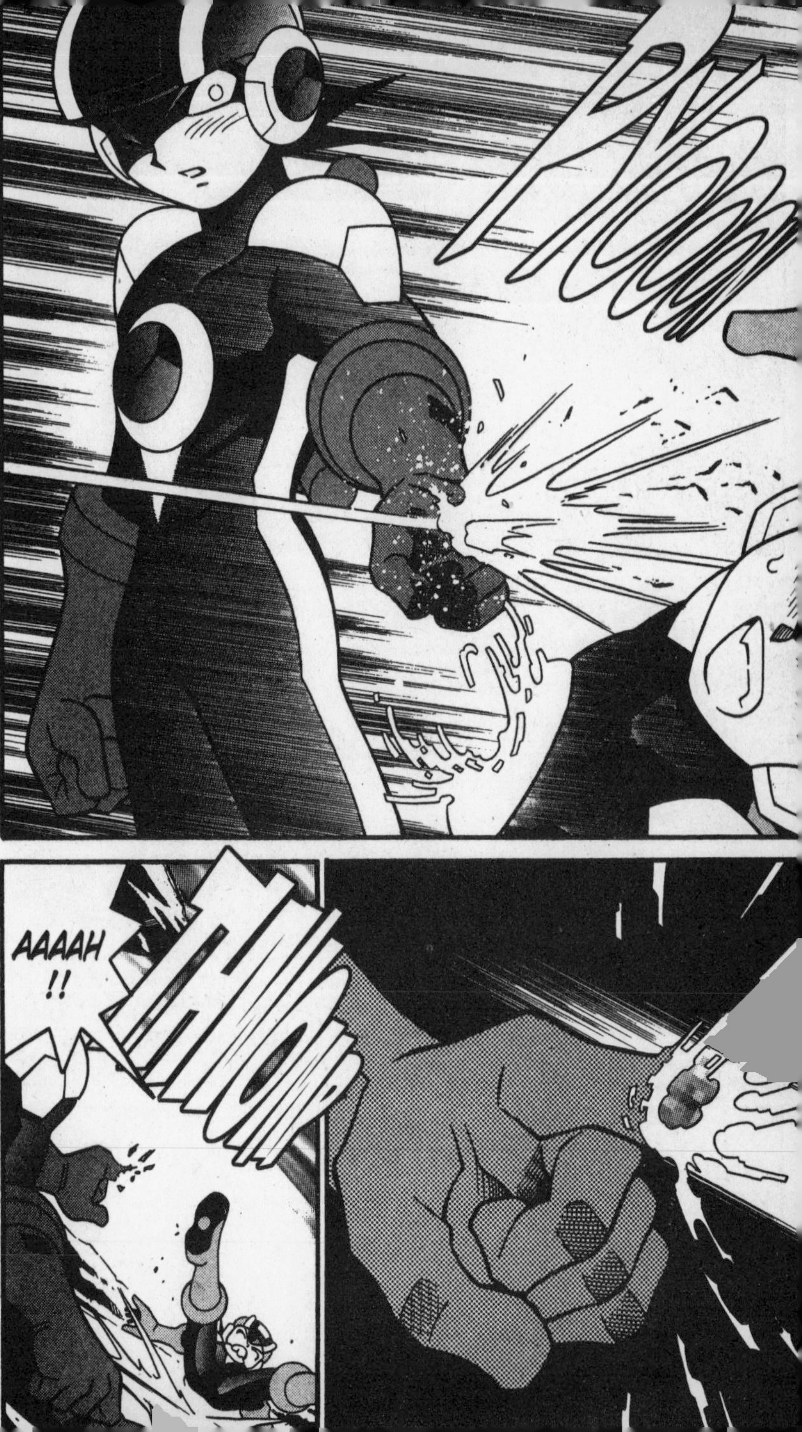
THWOMP
AAAAH !!

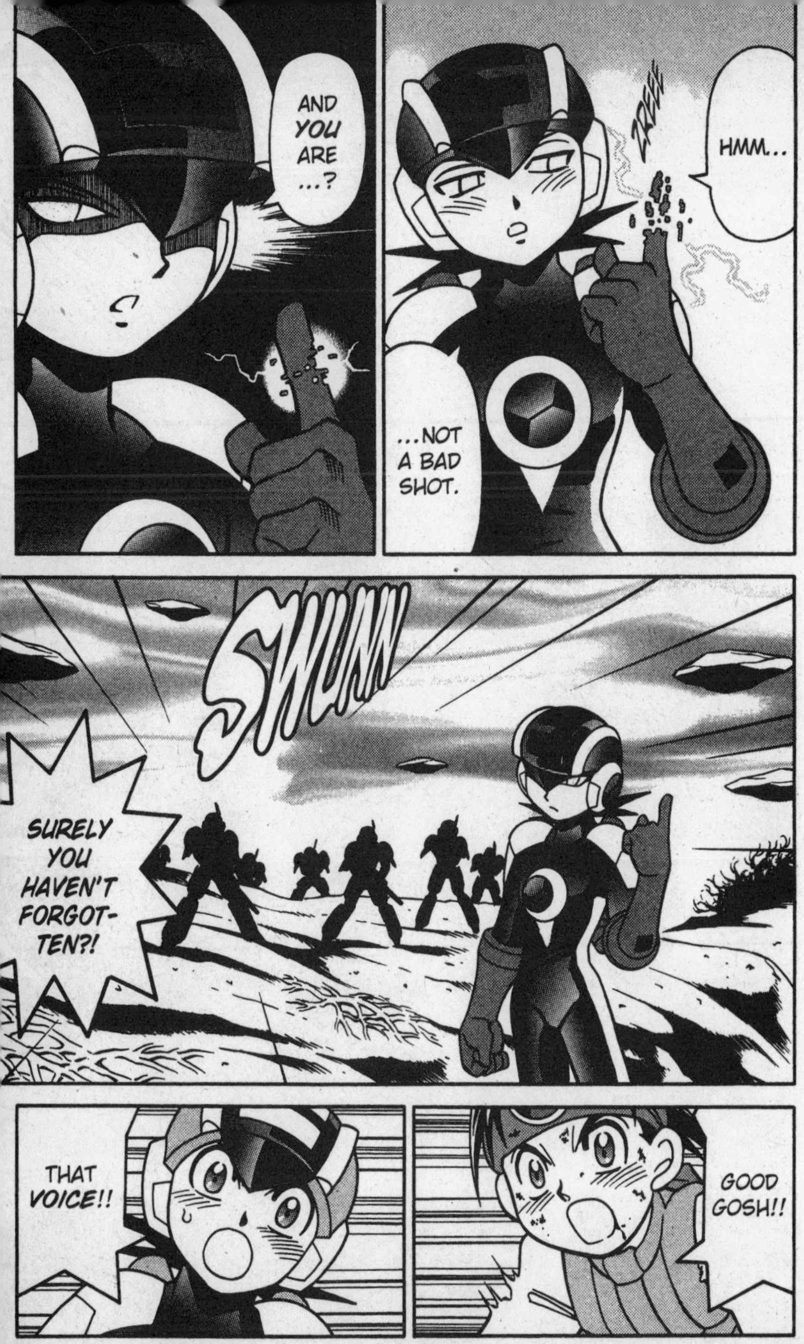
HMM...
ZREEE
...NOT A BAD SHOT.
AND YOU ARE ...?
SWUNN
SURELY YOU HAVEN'T FORGOT-TEN?!
GOOD GOSH!!
THAT VOICE!!

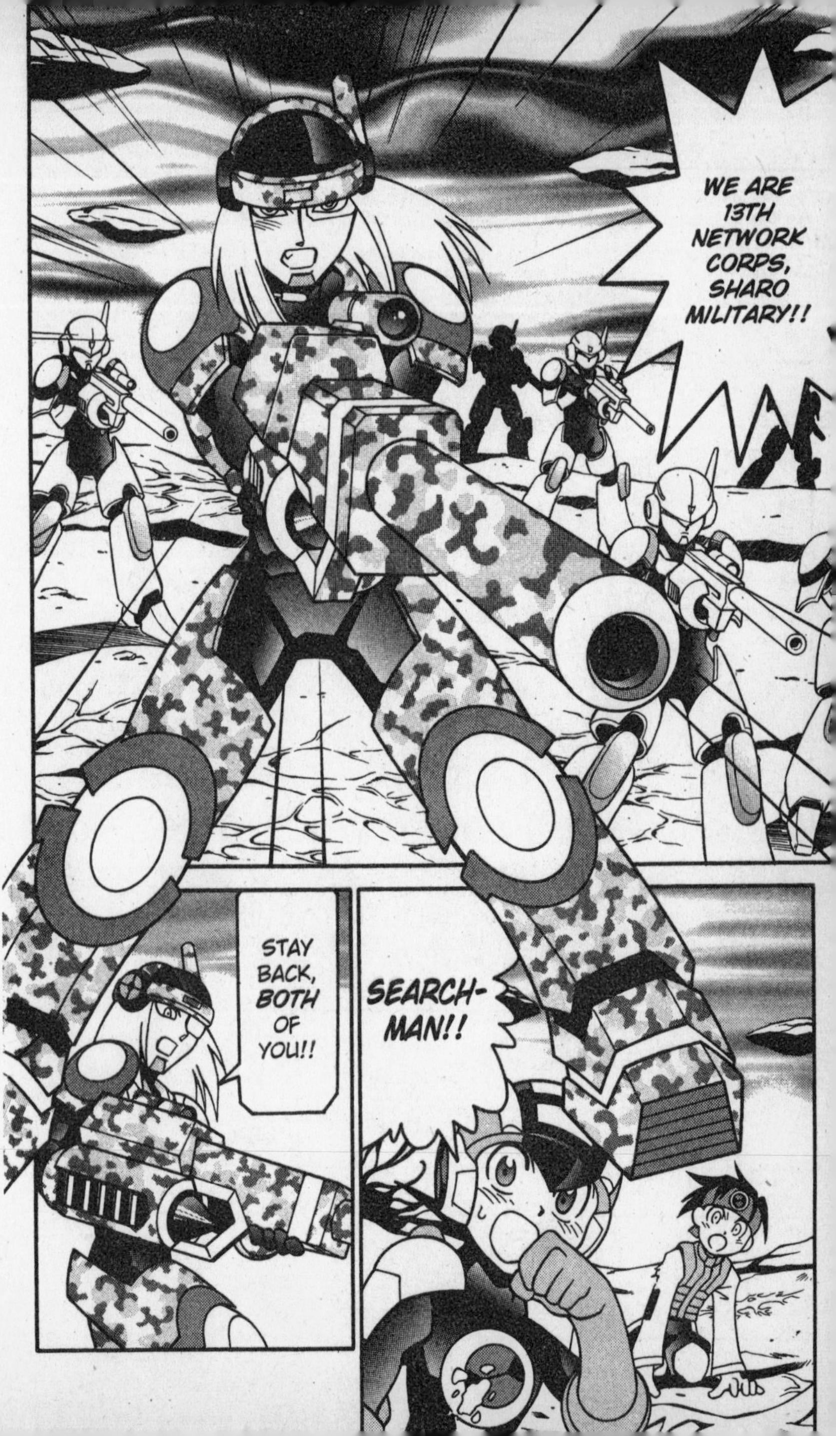
WE ARE 13TH NETWORK CORPS, SHARO MILITARY!!
SEARCH-MAN!!
STAY BACK, BOTH OF YOU!!

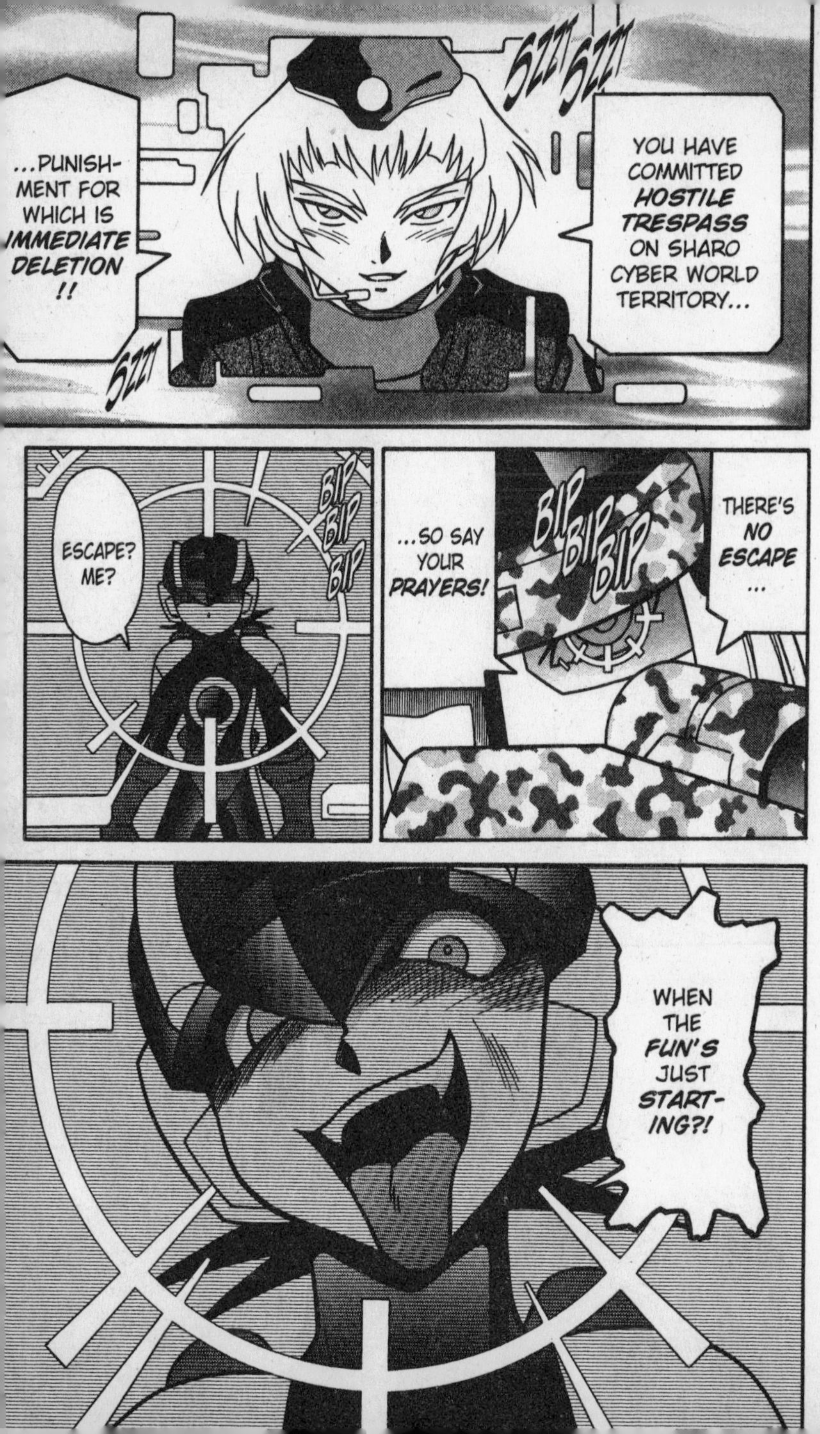
SZZT SZZT
YOU HAVE COMMITTED HOSTILE TRESPASS ON SHARO CYBER WORLD TERRITORY...
...PUNISHMENT FOR WHICH IS IMMEDIATE DELETION !!
SZZT
THERE'S NO ESCAPE ...
BIP BIP BIP
...SO SAY YOUR PRAYERS!
BIP BIP BIP
ESCAPE? ME?
WHEN THE FUN'S JUST STARTING?!

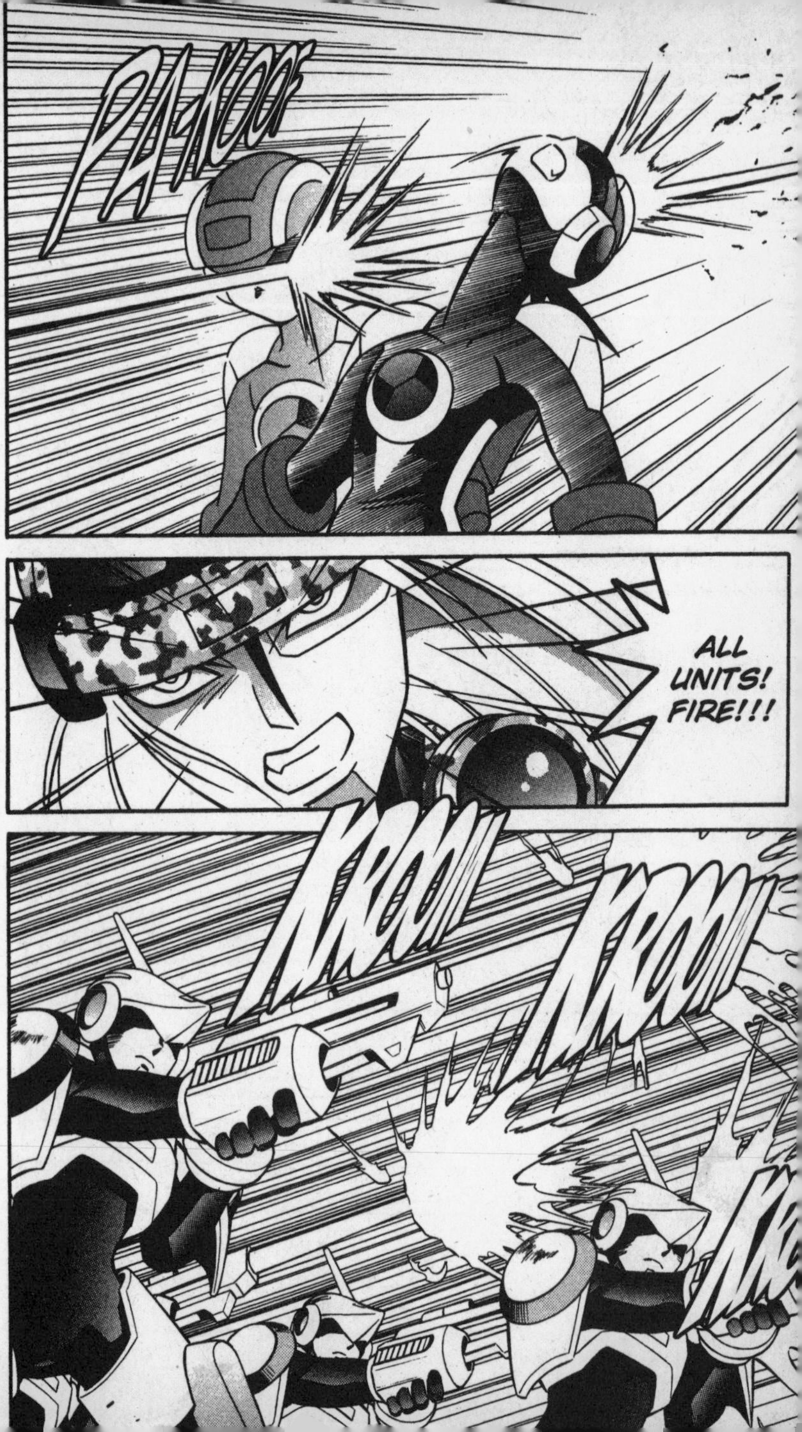
PA-KOOF
ALL UNITS! FIRE!!!

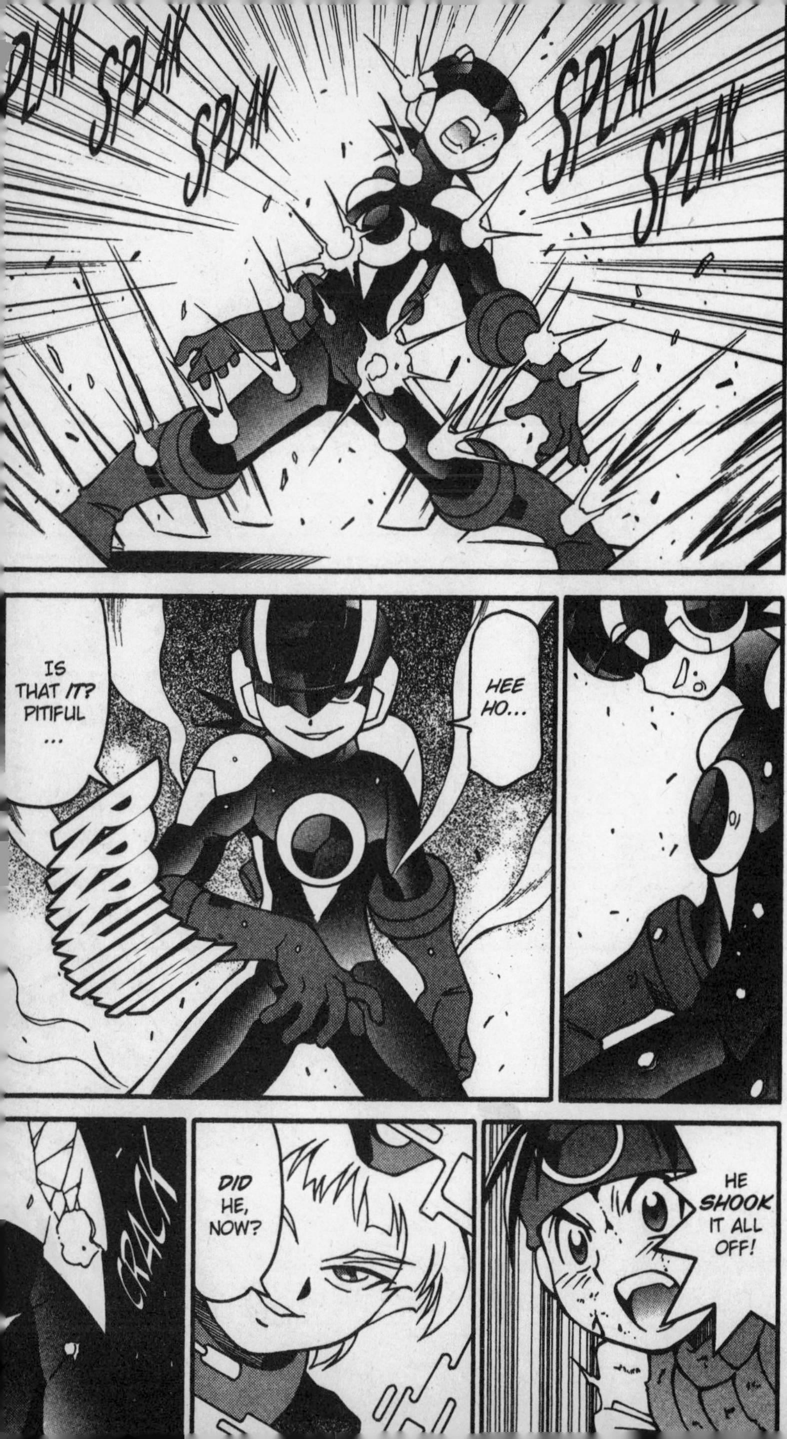
SPLAK
SPLAK
SPLAK
SPLAK
SPLAK
HEE HO...
IS THAT *IT?* PITIFUL ...
HE *SHOOK* IT ALL OFF!
DID HE, NOW?
CRACK

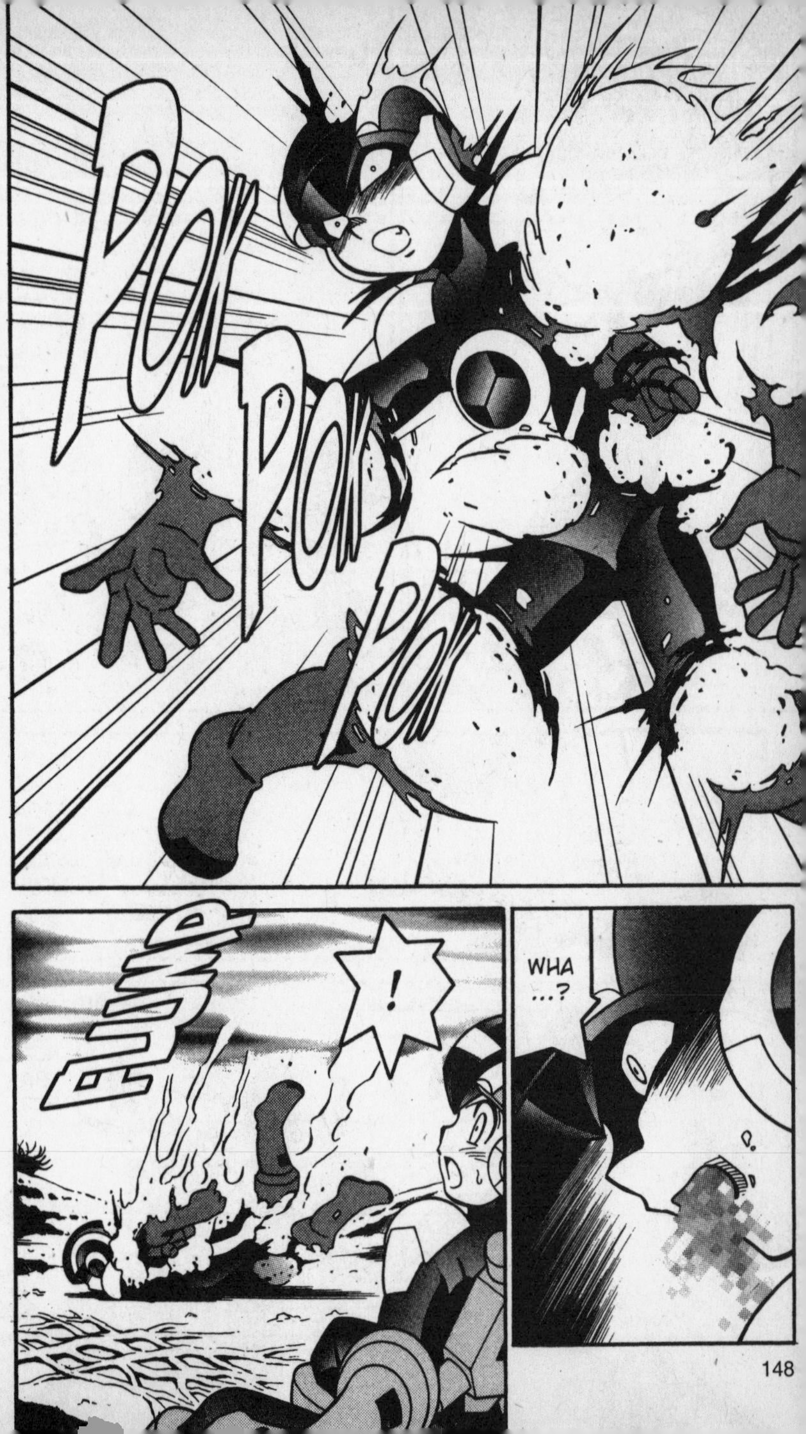
POK
POK
POK
WHA ...?
!
FLUMP

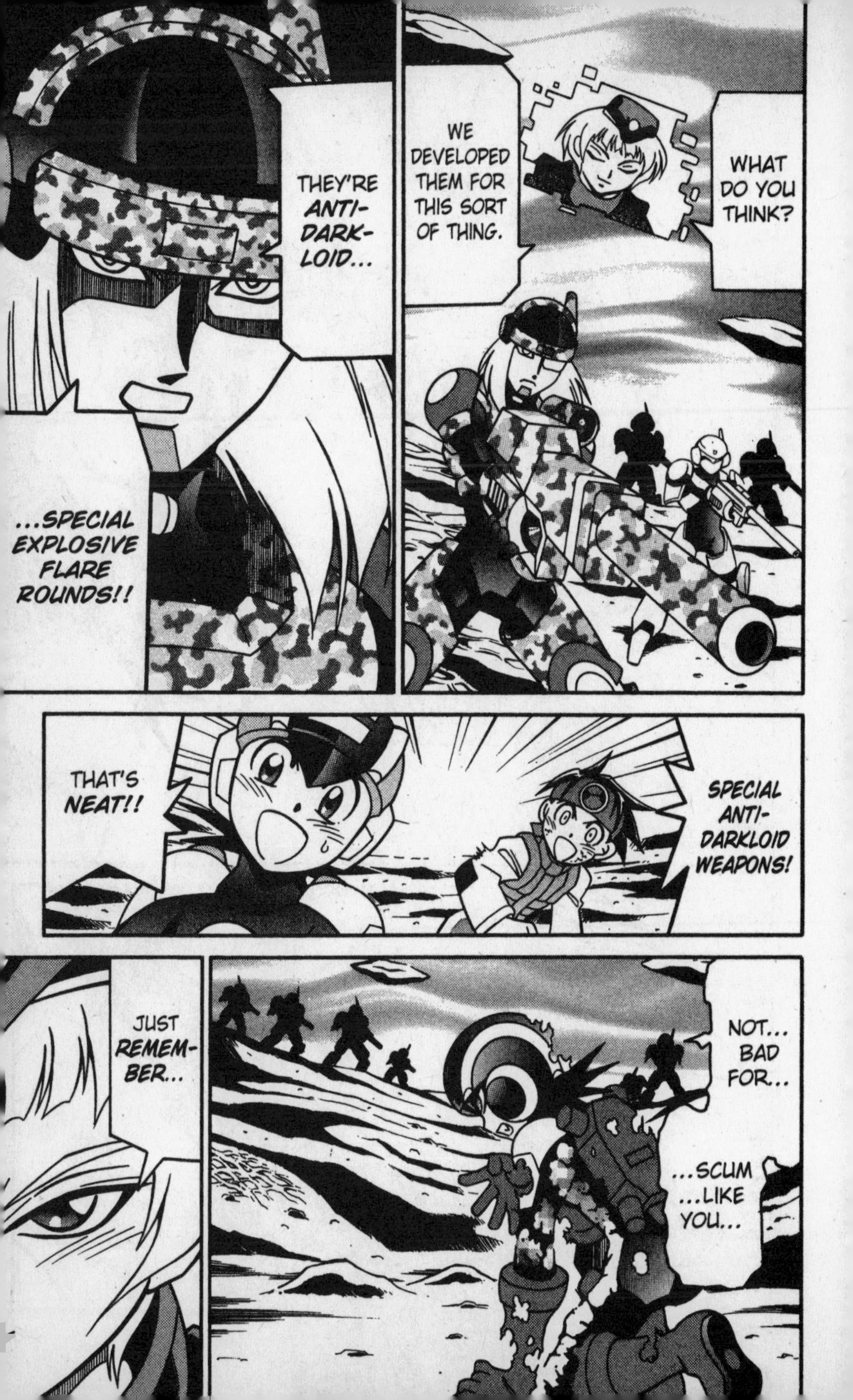
WHAT DO YOU THINK?
WE DEVELOPED THEM FOR THIS SORT OF THING.
THEY'RE ANTI-DARKLOID...
...SPECIAL EXPLOSIVE FLARE ROUNDS!!
SPECIAL ANTI-DARKLOID WEAPONS!
THAT'S NEAT!!
NOT... BAD FOR...
...SCUM ...LIKE YOU...
JUST REMEMBER...

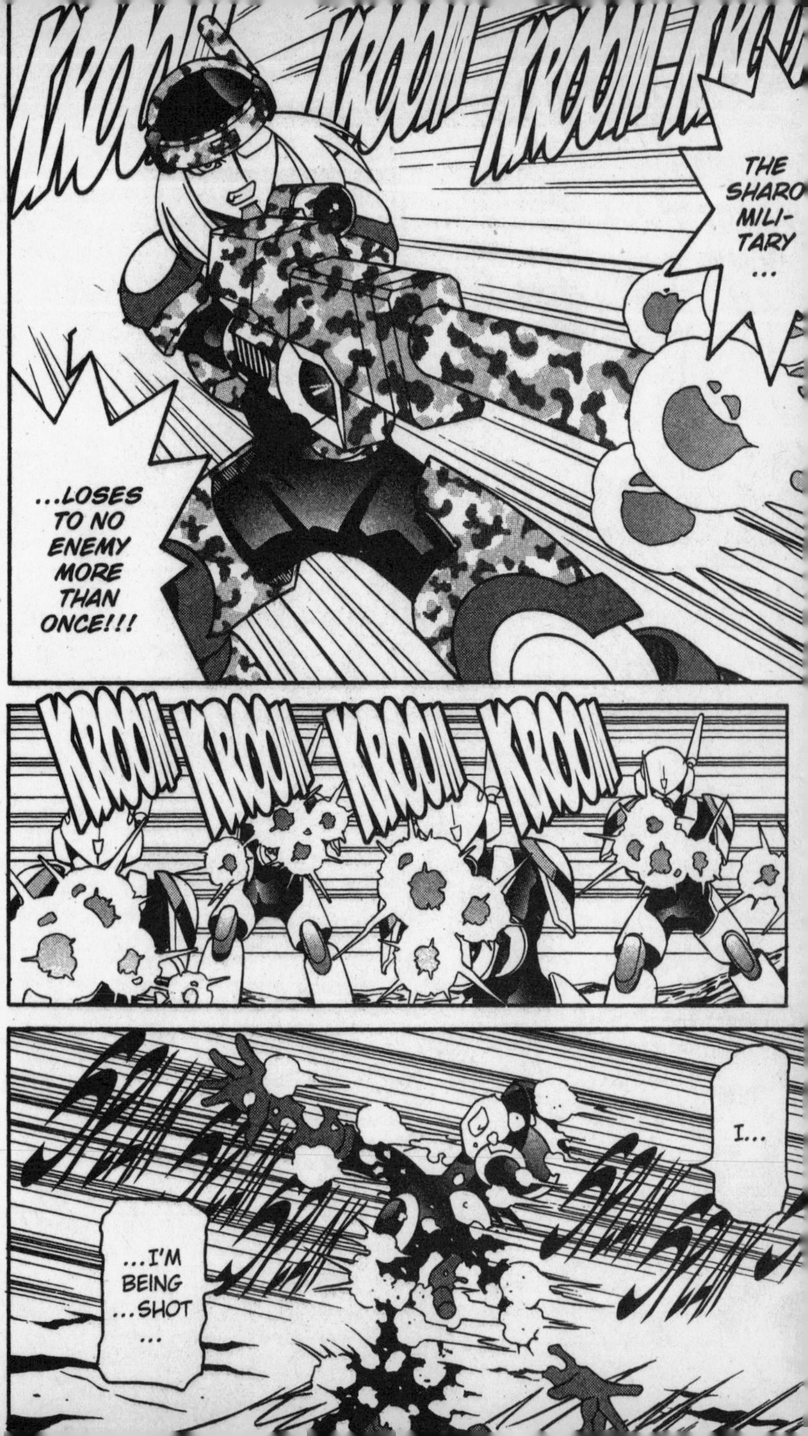

KRAOOM KRAOOM KRAOOM KRAOOM
THE SHARO MILI-TARY ...
...LOSES TO NO ENEMY MORE THAN ONCE!!!
KRAOOM KRAOOM KRAOOM KRAOOM
I...
...I'M BEING ...SHOT ...

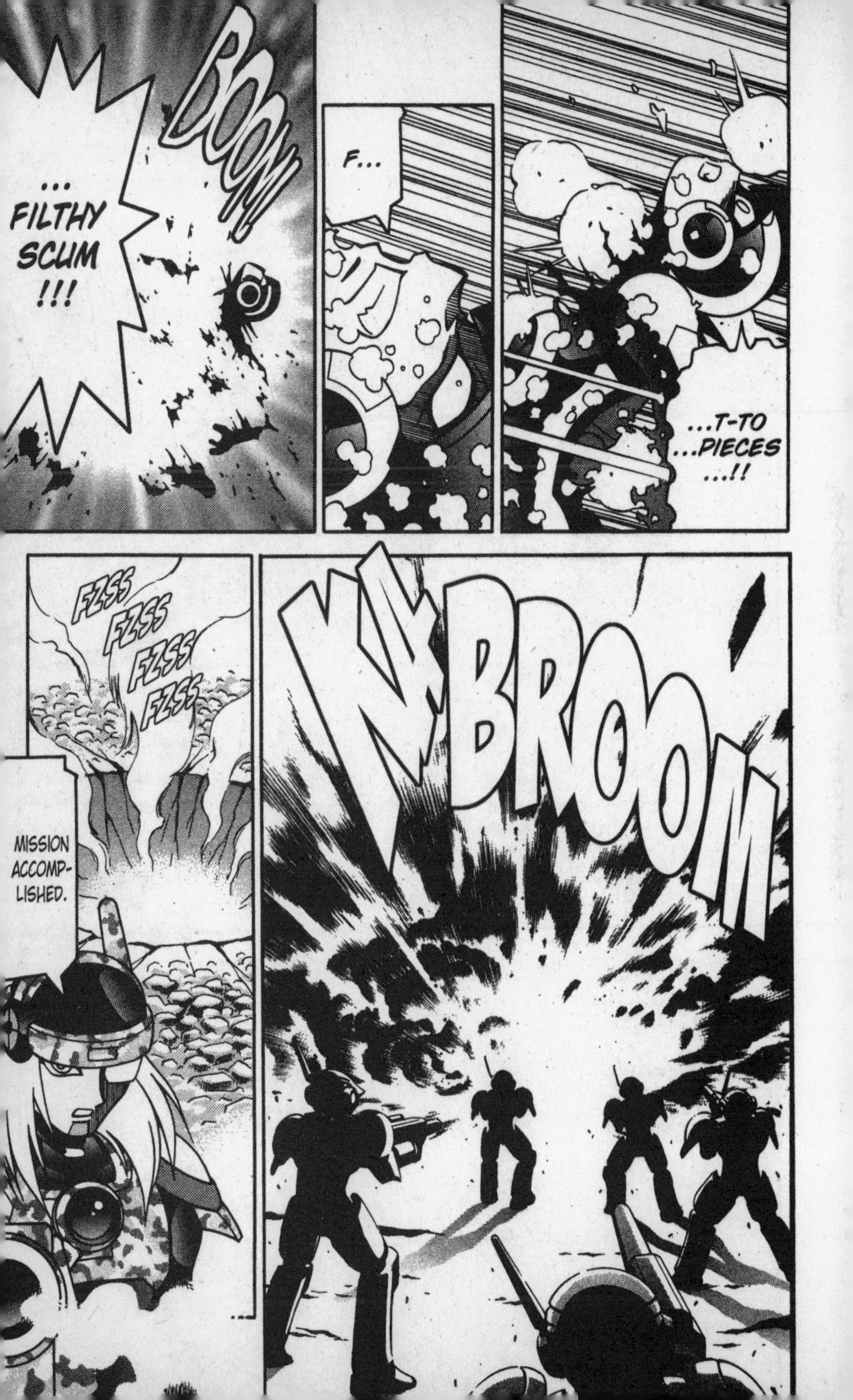

...T-TO
...PIECES
...!!
F...
BOOM!
... FILTHY SCUM !!!
BROOM
FZSS FZSS FZSS FZSS
MISSION ACCOMP-LISHED.

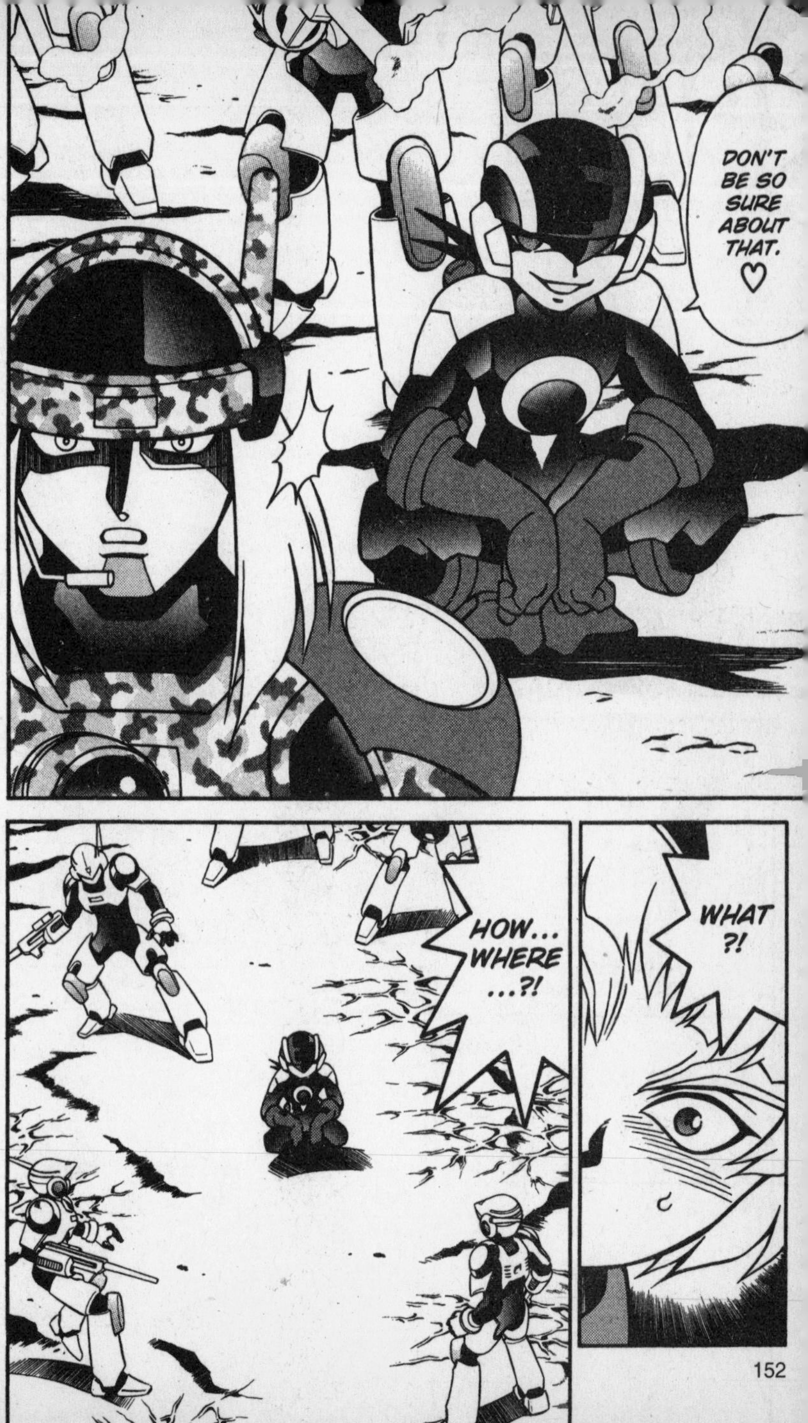
DON'T BE SO SURE ABOUT THAT. ♡
WHAT ?!
HOW... WHERE ...?!

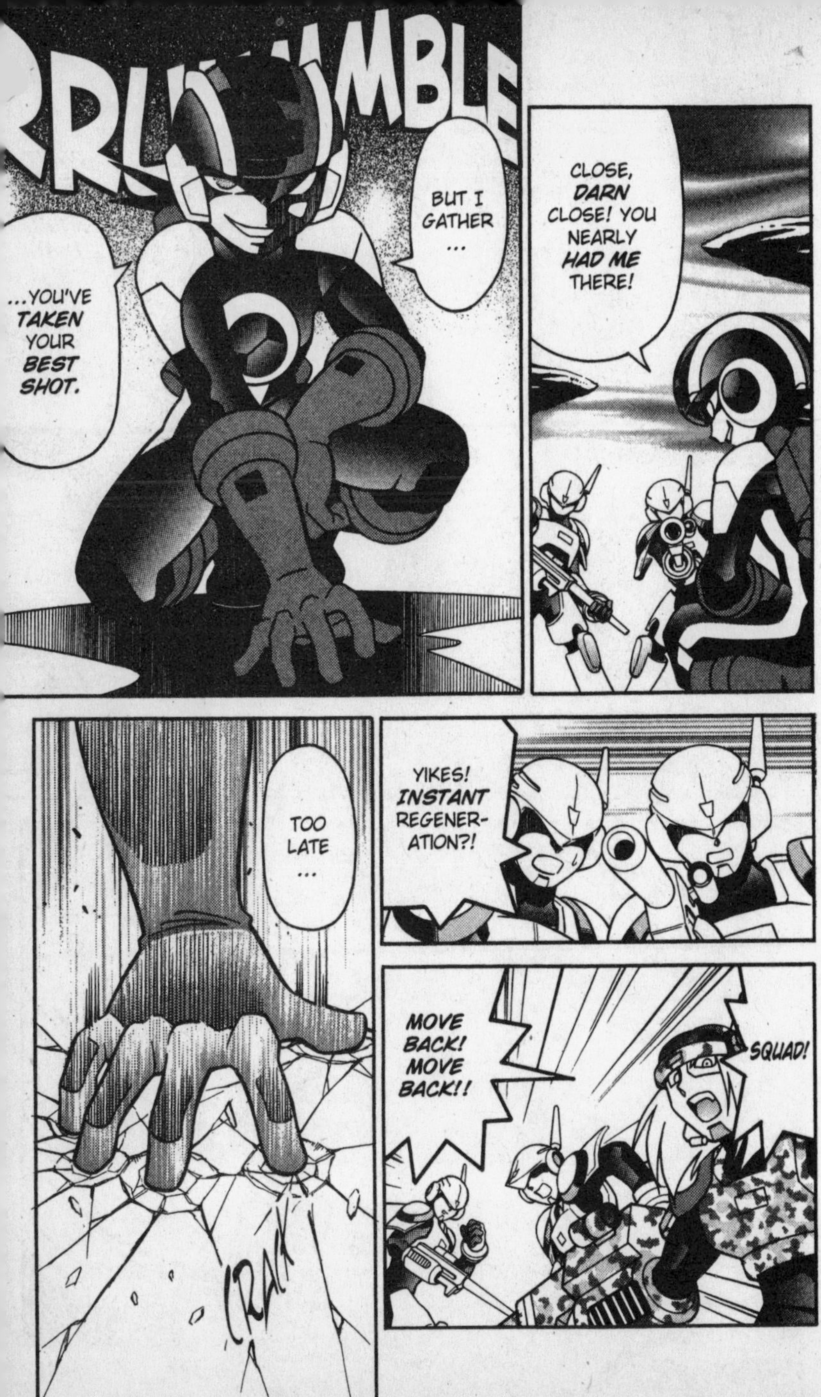
CLOSE, DARN CLOSE! YOU NEARLY HAD ME THERE!
RRU MBLE
BUT I GATHER ...
...YOU'VE TAKEN YOUR BEST SHOT.
YIKES! INSTANT REGENER-ATION?!
SQUAD!
MOVE BACK! MOVE BACK!!
TOO LATE ...
CRACK

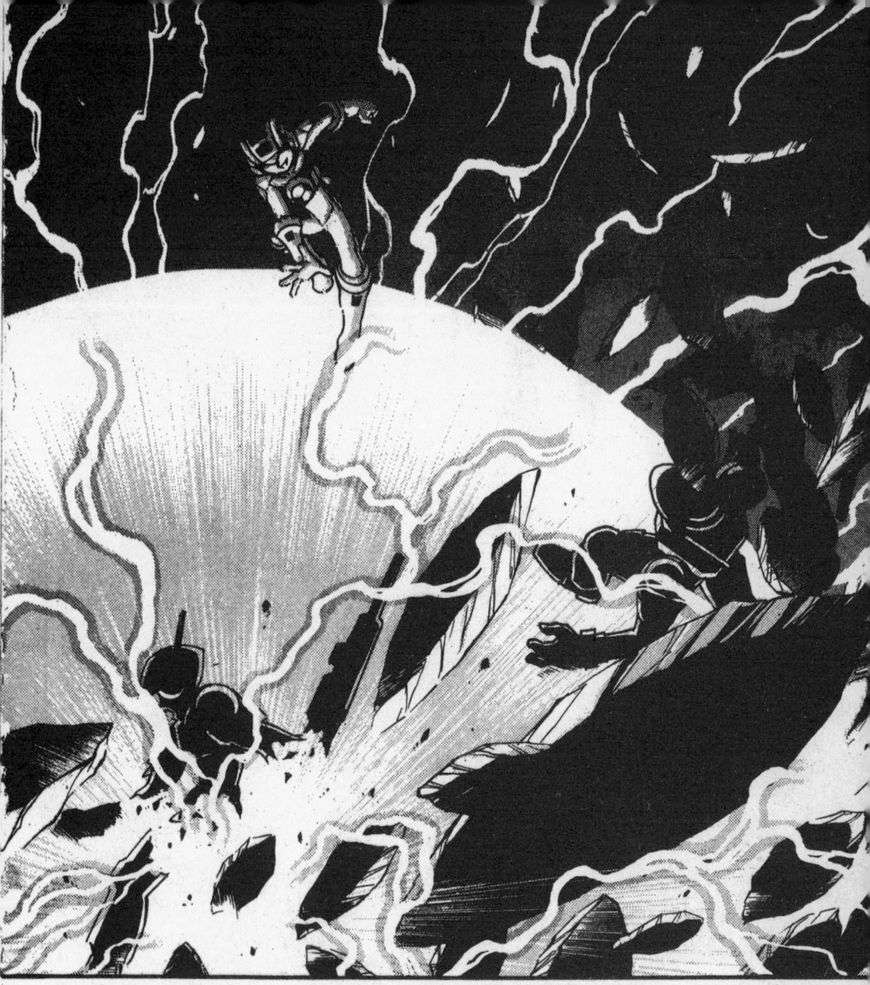

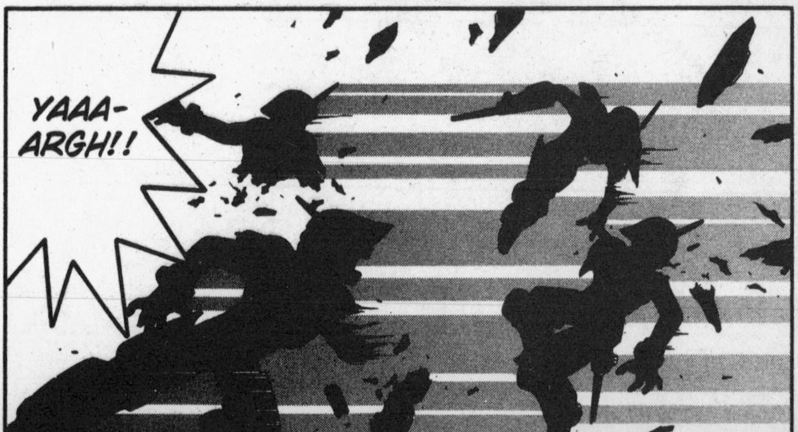
YAAA-
ARGH!!

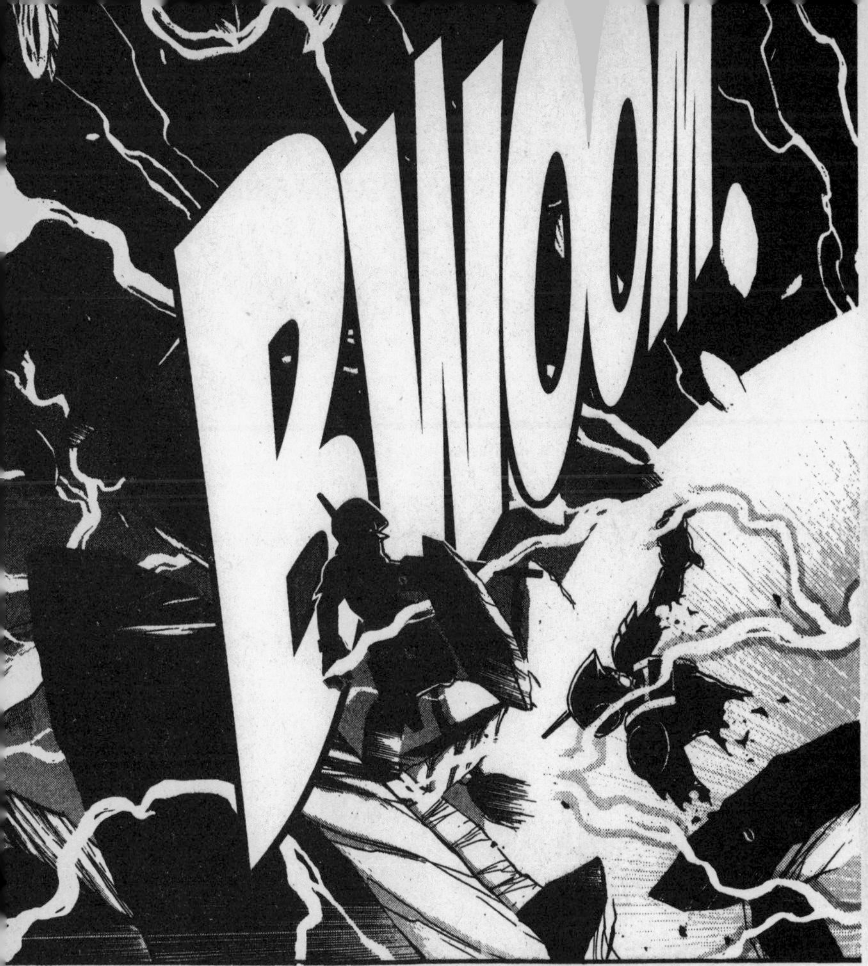
BWOOM!

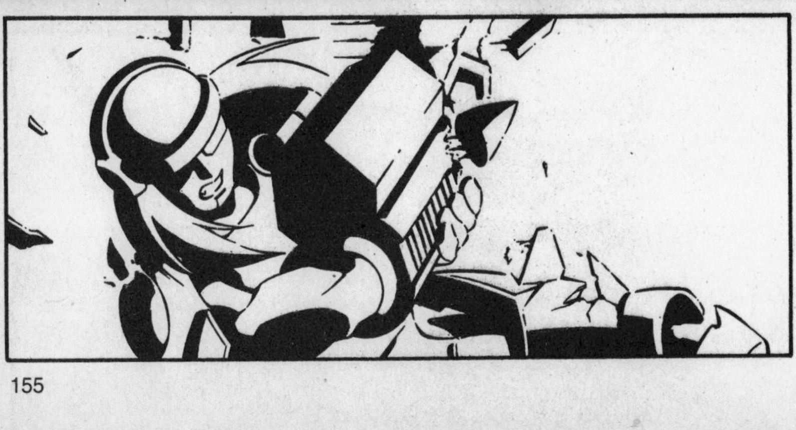

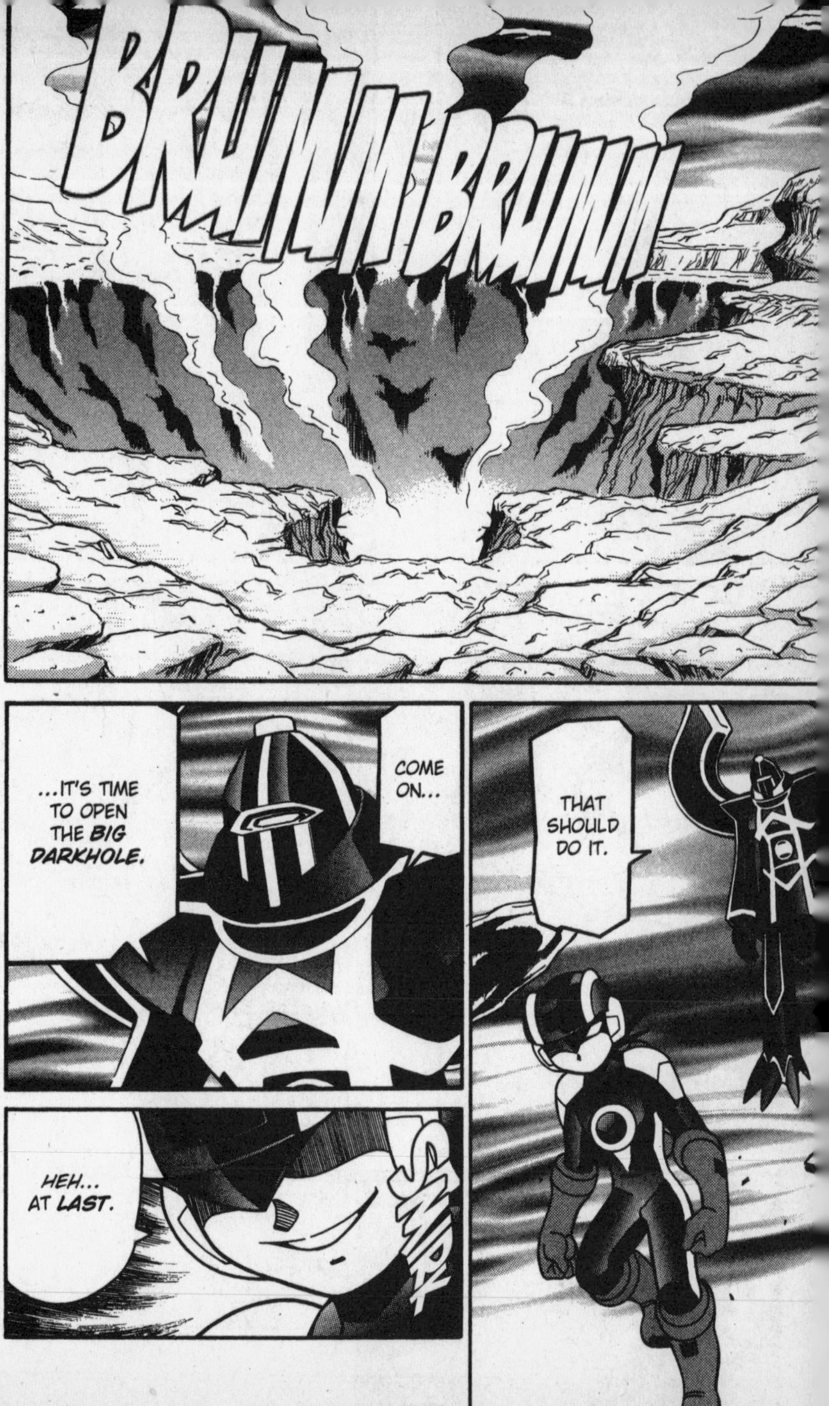
BRUMM BRUMM
THAT SHOULD DO IT.
COME ON...
...IT'S TIME TO OPEN THE BIG DARKHOLE.
SMIRK
HEH... AT LAST.

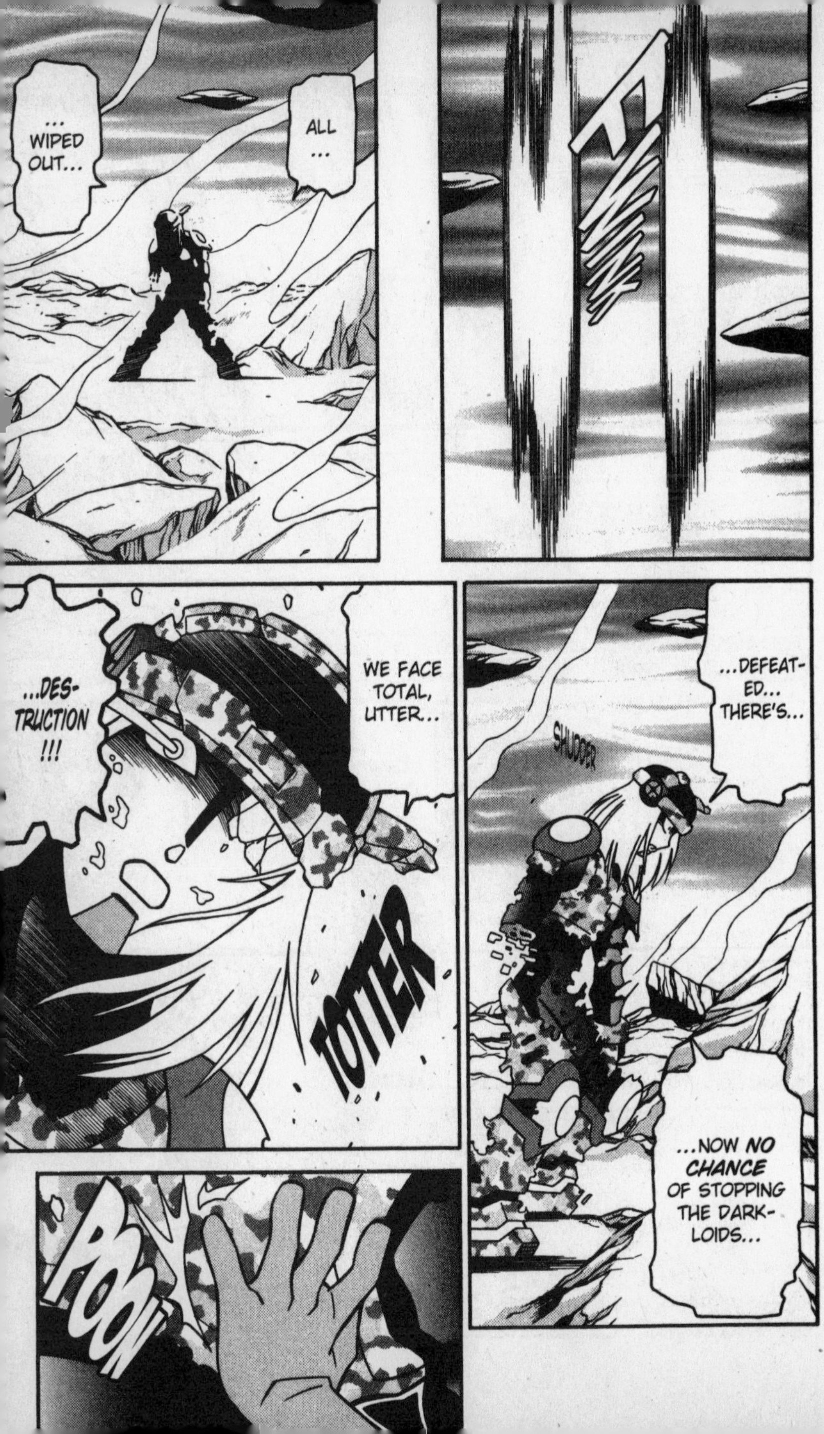
ALL ...
... WIPED OUT...
...DEFEAT-ED... THERE'S...
SHUDDER
...NOW NO CHANCE OF STOPPING THE DARK-LOIDS...
WE FACE TOTAL, UTTER...
...DES-TRUCTION !!!
TOTTER

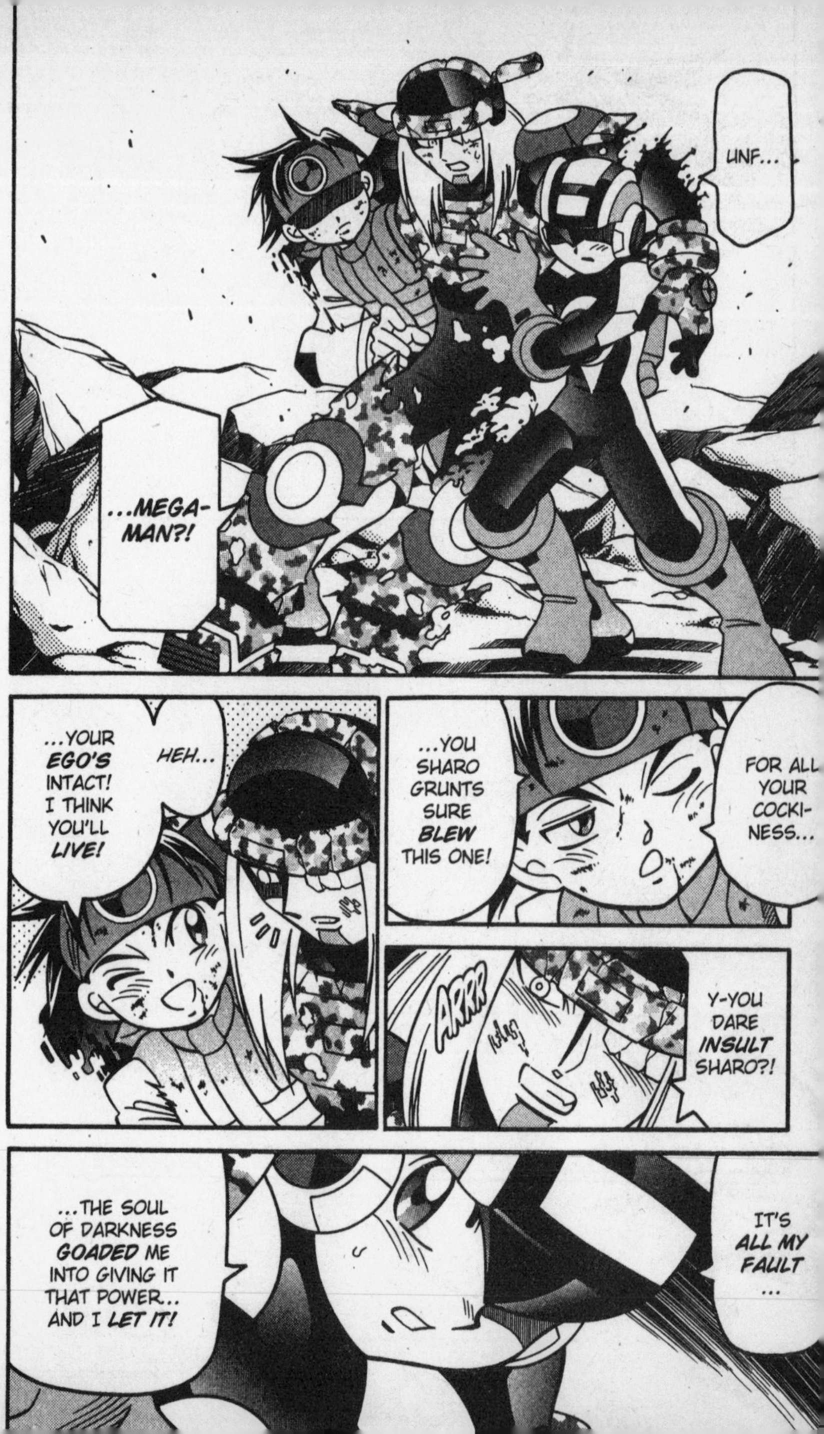
UNF...
...MEGA-MAN?!
FOR ALL YOUR COCKINESS...
...YOU SHARO GRUNTS SURE BLEW THIS ONE!
ARRR
Y-YOU DARE INSULT SHARO?!
HEH...
...YOUR EGO'S INTACT! I THINK YOU'LL LIVE!
IT'S ALL MY FAULT...
...THE SOUL OF DARKNESS GOADED ME INTO GIVING IT THAT POWER... AND I LET IT!

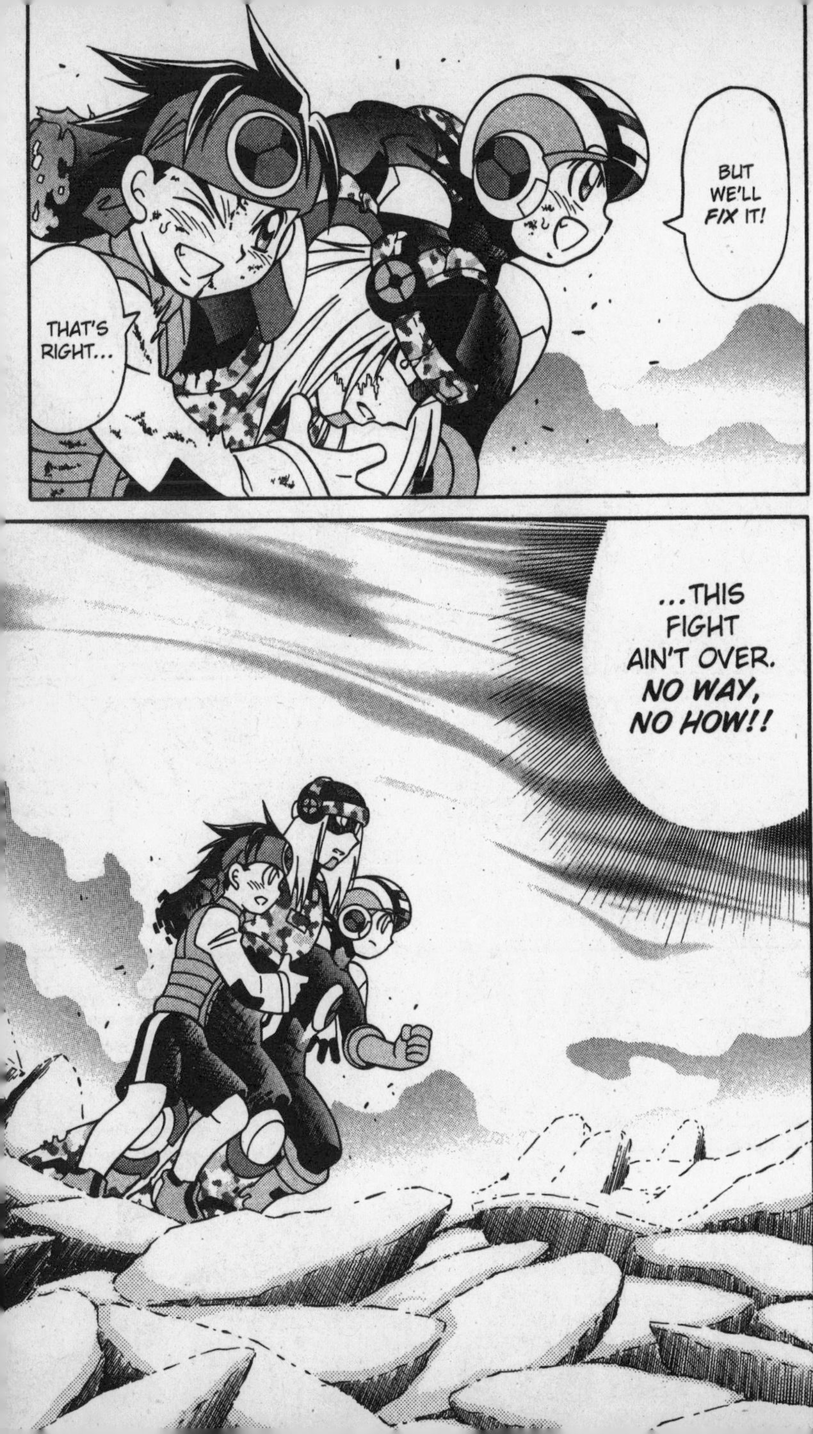
BUT WE'LL *FIX* IT!
THAT'S RIGHT...
...THIS FIGHT AIN'T OVER. ***NO WAY, NO HOW!!***

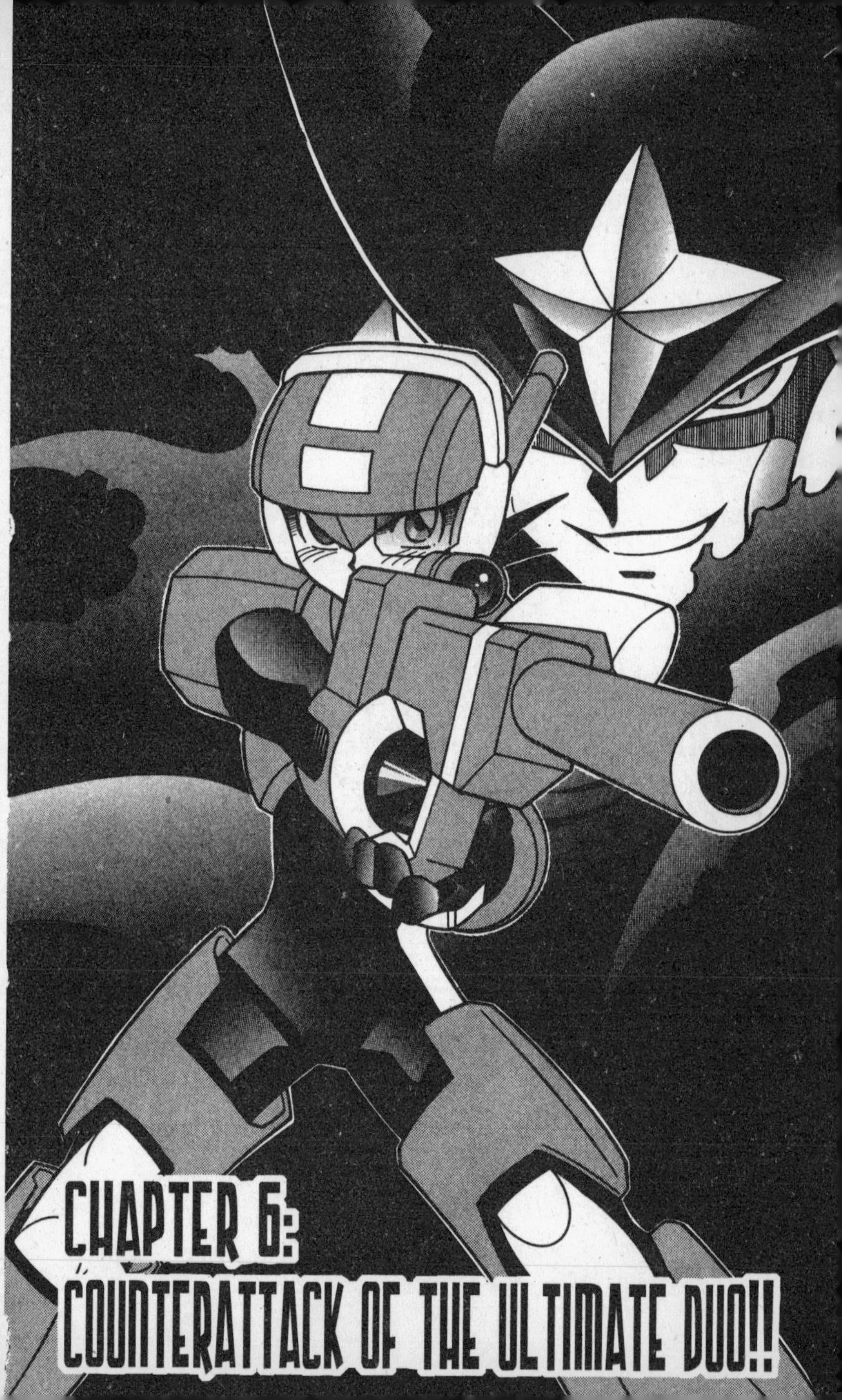
CHAPTER 6:
COUNTERATTACK OF THE ULTIMATE DUO!!

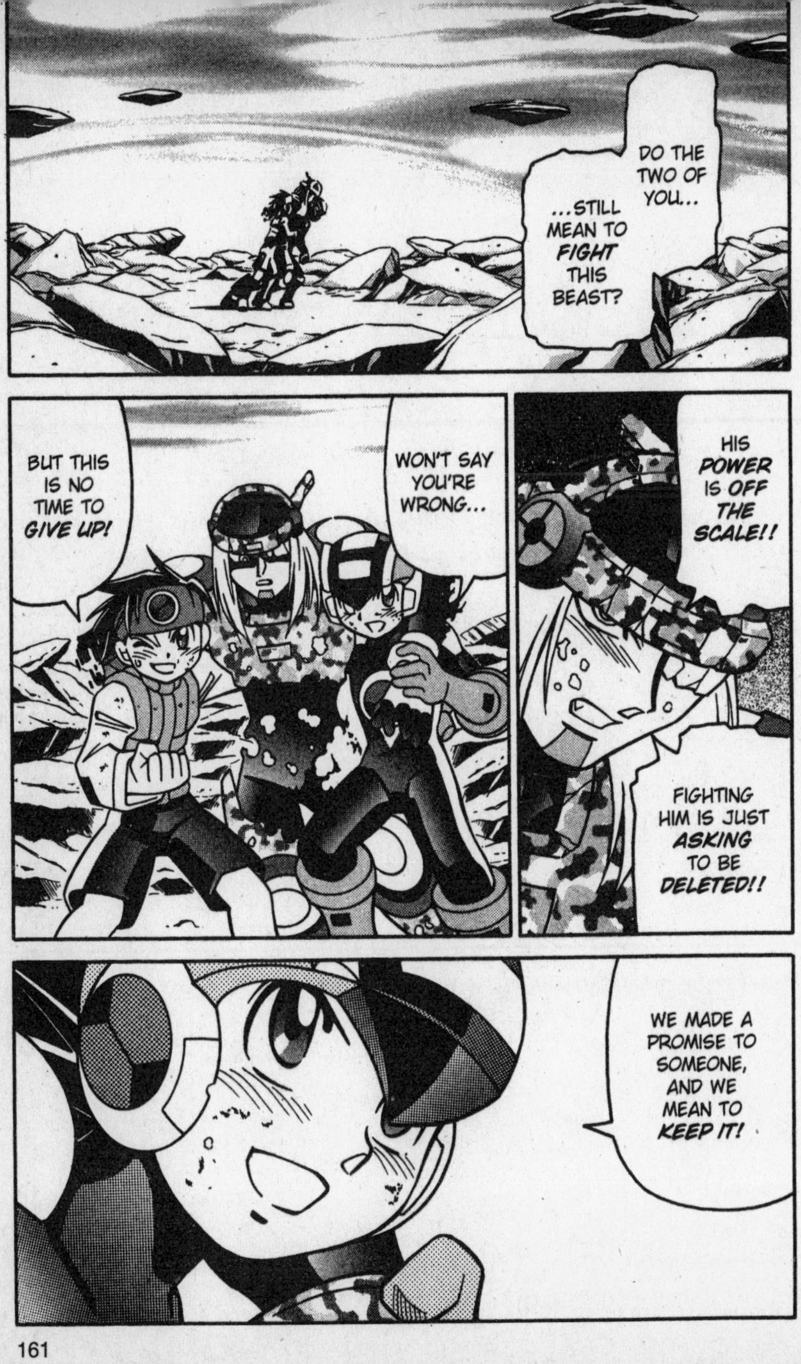
DO THE TWO OF YOU...
...STILL MEAN TO **FIGHT** THIS BEAST?
HIS **POWER** IS **OFF THE SCALE!!**
FIGHTING HIM IS JUST **ASKING** TO BE **DELETED!!**
WON'T SAY YOU'RE WRONG...
BUT THIS IS NO TIME TO **GIVE UP!**
WE MADE A PROMISE TO SOMEONE, AND WE MEAN TO **KEEP IT!**

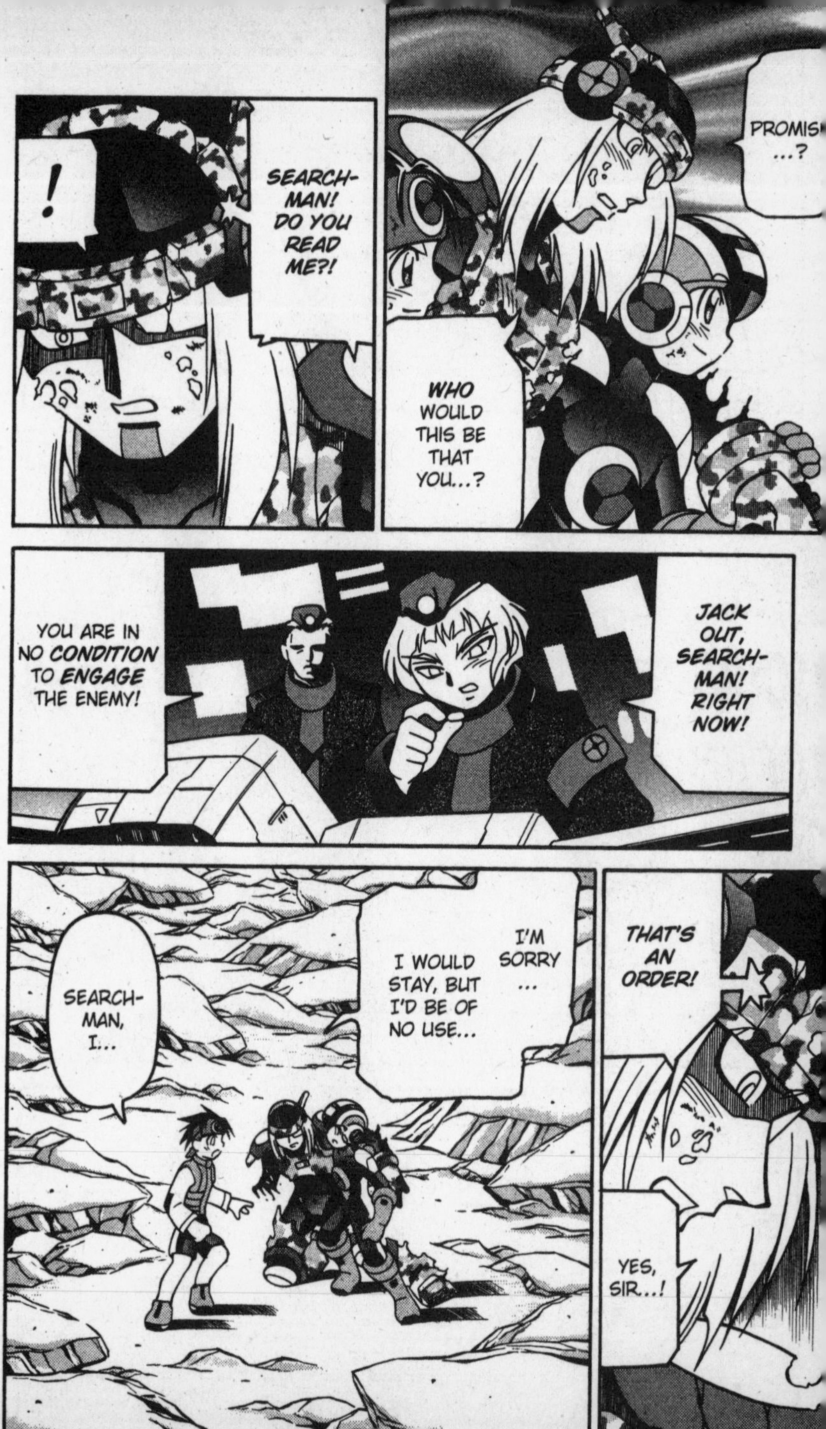
PROMIS ...?
WHO WOULD THIS BE THAT YOU...?
!
SEARCH-MAN! DO YOU READ ME?!
JACK OUT, SEARCH-MAN! RIGHT NOW!
YOU ARE IN NO CONDITION TO ENGAGE THE ENEMY!
THAT'S AN ORDER!
YES, SIR...!
I'M SORRY...
I WOULD STAY, BUT I'D BE OF NO USE...
SEARCH-MAN, I...

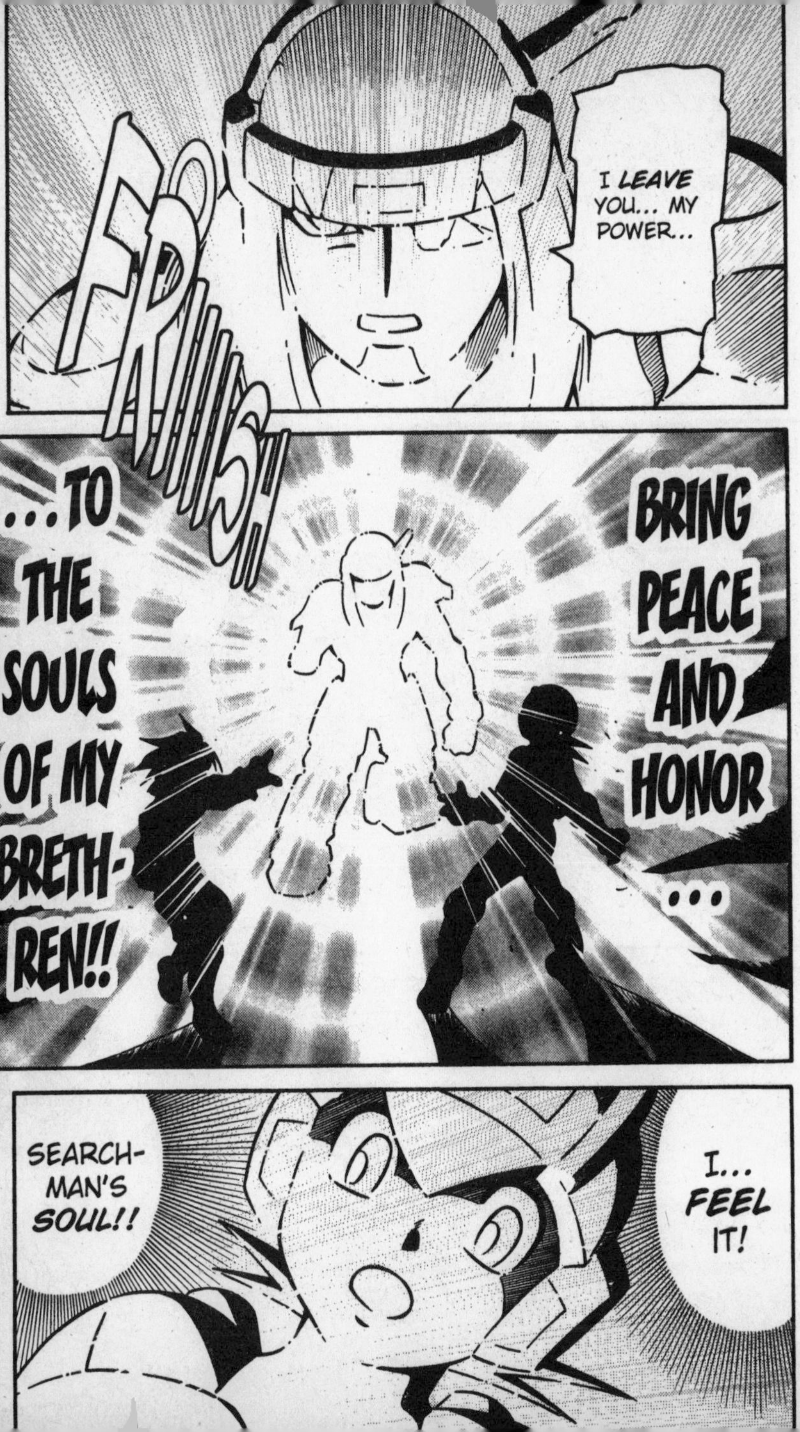
I LEAVE YOU... MY POWER...
FRIIISH!
BRING PEACE AND HONOR...
...TO THE SOULS OF MY BRETH-REN!!
I... FEEL IT!
SEARCH-MAN'S SOUL!!

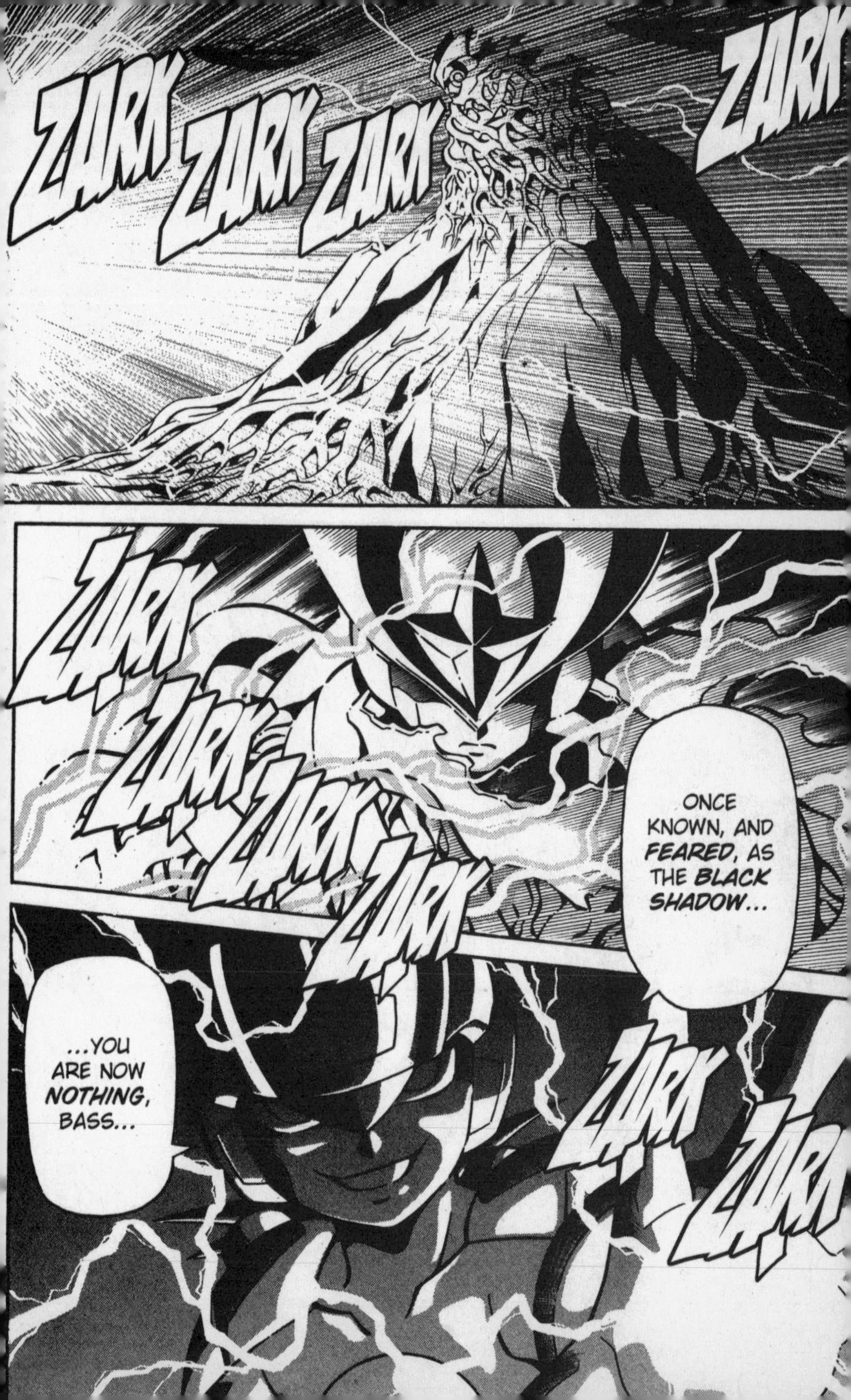
ZARK
ZARK ZARK ZARK
ZARK ZARK ZARK ZARK
ONCE KNOWN, AND FEARED, AS THE BLACK SHADOW...
...YOU ARE NOW NOTHING, BASS...
ZARK ZARK

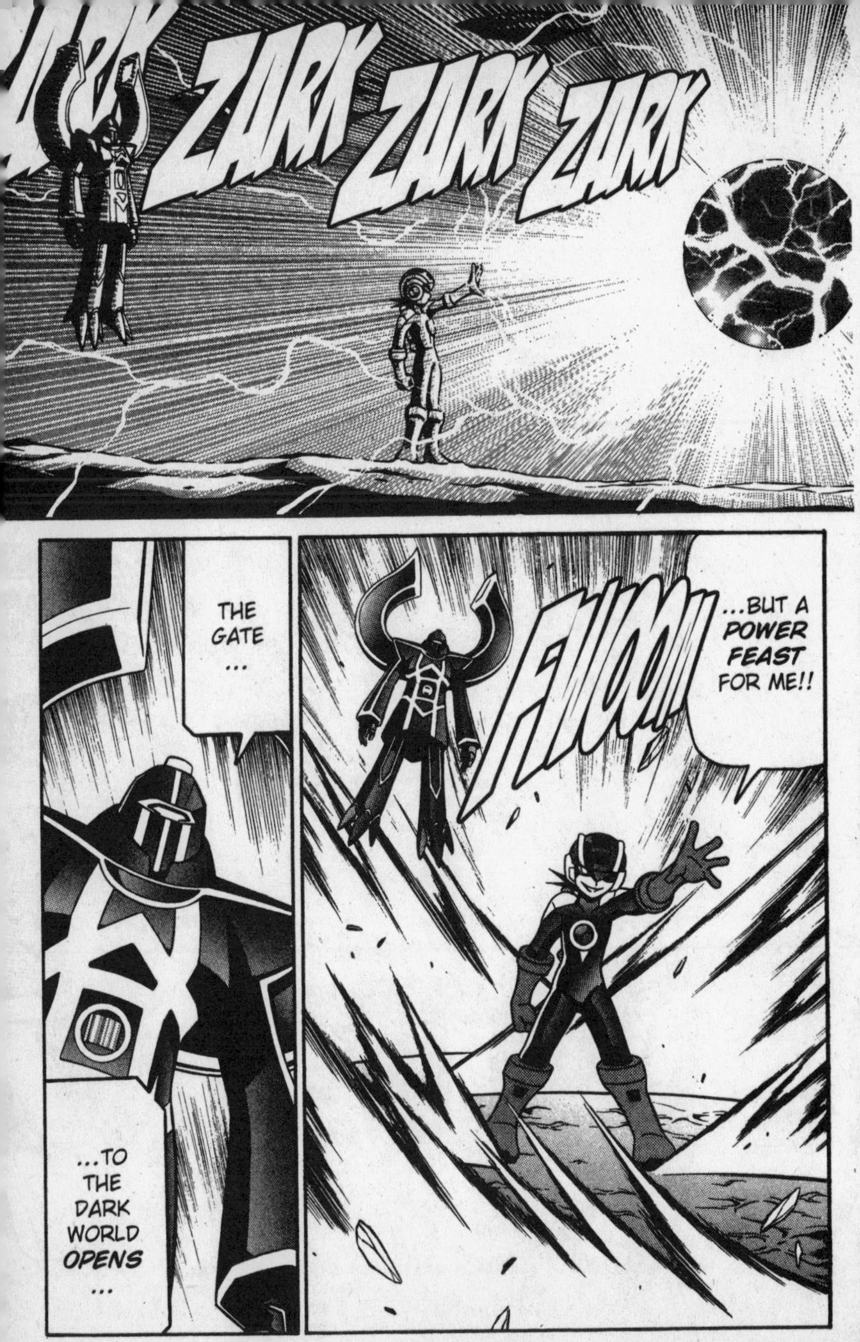
ZARK ZARK ZARK
FWOOM!!
...BUT A POWER FEAST FOR ME!!
THE GATE ...
...TO THE DARK WORLD OPENS ...

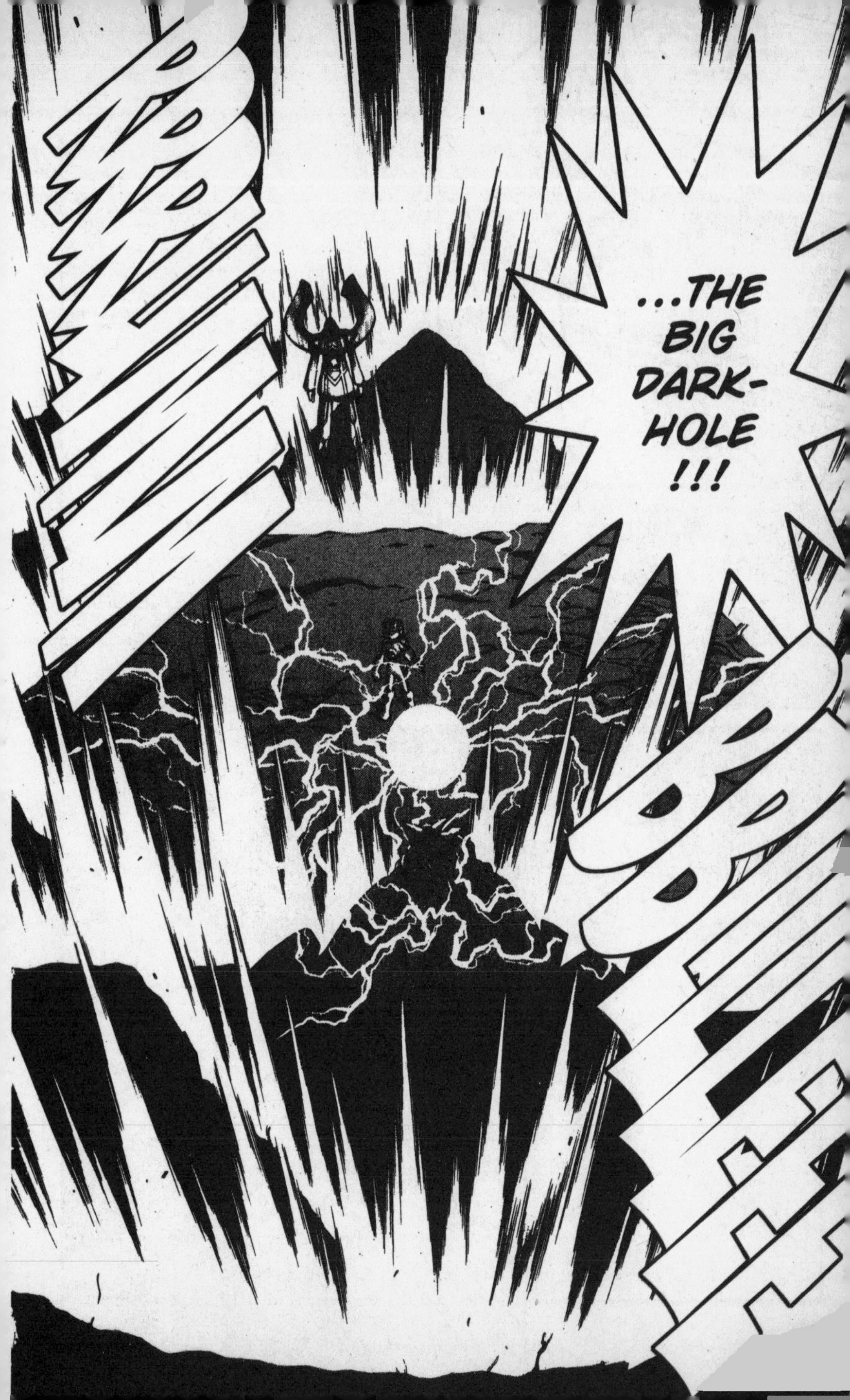
...THE BIG DARK-HOLE !!!

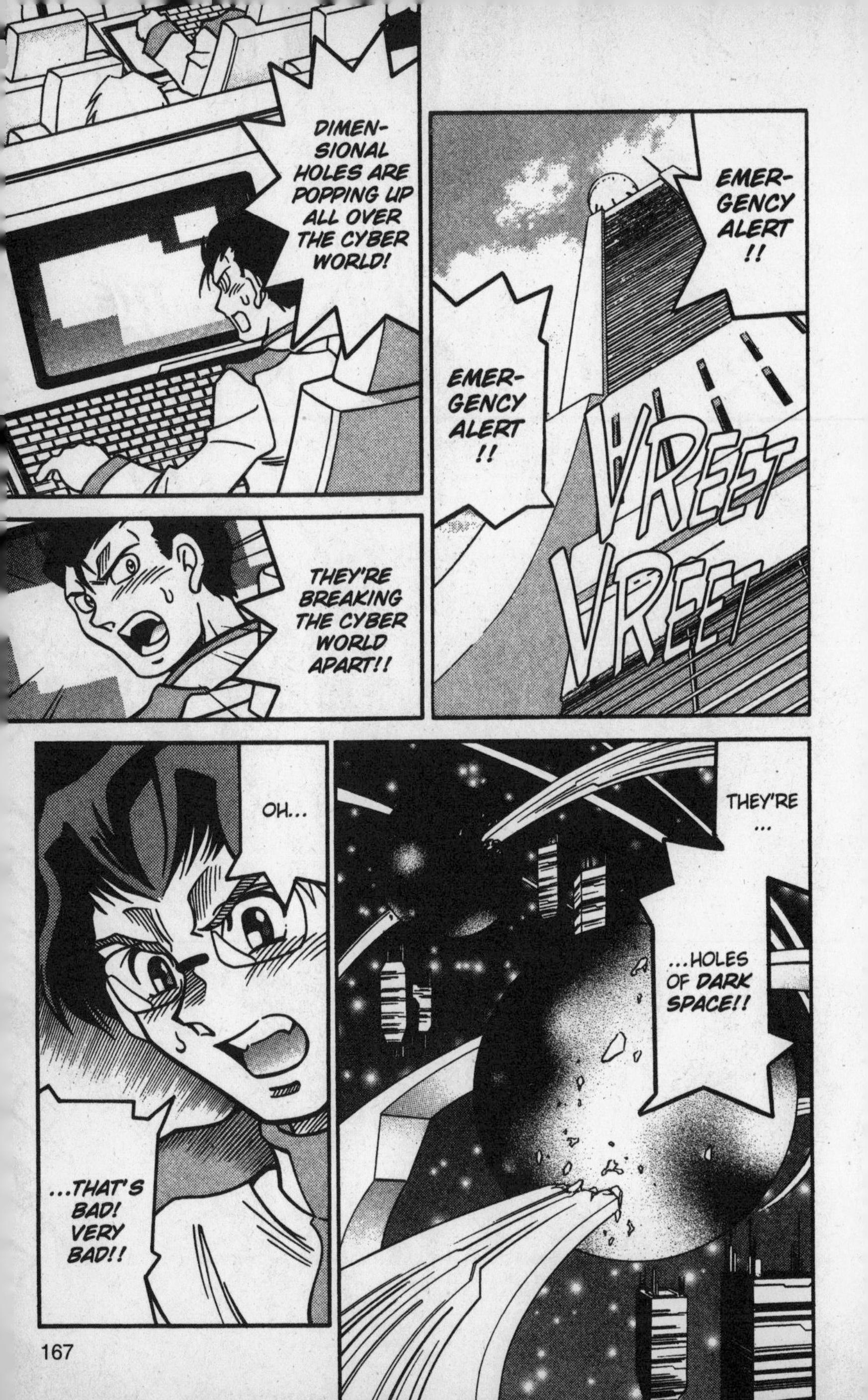
EMERGENCY ALERT!!
EMERGENCY ALERT!!
VREET VREET
DIMENSIONAL HOLES ARE POPPING UP ALL OVER THE CYBER WORLD!
THEY'RE BREAKING THE CYBER WORLD APART!!
THEY'RE...
...HOLES OF DARK SPACE!!
OH...
...THAT'S BAD! VERY BAD!!

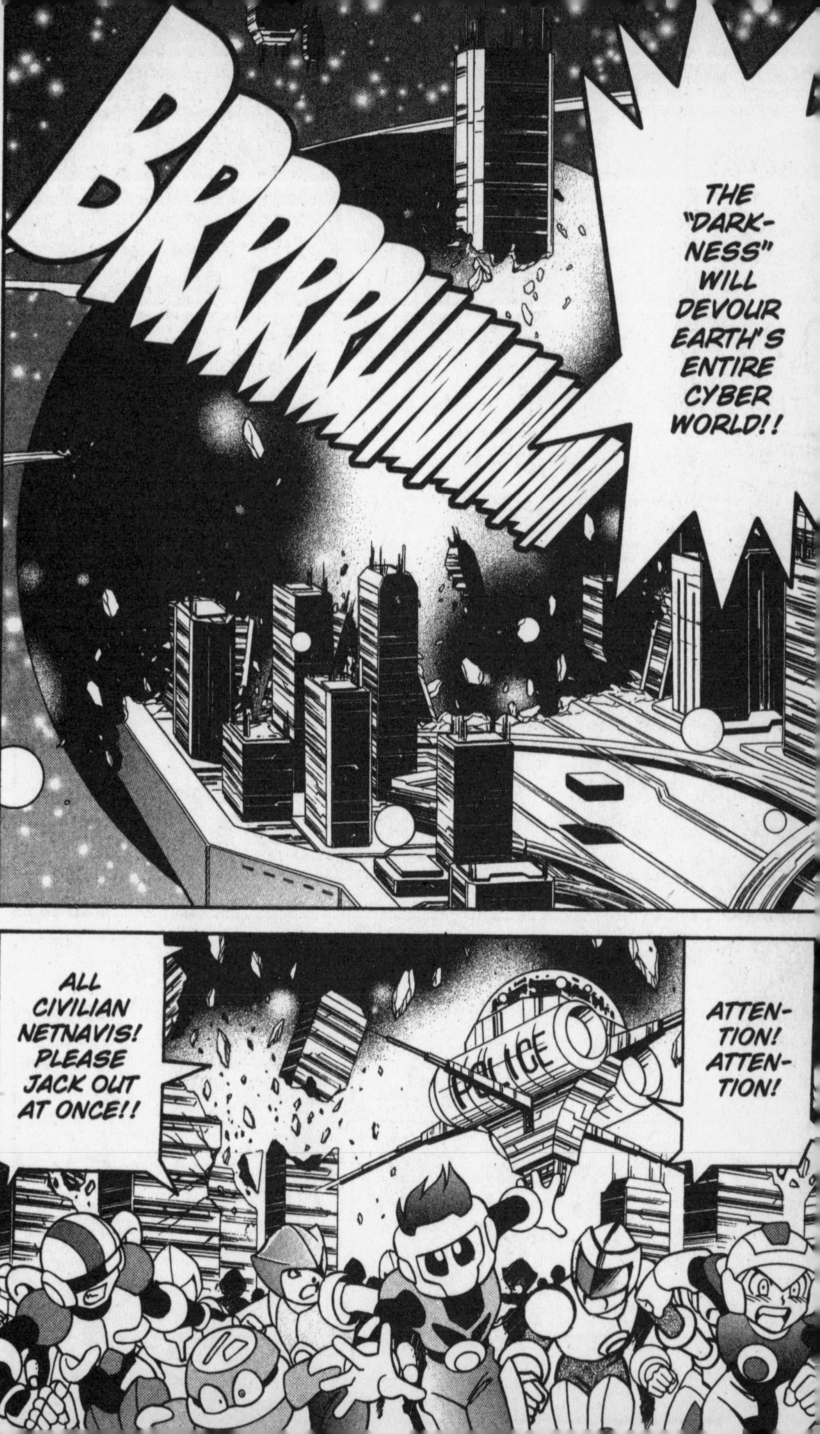
THE "DARKNESS" WILL DEVOUR EARTH'S ENTIRE CYBER WORLD!!
BRRRUMMMMM
ATTENTION! ATTENTION!
ALL CIVILIAN NETNAVIS! PLEASE JACK OUT AT ONCE!!
POLICE

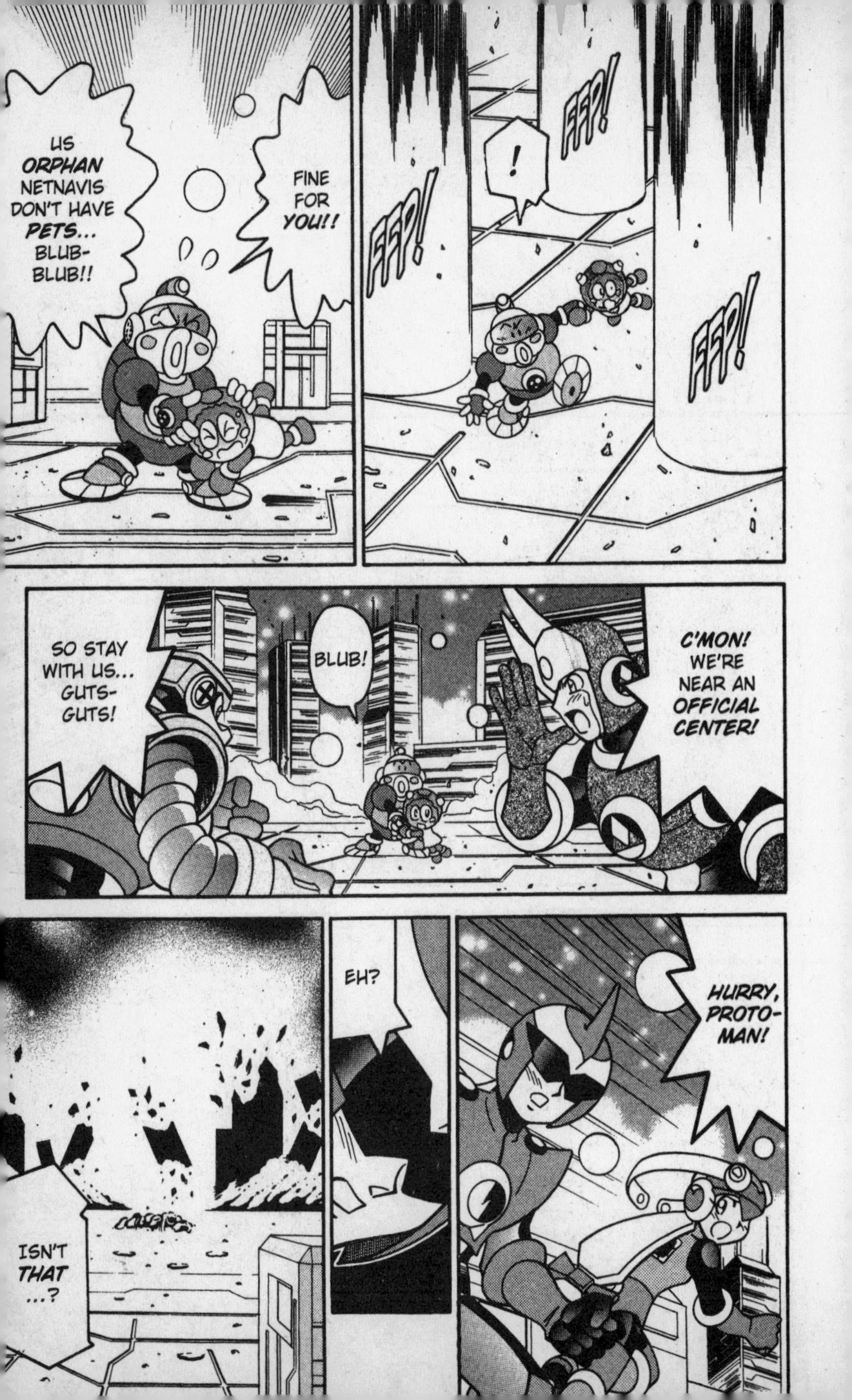
FFP!
!
FFP!
FFP!
FINE FOR YOU!!
US ORPHAN NETNAVIS DON'T HAVE PETS... BLUB-BLUB!!
C'MON! WE'RE NEAR AN OFFICIAL CENTER!
BLUB!
SO STAY WITH US... GUTS-GUTS!
HURRY, PROTO-MAN!
EH?
ISN'T THAT ...?

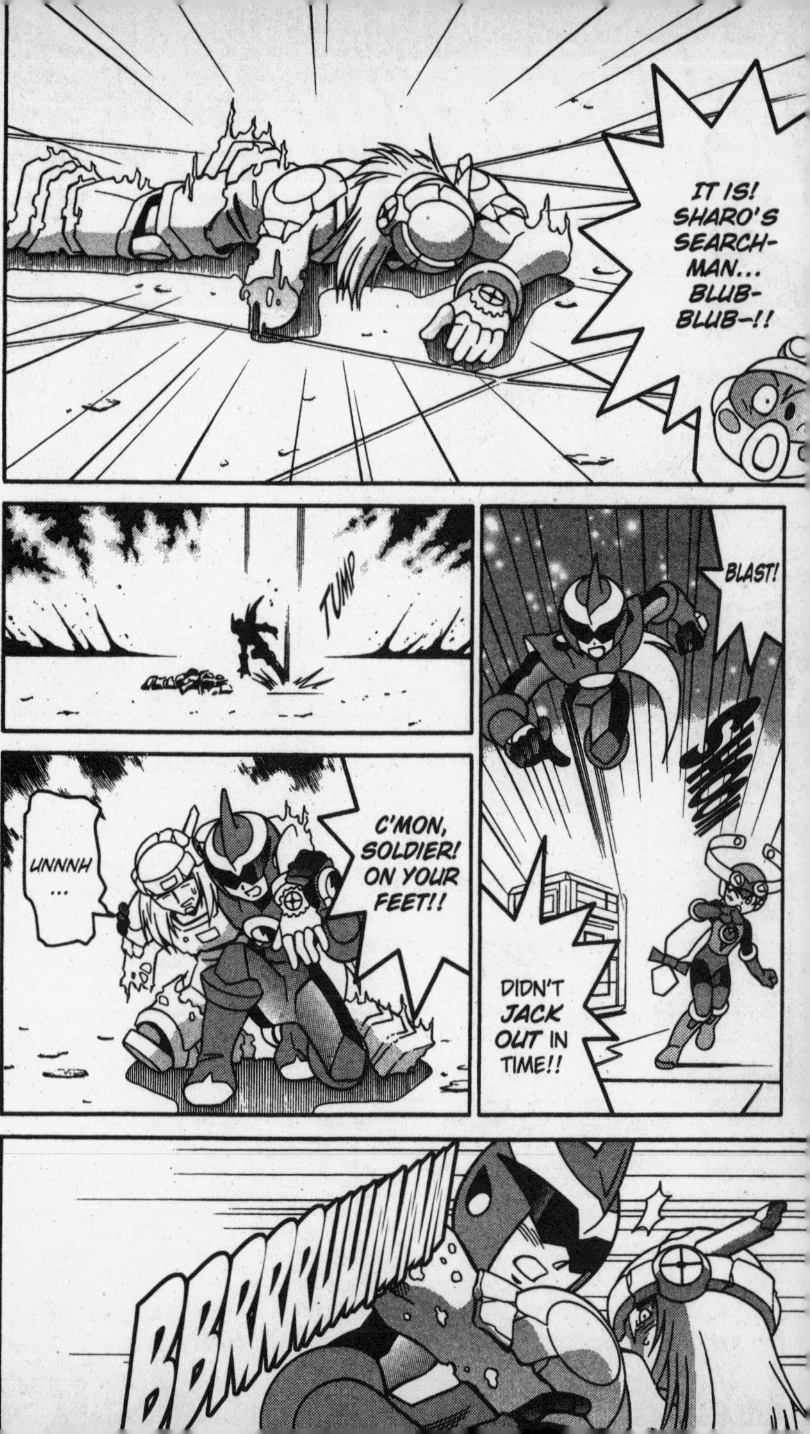

IT IS! SHARO'S SEARCH-MAN... BLUB-BLUB-!!
BLAST!
DIDN'T JACK OUT IN TIME!!
TUMP
C'MON, SOLDIER! ON YOUR FEET!!
UNNNH ...

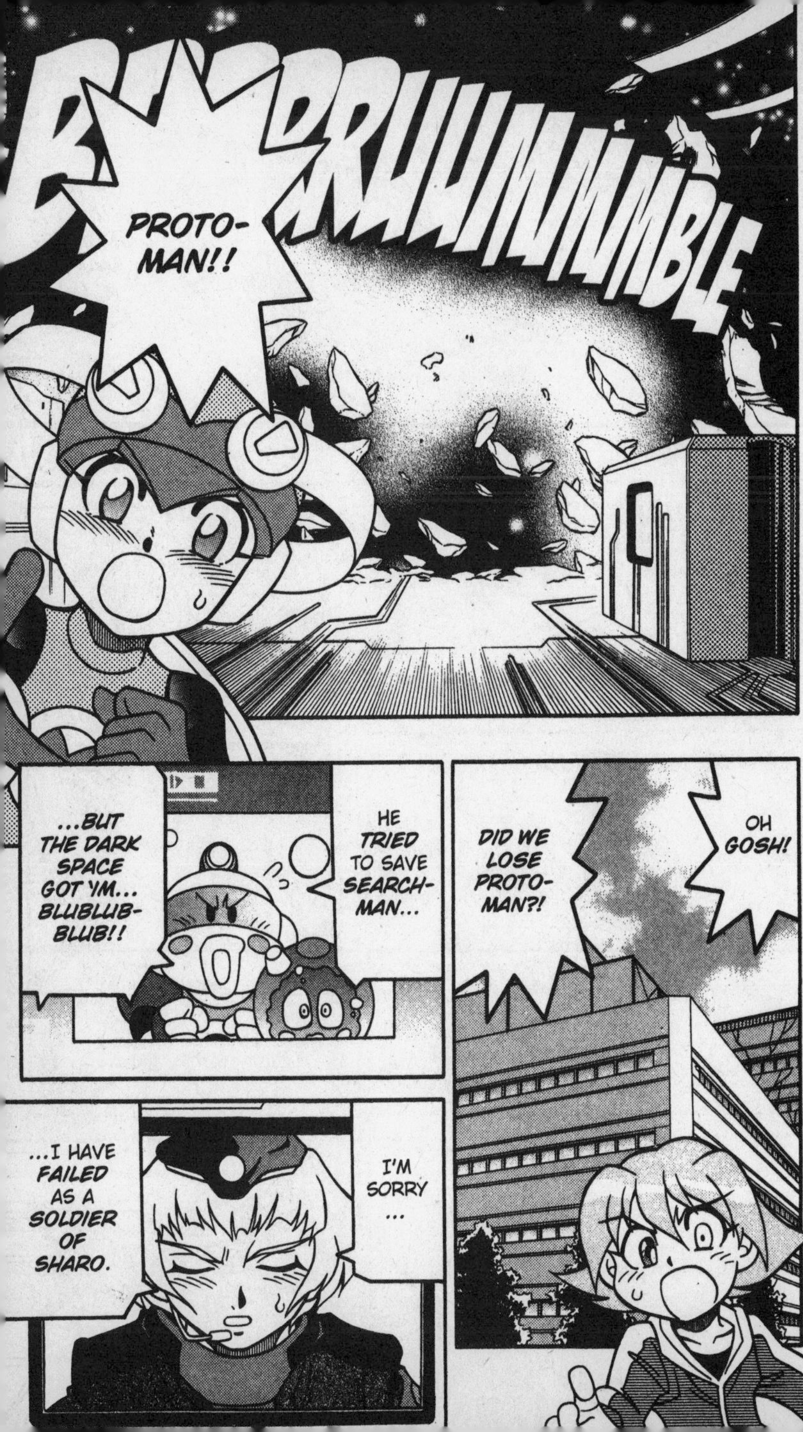
PROTO-MAN!!
OH GOSH!
DID WE LOSE PROTO-MAN?!
HE TRIED TO SAVE SEARCH-MAN...
...BUT THE DARK SPACE GOT 'YM... BLUBLUB-BLUB!!
I'M SORRY ...
...I HAVE FAILED AS A SOLDIER OF SHARO.

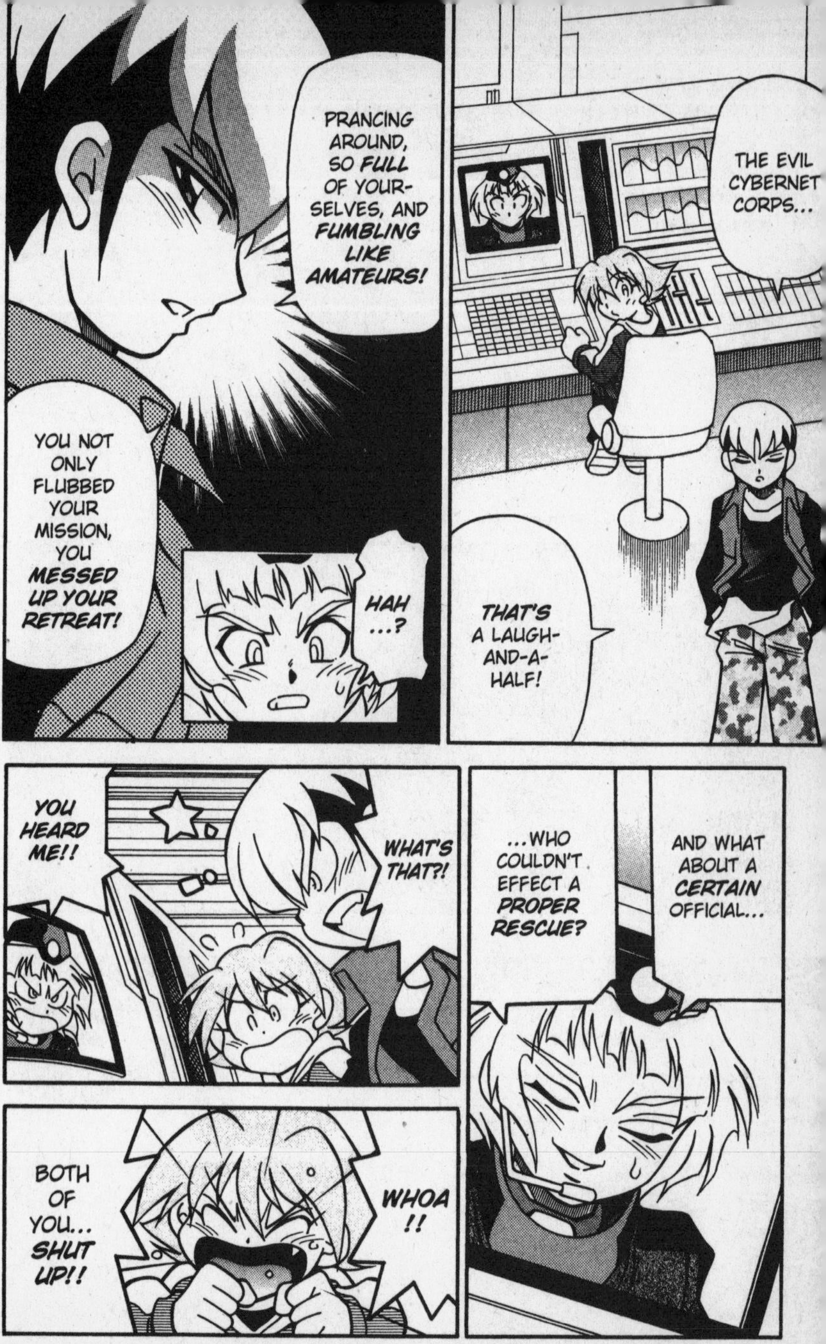
THE EVIL CYBERNET CORPS...
THAT'S A LAUGH-AND-A-HALF!
PRANCING AROUND, SO FULL OF YOURSELVES, AND FUMBLING LIKE AMATEURS!
YOU NOT ONLY FLUBBED YOUR MISSION, YOU MESSED UP YOUR RETREAT!
HAH ...?
AND WHAT ABOUT A CERTAIN OFFICIAL...
...WHO COULDN'T EFFECT A PROPER RESCUE?
WHAT'S THAT?!
YOU HEARD ME!!
WHOA !!
BOTH OF YOU... SHUT UP!!

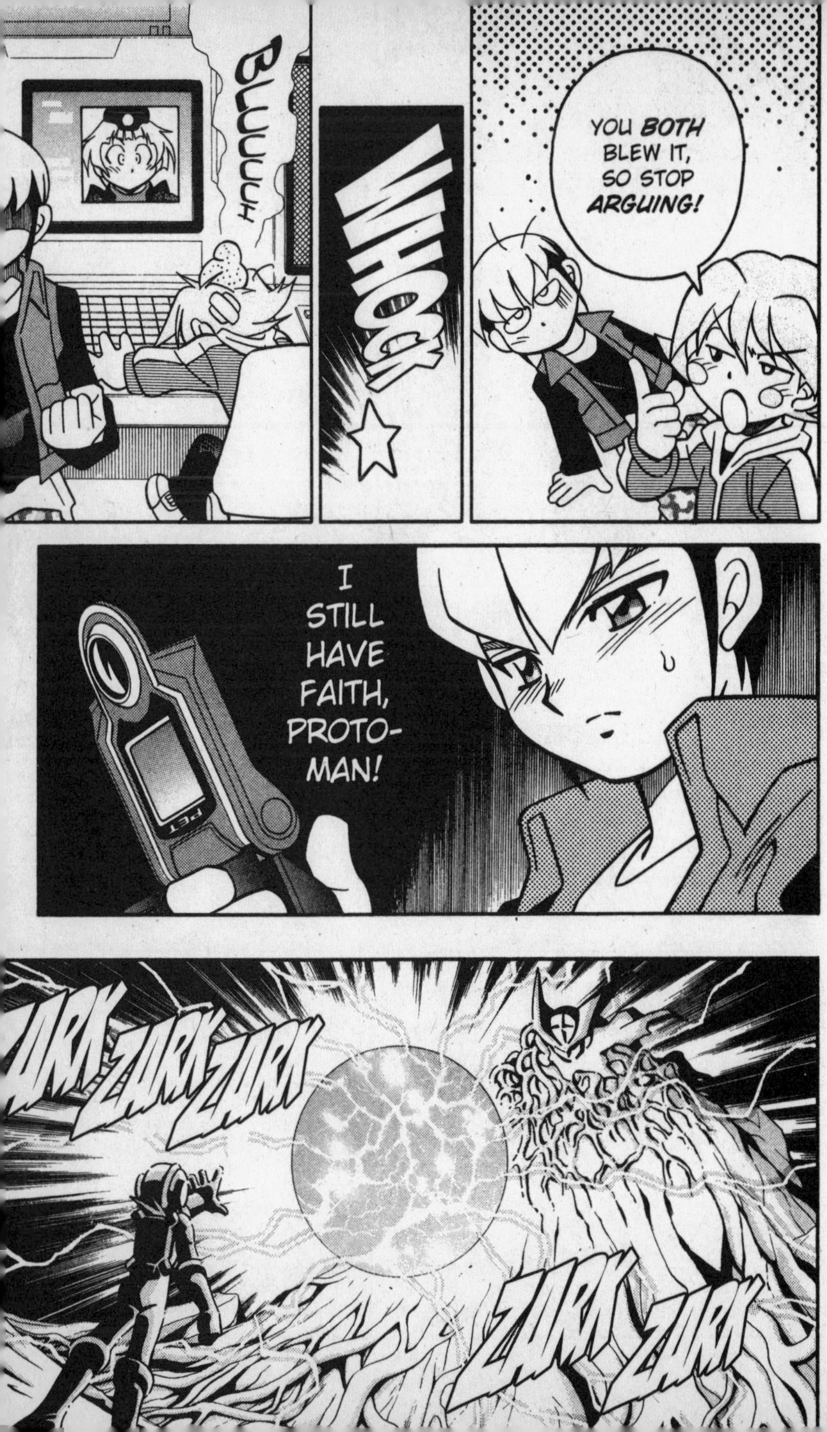
YOU BOTH BLEW IT, SO STOP ARGUING!
WHOCK!
BLUUUUUH
I STILL HAVE FAITH, PROTO-MAN!
PET
ZARK ZARK ZARK
ZARK ZARK

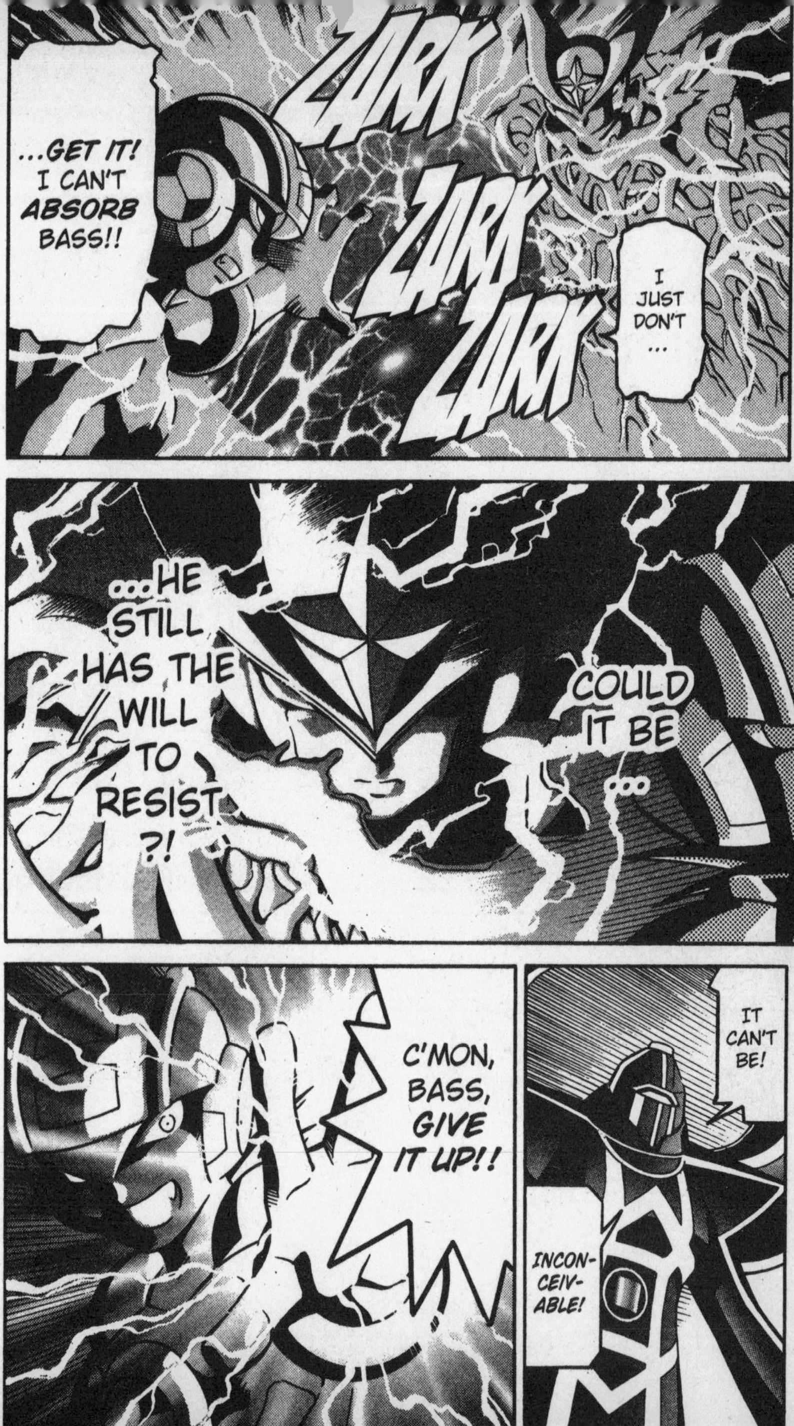
ZARK
I JUST DON'T ...
...GET IT! I CAN'T ABSORB BASS!!
ZARK ZARK ZARK
COULD IT BE ...
...HE STILL HAS THE WILL TO RESIST?!
IT CAN'T BE!
INCON-CEIV-ABLE!
C'MON, BASS, GIVE IT UP!!

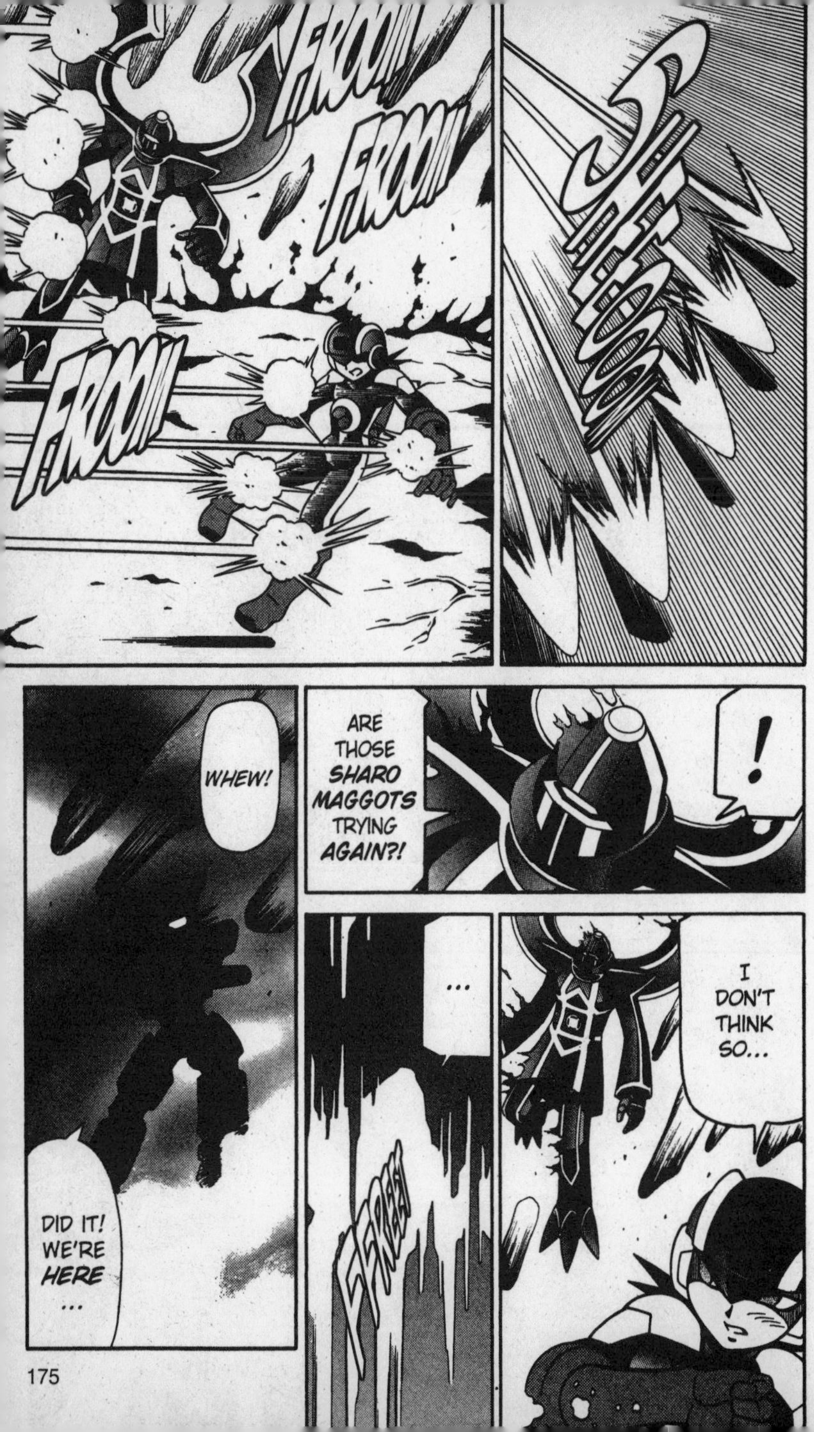
FROOM
FROOM
FROOM
!
ARE THOSE SHARO MAGGOTS TRYING AGAIN?!
I DON'T THINK SO...
...
WHEW!
DID IT! WE'RE HERE ...

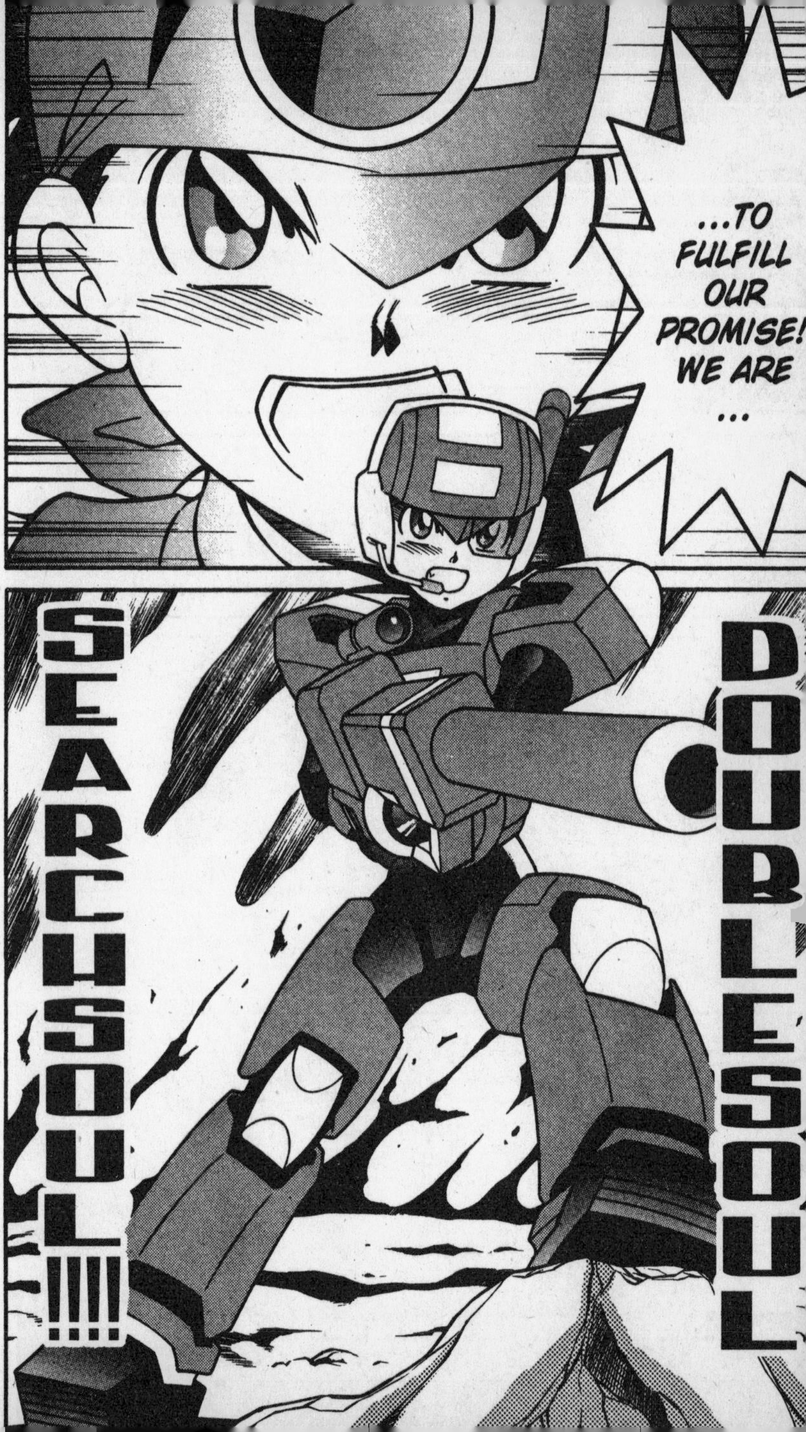

...TO FULFILL OUR PROMISE! WE ARE ...
DOUBLESOUL
SEARCHSOUL!!!!

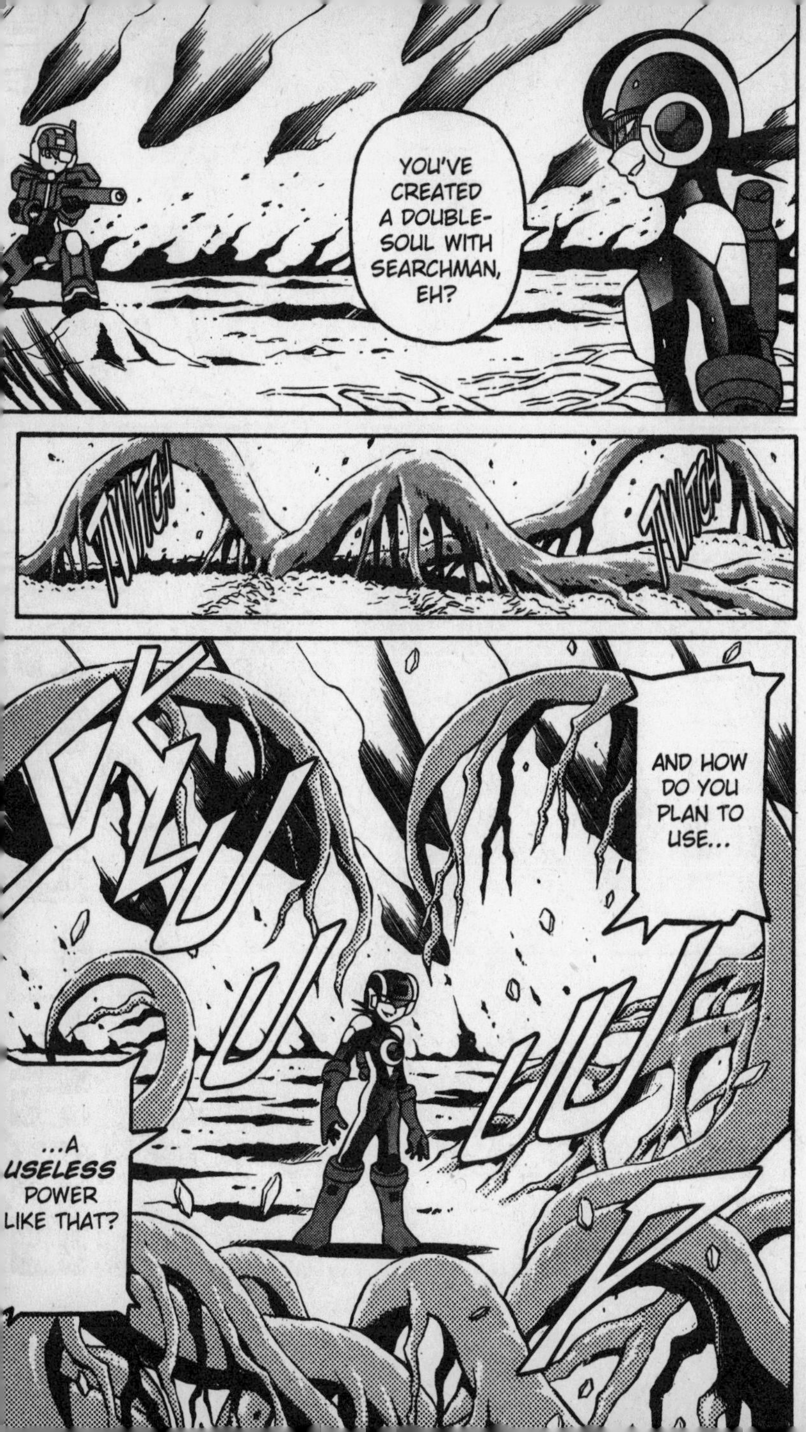
YOU'VE CREATED A DOUBLE-SOUL WITH SEARCHMAN, EH?
TWITCH!
TWITCH!
AND HOW DO YOU PLAN TO USE...
...A *USELESS* POWER LIKE THAT?

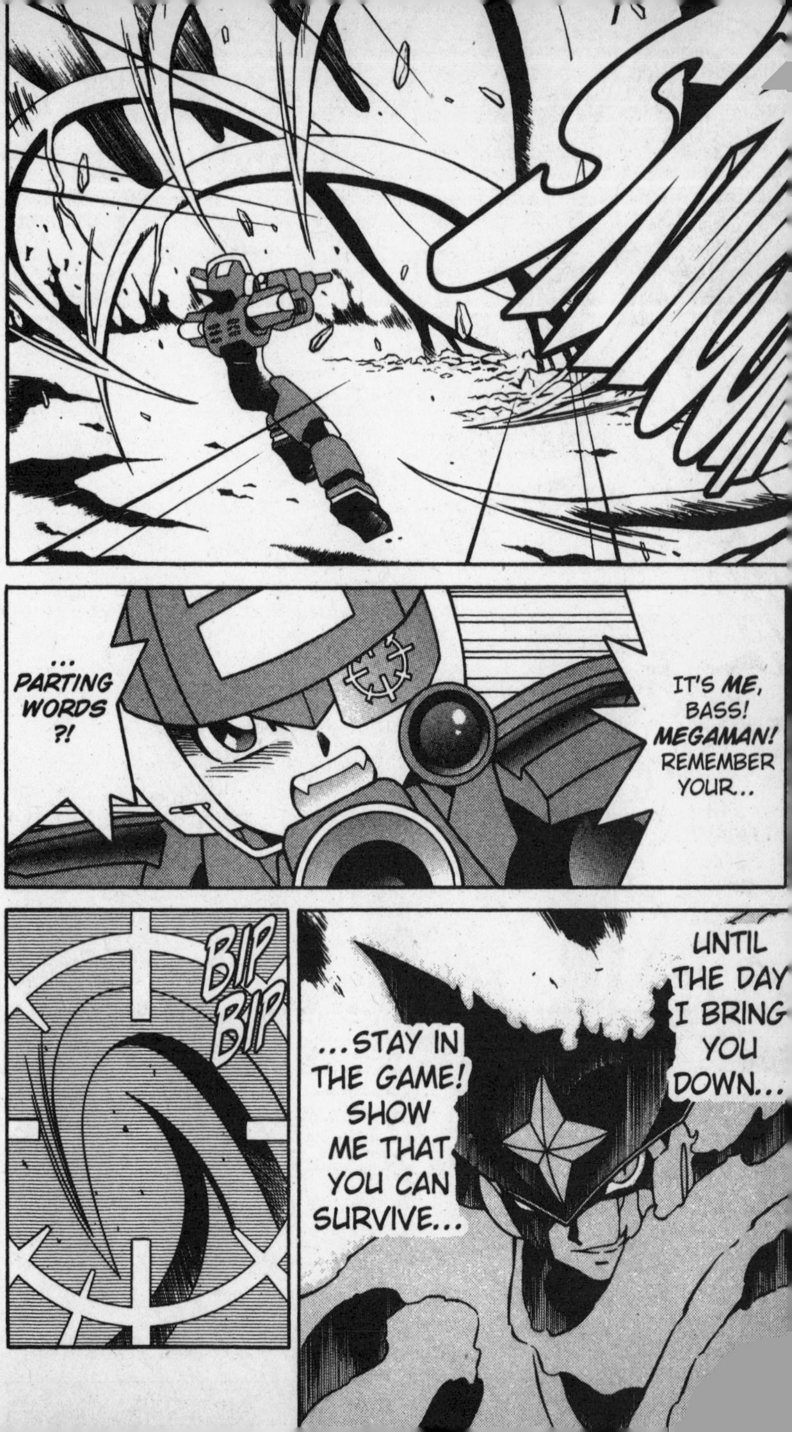
IT'S ME, BASS! MEGAMAN! REMEMBER YOUR...
... PARTING WORDS ?!
UNTIL THE DAY I BRING YOU DOWN...
...STAY IN THE GAME! SHOW ME THAT YOU CAN SURVIVE...
BIP BIP

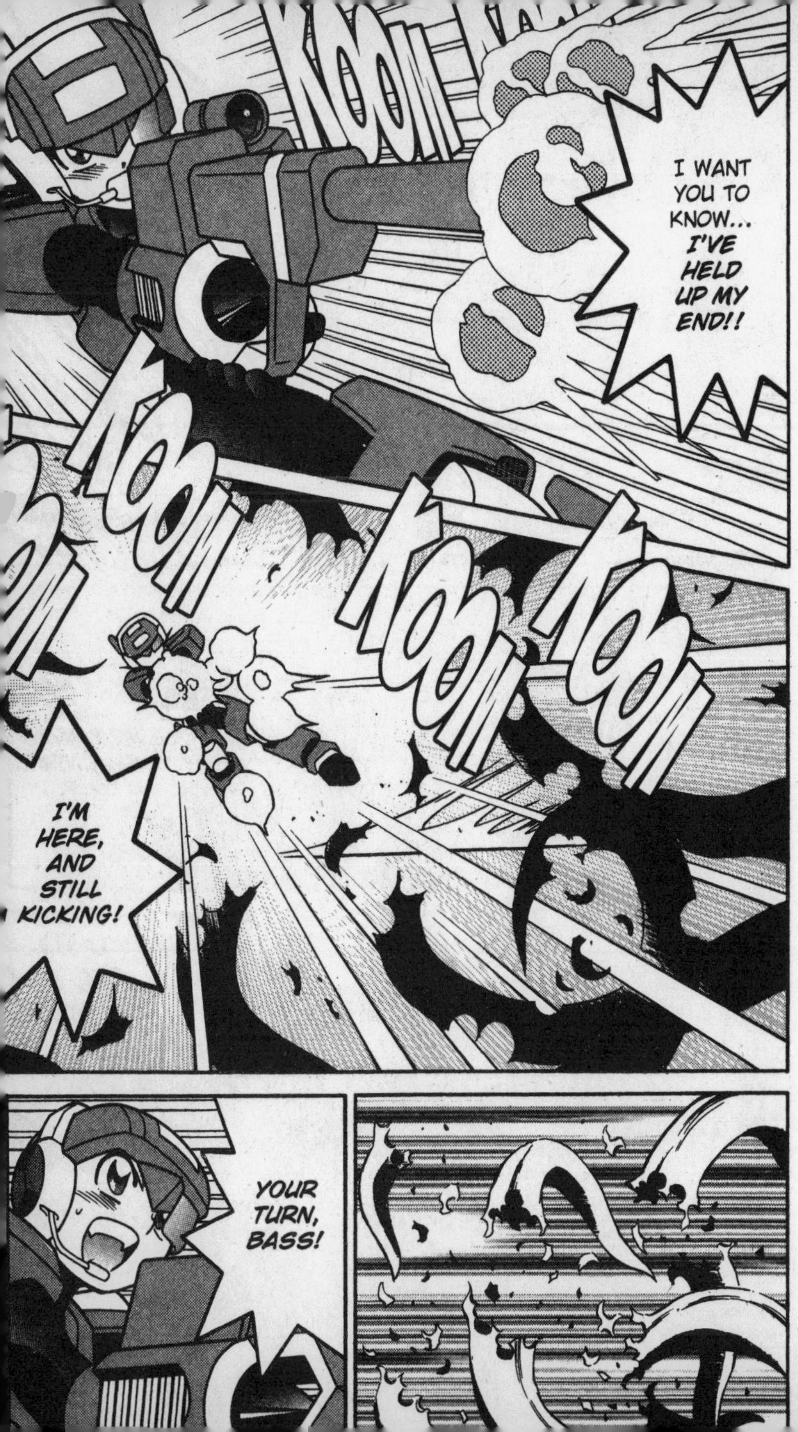
KOOOM
I WANT YOU TO KNOW... I'VE HELD UP MY END!!
KOOOM
KOOOM
KOOOM
KOOOM
I'M HERE, AND STILL KICKING!
YOUR TURN, BASS!

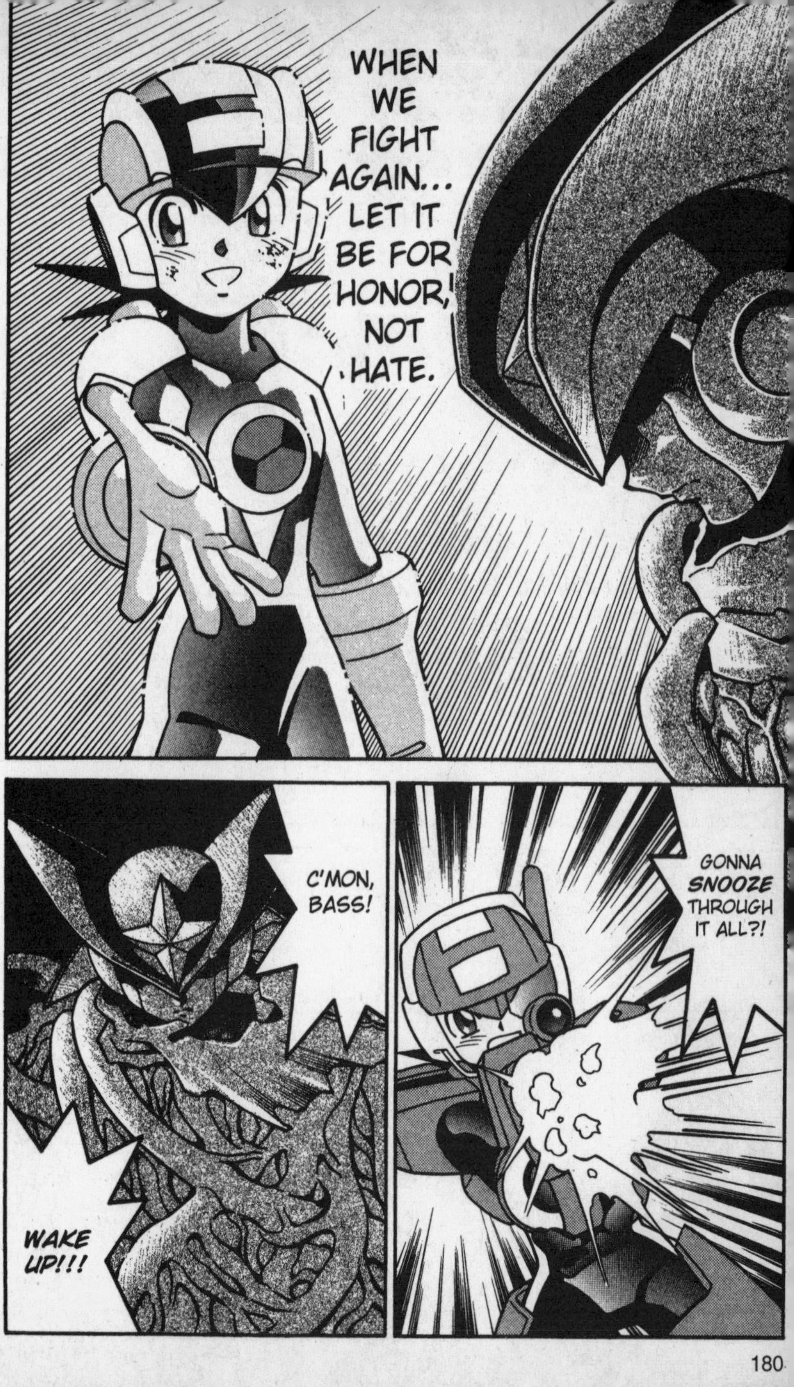
WHEN WE FIGHT AGAIN... LET IT BE FOR HONOR, NOT HATE.
GONNA SNOOZE THROUGH IT ALL?!
C'MON, BASS!
WAKE UP!!!

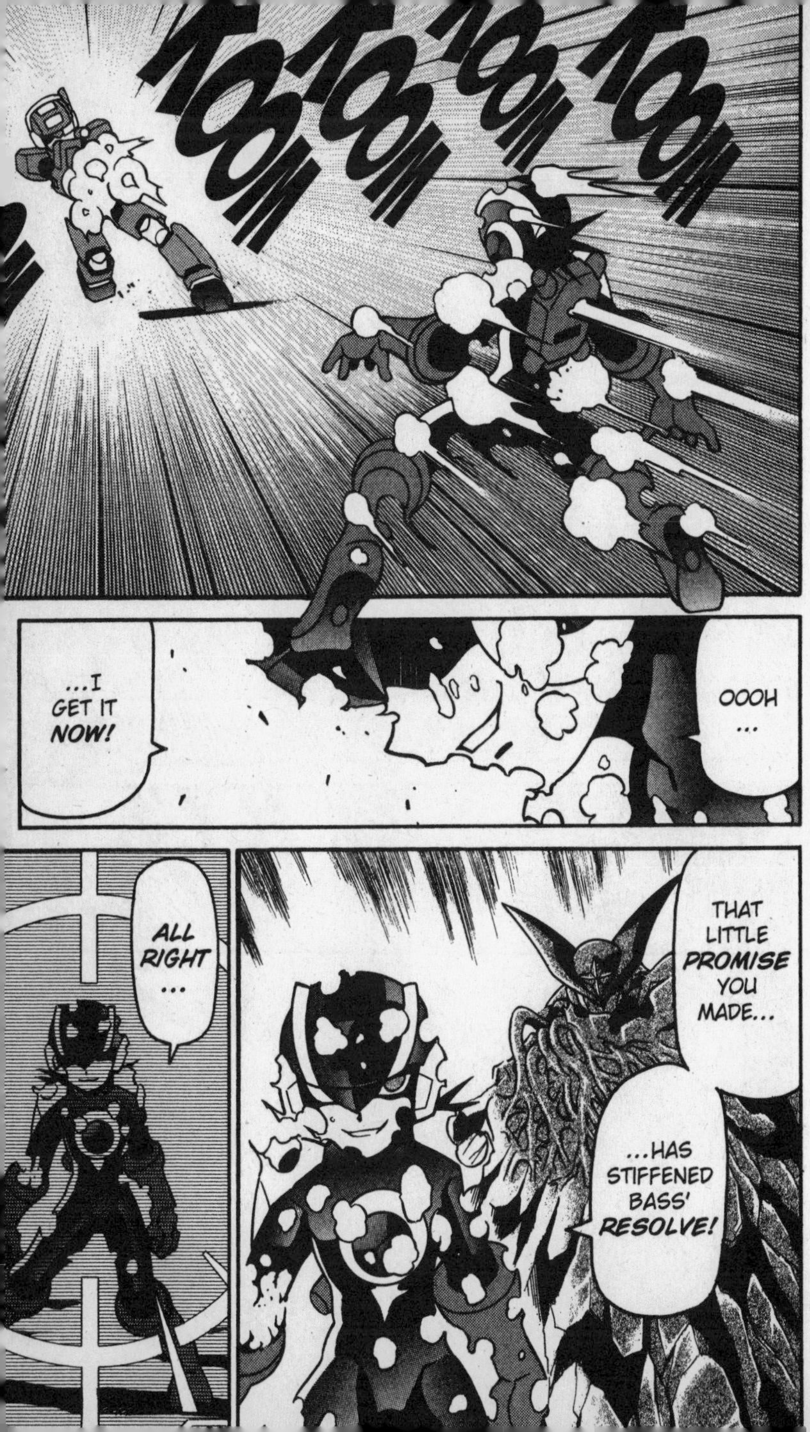
VOOOM VOOOM VOOOM VOOOM
OOOH...
...I GET IT NOW!
THAT LITTLE PROMISE YOU MADE...
...HAS STIFFENED BASS' RESOLVE!
ALL RIGHT...

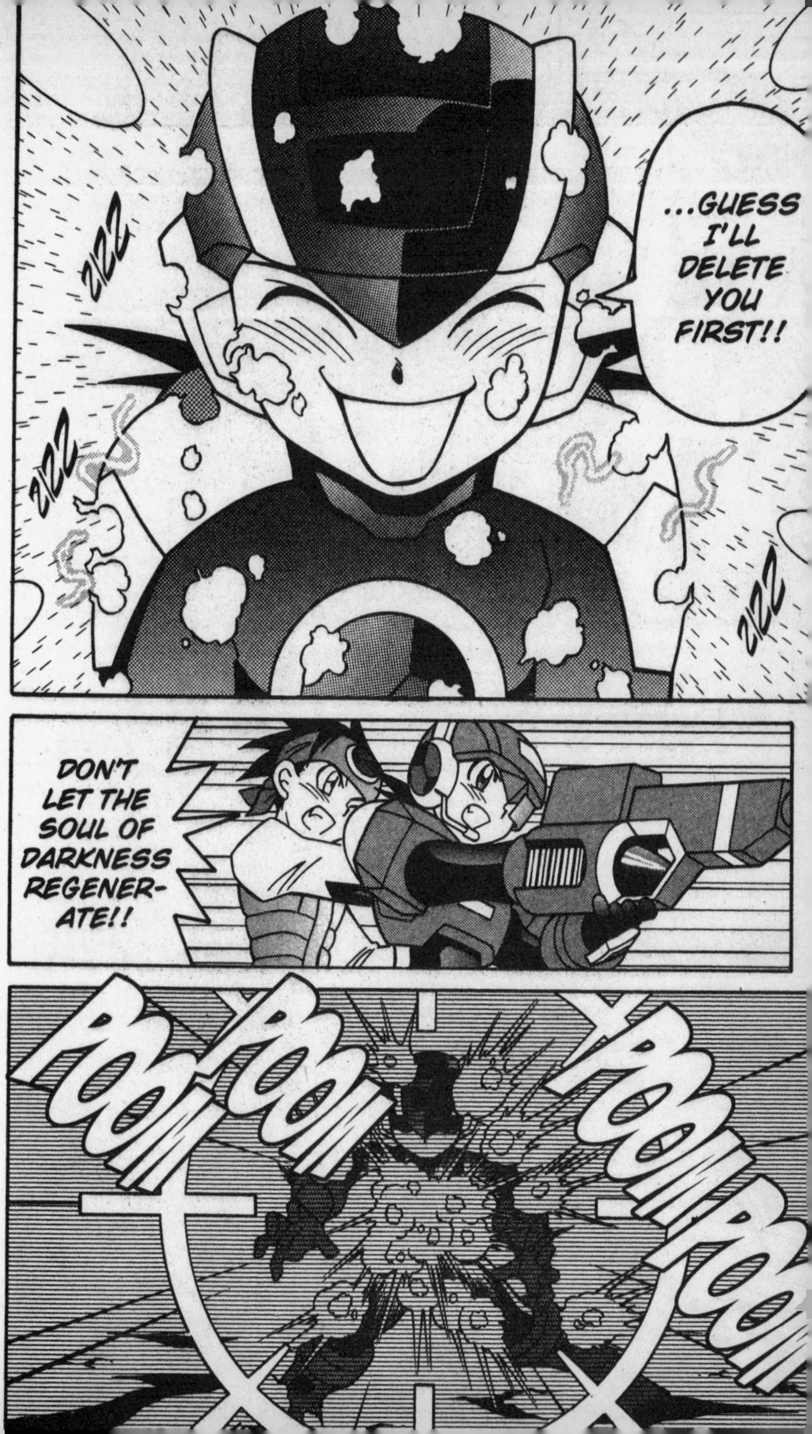
...GUESS I'LL DELETE YOU FIRST!!
ZIZZ
ZIZZ
ZIZZ
DON'T LET THE SOUL OF DARKNESS REGENER-ATE!!
POOM POOM POOM
POOM POOM

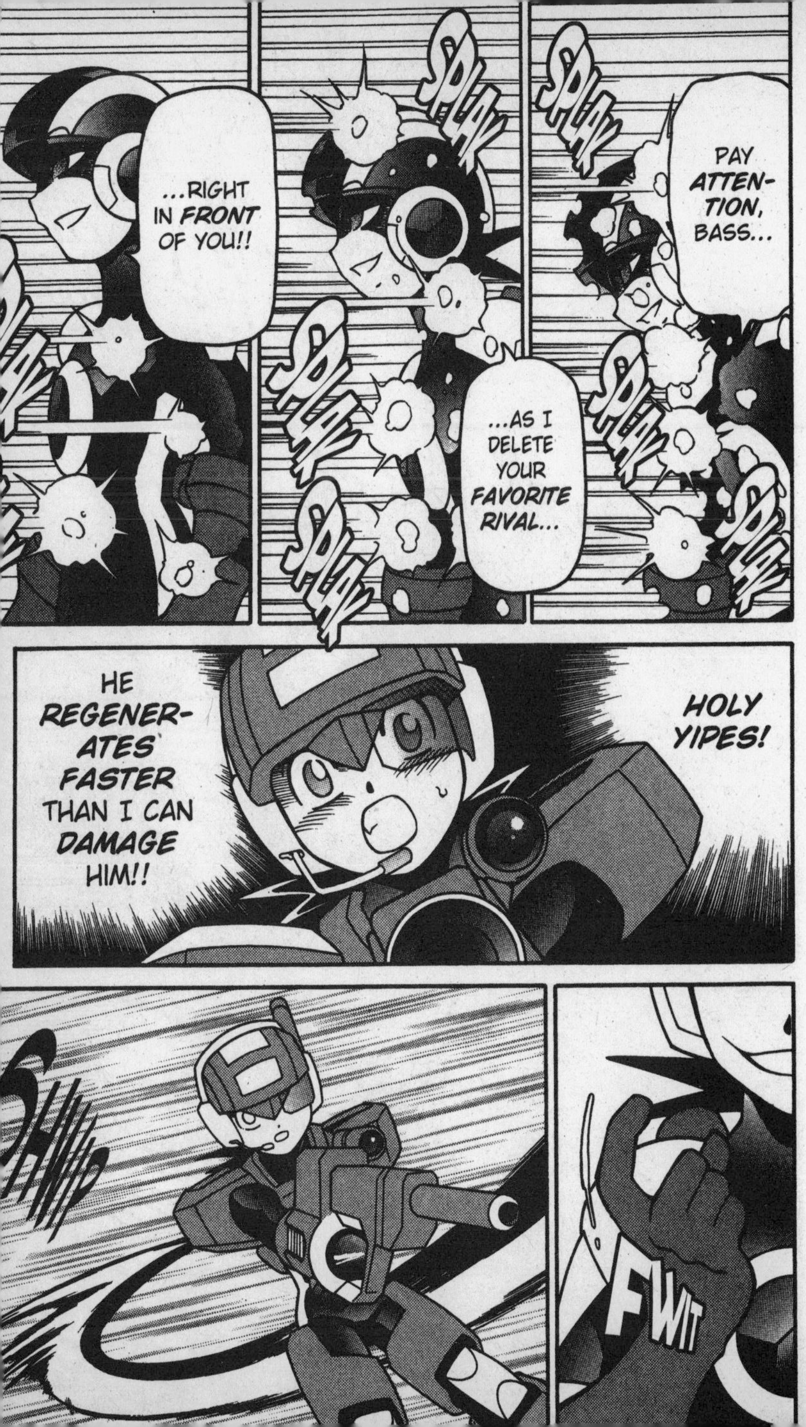
SPLAK
PAY ATTENTION, BASS...
SPLAK
SPLAK
SPLAK
SPLAK
...AS I DELETE YOUR FAVORITE RIVAL...
SPLAK
SPLAK
...RIGHT IN FRONT OF YOU!!
HOLY YIPES!
HE REGENERATES FASTER THAN I CAN DAMAGE HIM!!
FWIT
SHWIP

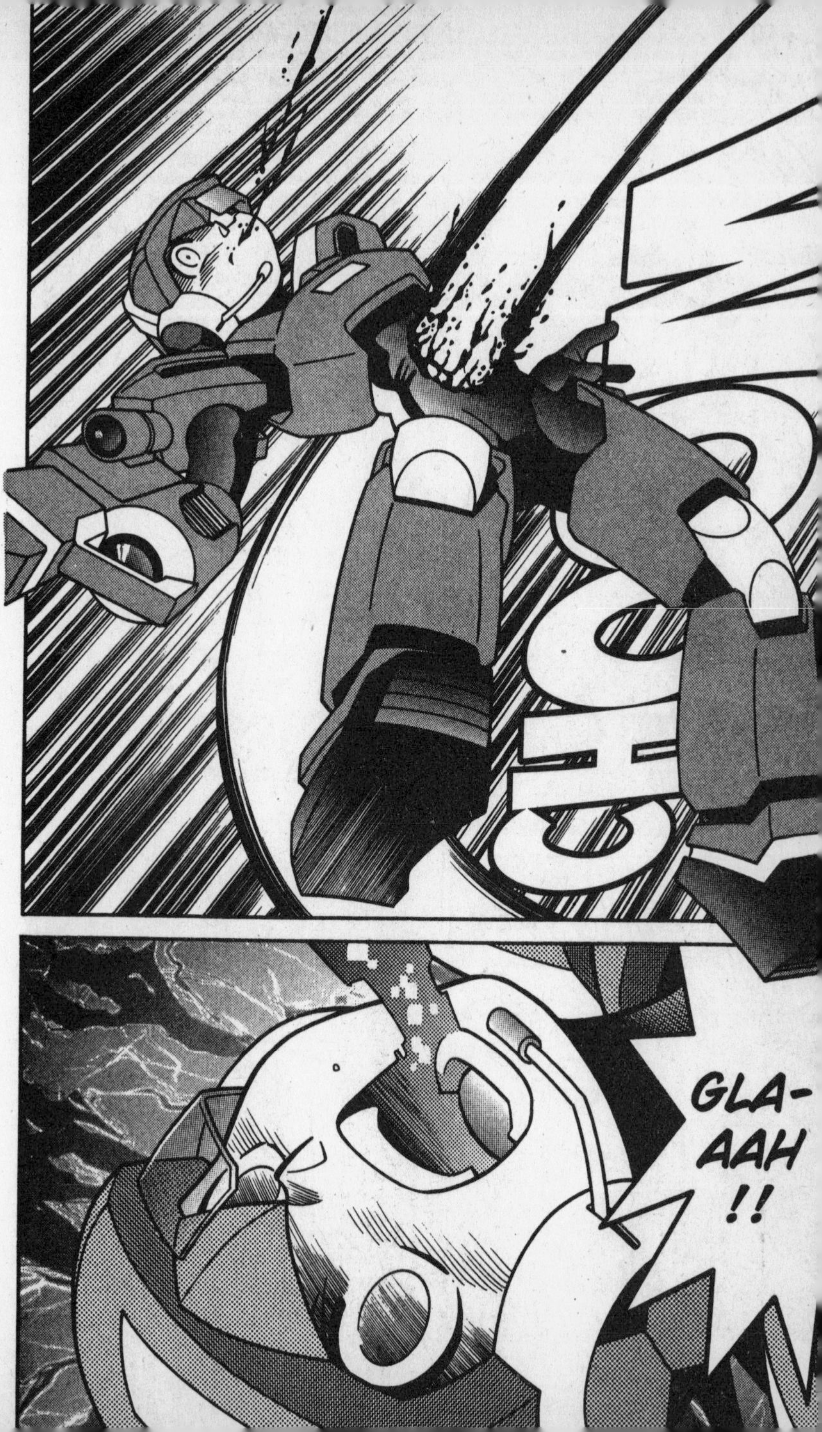
GLA-
AAH
!!

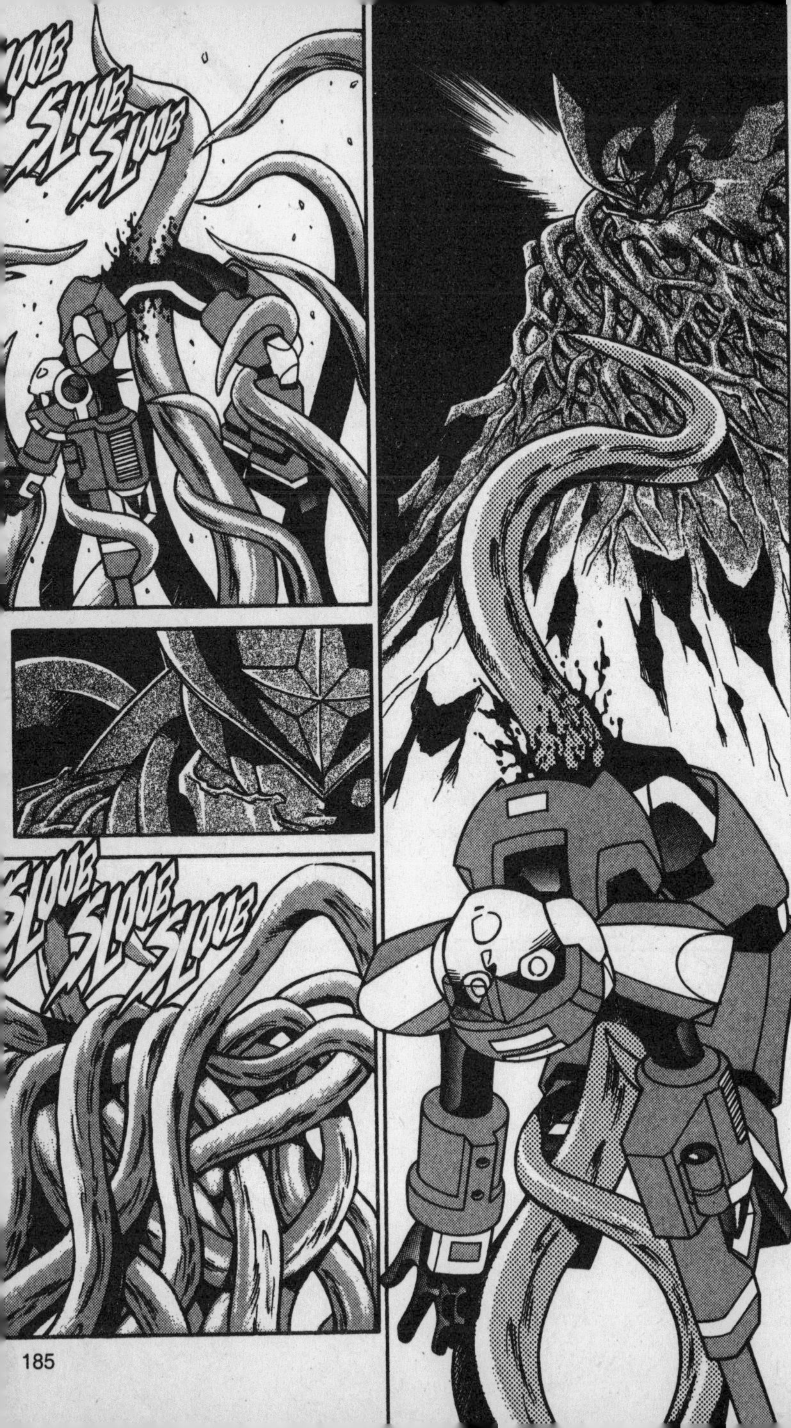
SLOOB SLOOB SLOOB
SLOOB SLOOB SLOOB

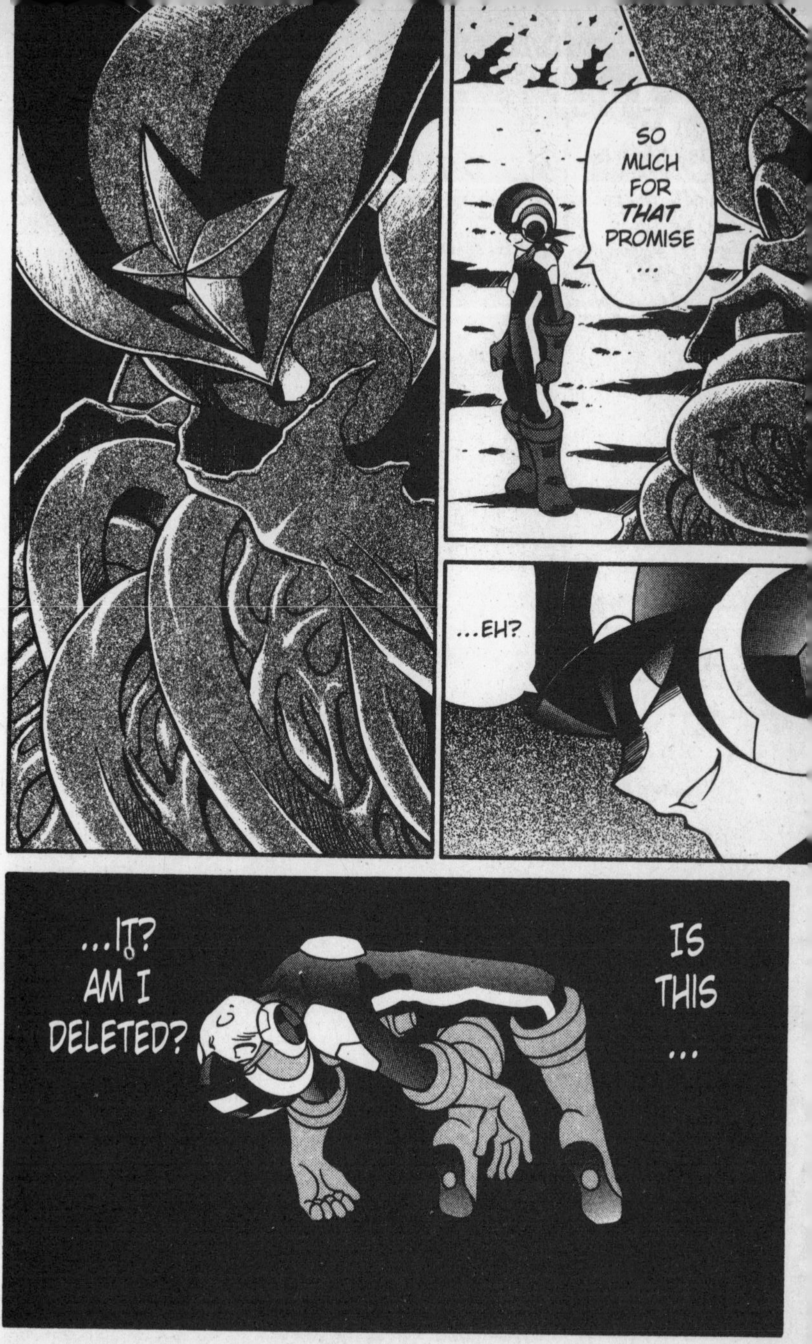
SO MUCH FOR THAT PROMISE ...
...EH?
IS THIS ...
...IT? AM I DELETED?

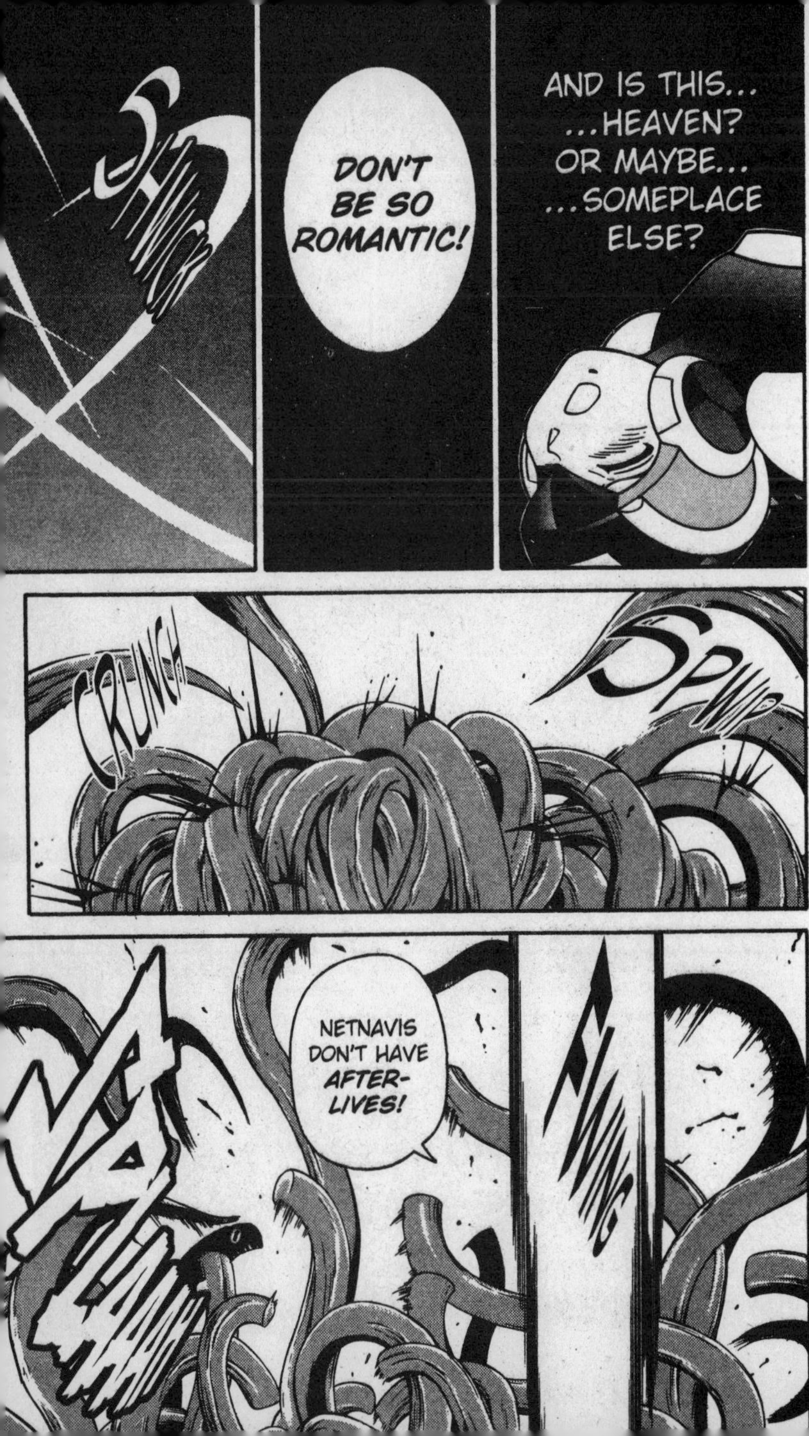
AND IS THIS... ...HEAVEN? OR MAYBE... ...SOMEPLACE ELSE?
DON'T BE SO ROMANTIC!
CRUNCH
NETNAVIS DON'T HAVE AFTER-LIVES!

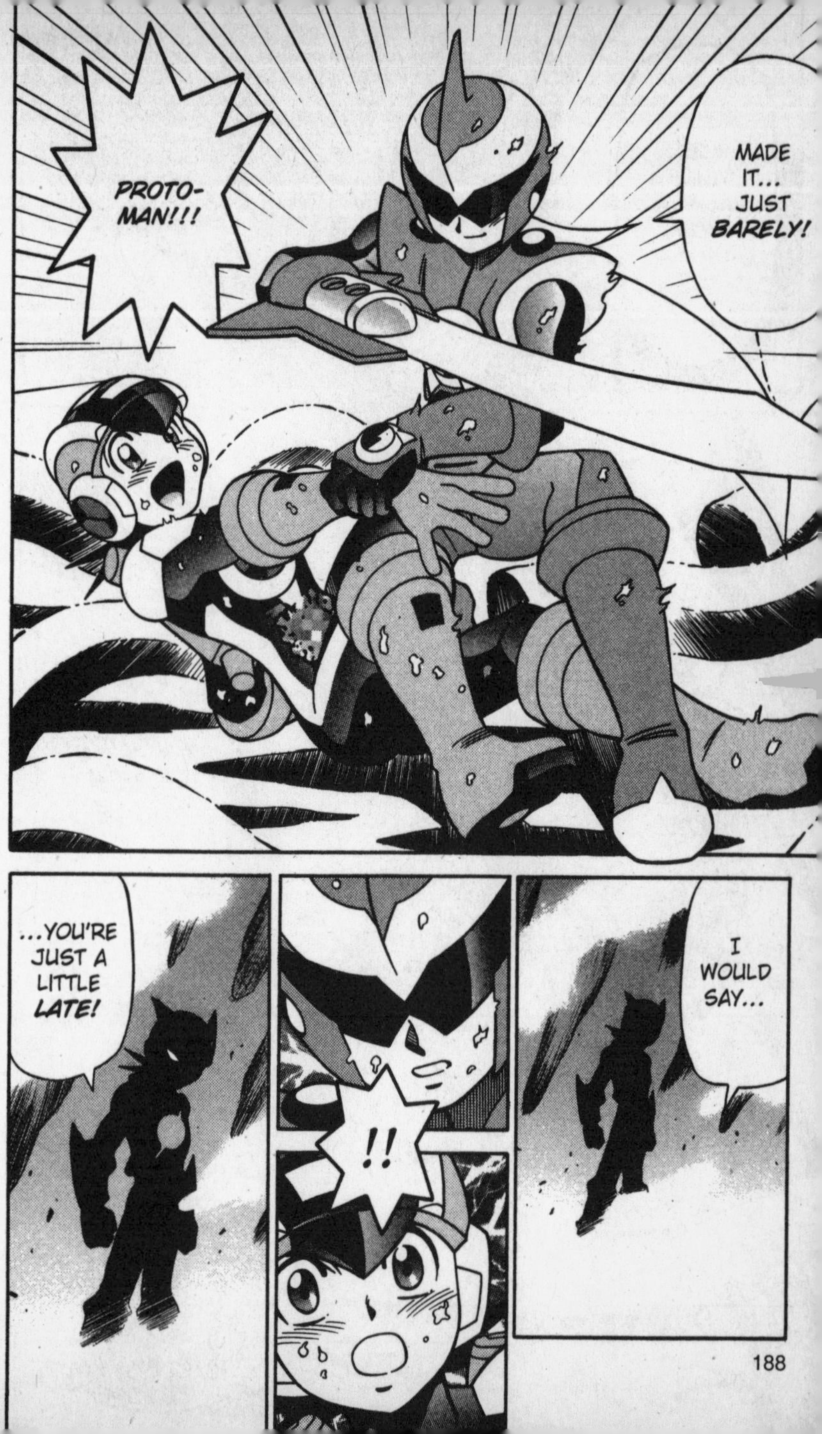
MADE IT... JUST BARELY!
PROTO-MAN!!!
I WOULD SAY...
!!
...YOU'RE JUST A LITTLE LATE!

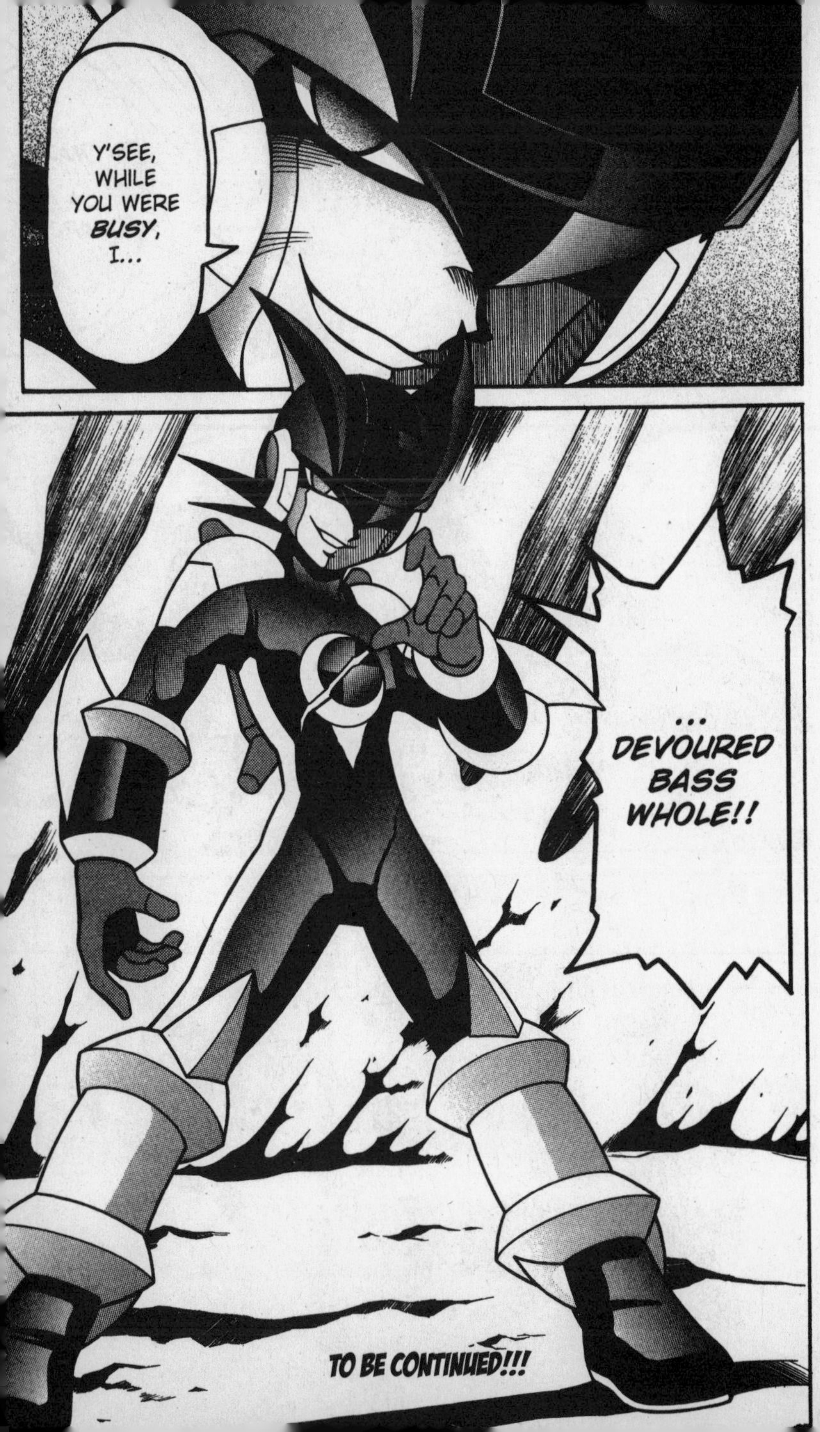
Y'SEE, WHILE YOU WERE BUSY, I...
...DEVOURED BASS WHOLE!!
TO BE CONTINUED!!!

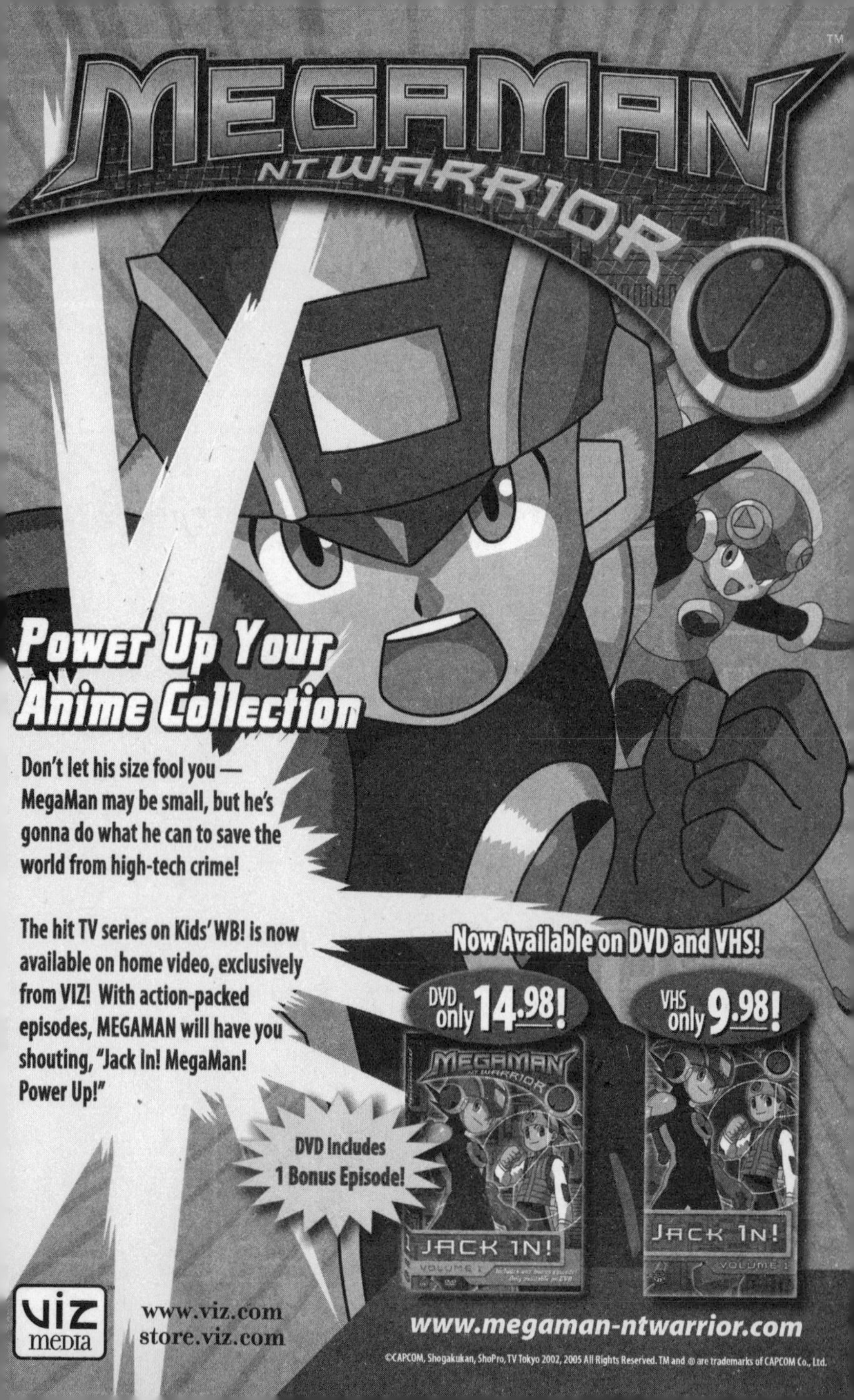
MEGAMAN NT WARRIOR™
Power Up Your Anime Collection
Don't let his size fool you — MegaMan may be small, but he's gonna do what he can to save the world from high-tech crime!
The hit TV series on Kids' WB! is now available on home video, exclusively from VIZ! With action-packed episodes, MEGAMAN will have you shouting, "Jack In! MegaMan! Power Up!"
Now Available on DVD and VHS!
DVD only 14.98!
VHS only 9.98!
DVD Includes 1 Bonus Episode!
MEGAMAN NT WARRIOR
JACK IN!
VOLUME 1
JACK IN!
VOLUME 1
VIZ MEDIA
www.viz.com
store.viz.com
www.megaman-ntwarrior.com
©CAPCOM, Shogakukan, ShoPro, TV Tokyo 2002, 2005 All Rights Reserved. TM and ® are trademarks of CAPCOM Co., Ltd.